Rav Avraham Itzhak HaCohen Kook

SUNY Series in Judaica:
Hermeneutics, Mysticism, and Religion

Michael Fishbane, Robert Goldenberg, and Arthur Green, Editors

Rav Avraham Itzhak HaCohen Kook

Between Rationalism and Mysticism

Benjamin Ish-Shalom

Translated from Hebrew
by
Ora Wiskind-Elper

STATE UNIVERSITY OF NEW YORK PRESS

Production by Ruth Fisher
Marketing by Theresa A. Swierzowski

Published by
State University of New York Press, Albany

For information, address the State University of New York Press,
State University Plaza, Albany, NY 12246

Library of Congress Cataloging-in-Publication Data
Ish Shalom, Binyamin.
    [Rav Ḳuḳ. English]
    Rav Avraham Itzhak Hacohen Kook : between rationalism and
mysticism / Benjamin Ish-Shalom.
        p.   cm. — (SUNY series in Judaica)
    Translation of: ha-Rav ḳuḳ.
    Includes bibliographical references and index.
    ISBN 0-7914-1369-1 (cloth). — ISBN 0-7914-1370-5 (pbk.)
    1. Kook, Abraham Isaac, 1865–1935—Teachings. 2. Orthodox
Judaism. 3. Mysticism—Judaism. 4. Philosophy, Jewish. I. Title.
II. Series.
BM755.K66I8513   1993
296.8'32'092—dc20   92-8087
                                                                    CIP

In memory of my mother
Pnina Malka, ע״ה
Whose soul ever strove for freedom

CONTENTS

The spiritual-social processes and the problems confronting the State of Israel today are rooted in the events of the late nineteenth and early twentieth centuries, when the Zionist movement came into being and the major ideological camps crystallized within Jewish society in Eretz Israel. Many of the difficult questions that have troubled Israeli society for years—such as relations between the "religious" and the "secular," the problem of state versus religion, issues between ultraorthodoxy and religious Zionism, the phenomenon of becoming observant, the question of peace and greater Israel, problems of "mysticism" and political rationalism, the nature of Jewish identity in Israel—are linked to the figure, works, and thought of Rabbi Abraham Isaac HaCohen Kook (1865–1935), the first chief rabbi of Eretz Israel, and one of the most prominent leaders of the Jewish community in the period of the Second Aliyah.

Rav Kook was the spiritual and halachic authority who laid the foundation of religious Zionism. Discontent with the "Mizrakhi" political pragmatism, he envisioned Zionism as a movement of return and all-encompassing Jewish renaissance. The contention voiced by Dr. Benjamin Ze'ev Herzl that Zionism had nothing to do with religion served to reassure the ultraorthodox apprehensive about the influence of the Zionist leadership and ideology in the domains of culture and education and paved the way to cooperation between the "haredim" and the "free ones" in the Zionist Organization. Rav Kook, however, adamantly opposed this policy. In writing and in speech, he did his utmost to convince the leftist and rightist camps their way was wrong, that Zionism would reach no glory by alienating itself from tradition.

It seems that Rav Kook's influence was greater after his death than during his life. With his novel approach and fearless independence, he was a sharp contestor of the Zionist movement, despite his enthusiastic support of its ideas; and as an aggressive disputant of the ultraorthodox community (the Old Yishuv), despite his deep identification with their ways, as well as an uncompromising critic of the pragmatist approach of the "Mizrakhi," regardless of the encouragement and backing he gave them.

Years pass, and echoes of the polemics of those days die away. The image of Rav Kook has become a symbol for many and varied groups, each of which holds him and his vision as a paragon for their opposing paths. It is the way of the world that, as historical distance increases and complex, dialectical thought leaves the intimacy of the artist's home, entering the public domain, elements and motifs are extracted from it and celebrated as ideals in and of themselves, generating social and religious movements in their turn. Is taking one ideal from a comprehensive teaching not tantamount to taking its soul? Can the intellectual breadth, the spiritual greatness, the freedom and daring of Rav Kook really be inherited in this way?

Rav Kook was a legend in his own lifetime. As Joseph Klausner said, "There was no man in the land of Israel—aside from Bialik—who had a public of such devoted admirers as Rav Kook; yet while Bialik, who was not a man of war, had few enemies, Rav Kook was beset with ideological antagonists because he never recoiled from potential persecution or insult."[1]

His personality was a mystery, and remains largely so. In an article of 1946, Joseph Klausner writes:

> I do not hide it from my readers: once I could not understand Rav Kook and his ways. On the one hand—a scholarly and educated rabbi, concerned with the upper and lower worlds, always talking about "holy" and "holiness," triumphs the supreme cause of building the nation and the land and its tolerant even toward wrongdoers in the religious sense, if only they will restore the House of Israel in his own land; and on the other hand—a rabbi who issues proclamations about the Ashkenazi ban on Yemenite ritual slaughter, writes a book about wearing the "head phylactery," is not satisfied even with the piety of the "Mizrachi" and fights for women's voting rights. I saw the great Rav, head of the rabbis of Eretz Israel, yield to the highest authorities and to Storrs himself. . . . Where is the eminence and courage of this great rabbi?
>
> Then I saw him *oppressed*—and suddenly his personality stood before me in its full stature. For only he who remains loyal to his own path in times of trouble, neither bowing to his at-

tackers nor seeking peace with the fortunate wicked—this and this alone is *true* greatness. And Rav Kook was oppressed from the moment he came to Eretz Israel until his dying day.[2]

Why was Rav Kook afflicted to the bitter end? What in his world-view aroused contestants Right and Left? What were his truest, most profound motives? Have his disciples, students, and devotees really plumbed the depths of the revolution concealed in the leaves of his writings? Are there indeed people who carry his torch? Does his teaching bear a message relevant to us? Can it show us the resolution of an age-old conflict?

This work endeavors to understand Rav Kook's spiritual world by dissolving the mist enveloping his writings. The work presents and analyzes the systematic elements in Rav Kook's teaching and reveals the spiritual interests and fundamental approaches of his religious thought. Speculative efforts may be demanded of the reader, for the object of this work is not a historical-biographical description nor a general overview of Rav Kook's outlook. Rather the book invites the reader to an unmediated encounter with his theoretical writings in their unique style and powerful expression; there is no better testimony to the inner world and the struggles of their author. It is an attempt to grapple directly and critically with the essential elements of Rav Kook's faith and views, to appreciate his state of mind, and to create tools enabling understanding of his attitudes on a wide variety of subjects.

The writings of Rabbi Abraham Isaac HaCohen Kook are a unique phenomenon in the history of Jewish thought. Even for the scholarly and experienced reader, they often seem impenetrable and strange both in content and form.[3] in these two areas, content and form, Rav Kook does not tread the paths broken by his predecessors in Jewish cogitation, whether philosophical, kabbalistic, or Hassidic; his unmethodical style appears figurative and obscure, or lacking an explicit framework of intellectual coordinates.[4] He does not use known philosophical terms or even classical kabbalistic symbolism with any consistency or method, although he was intimately familiar with both realms.

Rav Kook was ardently esteemed in the circles of his students and intimates, both during his life and after his death. Yet none of them fully understood him and recognized his direction in truth. Rav Kook himself voices this lack in a letter dated Tevet 5668 (1908): "I have no one with whom to share my heart, neither among the old nor the young, no one who can come close to the core [literally, seat] of my desire, and this troubles me greatly."[5] It goes without saying that members of the Old Yishuv and the New Yishuv alike, to whom Rav Kook's outlook and intentions were completely alien, regarded him with various attitudes, ranging from honor, astonished respect, and sympathy to opposition or harsh derision and even open animosity, but none of them out of understanding of his views.[6]

Much has been written about Rav Kook's life and works, yet a comprehensive philosophical-theological study penetrating to the depths of his thought has yet to be made. It is no simple matter to characterize Rav Kook's oeuvre. Is his thought philosophical? Was he a mystic, and can he be seen as a kabbalist? The answer, in each case, seems to be yes and no. It depends both on a definition of terms and the method of interpretation used to distinguish essential from super-fluous; and we must admit that even a method of interpretation founded on critical and "objective" criteria, particularly when dealing with material at times ambiguous, cannot preserve itself entirely from an irremediable undertone of subjectivity. These questions serve only to point to the complex nature of Rav Kook's work.

In one of his essays,[8] Gershom Scholem distinguished between the concepts of "mystic" and "kabbalist" and wrote that he sees Rav Kook as a "prime example of a great Jewish *mystic*."[9] A few lines later he adds: "The reader of Rav Kook's book *Orot Hakodesh* ("The Lights of Holiness") realizes immediately that the author *is no kabbalist*." Adin Steinssalz, in contrast sees Rav Kook as *"a man of kabbalah* who seems to flee from any clear kabbalistic statement" and claims that his book *Orot Hakodesh* is a *"kabbalistic book* deliberately written in non-kabbalistic terms."[10] And Hillel Zeitlin also sees Rav Kook's thought as "kabbalah."[11] S. H. Bergman holds Rav Kook was "more a *poet* than a systematic thinker,"[12] and even Rivka Schatz sees him not as a philosopher "with a system complete in itself," but more as a *"harbinger."*[13]

In the present discussion I wish to propose an alternate approach to an understanding of Rabbi Abraham Isaac HaCohen Kook's teaching. Although his thought should not be perceived as a systematic philosophy in the conventional sense of the term, a thorough study of his writings introduces us to an *inclusive world-view, possessed of internal structure and logic, whose details become comprehensible and clear in light of the principles on which it is founded.* In this sense, what we have before us may not be a systematic philosophy, but we must nonetheless try to uncover it through the veil of unsystematic formulation in which it is enveloped.[14]

The various approaches to Rav Kook's oeuvre serve, in any case, to evince the multiplicity of its aspects and warn against confining it within a narrow definition or applying a particular label to it in the name of simple convenience. The entirety of his writings reveal a many-faceted personality, experienced in the most intensive religious life and rent by opposing tendencies. His is the figure of a mystic with clear philosophical orientation, who developed an original and revolutionary conception of the very mystical-kabbalistic tradition on which he draws.

In the contradictions in Rav Kook's internal world are expressed in many domains: in the tension between talmudic scholarship in the Lithuanian style and his sympathy for mystical meditation; between concern for halacha and strict conservatism regarding its details, and the hint of anarchy and antinomism voiced in his speculative writings; between the profusion of reflections and remarks couched in poetic and hazy figures and orderly, rational thought phrased with the greatest fluency; between a sense of certainty in describing a specific picture of the world and skepticism of the very possibility of true awareness; between a tendency to extreme mystical exultations and a conscious effort to maintain spiritual balance; between a feeling of vitality and strength to one of muteness and helplessness; between the experience and aspiration to boundless freedom and the awareness of limitation and obligation.

In sum, the personality before us is composed of opposing forces, compelled by a sense of responsibility and supreme effort to neutralize and restrain extremist tendencies and to resolve differences through conceptual explanation, the basic assumption being that reality is too rich and too complex to be perceived or described by a single theory or discipline, With characteristic openness, Rav Kook writes:

> Whoever said of me that my soul is torn put it well, for torn it is indeed. Our minds cannot conceive of a man whose soul is not torn. Only the inanimate is whole. But man's aspirations contradict one another, and battle is constantly waged within him. All of man's efforts are to unite the opposing forces of his spirit by means of a general idea, whose greatness and sublimity holds everything and leads to perfect harmony. That, of course, is an ideal we strive for, though not every child born of woman can reach it. Still, our efforts can bring us closer and closer, and that is what the Kabbalists call "yikhudim."[15]

If we are to keep our understanding of Rav Kook and his works from becoming one dimensional, we must found our study on a systematic analysis of his speculative writings, as well as on the link between his theoretical teaching and personal experience from a phenomenological point of view—all this with an eye to the historical background, placing the issues in their proper context.

This book is based on the doctoral dissertation submitted to the Hebrew University of Jerusalem in 1984. Yet my interest in Rav Kook's thought has its roots in the fertile years of study I spent in Yeshivat Har Etzion of Gush Etzion. That *beit midrash,* with its entrenched Israeli and Zionist spirit and its atmosphere of openness and freedom, allowed me to combine my admiration for the personality and thought of that great and unique spiritual leader with an unconfined and critical reading and evaluation of his writings, an act of unspoiled love and a combination not to be taken for granted.

The opportunity given me by the Hebrew University of Jerusalem to teach Rav Kook's writings has allowed me to put texts usually considered unsuited to systematic philosophical analysis to the test of understanding and rational criticism. I am grateful to my students— alert, attentive and critical—who challenged me to confront these texts, clarifying and formulating the principles contained in them. And to my teachers and colleagues in philosophy and Kabbalah at the Hebrew University, who helped me gain understanding through years of open and fruitful discussion.

I owe a special debt of gratitude to Professor Rivka Schatz-Uffenheimer of blessed memory, who guided me in my doctoral dissertation and whose advice and insight contributed directly and significantly to this work.

The help of Professor Nathan Rothenstreich for his encouragement to publish this book is also greatly appreciated. The Warburg scholarship given me and the grant provided by the Memorial Foundation for Jewish Culture allowed me to devote my energy to research. Their generosity was a great help to me.

My research included study of all of Rav Kook's published works; I was allowed access to the unpublished manuscripts as well, many of which reach the public here for the first time.

I wish to thank Mr. David Kerschen, chief librarian of Beit Morasha of Jerusalem, who revised the bibliography of the current English edition and who kindly undertook the task of proofreading the final draft.

Special thanks go to Professor Arthur Green, Ruth Fisher, and SUNY Press for making an English version of the book possible.

Finally, I wish to thank Dr. Avraham Shapiro for his careful attention to the original hebrew edition of this work, and the publishers of Am Oved, who accepted the book for publication.

To my wife Rivka, my true partner in the task of writing—my learning is yours.

PART ONE

Introduction

1

In the Grip of Contradiction

Formative Influences and Sources

Three years after Rav Kook's aliyah to Eretz Israel (in 1904) and
settled in Jaffa as the rabbi of the New Yishuv, his son, Zvi Yehuda
(later head of Yeshivat Mercaz Harav) sent the author Y. H. Brenner a
small book entitled *Ikve Hatzon*, written by Rav Kook. The book was
accompanied by a letter that reveals an interesting aspect of the complicated relations between Rav Kook and his surroundings.[1] This letter describes the sources of his thought and the influences forming
his personality, presents the prime motives of his writings and actions, and cites the essential force that guided the composition of *Ikve
Hatzon*. It is a document of rare style in its description of the experience of Rav Kook's encounter with the reality of Eretz Israel, and its
influence on him from the perspective of someone who knew him
intimately.

Rabbi Zvi Yehuda Kook writes to Brenner,

> Not as the author's son, enamored of his father's ideas and eager
> to disseminate them, but rather as a youth of our generation and
> its ideals of the "camp that remains," who offers some delicacies
> to be enjoyed by his contemporary and friend (if I may) whom
> he recognizes from afar as one of his own and close to his soul,
> another idealistic youth of the "camp that remains."

The spiritual attachment and identification Rav Kook's son felt for this
great writer of the Second Aliyah and representative of the radical

3

trend to reject traditional Judaism teaches us something about the spirit he absorbed in his father's house. He describes Rav Kook himself in the letter:

> My father, may his light shine, is the author and one of the most devout rabbis. In addition to his learnedness in "Torah," he has been called a *"zaddik"*—he is also a scholar and free-thinking philosopher, impeded by nothing, in the full sense of the term. He has taken great care to search out and understand the philosophical teachings of the nations, to penetrate to the very foundations of our Torah, and to reach the inner chambers of the Kabbalah. And with a broken and seething heart he has regarded the shards of his beloved people, torn to shreds. He recognizes the source of all the misfortune in lack of understanding among brothers. . . . Until, for example: Judaism has become synonymous, for many, with hatred for life, idleness and worse, while enlightenment and knowledge and living aspirations have become synonymous, in the eyes of the elders [the ultraorthodox], with heresy and apostasy and contempt for the holy. The fissures made by such things have grown wider and wider leading to our situation today, unlike anything we have ever had before. Ever! He came to Eretz Israel—three years ago—and saw the degeneracy of these fissures. And he determined to enter public life, to work with all his strength for the benefit of his people. In his few books he publishes and reiterates his ideas, in varied aspects and perspectives (as long as his money lasts), and in his learned manner he is willing to speak and speak with whomever he finds worthy. He rises early and speaks, rises and writes. And despite the many disturbances—particularly from the older generation—he has already done a great deal—relatively speaking.

Indeed, Rav Zvi Yehuda aptly describes his father, on one hand, as one of the "most devout rabbis" and as a "free-thinking philosopher impeded by nothing," on the other. Anyone familiar with the state of Jewish society in those days can see the paradoxality of that description. How can these characteristics be combined in a single personality? In what soil can such a rare and noble sort of leadership take root and flourish? We are compelled to devote some words to the question of Rav Kook's sources and the historical-cultural context in which his spiritual world was formed and his thought engendered. Research of Rav Kook's sources is particularly problematic. Rav Kook drew nourishment from various cultural and spiritual worlds, a fact that has allowed many scholars to emphasize one source while ignoring another. Thus any attempt to present his complex thought as engendered in a single cultural realm leads to grave misunderstanding of his teaching.

Rav Kook's earliest education was in the Lithuanian scholarly tradition, his family linked both to the Mitnagged rabbinate and to Chabad Hassidism.[2] He was born on 15 Elul 5625 (1865) in the town of Griva in Latvia to Shlomo Zalman, an outstanding Torah scholar and strictly observant Jew, and Pearl Zlata, daughter of one of the first followers of the Hassidic rabbi "Tzemakh Tzedek" of Lyady (1790–1866). Until his bar mitzvah, late in 5638 (1878), he studied Torah in his parents' home, where he also gained a love for Eretz Israel and the Hebrew language. For the subsequent eight years he moved from place to place, absorbed in learning the many aspects of Jewish teaching. He became known as the "ga'on of Griva" and later as the "ga'on of Ponevezh" (after the city of his future father-in-law, Rabbi Eliyahu David Rabinovitz-Te'omim [ADeReT]. For approximately one-and-a-half years he learned in the famed yeshiva of Voloshin, where H. N. Bialik was also a student. During this period he was influenced by the Natziv, head of the yeshiva, and by his father-in-law, the Aderet.

Even in those days the young Rav Kook was troubled with the problems of his divided people; Hassidim and Mitnaggdim, Maskilim and Hovevei Zion. He was driven to action by the force of a "noble and powerful cause," as he put it, and strove to develop religious and rabbinic literature toward responsibility for the nation as a whole and care for its needs. In 5648 (1888) he began to publish a journal by the name of *Itur sofrim* with the aim of "building a home for rabbinic literature" and "unifying all dissention in the name of the nation's honor and renaissance."[3] The life of the journal was short, due to Rav Kook's inability to deal with organizational problems, yet it marked the beginning of his public action. Rav Kook was then invited to serve in the rabbinate of the town of Zaumel, and after seven years, in 5655 (1895) was called to serve as rabbi of the community of Bausk. His predecessor (until 5650, 1890) was Rabbi Mordechai Eliasberg, one of the earliest ideologues of religious Zionism; and in Bausk Rav Kook's national view began to crystallize. In the years 5661–5664 (1901–1904) he wrote a few articles, of clear publicistic nature, dealing with the question of nationalism and the polemics between the rabbis and the Maskilim and secular Zionists.

Rav Kook's profound absorption for so many years in the treasures of Jewish and traditional literature of all periods, particularly with kabbalistic teaching, clearly informs all his works. Yet in light of his traditional education, his bond to European contemporary philosophy is most remarkable.[4] His interest in the writings of the great philosophers of the nineteenth and early twentieth centuries was, admittedly, that of a self-taught amateur, but their influence on him is not to be measured solely by his direct dealing with them. His reactions to various philosophers will be discussed in detail later, for they are of essential significance. Here, I would like to demonstrate that no less that his explicit reactions to certain philosophical theories, the whole of Rav Kook's thought comprehends the states of mind and trends, the zeitgeist prevalent in Europe of his period.[5]

Nonetheless, Rav Kook unreservedly accepted neither the philosophical concepts nor the modes of thought of the Mitnagged rabbinate, nor the Mussar movement or Hassidism, nor the writers of the Haskalah. He borrowed tools from no one, rather creating his spiritual world by adapting, and vitally changing, values and meanings, intermingling domains in an original synthesis.

No thorough and encompassing study addressing the question of sources with any degree of conviction has yet been made. Some scholars have stressed Rav Kook's dependence on Lurianic mysticism and that of its followers, on the writings of R. Shneur Zalman of Lyady or R. Hayyim of Volozhin,[6] and some have traced his sources to the Hassidism of the Ba'al Shem Tov.[7] In opposition to these views, the claim has been made that Rav Kook's thought is not to be seen as continuation and simple conclusion of Lurianic Kabbalah, but rather that he should be viewed as a "modern writer of the late nineteenth and early twentieth century in the whole of his mood."[8]

These divided opinions are voiced in recent research as well, primarily in the manner of understanding Rav Kook's language and the place of kabbalistic symbolism in his writing. The claim has been made, on one hand, that the classical schema of kabbalistic symbolism serves as the basis on which his theological attitudes are formulated and is thus the key to their reconstruction;[9] another scholar, in contrast, claims Rav Kook's theological views are not anchored in Kabbalah and that he began "to clothe his ideas in kabbalistic garb" only later to win legitimacy "empowered by kabbalistic sources in the tradition." This scholar believes Rav Kook may have been impelled to look for *asmakhtaot* (scriptural proof-texts) in kabbalistic literature for want of support in classical Jewish sources.[10]

Both of these polarly opposed approaches seem to me slightly exaggerated. Each magnifies one aspect of Rav Kook's work and ignores, or at least minimizes, all other aspects. One cannot lose sight for a moment of Rav Kook's vital connection to modern Western philosophy, on one hand, and to traditional Jewish literature as well

Kabbalah, on the other. Scrutiny of his writings leaves no doubt of this double connection, and the previously mentioned letter of R. Zvi Yehuda to Brenner is definitive testimony. In the same letter, Rav Kook's son states that his father had "taken great care to search out and understand the philosophical teachings of the nations, . . . even reaching the inner chambers of the Kabbalah." Yet this general statement is not sufficient and, at the end of his letter, in his presentation of the contents of the book *Ikve Hatzon,* he does not hesitate to state his claim that the two essential essays of the book, "Knowledge of God" and "Service of God," are based on lectures given by Professor Hermann Cohen and published in the journal *Hashilo'ah.*[11]

The chronological dimension of Rav Kook's writings is very difficult to expose. His major works were not edited by his own hand, and the material they include is undated. There is a tendency to distinguish between his "early works" and "late works,"[12] the dividing line being his aliyah to Eretz Israel in 1904. This distinction, in and of itself, is indeed justified, although the facts do not necessarily lead to the conclusions often drawn from it.[13]

The years 1904–1906 were a turning point in Rav Kook's understanding of secularism and view of the *halutzim* (pioneers) of the Second Aliyah. His close contact with the members of the New Yishuv and their activities after his arrival in Israel induced him to alter the tactical attitude of tolerance toward the Maskilim and Hovevei Zion he had held in the Diaspora; once in Eretz Israel, he identified profoundly with the *halutzim* as he came to understand their motives. A fertile period of creativity then began, yet the foundations of his metaphysical outlook remained unchanged, and his attachment to Kabbalah never became a tactical matter or later trait in his thought. Even before his aliyah, Rav Kook studied Kabbalah regularly with R. Moshe Isaac Rabin, the *dayan* of Ponovitz,[14] and spoke of the subject with R. Mordechai Rosenblatt, rabbi of Ashmina, with R. Shlomo Elyashiv, author of the book *Leshem shevo ve-akhlama,* and with R. Pinkhas Lintop.[15] Moreover, formulations similar to his "early" writings are extant in the period after Rav Kook's aliyah to Eretz Israel as well.[16] Thus, for the purpose of study, the more fruitful distinction would not be between his "early" and "late" writings but rather between his writings of a publicist and contemporary nature, which were, on occasion, clearly polemic, due to the circumstances in which they were written, and his speculative, philosophical-mystical works, in diary form, spontaneously written and never intended for publication. The latter are a more authentic reflection of Rav Kook's views, for they were composed without relation to a concrete dispute and without the burden of responsibility borne by a rabbi responding to letters or making a public statement, obliged, as always, to take an apologetic stand on current issues.[17]

Thus we see the building blocks of Rav Kook's thought—the major metaphysical structures and most of the formulations, terminology, and symbols—were quarried in the literature of Jewish tradition, particularly the Kabbalah. Nonetheless, this study makes evident that *theosophy is not the focus of his interest*. For Rav Kook it is a tool, a sort of ideological model whose main importance is as an object of morality, serving, perhaps, as a moral foment and stimulant. He is bound to no single metaphysical paradigm as the true and exclusive description of reality. As we will show, he himself explains this fact both through epistemological and phenomenological considerations. The fundamental spiritual and intellectual interests spurring his writing are quite far from the horizon of thought and concerns of the medieval or Kabbalist thinkers[18] and cannot be understood by ignoring the non-Jewish cultural climate to which Rav Kook was so attentive. He adopts the basic dialectical model of Lurianic Kabbalah, yet as we said, theosophy is not his object and his discussion extends beyond that domain. The metaphysical structures borrowed from Lurianic doctrine serves the needs of ethical mysticism, born of Rav Kook's reactions, as mystic and Jewish theologian, to the problems posed by modern European culture and philosophy.

It is interesting, in this context, to note the surprising resemblance between Rav Kook's reaction to European cogitation and that of another philosopher and theologian of his time, propelled as well by profound religious and moral motives, whose theological formation was also greatly influenced by nineteenth century philosophy. The man in question is Albert Schweitzer, whose thought is also characterized as "ethical mysticism" and in it a concept of self-perfection is central as well.[19]

The similarity, in other aspects, between Rav Kook and Leonhard Ragaz[20] and Teilhard de Chardin[21] has already been pointed out. For Schweitzer and Ragaz, as for Rav Kook, the interest of freedom is primordial. In Ragaz's view, the church and theology would like to imprison God within the narrow confines of ecclesiastical thought, while the holy spirit in fact finds true expression out in the wide world. The kingdom of heaven, which is in effect the kingdom of justice, freedom, and social equality, comes into being wherever God's will is realized in human freedom.[22] As our discussion progresses, we become more and more aware just how closely these views resemble those expressed by Rav Kook. He addressed the subject directly in one of his letters: "We would not regret it if some quality of cultural justice could be built without any spark or mention of God, for we know that the very aspiration to justice, in any light, is itself the more luminous divine influence."[23] (*Igrot Rayah,* vol. 1, p. 45).

This most interesting phenomenon captures our attention: the works of an entire group of religious thinkers, priests, or theologians, whose works exemplify a special type of thought originating in the late nineteenth and early twentieth centuries.[24] They are thinkers and mystics who were not prominent in their own time, yet who created a new theology by confronting contemporary ideological trends.

This tumultuous period was heady with "isms," and their influence was decisive: rationalism and idealism here, Darwinism and Vitalism there, and in between existentialism, materialism, and nihilism. All were marked by the indelible stamp of the period—the striving for freedom.

This aspiration, the underlying impetus of the French Revolution, not only set in motion the wheels of national and civil liberation movements[25] but was the spirit and philosophy that "sprouted and burst forth everywhere, audible from every mouth, expressed in the verses of poets and the words of practical men no less than in philosophical formulations on the subject."[26] Even the scientific determinists of the rationalistic eighteenth century held that understanding of necessity is liberating, and no less than they, Herder, Hegel, and Marx, who replaced obsolete, mechanical models of life with vitalistic ones, believed that understanding the world is liberation.[27] The idea of freedom roams, in the history of modern philosophy, from rationalistic theories to nonrational or mystical approaches.

As for Rav Kook, some of the concepts prevalent in the intellectual atmosphere of the times influenced him only indirectly. But other circles and methods undeniably received his attention in one way or another, positively influencing some of his views. This is especially true of philosophers whom he mentions by name, such as Spinoza, Kant, Schopenhauer, and Bergson.

In any case, in this book I have tended away from any excessive comparative investigation, as I am skeptical of its relevance and contribution to an understanding of Rav Kook's conception. In many cases, the attempt to isolate his sources definitively remains in the domain of speculation, as his writings are rich with associations to the whole treasure house of Jewish creativity, and the direct provenance of ideas from an earlier source usually cannot be traced through any quotation, paraphrase, or use of a particular term. Rav Kook's writing was spontaneous, with an awareness of his originality and novelty, and his sources are assimilated in his spiritual world, evading the scholar's attempt to isolate them. Success in the search for the origins of terms, citations, and paraphrases does not imply success in locating ideological sources, for the two are not identical. His use of terms and symbols is completely free. Similarity between various systems of thought, after all, does not necessarily testify to a formal link between them.

Of interest, on this point, the account by R. David Cohen ("Hanazir"), editor of *Orot Hakodesh* (Lights of Holiness), of a conversation he held with Rav Kook on the concept of completeness in the latter's teaching:

> Yesterday evening, when the Rav, may he live long and happily, showed me the article by Rimon, which cites the lack of philosophical concentration in Rav Kook's writings . . . he also set the fundamentals of his method before me: God's completeness is absolute, for He contains no deficiency (this is a great philosophical rule). Yet on the other hand, the exaltation and ascent ever higher in holiness—this is also completeness. And if there is no transcendence there will be no completeness. For he said, like R. Azriel: that the boundary of Ein Sof (infinity), the final level which lacks nothing, is completeness. And when I remarked that the essential difference in R. Azriel's system is movement, he agreed, saying it is surely so and the similarity is merely external. Just as, in completeness, there is completeness from deficiency so there is completeness from transcendence. This, then, is the fundament of his entire method: exultation in the human spirit, development leading to perfection through the generations, *tikkun*, all is by grace of the highest holiness, and movement is there, in the idea of transcendence.[28]

Interestingly, one could assume the sources of Rav Kook's concept of divine completeness are found in Lurianic Kabbalah,[29] and Rav Kook himself who, in citing his point of origin on the issue, chose to mention R. Azriel from Gerona and, when challenged by the differences between them, retracted his claim. This conversation seems to prove quite clearly that Rav Kook was not conscious of his sources. In his highly original thought, ideological elements originiating in many sources are reformulated, and it is difficult to speak of conscious need for specific sources.[30]

I must stress that I do not claim the question of sources is completely fruitless, and in the source of our discussion we will consider Rav Kook's relation to the mystical and philosophical literature preceeding it. Revelation of the sources for quotations, terms, expressions, paraphrases, and symbols Rav Kook uses does often illuminate and enrich our understanding of his words. Yet scientific responsibility does not allow us to treat such sources with more seriousness and precision than they deserve; and, as we have said, we must take care not to upset the balance between comparative study and penetrating discussion of his theoretical teaching itself and its essential tendencies.

The "Old Yishuv" and the "New Yishuv"—Unbridgeable Distance

The social and religious reality Rav Kook encountered in Eretz Israel upon his arrival in 1904 was no less complex and intricate than that which he had left in Russia. In essence, the roots of the situation in Eretz Israel can be traced to processes and changes experienced by European Jewry throughout the nineteenth century.[31] In that period, the Jewish population of Eretz Israel was divided into two separate societies, whose differences were substantial both in mode of life and world-view and its characteristic ideology. One society, called the *Old Yishuv*,[32] was an Orthodox group whose motives for aliyah had been religious and spiritual; that is, to study Torah and pray in the Holy Land. According to this population's conception, it had no responsibility for the country's physical, economic existence; full responsibility was borne by Jews of the Diaspora. They maintained that their Torah study and prayer in the Holy Land enabled Diaspora Jewry to exist; those Jews in the *galut* thus had the duty to provide for the Jews living in the Holy Land, and their support was demanded not as an act of mercy but as a lawful obligation.[33] This view was even formulated as halacha by R. Moses Sofer (the Hatam Sofer), who wrote: "It is up to us to maintain the habitation of Eretz Israel, not to aid [those settled there] but in order, ourselves, to perpetuate the Torah, for were it not for the Jews there, Torah itself would disappear, Heaven forfend."[34]

The other society, called the *New Yishuv,* came into being with the First Aliyah (of 1882) and was based on an ideology diametrically opposed to that of the Old Yishuv. Whereas the Old Yishuv saw the anomaly in its economic structure as a positive phenomenon, justified by the divine values of its faith, the New Yishuv could justify its existence only by successfully creating a society with a "normal" economic structure, operating self-sufficiently and supporting itself by its own labor. The economic support received from the Diaspora was considered, as a matter of principle by the New Yishuv, no more than temporary; its purpose was to help found an active society, living by the fruits of its labor, whereas the Old Yishuv regarded the "haluka," its economic support, a permanent situation by definition.

The economic dependence of the Old Yishuv upon the Jews of the Diaspora not only caused unhealthy relationships between "the position of the receivers" and "the position of the benefactors" but engendered ideological dependence of that population upon the rabbinic authority of the Diaspora, thus transferring the schism and disagreements of the Diaspora to public life in Eretz Israel.

One of the major bones of contention with the Orthodox community was naturally the problem of education and general knowledge. Every attempt to introduce changes or reforms in the arrangement of educational institutions was considered heresy, even if the initiators were accepted figures in the Orthodox community or supported by eminent rabbis. The majority of the public was usually swept along by the fanatic element, which did not refrain from using means of terror and violence.[35]

When Baron Rothschild proposed, in 1843, to provide the children of Jerusalem with the opportunity to learn some secular subjects, his suggestion was met with outrage.[36] The question of education reached a crisis stage some years later. In 1856, the Jewish Austrian poet, Ludwig August Frankel, arrived in Jerusalem with the intent of establishing a school there in the name of the aristocrat Lemel, where general subjects would be studied in addition to religious. The Sephardi head rabbi, R. Hayyim Nissim Abulafia, gave his approval and determined that nothing in the institution was in contradiction with the Jewish faith. The Ashkenazi community, however, violently rejected the idea, expressed vehement opposition, and even imposed the most radical measure of *herem* (ban); the announcement was written and signed by the rabbis of the Ashkenazi community.[37] It was applied to all of Eretz Israel and to anyone who would ever be there, forevermore, and was impossible to lift or nullify.[38]

Thus it can easily be argued it was the extremists who determined the public atmosphere in the Old Yishuv[39] rather than the rabbinic body, who for practical reasons were more moderate in their relationship to the Maskilim. This situation laid bare the leadership of the Old Yishuv in all of its weakness, for they essentially upheld the extremist position and thus, even when practical considerations made this group's actions objectionable, the rabbinic body could not stand firm and restrain them from their extremist ways. A prime example of the weakness of leadership can be found in the arrest of Eliezer ben Yehuda in November 1893. Ben Yehuda was an ardent antagonist of the Old Yishuv, and the Orthodox establishment tried to get rid of him by denouncing him as guilty of high treason. The strident criticism of the entire Jewish world and opposition to this act, however, forced its instigators to retract their accusation and to disavow what they had done.[40]

In fact, there was an additional cause for the tension between the Old Yishuv and the New. At the time of the First Aliyah (1882), the Old Yishuv was embroiled in a crisis in its relationship to the Diaspora communities. The development of the New Yishuv, which was of a mostly traditional nature, harbored within it a potential alternative to the aid sent by Diaspora Jews and received in Israel.[41] But the Old Yishuv feared their income from the "haluka" of Diaspora Jewry would be harmed, an event that could endanger their very existence in its traditional state. Non-observant Zionists were a minority in the Jewish community at that time, and the sharp disagreements thus occurred, for the most part, between Hungarian extremists and the Orthodox of German origin.

The situation began to change when the Zionist Organization was founded in 1897, and even more drastically in the period of the Second Aliyah (1905–1914), with its socialistic orientation and actively antireligious approach.[42] For the Old Yishuv, this aliyah symbolized the image of the secular Jewish settlement that was growing in Eretz Israel. The *halutz* (pioneer), a heroic figure in the eyes of secular Zionism and emblem of the modern Jew building Eretz Israel, was in the eyes of the Old Yishuv a symbol of all the dangerous evil of Zionism, the idol of a goddess set up in the king's palace.

The New Yishuv, for their part, viewed the Old Yishuv in the most negative light imaginable. Zionism, which sought to create a "normal" Jewish society in Eretz Israel, living from its own labors, whose sons would engage in creative occupations such as agriculture, crafts and industry, saw the Old Yishuv as a degenerate and corrupt society.

The question of the Second Aliyah's attitude to religion and tradition is a complicated one.[43] Its members had already been caught up in the process of secularization that had swept over Europe as a whole and over European Jewry in particular. They wished to find their Jewish identity in Jewish *nationalism*, which they saw as an appropriate substitute for religion. The close affinity between the religious and national aspect of Judaism gave the Jews of the Second Aliyah the impression of cultural continuity and a sense of Jewish identity, which also encouraged them to adopt an attitude of hostility or undisguised indifference and denigration toward religion.[44]

This fact made imperative a distinction between the concept of "religion" and the concept of "tradition." Although the opponents of

religion were adamant, many were uncertain in their view of tradition, and there were those who saw it as a key to the preservation of
historical continuity.[45] Just the same, the keeping of Jewish traditions
also went through a process of secularization, initiating changes in
behavioral norms and modes of living. As a result, Shabbat eve became a "cultural activity," festivals were the occasion for excursions or
days of leisure, and there were even attempts to create new
holidays—the First of May, Herzl Day, and so on.[46]

Even the Hebrew language itself underwent a process of secularization, and concepts with clear traditional significance such as
geula, kedusha, mitzvah, Torah, brit, and *korban* (sacrifice) acquired new
meaning in keeping with the new world-view. Thus "geula" (redemption) was understood as human liberation from supreme powers and
from religion, and the festival of redemption was the First of May.[47]
Use of the term *kedusha* (holiness) became at times a paraphrase of the
traditional Kiddush and the Kaddish, from which the name of God
was deleted and replaced by "the Jewish People" or "the *halutzim.*"
The Passover Haggadot composed by the kibbutzim are characteristic
of these changes. One such Haggadah contains the following Kiddush for Passover: "The sixth day. And the creation of heaven and
earth was complete. . . . Let us sanctify and bless . . . the halutzim of
our people and their aliyot, who planted the fields of our birth-
place . . . and may we celebrate more joyous holidays . . . and the
pioneer effort be sanctified, for its creation of a society of egality and
unity . . . which encouraged us and brought us proudly to our Land,
preserved us and caused us to reach this time. . . ."[48] In the Haggadah of Kibbutz Na'an of 1944, the following Kaddish appears:
"Yitgadal veyitkadash ha'adam ha'ivri" ("Glorified and sanctified be
[God's great Name] the Hebrew man").[49]

The *mitzvot* were conceived by socialistic Zionism according to
the same principle, and at the founding meeting of "The Council of
Teachers for the Jewish National Fund" that took place in 1927, the
"614th Commandment" was invented: every boy and girl from the
nine years and older was obligated by the commandment of nationalism to contribute regularly, on a monthly basis, to the Jewish National
Fund.[50]

Alongside this tendency there arose another, more radical
trend, which Buber and Bergman called a *process of collective assimilation.* Its nature was lucidly expressed by Joseph Hayyim Brenner, one
of the great authors of the Second Aliyah: "We want their [non-
Jewish] culture in our own streets, on our own land, within our
people, and what we would do were we intermingled with them we
are prepared to do amongst ourselves in our own way.[51] Above all we

want to be vital and alive, without the yoke of Torah and mitzvot and without the lies of faith and religion . . . "[52] In any case, common to all members of the Second Aliyah was the aspiration to liberation from the burden of Diaspora existence, escape from the religious commandments, and intellectual and creative freedom.

Paradoxically, despite the great social and spiritual disparity between the Old Yishuv and the Second Aliyah, confrontations between them were few. The arena of life and its struggles for the Jews of the Second Aliyah was principally on farms in the regions of Judea and the Galilee, and the geographical distance separating them from the extremists of Jerusalem certainly also contributed to the minimum of conflicts. Even in 1910, six years after the beginning of the Second Aliyah, David Ben Gurion wrote:

> The two parts of the Jewish population of Eretz Israel are separated by a yawning chasm, the small part being the New Yishuv, and the larger part the Old Yishuv . . . gangs of public robbers, commonly called *memunnim*, Gabbais, heads of kollels . . . who exploit the power they gain from the *haluka* to prevail over the public and enslave it, to annihilate every free idea and crush every attempt for liberation. . . . This sector is dead and buried, a population of obscurantists and schnorrers . . . [53]

No arguments were conducted with the New Yishuv. The *halutzim* simply recoiled from them. On veteran settlements, in contrast, differences of opinion and conflicts began to erupt between the original members, who were observant for the most part, and the newer arrivals of the Second Aliyah. This friction stemmed mainly from the markedly different style of life of the new workers as opposed to that of the veterans and from the observant Jews' suspicions their children would be influenced by the life-style of the "free ones." This suspicion had a legitimate basis, although the new workers did not try actively to demonstrate their "atheism" and arouse the rage of the veteran members.[54]

The Problem of Education—Tradition versus Innovation

Parallel to this development, disagreements within the Orthodox camp, between Jerusalem extremists and German immigrants, continued to escalate, reaching a climax in the early 1930s with the German Orthodox Aliyah to Eretz Israel. The members of Agudat Israel who immigrated to Israel did not wish to send their sons and daughters to the educational institutions controlled by the Orthodox Agudah population of Jerusalem. Moshe Blau, one of the heads of Agudat Israel in Jerusalem, visited Germany and wrote to M. Porush, also a head of Agudat Israel in Jerusalem, of the intent of R. Samson Breur "to immigrate and settle in Eretz Israel." "He is by profession an outstanding educator, distinguished Torah scholar, God fearing, and plans to open a school there that will include, to a certain extent, general studies. The priority, of course, will continue to be religious studies."[55] M. Porush responded: "Even if the learned rabbis of the High Court of Justice (may they live long and happily) were to agree to such a thing, would it be possible to contain Amram Blau or Asher Zelig Margolioth, and prevent them from making a scandal?!" And in another letter: "Our extremists have revived. They suspect the Germans [members of Agudat Israel of German origin] will introduce innovations in Agudah . . . and they are meeting in groups trying to strengthen their position.[56]

But without waiting for the approval of Agudat Israel of Jerusalem, the school Horev opened in Jerusalem in January 1934, designated for the children of German immigrants. The school offered its pupils a broad general eduation. Moreover, in the younger classes boys and girls studied together. The older children learned in separate groups, but classes were conducted in the same building and the playground was shared by both sexes.[57]

The school's opening occasioned renewed outbreaks of controversy, and the following statement appeared on an announcement board:

> How can we express our shame and disgrace? . . . Our brothers, the people of Agudat Israel, have opened in Jerusalem, the Holy City, a school called "Horev" which threatens the world's destruction. Boys and girls, young men and women learn there together in mixed classes, a thing unknown even in the schools of the Maskilim. Yet another mixture takes place there—the teachers are both male and female, with no assurance against forbidden acts of closeness and *yihud*, may G-d protect us, woe to our ears etc. The place has all the impure signs of a school: writing on blackboards, ringing of bells as in a church, learning from Landkarten, called maps . . . and the herem was violated by no other than Agudat Israel, who permitted itself what has been forbidden for eternity.[58]

Throughout his life and in his world-view, Rabbi Abraham Isaac HaCohen Kook acted as an intermediary between the struggling camps. He was a conservative rabbi of the old style, but at the same time the horizons of his thinking were no less broad than those of the Maskilim of his generation. His position found expression both on the essential theological level and in a practical sense. He phrased his view of the ultraorthodox approach in no uncertain terms:

> The enslavement of the intelligence and its stupefaction result from certain influences, and the more holy the influences, the greater the damage done, amounting to the corruption of the world, and resembling more and more the villainy of false prophecy in God's name, actions of wickedness and impurity, idol worship and abomination. Thus when the attempt to stupefy the intelligence is presented in the name of faith, of fear of Heaven, or diligence in Torah and fulfilling of mitzvot, it becomes a terrible lie and a filthy impurity. Then the holy ones of the Most High, God's pure servants, must go forth to redeem the world and Israel, the Torah, and all that is holy to the Lord from these destroyers. Let them be who they may: liars who want only to cheat their fellows or fur-cloaked deceivers, weak of spirit and small of mind, whose own intellectual light has been obstructed, their feelings dulled, and their imagination coarsened, who purposefully and thoroughly trample down the reality before them, their own faith enrooted in mere fables of faith. . . . And thus souls stumble and fall, and human beings live the lives of beasts, degradation without knowledge or understanding, without human honor, that most basic element in recognizing the honour of Heaven that fills the world, that gives life to all, and animates spirit and soul.[59]

Although Rav Kook's principles regarding general culture and the Haskala did find expression in the practical issues currently being confronted, they were formulated with much less freedom than that expressed on the theoretical level. He wrote explicitly that the *herem* prohibiting general studies was very harmful, and that "it was impossible to exist and to endure the new conditions of life without language and science. All of those who have thrown off the yoke of Torah and *mitzvot* educate their children in schools and prepare them to the utmost for the battle of life, while the children whose parents are bound to the holiness of Torah and faith lag behind them, exhausted, on the paths of life."[60]

At the time of his aliyah to Eretz Israel, Rav Kook had already reached the conclusion that "we must pave a new way to the revival of Judaism,"[61] necessitating a new approach to education, which would include study of history and philosophy, criticism and poetry, so that these academic domains do not remain the control of "those who desire the very destruction of the Torah and of faith in the Lord."[62] Yet Rav Kook refrained from public opposition to the *herem* and revealed his opinion only to a choice few that pupils must be trained "for the battle of life with the most essential languages and sciences."[63]

When Rav Kook was requested to relate to the possibility of establishing institutions where general subjects would also be studied, he responded by expressing his fear of open confrontation with the rabbis of Eretz Israel: "Certainly I will not be able to participate formally in such an establishment. I cannot distance myself too much from the boundary drawn by earlier rabbis limiting general education, especially in Eretz Israel. But the bitter truth that appeals to every heart compels me at the very least to take an interest in that holy institution."[64] In a distressed letter to Israel he explained:

> As one of the rabbis of Eretz Israel I cannot very well take formal part in this issue [the founding of a religious gymnasium], despite my belief in its holiness, due to the line of thought that reigns among the rabbis of Eretz Israel, imposed by previous generations, to stand in strict opposition to the influence of the Enlightenment, even when its ends seem to be elevated. True, emulated rabbis of our generation outside of Israel have recognized the situation, and many of them will gladly support it as a last resort.[65]

Moreover, Rav Kook was convinced that had the rabbis of the previous generation who had imposed the *herem* been familiar with the present situation, they would surely have been in favor of the establishment of the new schools.[66]

Political and sectarian pressures and the fear of a violent clash with the rabbis or Eretz Israel sometimes caused Rav Kook to phrase his words with great caution and even obscurity, in a tone that could be understood as a withdrawal from his positive attitude toward general education.[67] Nevertheless, his activity in favor of the establishment of new institutions in which general subjects would be studied, as in the schools in Germany of Rabbis Hirsch and Hildesheimer,[68] reflected his basic position, although this activity came only after much hesitation, difficult deliberation, and prolonged postponements.[69] The situation of Eretz Israel, in Rav Kook's eyes, held many latent dangers. The country's orthodox Jews continued to ignore the modern way of life and new developments, thus bringing on its own degeneration, whereas the Zionist *halutzim* had become willing captives of a foreign culture, attempting to clothe it in Jewish garb and unaware, in his eyes, that the soul of Israel could not be thus redeemed. An unprecedented rescue operation was therefore imperative, necessitating the establishment of new educational institutions, whose program of study would include all the disciplines demanded for the creation of a modern, improved society.[70]

Rav Kook thus supported the new school "Tahkemoni" of Jaffa, both in principle and in fact, and supervised it with consistency and rigor.[71] To his deep sorrow, the school did not fulfill the hopes invested in it, and his relation to Tahkemoni changed only a few years after it was founded. He did continue to support it as the "least of possible evils" and even agreed to allow the study of German as a foreign language, but no longer saw it as a institution from which the future spiritual leadership of the Jewish people would emerge.

In the polemics related to his support of Tahkemoni, opposing the *herem* on secular studies imposed by the rabbis of Jerusalem, Rav Kook made an effort to take a defensive stand in order not to agitate the controversy. In a letter to Rabbi Jehiel Michel Tykocinski (of blessed memory), Rav Kook wrote:

> I have never considered actively breaching the limits imposed by our predecessors in Eretz Israel to arrange the foundation of schools in which secular subjects and foreign languages would be taught even in the most pure holiness, and even by God-fearing and complete teachers, for discretion is the better part of valor. . . . Only when I saw honorable people acting for altruistic ideals had come to found such an institution . . . did I decide that we must proceed cautiously so as not to prohibit their doing so . . . [72]

This statement, like many similar statements voiced by Rav Kook, may testify not only to his apprehensions about causing controversy but also to the indecisiveness of his position, to his ambivalence regarding the new institutions. Nevertheless, his awareness of the deep crisis oppressing Judaism did not allow Rav Kook to stop his vigorous activity on behalf of education in the new style. The crown of his labors in Jaffa was the foudation of an advanced yeshiva of a new type, with unique educational goals, in which general subjects would also be studied.[73] Rav Kook hoped that the yeshiva would impart its spirit to the New Yishuv, the general nonobservant public, and would also influence the old-style yeshivot.

In 1907, approximately two years after his aliyah to Israel, Rav Kook began actions preparing the establishment of the yeshiva. In letters sent to rabbis, leaders, intellectuals, and educators, he presented his plan and submitted a long list of reasons justifying the establishment of the yeshiva and clarifying its aims. Following are some of his basic reasons:

A. It is appropriate that, parallel to the material development experienced by the population of Eretz Israel, a spiritual renewal also take place that will influence the image of the New Yishuv now being fashioned.

B. The spiritual leadership of the New Yishuv will blossom within the walls of the yeshiva.

C. The students of the yeshiva, who will occupy themselves, among other things, with the search for solutions to contemporary halachic problems, will consolidate a body of scholars, men of action, cultured and well-mannered, in Eretz Israel.

D. The yeshiva will provide the nation with all that it lacks spiritually, including literature and poetry, so that people with literary gifts will not be restricted to the circles of those who have rebelled against Judaism.

E. The yeshiva will emphasize the spirit of nationalism, and this will prove that even Orthodox yeshiva students of Eretz Israel do not lack nationalistic feelings.[74]

According to Rav Kook's plans, the yeshiva was to have been divided in two parts. The lower division was to serve as a sort of seminary for teachers and the upper division would be devoted to Torah for its own sake, rather than for practical ends. The program of studies of the lower division was to include religious studies in addition to general academic disciplines. General studies would include foreign languages, "Western and Eastern."[75] Rav Kook saw a practical advantage in the knowledge of Arabic and Turkish, for educated Torah scholars who also mastered those languages were likely to receive certain high government positions and could thus help improve the situation of the Jewish people in Eretz Israel. He did not feel graduates of the yeshiva were obligated to become rabbis. On the contrary, studies at the yeshiva would prepare them to work in all realms of life. In the upper division, the program of studies would include, in addition to traditional Jewish studies, subjects such as Jewish philosophy, Kabbalah, Aggadah, Midrash, ethics, and "all aspects of historical investigation." Another difference between this yeshiva and others was in its aesthetics. All the yeshiva's external arrangements, from its construction to the students' dress and manners "must be in good taste."[76]

Rav Kook feared sharp opposition to the yeshiva from the Old Yishuv, and preferred not to establish it in Jerusalem. He tried to summon the widest possible support of rabbis and leaders both in Israel and the Diaspora. In this battle, as always, Rav Kook struggled alone. He describes the situation in one of his letters: "It is very difficult for me to reach a compromise with my learned contemporaries, may God preserve them. . . . I am attacked right and left . . . but whom shall I speak with, and who will agree with me; who is willing to forsake his honor for the honour of God and his Torah and the sanctity of his beloved land?" (*Igrot Rayah,* vol. 1, pp. 310–311). Yet he did not flinch from the anticipated opposition, explaining even to those against his plans that the yeshivot that rely only on "*pilpul* (Talmudic dialectics) and excessive expertise will not be able to withstand the destroying stream."[77]

From "Zion" to "Jerusalem"

The revolution Rav Kook wished to initiate in the domain of education was aimed both at content and style. The particular emphasis on the aesthetic side of the yeshiva's arrangement and management emerges from an understanding of the repulsion and aversion aroused in the *halutzim* by the ghetto-like image of members of the Old Yishuv. Rav Kook's description, in one of his letters, leaves no doubt of where his sympathy lay. He writes:

> The spirit of the New Yishuv cannot bear the attitude, the sytle and the characteristics of the students of the Old Yishuv. This is true not only of rebels who have thrown off Torah and *mitzvot* but also of a large portion of reasonable people, learned and God fearing. The vital movement of the New Yishuv, the *joi de vivre* and courage of heart, broadening of knowledge, and national pride imbuing it cannot bear to see the hunched back, the drawn and melancholy face that summons fear and faintness of heart, the vague eyes and the despair and hatred of life behind them. The alien Eastern garb [= the Hassidic garment of Eastern-European Jews], combined with the depression of poverty, strikes terror and contempt in anyone accustomed to European life . . . [78]

Rav Kook's positive relation to the *halutzim* did not keep him from fierce struggles with them over issues he thought important, but his criticism never amounted to unconditional rejection of an activity or movement. Even his style reflected his basic relation, as he said: "I raise my voice about impurity whenever necessary, but I say what I must calmly and collectedly." This fact made continual dialogue possible with the leadership of the people of the Second Aliyah. He had a learning connection with Eliezer ben Yehuda, who, despite his ideological polarity to Rav Kook, would seek his advice on linguistic matters;[79] and with Hayyim Nahman Bialik[80] as well, who sent Rav Kook his commentary on the Mishna for his opinion of it. Rav Kook, for his part, was always interested in having his writings appear and read by the *halutzim* public,[81] and indeed, the writers of the Second Aliyah did not regard his essays with indifference. They valued his moderation and benevolence though they could not identify with his religious and mystical conception. Some expressed their respect for Rav Kook unequivocably, like Berl Katznelson, who said: "Two great Jews live in our midst here in Eretz Israel: Rav Kook and Yosef Hayyim Brenner."[82] Yet there were others who poured their fury and scorn upon him. When the subject of election of women to the Temporary Council Committee was under discussion, the newspaper *Hapo'el Hatza'ir* reacted in an aricle about the "meeting of the rabbis of Eretz Israel" in the following manner:

> If the holy Abraham Isaac HaCohen Kook, servant of holy worship in the Holy Land, etc. would like, in his great humility, to be the leader and Light of the Exile, no less,—why shouldn't he be; who is stopping him? . . . As far as we are concerned, he can occupy himself with philosophy and prayer too, and he'll always find a band of loafers who will lick their fingers with joy over his wisdom and profundity; but he'd better not dare bring that wisdom and profundity of his into our lives, to our harm and the impediment of the Hebrew Yishuv . . . [83]

Yosef Hayyim Brenner himself was ambivalent in his relation to Rav Kook and used to review his writings in *Hanir*, of which he was editor. In the end, Brenner reached the conclusion there was no sense or call for mockery. Something was happening in Rav Kook's circle. He found that "orthodoxy and enlightenment are being combined, and the holy stockings on the heels of the hypocrisy of necessity have been placed in European sandals; with his writers [of Rav Kook's circle], and especially in some famous lines of Rav Kook himself, we even feel our dialogue is with a thinking man, indeed with stormy and yearning souls."[84]

The reserved respect Brenner felt toward Rav Kook did not moderate his criticism. He rejected Rav Kook's religious-national view as "the fruit of the thoughts of a nebulous, mystical soul," and he could not agree with the invariable conclusions leading to faith and *mitzvah:* "[After] all his confused assumptions and untenable visions . . . he concludes with the verse, 'The just shall live by his faith.' . . . The adornments of 'unity and duality' [*Akhdut ve-Shniut*] are superfluous, and so are all the gyrations of "the essence of unbelief" [*Mahut ha-Kefira*]."[85]

A clear example of Brenner's complex relationship with Rav Kook is found in his criticism of the collection "Hatarbut haIsraelit" 5673 (1919):

> The thoughts of the author of this collection are not our thoughts, and the ways of he who penned "Hatarbut ha-Israelit" are not our ways. . . . The *exalted* world-view (we invoke this word in full recognition of our responsibility) expressed in all the "sperm" [play on the title *zer'onim*, also meaning "seeds"] of the honored Rabbi Avraham Isaac HaCohen Kook in that book is untenable as far as we are concerned, we who sit so low. Our own place of rest is not "in the Lord alone"; and we have no such place and have ceased searching for it. Our intellectual restlessness prevails over us. . . . What is more, sometimes we don't believe even he [Rav Kook] knows rest. The writer of the chapters "Haneshamot shel olam hatohu" ["Souls of Chaos"] and "Yisurim memarkim" ["Suffering Cleanses"] bears witness that the spiritual embellishments of the apostates and the "destroyers" are not foreign to him. . . . In any case, as for the literary side . . . The articulation of the author of *Zar'onim*, the poem "Lachashei he'havaya," the preface "Israeli Culture" . . . which is a culture of true literature—of this there is no doubt. The man on the street does not speak this way; his is the language of thinkers and serious men![86]

The essay Rav Kook composed together with Rabbi Yoseph Hayyim Zonnenfeld and a group of rabbis of the Old Yishuv on settlements in the Galilee also received mixed reactions from the members of the Second Aliyah. The people of Merhavia recall the visit of the rabbis thus:

> The delegation of rabbis who stayed with us a few days and nights. . . . We explained to them that the Arabs usually choose to attack us on Shabbat night, and so we must defend our property and our lives. . . . Rav Kook, of blessed and saintly memory, responded gently . . . that if, indeed, we are certain it

is a case of *pikuakh nefesh* [saving endangered lives], we are obligated to defend the place, even if it comes to desecrating the
Sabbath . . . —People of Merhavia who were estranged from
tradition—he won their deep respect . . . [87]

In contrast, there were those who contended that the delegation
of rabbis "did not receive much attention" and that "the farmers and
laborers . . . are too busy with plowing and planting, with protecting
their souls and their property, and had no desire to hear the 'moral
staff' of Rav Kook and his companions. So the rabbis left just as they
came, having changed nothing, their mission unsuccessful."[88]

Yet disagreement between Rav Kook and the leadership of the
Zionist movement went far beyond specific contemporary issues. The
dispute turned on an understanding of the very objective of the Zionist movement, and a view of the revival undertaking either as a solely
political creation or, rather, as the beginning of a more comprehensive and general renewal—social, cultural, and religious. Rav Kook
sought dialogue with the heads of the Zionist movement both in
public challenges and in writing, as well as in personal discussions.[89]
The fact that, in his eyes, the Zionist movement was concerned only
with the physical revival of the nation,[90] with restoring the body
without renewing the spirit, led him to decide that a second powerful
movement must arise parallel to the Zionist movement, which would
concentrate on the spiritual and cultural edification of the nation. This
movement was to be called *Degel Yerushalayim* ("The standard of Jerusalem"), and at its heart was to be a spiritual center that would rein-
force and cultivate spiritual leadership for the entire people. In a letter
to R. Hayim Hirschensohn on 14 Kislev 1920, Rav Kook wrote:

> And as for our Movement for National Revival itself, I
> believe that since the days of Herzl and until the present time,
> only the secular side of the issue has begun to be realized, which
> is a very pleasant and honorable thing, and the secular is des-
> tined to become the base of the holy, for which all of Israel's
> delight will be contracted. And in order to complete the revival
> movement and elevate it to the highest plane, we must now
> create the holy side of the movement, which would appro-
> priately be called "Jerusalem" as the name of the city in which
> God is present. Just as the name "Zion" signified the secular
> aspect of statehood, so the name "Jerusalem" will signify the
> idea of sanctuariness, for all the pure ideals ready to issue from
> it to Israel, and to man. The two movements will proceed to-

gether in friendship and mutual aid, but free as well and unoppressed. Then the light of honor will shine from each side and illuminate the other, and we will enjoy the brilliance of the secular together with the splendor of the holy, emerging and radiating from "Zion" and from "Jerusalem." To this end, our center has been founded here and now, and named "Histadrut Yerushalayim" ["The Jerusalem Agency"], which proclaims every Jew must be a Zionist in order to do the secular work of the nation, and must be Jerusalemite in order to do her holy service. And each agency must be managed by powers suited to it; the secular Zionist Agency by nonobservant people expert in their fields, and the holy Jerusalem Agency by sanctified people expert in their fields.[91]

The movement "Degel Yerushalayim" was in fact established and branches of it were even opened in some European cities and the Soviet Union, but its life was short. When Rav Kook returned to Israel after the war, he assumed the Jerusalem rabbinate and decided to realize his former dream to establish an advanced yeshiva of a new nature, this time not only for the benefit of the New Yishuv, but for the sake of the entire Jewish nation scattered throughout the world. Rav Kook did not believe the necessary changes could be effected within existing establishments, and thus sought to found a new yeshiva.[92] This yeshiva was to be a "Holy Center" for the entire nation in the Diaspora, and young strength both from Eretz Israel and the Diaspora would be concentrated in it.[93]

In 1921, Rav Kook founded "The Mercaz" ("Center"), which was to be a modest beginning to the establishment of the big "Central Universal Yeshiva", or as Rav Kook called it, *Hayeshiva ha-Clallit*[94] or *Mercaz ha-rav*.[95]

The curriculum of the yeshiva was to include the disciplines of halacha, Midrash, Aggadah, principles of interpretation and halachic ruling, Bible, with the support of all disciplines and knowledge that "leads to probing the depths of Torah and her holiness," Jewish history, history of Eretz Israel, ancient and modern Jewish philosophy, written and oral expression. The development of expressive ability, both oral and written, was one of the important challenges Rav Kook sought to address within the framework of the new yeshiva. He maintained literary style should be developed to "accustom and teach our students, the future shepherds and leaders of Israel, to write in clear and beautiful style . . . then our students will know how to stand in the breach and respond with eloquence to any raging wind or tempest." Moreover, it was necessary "to develop the gift of speech to its fullest, and thus the vital homiletic ability of our students."[96]

At the conclusion of their studies, students were to return to their homes in the Diaspora to serve as rabbis, authors and educators, thus realizing the goals of the yeshiva: "To bring our people, God's people, out of secular narrow-mindedness, out of the limitations of the galut, out of the spiritual bondage that bows down before every foreign idea and mistaken opinion, and to spread rays of light in the vast darkness of the exile, to the eyes of God's entire people."[97]

The curriculum that Rav Kook proposed for the Central Universal Yeshiva was not yet entirely satisfactory, and he recognized the contribution offered by academic studies and the cross fertilization likely to ensue from close connections between Torah scholars and academicians. In a letter to his student Benjamin Menashe Levin, who began university studies, Rav Kook wrote:

> I send you my most heartfelt blessing on the occasion of your entrance into the university. I wish you success, the horn of light be raised to its highest, to Torah and to Israel, with God's help. . . . What would make me most happy in your entrance to the labor so necessary to our generation is to exalt the Lord's name and to wave the flag of Israel on high, by the wise of heart who have learned academic methods. Thus it is very good that we can unite, for the views and the internal perspective of people such as myself may be of much benefit, with God's blessed help, to those armed with knowledge of the European sort, just as we will benefit by the path and style of those educated in the houses of Yaphet (universities) as well.[98]

Rav Kook related to the details of the academic disciplines as well; in his mind, philosophy, Semitic languages and literature, and national economics were particularly important. Indeed, for the sake of scientific completeness "things hidden in the other realms of knowledge" should also be studied.[99] But in any case these disciplines would be the instrumental ones in confronting the essential challenges, both spiritual and practical, posed by the age.

Rav Kook was not of the opinion that these disciplines must be studied within the yeshiva, but his relation to the university was complex. Still, he was aware the horizons and capacities of the yeshiva's students must be broadened. His program outlined a necessary minimum, guided by the intent not to harm the traditional character of the yeshiva, on the one hand, and yet, on the other, to respond to the challenges of the times. The education program he envisaged for the Central Universal Yeshiva was never realized.

In sum, Rav Kook did not succeed in initiating revolutionary changes in his society. Under the circumstances, even the little he did accomplish is seen as a breakthrough (or, in the eyes of the ultra-orthodox, as a breaking of boundaries). His unequivocally positive attitude toward secular studies and the necessity of dealing with the new reality has not yet been accepted by the ultraorthodox population of Eretz Israel. Nonetheless, after Rav Kook's death, far-reaching changes did occur in the structure of education and ways of thinking, even within the circles of Agudat Israel.[100] The founding of a chain of high school yeshivot, which include wide general eduation in their curriculum and, in their wake, the "Hesder" yeshivot, which combine Torah study with I.D.F. army service,[101] reflects a process of increasing recognition of needs and willingness to confront reality. The ideology of the Hesder yeshivot is founded on the teachings of Rav Kook.

In the long term, his theoretical teaching, in all its complexity, originality, and daring served as a gateway of hope for the renewal of traditional Jewish creativity, for it earnestly grappled with the question of the meaning of religion in the modern world. And yet, for many years Rav Kook's teaching did not leave the four walls of the *beit midrash*, a sort of inheritance hidden out of love. Almost secretly, a body of young spiritual leaders gradually formed, awaiting the time for action. The hour arrived at last—the Six-Day War and, even more, the Yom Kippur War—and a tremendous force of spiritual energy was released, creating and empowering an activist social-ideological movement commanding attention: pride and support from one side, fear and opposition from the other. Unfortunately, because Rav Kook's teaching has entered the public domain, his name has become associated with an ideology characterized not by complexity and multidimensionality but by fanatic adherence to a single idea.

Parallel processes are currently taking place in Jewish society in Israel: religious and antireligious extremism, on the one hand, and a longing for openness, tolerance, and pluralism, on the other. Political moderation opposes messianic fervor. Each waves the banner of Rav Kook's writings and finds support in them. Some emulate his conservatism and extremism, whereas others celebrate his openness, moderation, and modernity.

The disparity between the radical nature of his thought and his conservative approach to practical halacha is one of the enigmas to be confronted in this book.

PART TWO

Elements of Reality and Perception

2

Reality and Truth—Epistemology and Ontology

Any attempt to describe and analyse Rav Kook's thought in a systematic manner must include thorough consideration of central epistemological and ontological issues, for such concerns are vital to his original and uniquely Jewish attitude on metaphysical questions and serves, as well, as the basis of his outlook on a wide range of subjects.

Exploration reveals that Rav Kook followed no precise and consistent epistemological theory, although he does show a clear inclination toward a certain view of the world whose fundamental elements are kabbalistic and neo-Platonian. The absence of a consistent epistemological theory in Rav Kook's thought is no accident; one could even say it is essential, rooted in his own theory of knowledge and extensively substantiated. This personal epistemology is founded on the possibilities inchoate in kabbalistic theology, yet the principle attitude characterizing it is of post-Kantian nature; that is, his view expresses a mood that took root in modern Western thought after Kant, according to which cognition in the mystical realm is impossible. In the following discussion, we will try to uncover and examine the ontological and epistemological elements composing the picture of reality Rav Kook conceived.

Certainty and Doubt

In his conception of reality, certainty and doubt are interdependent. Despite the atmosphere of certainty pervading his writings, one

31

cannot ignore the threads of doubt that run through it in everything concerning precise formulation and definition of the image of reality. Rav Kook expressly avers the existence of a realm in which our knowledge is no more than an assumption:

> Love of pure knowledge must be constrained that it not hinder us from continually desiring what is higher and more sublime than our pure knowledge, to what we can attain only by direct *speculations,* hidden feelings, and at times by *meditations of the heart and imaginings, like visions and waking dreams;* for just as they can harm us when out of laziness and used by science to gain possession of its clear knowledge, so they can ennoble us, grounding the parts familiar to us with greater clarity, and elevating our entire being when they come from things exalted beyond the grasp of our knowledge. And we, spurred by our desire for peace, our soul full with longing for spiritual radiance, are driven to search even in what is hidden from us, beyond our clear understanding, until we bring ourselves to *speculate,* to indulge in spiritual luxuries for precious ends, by means of cogitations of the soul, *aided by imagination,* which also becomes sanctified and carved in scientific form, using its strength in a worthy manner. And about this it is said, "contemplate what is permitted to you."[1]

Rav Kook's words may be interpreted as a reaction to the "scientifistic" mood of empiricism and logical positivism. He was still caught up in the tension between his modern, post-Kantian view, conscious of the limitations of human understanding, concerned with the complete subjectivity of knowledge,[2] sensitive to positivistic criticism against all metaphysics and his intuitive tendency toward a very particular vision of reality.[3]

Esteem of pure science does not, in Rav Kook's eyes, mandate the abandonment of metaphysical speculations. Just as science is of foundational value in a certain realm, so speculations, in another realm, play a role in attaining what Rav Kook calls *precious ends.* And not only "direct speculations" but "hidden feelings" as well, "meditations of the heart and imaginings, like visions and waking dreams," all these can be thought of as levels of knowledge in a domain beyond the grasp of science. Metaphysical speculations are legitimate, he affirmed, as long as there is awareness of their place and limitations:

> If only the content is not changed, letting a speculative concept be held as a scientific one, or an imaginary idea as

something speculative, intellectual, and so on, for then one can be snared in the net of error. But when one is cautious of the *limits of his understanding*, and knows how to go beyond the revealed to the concealed, *to things so lofty and sublime that his only access is through speculation and imagination*, then man himself will discover the power of heaven, and the supernal light will shine on him, for his way is before the Lord.[4]

This does not imply that Rav Kook's approach is phenomenological, or at least not radically phenomenological. He believed fully in the existence of absolute reality. But in his opinion, the exact image, the way of being of this reality is not at the moment given to scientific understanding and, unavoidably, must be approached by means of conjecture and imagination.

Rav Kook holds that hypothesis and imagination are not inferior to science as means to knowledge, but rather the opposite. If different kinds of knowledge were arranged on a scale, science would be at the bottom, with speculation and imagination superior to it.[5] The difference among these kinds of knowledge is in the regions to which they are directed. Rav Kook expected that, as human knowledge increases, so the domain of science will broaden and things that were formerly no more than speculation will become known. The process of broadening in the realm of human knowledge is infinite, and thus the scale of types of knowledge remains; yet, as knowledge develops, there is a shift in domain among their various levels. As he said: "In time, some imaginary parts will become speculation, and some speculations will be clarified in knowledge and pure awareness; then the imaginings and the speculations will rise, becoming more noble and sublime. And man will go from strength to strength."[6] On the basis of this remark we can understand his comment that "remote suggestions," "like dreams," preceed the exact sciences, presaging their appearance.[7]

The graduation of levels of knowledge is not determined by the degree of certainty they impart, for "certainty alone, with all its holiness and splendor, is the groundstone of spiritual life only when it joins with the meaning of its content, and meaningful yet doubtful content may even be of immeasurably more worth than content that is lowly but certain. It is better to trust in God than in man."[8] The importance of a certain type of knowledge, then, is not in its degree of clarity but rather in the object to which it is directed and that it aspires to grasp. The "higher" is the object of knowledge or, in other words, the nearer it is to the level of the essence of being, to the thing itself, the more diminished the level of clarity and certainty; yet, at the same time the value and importance of the levels of knowledge increase. "By the strength of speculation and highest imagination, we rise to the source of wisdom and the place of understanding, higher than wisdom and understanding themselves. But where shall wisdom be found? And where is the place of understanding? God understands its ways, and he knows its place. (Job 28:12, 23)."[9]

In a more profound sense, Rav Kook's words imply it is a mistake to attribute to science the ability to attain certainty, as a skeptical approach can undermine any scientific theory. This same skepticism, sometimes aroused in one and even leading one to formulate an entire philosophical theory, originates, in Rav Kook's view, in the mind, "but emotion is deeper, and it stands in certainty."[10] Beyond this phenomenological statement, however, Rav Kook highly valued imagination as a means of gaining information in the metaphysical realm and, in his eyes, imagination has special importance, related to his conception of revelation.[11]

From the preceding introductory remarks, we see clearly that Rav Kook refrained from granting truth and certainty to metaphysical speculations and defining them as conjectures or even imaginings. This approach is also evident when he treats specific subjects; a fundamental uncertainty is audible in his phrases. One of the most prominent examples is in his discussion of the subject of "will." In one instance Rav Kook wrote: "Free will, illuminated by the supernal intellect, is the quiddity of being revealed within it, and that is the soul of Adam haRishon, the First Man in all its fullness."[12] Elsewhere, Rav Kook expressed the apparent opposite, saying that will "is not the essence of being."[13] In yet another place he broached the subject in a more skeptical tone: "Complete freedom and the will within it, burdened by nothing external, serve to *reveal* the very essence of life, that life which accepts the plan of good or evil fortune. . . . Perhaps free will is the essence of life. . . . We have no need to attribute essence to anything other than free will."[14] Thus we see that, on the subject of will, a central and vital element of his thought (to be discussed more extensively later), Rav Kook's conception is not unequivocal, clear, or precise. That is the rule, as we have said, for basic knowledge, because in the metaphysical realm we must rely on speculation alone; as a result, not only marginal details but the issues themselves vary in their formulation and definition in Rav Kook's writings.

He averred that our clear and evident knowledge of the divine is minimal: "Our main knowledge of God is: "One, Creator, Lawgiver."[15] Rav Kook did not indicate the source of this knowledge; as far as he was concerned, it should be seen as evident knowledge.[16] If we can be said to know anything about the divine, it is the three attributes mentioned previously. All other speculations, "all the riches of spirituality can only give interpretations and explicit descriptions of how to understand this information, to purify it and raise it to a higher ideal, more noble, intelligent, practical, more simple and sublime."[17] All speculations are interpretations of this evident knowledge, and because they are no more than interpretations, their status is relative, giving rise to no interpretations whose goal differs from that of the information itself.

One of the basic assumptions of Rav Kook's epistemology (which also never exceeds the bounds of conjecture) is the supposition of the "equivalence of values" [השתוות הצרכים], by which the various parts of reality are in total accord with each other, thus allowing particulars to illumine the whole, the spiritual to be learned from the material, and so on. He wrote: "Were it not for the equivalence of existence, no wisdom could develop. Because spiritual creation is so abundant, and wisdom gives life to all, the order of reality must of necessity contain equivalence of values, that one part points to another, the particularity to the general, the material to the spiritual, and the imagination to the intellect."[18]

In the spirit of this basic assumption, Rav Kook raised the following questions: "Why are events of being as a whole not compared to the events of man, the unique creature; why is being itself not explained by its most visible part?"[19] Indeed, the principle of parallelism justifies, in Rav Kook's eyes, the use of anthropomorphic terminology in describing all being.[20] What is interesting is that, although Rav Kook granted a high degree of truth value to the assumption of "equivalence of values," it remains for him no more than conjecture despite its ability to "bring us closer to truth." As he said:

> Our equalized values are not external values at all but rather internal, essential. And is essence not divine greatness, praise without end, high above the bounds of quantity and quality? And as for the ultimate value of this unestimable, this measure of truth, all is no more than one small point whose very disunity is inconceivable. It is like a single atom compared to the light of *En Sof*.[21] This *speculation* is what brings us *closer* to the lucidity of truth.[22]

Rav Kook's claim of the relativity and uncertainty of all metaphysical information leads to a fundamental question: What is the value of metaphysical speculations, and why should we deal with them? One aspect of the answer to this question is found in something hinted earlier: The importance of speculations in their truth content. We will return to this issue in the course of our discussion. At this point I would like to broach another aspect of the answer. Rav Kook seems to suggest the impetus to deal with metaphysical conjecture is connected to the need to fulfill spiritual desires. This quality of wish fulfillment is not part of the nature of science; on the contrary, it characterizes the sort of study Rav Kook called *mysteries of the Torah* ("razei Torah"). He wrote:

> Limited human science is a worthy tool for deracinating the alien roots of false imaginings, which must be uprooted—these imaginings are based in human ignorance and his tendency to evil. Yet the great happiness that pervades the heart with holy joy when his highest wishes are fulfilled comes about only through the mysteries of the Torah, which present man with the luminous mirror of his soul, vital and sublime, as it truly is.[23]

In the term *mysteries of the Torah*, Rav Kook refers not only to the *sefirot* of kabbalistic teaching but to those same speculations and thoughts common to the mind of every individual, and it makes no difference whether they are expressed in kabbalistic language or otherwise:

> Mystical thought is the freedom of Israel, of the Israelite soul. She is a unique soul, nourished by the dew of life of the People of Israel, thinking and imagining according to her nature, guided by the influences that caused her to think about those events, monumental in the history of Israel, of divine descent, supreme and pre-eminent, which appeared in that marvellous nation.
>
> When freedom ascents to its zenith, when the soul no longer suffers the burden or yoke of conventional opinion whose source is not in Judaism, then the ideas continually created by that pure holiness are themselves mysteries of the Torah. Whether they are phrased in the language and style commonly used by the masters of mystery or in another manner or literary style—it makes no difference.[24]

What we see here is a significant expansion of the term *Kabbalah*, evident in the conclusion of the preceding passage: "and the People of Israel [*Knesset Israel*] is itself the inheritance Moshe received from Sinai [קבלה למשה מסיני]."[25] Thus in Rav Kook's view, Kabbalah is not only a tradition of knowledge handed down from Adam to Moshe and to our own day, as the kabbalists held,[26] but also the original creation of the individual Jew. We find here an awareness and legitimization of innovation itself.[27]

In any case, the justification for dealing with metaphysical speculations is not necessarily in their degree of certainty and truth value, but rather in the essential role these suppositions play in the human spiritual world and in determining our way of life. To decide how to live, one needs an image of the world, some ideological model, which in Rav Kook's eyes bears great influence on the nature of human life: "Connection with any content breaks a path in life, and if that content is elevated and sublime, so will the paths of life be elevated and sublime as well; if the content is lowly and degenerate, the paths of life will be equally lowly and degenerate. But life will have paths wherever there is a permanent attachment to some content."[28] The picture of human reality is clearly connected to the human moral state "because human representations, however they relate to the image of reality, also undergo a special process in man's moral development."[29]

Rav Kook's view of metaphysical study as speculation, and the connection between human commitment in the metaphysical realm and the human moral state underlie his justification of the kabbalistic conception of emanation:

> The conception of emanation was not engendered, in the system describing it, by the conviction that creation ex nihilo is absolutely impossible, that all of existence was and comes into being by the spirit of the living God alone, the world's true Being in the divine alone, in supreme faith. The idea was conceived, rather, because absolutely nothing hinders us from representing reality in that manner; we thus have no more need for other ways, and we can easily think that all naturally emanates from God and nothing aside from Him is needed; hence those sages are ill at ease with the notion of being created from total nothingness in the simple sense.[30]

The idea of emanation, then, is possible, and that fact explains the tendency toward it; this very possibility makes it even more reasonable than any other idea (speaking of creation ex nihilo, meaning the godhead exceeding its own confines, for its possibility eliminates the need for any other idea). The idea of emanation can thus be seen as a speculation "bringing us closer to the brightness of truth," mainly by the grace of its simplicity. Yet the idea of emanation has another advantage, from an educational-moral perspective:

Indeed, the great miracle and depth of devotion, the high-est moral influence in all the wonders, simplistically called *ex nihilo*—these are abundant in the doctrine of emanation. Ac-cording to this teaching, which magnifies the understanding of His exclusivity to a higher significance, and the sense of faith in the depth of His great holiness tends more and more toward the melody of that wondrous vision, for it is better to take refuge in the Lord than to trust in man. Even Adam Kadmon, the Primal Man—the nothingness before his being had no refuge in God; God became his refuge only after man was created, and this is a flaw in the man's longing for the holy. But the most sublime of views says, "Lord, you have been our dwelling place in all gen-erations. Before the mountains were brought forth, and before ever you had formed the earth and the world, even from ev-erlasting to everlasting, you are God." (Psalms 90:1–2)[31]

In Rav Kook's opinion the moral meaning of the idea of creation ex nihilo is in one's connection to one's Creator and nostalgia for Him as one's refuge. In this sense, the idea of emanation is indeed compel-ling in its affirmation of an eternal attachment, without beginning and everpresent.

In other passages, Rav Kook points to the principle of freedom as the sole reassuring principle the heart can accept in establishing a picture of reality. In the following statement, he reacted to the idea, propounded by Nietzsche, of humankind's jealously of God:

It is very difficult to imagine God and His relation to the world and all its creatures when divine existence is represented as external to the world's existence, for then it would seem that God had somehow managed to be most fortunate of all, while all of creation is lacking, failed in its attempt to be like Him.

And for this reason the soul is inclined toward an image of all-encompassing unity that recognizes God alone, yet aware that no single manifestation is really God but rather everything, and the source of all and what is beyond that. But what sepa-rates the isolated manifestation from the divine is not truth in and of itself; only our blindness makes it seem so, for we are in-capable of distinguishing more than individual details, and our own reality, with all its deficiencies, is no more than blindness.

But even this belief does not suit the other conditions for happiness hidden in the caches of the heart. *What assuages the mind is the element of happiness in freedom,* justice free and com-plete, the absolute good, which in its freedom inclines to the good, it is necessary to existence, and every individual in his freedom can ascend to the source of his desire, and when he reaches for absolute good, *he will be drawn into the body of the King, and nothing will separate him from his God;*[32] "But your iniquities have made a separation between you and your God" (Isaiah 59:2).

Thus we realize true being is in the divine, and all of existence beneath God's supremity is no more than the descent of will in its incomplete choice, causing yet more loss, until at last all impurity will perish, and will in its freedom will rise to the absolute good, and the Lord will be one and his Name one. And this return of all to the divine is the supreme completeness of existence, its essence is inconceivable. The idea that all of being is divine, that nothing is wholly separate from God, is a delight to the heart. The *spiritual pleasure* caused by this idea is the *sign* of its truth.[33]

Rav Kook was not satisfied with the commonly accepted monotheistic view, which conceives a fundamental cleavage between God and the world, nor with the pantheistic view, which holds "the representation of God . . . nullifies the whole of existence."[34] The pantheistic-acosmic idea is rejected for, in Rav Kook's eyes, "the practical world cannot conduct itself" according to it.[35]

The more favored idea, Rav Kook believed, is that which sees the element of freedom, weighted with moral significance, as fundamental to existence.[36] This element he described as "justice free and complete, the absolute good, the free which, in its freedom, inclines to the good," and it provides the basis for liberty of the individual: "And every person, in this freedom, can ascend to the source of his desire."[37] This, then, is a return to the acosmic idea, although with an essential change in human consciousness: the existence of reality is not nullified relative to God, but rather the opposite; existence is intensified in God.[38]

Thus we find Rav Kook's approach to the ontological question is not unequivocal: in the practical sense, the monotheistic view is imperative, yet as far as truth is concerned, the pantheistic-acosmic idea is preferable, though it too is not suited to all "the other conditions for happiness hidden in the caches of the heart." Thus, as a sort of compromise, Rav Kook developed the element of "the happiness in freedom, justice free and complete, the absolute good, the free which, in its freedom, inclines to the good"; that is, the dynamic principle of being.[39]

Rav Kook's considerations in stating his metaphysical position are thus not solely epistemological. Certain spiritual and ethical aspirations shift the scales toward one picture of reality or another. This pragmatic attitude, combined with his epistemological consider- ations, preclude a measure of certainty allowing a consistent ontologi- cal conception to be formed.

It is important and interesting as well to note that Rav Kook sometimes regarded his own kabbalistic world-view reflexively; at these times he called the metaphysical speculations *conjectures*, aware of the uncertainty, relativity, and subjectivity characteristic of opin- ions in that domain. At other times, in contrast, Rav Kook compre- hended his self-reflection in the concepts and assumptions of his kabbalistic world-view, as in the following passage: "Even conjecture of the mysteries of Torah is of great importance. For everything de- pends on the supreme capacity, which has no limit or end. And its beauty and wonder is a revelation, somehow containing within it the light of all life. 'Thy testimonies are very sure: holiness becomes thy house, O Lord, for length of days' (Psalms 93:5)."[40]

Speculations are thus perceived as expressing and reflecting absolute truth, the "light of all life," that is, the source of being; and they are interpreted as testimony of their origin or as an appearance that is revelation.[41]

We can summarize our discussion in this way: Rav Kook's meta- physical view is a philosophical attitude that may be termed *mature;* its perspective regarding philosophy no longer allows it to remain bound to a particular metaphysical idea in absolute certainty of its truth and without seeing itself as obliged to justify that idea and demonstrate its reasonability—note: its reasonability and not its ne- cessity. Rav Kook tried his utmost to explain his preference, on well- known grounds, for one metaphysical idea over another. This fact does not prevent him from building a metaphysical picture of the world[42] and to speak of it, for the most part, with certainty, inspiring even the reader of his works with a spirit of certainty. Rav Kook himself pointed out this paradox and explained the source of both certainty and skepticism in the duality of the human personality: the source of certainty is in emotion, and skepticism in the intellect.[43] This does not imply the certainty of emotion is necessarily irrational. On the contrary, the mind demands the intelligibility and reasonabili- ty even of truths originating in emotion: "Limited human science is a proper tool to deracinate the alien roots of false imaginings, which must be uprooted."[44] Yet the critical mind is unable to construct a picture of the world whose certainty would allow one to navigate the course of one's life by it.[45]

Reality and Truth—The Ontological Status and Epistemological Value of Metaphysical Speculations

As we remarked previously, the necessity of existence is an evident truth in Rav Kook's conception. In the following discussion, we will see how deeply he explored the subject, boldly developing a number of its implications. In one instance, he treated the dispute between Maimonides and the theologians of the kalam on the issue, writing: "In holiness there is no exaggeration of reality. Everything that is represented and imagined and can be represented—all is common truth. That was the core of the method employed by the Mutakallimum, rejected by Scholasticism for not being able to explain themselves."[46] Others, however, have already pointed out this was not the disagreement.[47] Maimonides rejected the kalam's premise of the "different possibilities" devoid of relation to reality.[48] In Maimonides's view, what is possible is real, and although its reality may not be necessary, its way of being is indeed necessary.[49] Hence Maimonides's belief that all that is possible exists, but the assertion is attenuated by its reverse formulation: only what exists is possible. Reality, for Maimonides, means the laws of reality.[50]

Thus Rav Kook fully comprehended Maimonides's view and his dispute with the kalam. He presented the position of the kalam exactly as Maimonides understood it: "All that is represented and imagined and can be represented." The kalam spoke of the logical admissibility of the existence of various possibilities, whereas Maimonides identified logical possibility with reality and rejected the position of the kalam by describing their "possibilities" as imaginings. Rav Kook was imprecise in attributing to the kalam the necessity of existence rather than necessity of possibility alone. He himself adopted the necessity of possibility from the kalam and the necessity of existence from Maimonides and created the following formulation: "All that is represented and imagined and can be represented—that is what truly exists." This formulation indeed reflects Rav Kook's essential view, as expressed in the following passage:

> All that is born from the mind's intelligence is reality itself. And the more clearly it is conceived, the stronger and more active its reality. The higher and more encompassing the quality of intelligence, the more able it will be to vitalize and heal the spirit, that it may bear the fruit of life.
>
> The vital quality in *En sof* is divine intelligence; all that flows from its spirit, the more it is connected to the divine source, the stronger the living link between them will be. And

those truly devoted to God thus feel the vigor of their lives in divine thought. It is this vigor of life that strengthens, refining and instilling supreme happiness. "And I will rejoice in the Lord, I will rejoice in the God of my salvation" (Habakkuk 3:18).[51]

Here Rav Kook took yet another important stride. The "possible and the existing" refer to what exists in actuality as opposed to all that is possible in thought. Thus, Rav Kook's description of human thought as "flowing from the spirit" of "the divine intelligence," that is, from the *sefirah* of *hokhma* [the "wisdom" or primordial idea of God], already confirms its ontological status. All thoughts and speculations are possesed of real existence.[52]

This position is in fact mandated by the concept of God's completeness as Rav Kook understood it:

> As for the divine, everything already exists in reality, for all that was, is, and will be—all is in His spirit, knowledge and desire. . . . It is a basic principle that divine knowledge encompasses what is in reality, because there is nothing outside of reality as far as God is concerned. . . . Moreover, it is irrelevant to speak of God's knowledge encompassing what is not part of reality, for since His knowledge encompasses all, He is inherent in the most excellent aspects of reality, and the entirety of earthly realities are no more than tiny sparks in the light of that supernal reality.[53]

By seeing all absolute existence as evident,[54] Rav Kook must negate the possibility of "nothingness" [the *"En"*].[55] The idea of "nothingness" "is a relative matter," dependent on the perception of creatures;" that is, without real existence. The concept of "nothingness" allows one to recognize its opposite, "reality,"[56] but this too is a relative term. Our consciousness perceives not "nothingness" but rather what is real alone because the latter is a branch of divine knowledge, thus acquiring similar characteristics.[57]

Now that thoughts have been defined ontologically as real entities, nothing remains but to affirm their epistemological value as truths, for what exists is true by necessity:

> All thoughts are true in the divine, [and neither merit nor deficiency can harm him], for God's greatness is so exalted that all deficiency is in Him utter virtue, as in the opposition of the attribute of justice and the attribute of mercy, or the use of nega-

tive attributes for positive ends in moral life. Do not try to understand everything, for in truth no thought can grasp this in the least. And in any case, all thoughts are illuminated by its light, just as all of being exists in it.[58]

Thus, the concept of the infinite absolute leaves no room for the concept of "nothingness"[59]; or more precisely, if there is a place for the concept of "nothingness" it is because "there is nothing without a place"; or the concept of the complete [השלם] necessarily includes contradiction, comprehending both concepts of "nothingness" and "reality." "All deficiency is utter virtue"[60] because all oppositions and contradictions gather together beneath the wings of the method. The concept of the complete does not allow a single element to be removed from the method. When the real is identical with the true, the assertion is justified that "the possible speculations within the holy are the most sublime songs, and the supreme truth contained in them is revealed by them."[61] He said as well:

All thoughts are reasonable, systematically connected. Even those we recognize only in the sprouting of an idea, when we dig down to their root, we discover they have grown from the source of reason, for that is the nature of thought.

And in any case we know no thought in the world is meaningless; there is a place for everything, for all flows from the source of wisdom. If there are flawed or empty thoughts, those flaws and emptiness are no more than external; when we penetrate to their innermost nature we find the life in them, for wisdom is the source of life.[62]

The concept of the complete includes, as we have said, all oppositions, a problematic condition in terms of the laws of logic.[63] Rav Kook was aware of this difficulty and, in confronting it, laid the philosophical groundwork to a solution of the paradox in his conception of reality. His writings contain four different approaches to dealing with the problem of antimony, which can be traced to the following philosophical schools of thought.[64]

According the the first school, oppositions are no more than different aspects of a single reality. This contention is expressed in a letter to Shmuel Alexanderov written in Jaffa in 1908:

To my surprise, his honor responded to all I wrote on the subject of opposites with the well-known comment that two opposites cannot possibly exist in a single subject. And I was astonished, for that is just what is needed. The innovation I suggest is that, for highest thought, which penetrates to the depths of things, reality contains no opposites; every case where opposites are apparent, there is surely some invisible condition that, when clarified, reveals that the two contentions, seemingly expressing and representing opposites, actually are built on different aspects of a single contention, and it is the two opposites together that allow us to see the contention from both sides; the opposites, then, are not absolute—as far as they are concerned, there is not one subject, as their relations to the subject are different.[65]

The various and seemingly opposed aspects of reality are necessary of existence on a lower level of perception, but they do not bear witness to contradiction at the base of the absolute:

> Separate thoughts do not really contradict each other. All are in effect a unified revelation visible in different flashes. Just as bodies cast a shadow by obstructing and eclipsing the light, so the shadows of the spirit obstruct the brightness shining from parts parallel to them, and the shadows are the offspring of imagination not completely illuminated by the beams of the intellect.[66]

The second approach treats the issue of freedom, asserting that freedom and necessity are qualities characterizing various domains of being. That is, in Kantian terms, the thing-in-itself and phenomena, and in Rav Kook's words, "hidden" and "revealed" things. He wrote:

> Secret knowledge is based on the internal clarification of omnipotence of limitlessness in the possibility of infinite *gevurah* ["power, strength"]. Public knowledge is built upon the tendency to restrict force according to the same conditions emphasized by that restriction as it is revealed. In each domain, this awareness alone reigns, unrestricted, *there is no limit to ability in concealed things, and freedom is not manifest in what is revealed.*[67]

The third approach, following Maimonides's doctrine of attributes, nullifies the very meaning of contrary concepts on the following grounds:

> There is no harm in dismissing will from God, for it is a limited attribute; necessity is certainly more limited, or in any case no less so than will; thus a higher attribute than both will and necessity must be found, for which we have no representa-

tion or sign. Similarly, there is no harm in dismissing intention from this attribute, although chance is certainly dismissed, for it is lowlier and feebler in its essence than intention; in any case, both the concept of chance and intention point to a higher matter, the cause of the present activity, which is necessarily made manifest by God.[68]

Even if, for various reasons, we prefer to speak of necessity in relation to God Himself, we must know that "necessity is not necessity, but rather a matter beyond all will."[69]

The fourth approach is the most daring. It addresses the metaphysical paradox concealed in the concept of the complete and wishes to demonstrate that "the idea of transcending the laws of nature is understood in its possibility and suitability to all the lines of reasonable thinking."[70] Throughout logical analysis, the concept of "the complete" comes to be seen and represented as implicitly contradictory. This analysis lead Rav Kook not to a rejection of the concept of "the complete" but rather to an affirmation of the paradox. Here, then, is his argument:

> We understand two senses of completeness in the idea of divine, absolute completeness. One meaning of completeness is that its greatness and wholeness allows no additional virtue. But if there were no possibility of addition, that in itself would be a deficiency. For completeness is ever increasing; it contains an excess and delight and a sort of exaltation we so long for, a going from strength to strength, divine completeness thus cannot exist without this excess of added strength. In the divine is the ability to create, eternally and boundlessly to bring into being, ascending higher and higher in all its aspects; the essential divine soul of existence, life granting, is its constant uplifting, its divine element, calling it to find and perfect itself. . . . And because the darkness is so thick, consciousness does not know this exalted secret of the ultimate end, of divine completeness in ascent, propelled by all of creation, toward the infinite; thinking reason is plunged in gloom, for there is nothing but this completeness of rising, no absolute completeness, no other excess and ascent beside it, for all is already risen, all is complete and whole. That, then, is the obscurity in the methods of the daring modern philosophers (Bergson).[71]

This conceptual analysis demonstrates that the idea of the existence of absolute being is perceived as a completeness in which antinomy is intrinsic. The aspects of completeness and becoming complete, of freedom and necessity, of infinity and limitation, and so forth must exist. The concept of the "complete," according to his definition, does not permit the absence of even a single aspect: "Unlimitedness in its very essence contains limitation, and what is to become limited in and of itself is present in unlimitedness."[72] Rav Kook thus rejected binary logic and asserts that a thing can be both itself and different from itself simultaneously:

> In the divine, time is eternal, thus it is not time, or in any case it lacks no quality intrinsic to time. The boundary is in *En sof* [infinity], which is no boundary, or in any case it lacks no quality intrinsic to boundary. Change is staticity, yet it never lacks the quality of change.
>
> And we can speak of perception of God in terms of our understanding of time, boundary, and change, knowing His is the infinity of En Sof and staticity, and all that appears to be in time, bounded and changeful is a dark mirror, which receives, from the endlessness of *En-sof* and staticity, the truly luminous mirror.[73]

Rav Kook's view of two opposing and mutually existing elements in reality, the static and the dynamic and free, is a conscious polemic against the system of Spinoza, on one hand, and Bergson, on the other.[74] The position of both philosophers is logically consistent, their image of reality founded on one particular principle and rejecting all that opposes it. Rav Kook, in contrast, adopts both the core of Spinoza's system (that is, perception of the divine as unity and static completeness) and the basis of Bergson's method (that is, perception of reality as continuous movement, creative development, the principle of freedom). This position is engendered and justified through a logical analysis of the concept of "the complete." When the limitations of binary logic become manifest, its laws are easily broken.

Types and Stages of Perception

Rav Kook held that there are two kinds of perception or knowledge: "revealed knowledge"[75] and "sublime knowledge."[76] Knowledge of the "revealed" is a vital stage in understanding the "sublime," but the source of these two types of knowledge is different, as are the kinds of awareness directed to them. Knowledge of the "revealed" originates in discursive study or, as he put it, "the graduated way."[77]

Where, then, is the origin of "sublime" knowledge? Rav Kook's answer was

> As for sublime knowledge, we cannot ask how we know it. When, within the soul, we find a noble spirit and a treasure of *ordered bits of knowledge, fit together,* that is the highest of contemplations. All knowledge issuing from investigation is no more than a means to reaching this higher knowledge. . . . The best way to attain this higher quality is by cleaving to God with utmost strength, and by meditation on the mysteries of Torah.[78]

The intent here is not to isolated flashes of insight but rather an orderly and consistent method of thinking whose source is not in discursive understanding. We have seen earlier that "meditation on the mysteries of Torah" mentioned here as a means to perceiving "sublime knowledge," is not "Kabbalah" in the conventional sense but rather the metaphysical speculations each Jew conceives individually. If discursive knowledge is of no use in the metaphysical realm, there must be other kinds of knowledge with greater perceptive power, and the term *meditation on the mysteries of Torah* points to them.

Rav Kook distinguished schematically among three levels of perception":

> There is superior *thought, without articulation of letters and conceptual images,* without even the accompaniment of song and musical expression. *Second* to it is *thought embodied in images,* but these are abstract and inclusive, and cannot possibly define any particularity, until the *third* degree is reached, which can draw *particular meditations* from general oblivion, ready to be studied by all sorts of investigation.[79]

These levels of perception parallel three realms of learning, "revealed, concealed, and unities,"[80] and they form a line of thought rising from the particular and multiple to the unified and inclusive. Within this schematic construct, however, he proposed a more-detailed graduation of eight levels of perception: senses of the flesh, imagination, intelligence, divine inspiration, prophecy, luminous mirror, the supreme splendor of Adam haRishon, the living light after the final *tikkun* (restoration, leading to completeness).[81]

Let us begin our discussion of the levels of perception with the lowest. In three places, with slight variations, Rav Kook distinguishes among these spiritual levels, which he calls *cognitive stages:*

This is the order. The body and all its powers must be purified and strengthened, and after that comes the power of *imagination* in all its aspects, which must also be strengthened and cleansed, then *feeling* and all its branches, and above that is clear *intellect* with all its ramifications, and the light of supreme *attentiveness* which comes from the sparkling of exalted divine inspiration, supreme above them all.[82]

In another variation, the idea appears as follows: "Acts turn to *imaginings* through spiritual digestion, and the imaginings to *feelings*, and the feelings to *ideas*, and the ideas to a *fixed spiritual character* acting on all essential content."[83] In a third context addressing the issue, Rav Kook lists only three levels instead of four as in the two previous passages:

Imaginings, ideas, and *the appearance of the holy* beyond the intellect are three levels of the spiritual essence of man and the world, which are mutually connected. Each imaginary point corresponds to an intellectual point whence it draws its strength and by whose grace it ascends and unites with its source; and each intellectual point corresponds with a point of manifestation in the divine, beyond language and more sublime than all intellectual knowledge, whence it draws its own essence and strength to reach its own level. The unification of all these points of imagination, intellect and appearance in a perfect block forms a whole world of threefold holiness, each aspect illuminated by all three of its levels.[84]

The reason for the striking difference in the number of levels between the two earlier texts and the later one lies in the identification of feeling with imagination or at least its inclusion in the category of imagination.[85] Yet all three texts form a unified picture in the gradation of levels of knowledge, in which imagination and feeling appear at the bottom of the ladder, succeeded by intellect, and above them both is a higher level, designated in various ways; we will examine its nature shortly. Yet even the terms *imagination, feeling,* and *intellect* bear changing meanings throughout Rav Kook's writings, and we must examine each term in its particular context.

Let us begin with *feeling.* What are its attributes? It is said: "Feeling is quicker than the intellect. In feeling, the term 'God' is fertile and abounding with being even before a single one of the vast store of secrets concealed in it has been solved. This is not so for intellect. The mind needs to process; nothing comes without study and perusal."[86]

Feeling can thus be interpreted as intuition that grasps all the richness of matter, albeit unprobed and unrefined, whereas the fruits of intellect are born only after a process of study and investigation. The virtue of feeling, however, lies not in its speed alone. Rav Kook spoke of instinct in another context, and the strong similarity between the two texts suggests *feeling* may be equivalent to *instinct*. He wrote:

> Instinct is quicker and more precise than man's intellectual understanding, and man's distinctiveness is that all his insights can be raised to the supreme side of instinct; this is the source of its precision and speed toward the most high. Those who have true faith in God have the strongest instinct, and all cultured people will eventually return to them by way of more intermediate aims, such as the aspiration to morality, insight, building the nation and its honor, and so on. The cultured indeed have the strongest instinct, and every man of strong instinct is slack in matters demanding calculation and discretion. Thus the factions in the nation must combine, that they may come to understand each other, intensifying their instincts each according to his own particular and unique strength.[87]

The advantage of instinct over intellectual understanding is thus not only in its speed but also in its accurate grasp of the "most high."[88] On the basis of this superiority of feeling and its cause, we turn our attention to Rav Kook's words in a letter to Rabbi Shmuel Alexandrov:

> Let his honor not suspect me of being led by emotion devoid of intellectual enlightenment. I only stress once again that feeling is more intellectual when in its pure state, in that psychic vision we call intellect; even what we attribute to intellectual love is founded in feeling, and without this feeling, rationalists would not triumph in their ideas and moralists, moreover, would not triumph in their good deeds, for the intellect draws its proofs from another world, while feeling harbors all good in itself—it has no need to bring its bread from afar; yet the only way feeling can ever reach its goal is when the light of intellect shines upon it.[89]

Another matter is also clear: neither "feeling" nor "intellect" is used here in its normal sense. For if feeling in its pure state is more intellectual than the phenomenon called *intellect*, the nature of this feeling, or as Rav Kook described it, "the highest side of instinct," demands explanation. The meaning of the term *intellect* also needs to be determined, for on the one hand Rav Kook asserted instinct or feeling is "swifter and more precise" than the intellect, although on the other hand in the gradation of types of understanding, feeling is a rung below intelligence.

To clarify the concepts of "feeling," "imagination," and "intellect" we must return to the principle of parallelism mentioned previously in our discussion of "the equalization of values." Rav Kook conceived of types of knowledge as two parallel systems, lower and higher or, more precisely, a single, double-countenanced system.[90] "Feeling," "intellect," and "imagination" each has two aspects or two levels. Thus Rav Kook affirmed, on the one hand, that "all the truth and grandeur secreted in the wealth of imagination may be drawn out, little by little, through the narrow and refining channels of the intellect." Indeed, "our rational mind is but a humble pupil who explains but a glimmer of all the living light in the treasure house of our imagination, rich and holy, which lives a life of supreme reality, subduing real existence with the force of its own independent being."[91] In other contexts, however, Rav Kook sees the imagination as a yet unripe element of the intellect:

> The levels of intellect range from lower to higher. All the images of imagination are in actuality images of the intellect, but in the form of seeds that have not finished growing. Indeed, when the intellect is proven true and encompasses the essence of human life, then all the images of imagination at all its levels, and all those of the entire intellect will become attached to each other, as an organic body whose parts are all intertwined.[92]

To clarify this point, let us make a sharper distinction between the two systems: on the lower level, we have "our rational intelligence" which is no more than a "humble pupil" of imagination, in whose treasure house "lies all the truth and the grandeur." But we must note, this imagination is of the upper plane. The rational intelligence of the lower plane is, of course, beneath imagination in its higher aspect. Yet even on the lower level imagination exists, and Rav Kook described it thus:

> Imagination clothes itself in a special form when the intelligence acts upon it. This form is holy, gladdening (perfuming) the world and cleansing man from all his impurity. And whenever this form is obscured, and imagination is conceived by its own law, without the influence of imagination, then it becomes

the most sullied source of all misfortune and all sin and suffering in both private and public life.[93]

He said as well:

> The ascent of imagination occurs whenever it cleaves to holiness, but profane imagination has no more than its shadow, and is the source of mockery. The further it distances itself from original intelligence and the more it prevails, the weaker reality becomes for it, and the soul immersed in this imagination is tortured until it perishes.[94]

In contrast to the lower aspect of intellect and imagination, their higher aspect is described thus:

> . . . the full intellect, worthy of establishing the foundations of the imagination in life—that is the *divine intellect*, and from it come prophetic vision in the revelation of the Torah as well as the light of divine inspiration, the source of wisdom for of all who seek God, all the spiritual qualities activated by this influence, and the way of life by which they raise imagination from its baseness, illuminating it with the light of intelligence and human happiness.[95]

Regarding imagination, he said:

> Imaginings emerge from the soul's depths; they are fresh seed from the secret places of the spirit; a whole world is reflected in them. The correspondence between the soul and its imaginings and the world with all its creatures is no mere false vision. The great ocean of *imagination* is a *mirror of reality;* reality incribes its mark upon it, as thence is it taken as well.[96]

> Even when the intellect does not agree with the ideas of imagination, they retain their independent value, for imagination is a whole world in and of itself. Only its additional blessing allows it to become one with the intellect, and the two are joined together in their highest source, supreme beyond intellect and imagination alike.[97]

In the case of emotion and intellect in their lower aspect, Rav Kook asserted that "limited human science is a proper tool for eradicating the alien roots of *deceptive imaginings*, which must be uprooted."[98] On the lower level, "all existence described by its laws is no more than the product of our imagination, illumined only by the light of intellect from lower *hokhma* (wisdom), allowing the laws of nature to be ordered according to it."[99]

The relation between the intellect and imagination is usually preserved in both their upper and lower aspect, although their qualities differ. This divergence, however, is not significant, for "the division between imagination and intellect is not radical but gradual."[100] "Emotion is part of intellect, and is its lowest level; when it rises to practical action it claims its own emotional domain."[101] Intelligence and emotion are united, then, "in their highest source, sublime beyond intelligence and imagination alike"; that is, at the stage of nondifferentiation. Thus, when these aptitudes, intelligence and imagination, begin to act, they are two distinct and separate aptitudes. In kabbalistic symbolism, Rav Kook identified emotion with the *sefira* of *malkhut* (the "kingdom" of God), lowest of the *sefirot:* "In all of worldly life it [feeling] is the basic content of the letter *heh*, last letter of the name of God, which has become a holy name in and of itself."[102]

This view of imagination, or feeling, as an intellectual attribute does not blur its particularity when it is differentiated and functioning. As an aspect of the intellect, imagination is an inferior intellectual level, but when tried and functioning, its perceptive ability is superior to that of intellect, for the latter is a creative aptitude, the source of its perception within itself, whereas imagination is an instrument capable of receiving truths from a source beyond both itself and intellect:

> Imagination is the shadow of the intellect, and at times above intellect, not by its own virtue but because it is like a substance illumined by divine light. There are thus two unique attributes in imagination, whose law varies—on the one hand, the shadow of intellect it contains, and on the other, its ability to receive illumination. The shadow aspect of the intellect is original; and this power, though essential to it, is of inferior quality, as it is after all no more than a reflection of the intellect, certainly containing all its weaknesses as well as other weaknesses through the diminishment of reality that occurs between intellect itself and the shadow it casts. Its receptive ability makes it open to the most exalted appearances, yet in this it is not original but rather merely a receptacle for whatever is placed in it. What it does receive, however, comes from such a sublime and noble source that it has no need to consider the weaknesses of the intellect.[103]

One conclusion alone can thus be drawn. Because both the intellect and imagination, in their various aspects, have certain advantages and disadvantages relative to each other, perception must by necessity be nurtured by them both:

> Science is built on two bases, the imaginary and the intellectual. These are the two elements composing science; and in their balanced combination they stand in a state of effervescence, combatting each other; and in their effervescence all the branches of the human spirit are renewed. The higher disposition of the intellect weakens the imagination, ruining the balance of science. The disposition of imagination, meanwhile, blurs the intellect, and particular deficiencies become apparent in the system of scientific knowledge. A sound science is produced from the balanced combination of imagination and intellect.[104]

Modern culture is not aware of the indispensibility of imagination in enriching the human spirit and knowledge, and imagination is thus relegated to a position of inferiority:

> Imagination has qualities that intellect lacks. Imagination instills the world in us in its spiritual form, making our spiritual essence more complete, but as it prevails, it obscures the outline of the real world. The endeavours of culture have greatly enriched practical science, as well as the spiritual founded upon it, but the world of imagination and all its vitality has been greatly diminished. Thus the present personality is much inferior to the former one, especially that of great individuals, whose imagination prevailed, gaining its rightful share from the practical intellect. And now we can justly claim as well, despite all modern intellectual advancements: if our ancestors were as angels, we are as human beings, and if they were human, we are as donkeys.[105]

In sum, the conclusion reached from Rav Kook's conception of the absolute source of cognition, thoughts, and imaginings allowed him to treat entities conceived through previously mentioned channels as absolute truths, on one hand, yet with awareness of the limitations of cognition to maintain a relativistic attitude from an epistemological point of view. In this way, Rav Kook burst the bounds drawn in the Middle Ages to circumscribe the epistemological problem. He no longer spoke of the impossibility of knowing God nor did he propose a doctrine of negative attributes. His claim of the relativity and subjectivity of cognition is rooted in the realm of modernity, and on this issue he was definitively post-Kantian. Even his inclination to attribute ontological status to speculations is a mystical variation of penetrating discussions in modern philosophy concerning the possibility of error in a monistic system, whether formulated as pantheism or as a kind of idealism.

Let us turn to an examination of the higher levels of perception; that is, divine inspiration or prophecy. *Divine inspiration (ru'akh ha-kodesh)* is a general term for mystical levels of perception and also signifies the impelling spirit on the practical, imaginary, and intellectual plane—a spirit whose source is divine. Thus one can speak of different sorts of "divine inspiration":

> There is the divine inspiration of an *act*, which arouses the highest spirit to action, . . . and it truly stems from the supernal will in managing the entire world. In the divine inspiration of *imagination*, imagining power is illumined, glorious, lucid, holy and sublime . . . in the divine inspiration of the *intellect*, all ideas and disciplines flow forth as a perennial spring, . . . and *the most sublime divine inspiration* is *ru'akh ha-kodesh in itself* [a lower degree of prophecy], in which all these shine as one.[106]

The highest divine inspiration is thus the totality of mystical perceptions undistinguished by particular content. "It contains no articulation or conceptual images."[107] Such divine inspiration is described as sudden moments of illumination that appear and disappear like lightning, in contrast to the unceasing perceptions of the natural intellect. The differences between one perception and the next depend on "the quality of the flashes and their closeness to each other, until even the continuous form of an image is none other than the prolongation of frequent flashes, whose intervals are not sensed."[108] For this reason mystical perceptions cannot be constant or continual. "Prophecy is intermittent light."[109] Nonetheless, this quality does not characterize all levels; Moses's prophecy, for example, is described in the Torah as continuous.[110]

Perhaps the difference in interval, constancy and continuity between prophecy in general and that of Moses can be traced to their separate sources:

> *Prophecy* and *divine inspiration* come from the word of God, to the inwardness [in the manuscript: "from the inwardness"][111] of man, and within him they emanate to all that concerns the entire world. *This is the case* of *aggadah*, for it flows from the *soul* of man, presenting itself in the external aspect of the world. *But the Torah* comes from *the light of highest truth*, containing no distinction between man's inwardness and worldliness and its source. From high to low, all is surveyed and known. "With him I speak manifestly, and not in dark speeches; and the similitude of the Lord does he behold" (Numbers 12:8)—this prophecy alone can yield the Torah. And in this the Torah is supreme beyond all prophecy, and Torah sages are superior to prophets by grace of the divine content whence they draw their spiritual vitality.[112]

What, then, is the nature of prophecy and divine inspiration? How do they differ from the Torah, on one hand, and from the natural intellect, on the other? We may say that prophecy and divine inspiration emerge, like *aggadah*, from "man's inwardness," from "the soul of man." They remain in the domain of absolute subjectivity despite their origin in the "word of God." Hence they are characterized by lack of constancy and continuity: "Prophecy is intermittent light."

The rational intellect, in contrast, gains its perceptions gradually and builds its judgments according to the necessary laws of understanding. It is characterized by constancy, "as a sort of uninterrupted divine light, yet without heavenly manifestation it does not reach the distinct clarity of entities grasped in spiritual images, and it can have no role in directing life in the widest sense for all time."[113]

Only in Moses's prophecy, that is, the Torah, a direct manifestation of divine truth, does a unity of particulars and universality reign: "in it, nothing distinguishes the inwardness of man from all of eternity and its source, and complete harmony abides between the dimension of subjectivity and that of absolute objectivity." Thus "this prophecy alone can yield the Torah." Here we find the level of the "luminous mirror" that "contains all in general appearance and particular prominence."[114]

In any case, a clear affinity is discovered between the constancy and objectivity of the Torah and that same quality in the natural intellect; life must thus be built on the steadfast foundation in which Torah and understanding are united. Between the two there is also room for "the brilliant lights of prophecy and divine inspiration," which are like a "bursting into song," exciting and uplifting, yet in and of themselves are unable to serve as the basis of a full life.[115]

Above the level of the "luminous mirror," which is, once again, Moses's prophecy as expressed in the Torah, is a higher level called *the divine brightness of Adam haRishon* [the Adam of the Bible].[116] We may learn something of this stage through the following passage:

> There are three levels on which the private and collective completeness of Israel must be founded: the return to nature, to human morality, and to the element of nation. Supreme holiness touches all three.
>
> The highest service of God is directly linked to nature. This supreme holiness is profaned by man's foulness, which destroyed the rite of nature by making it an idolatrous monster when it should rightly be a steadfast basis of exalted idealism. The divine brightness of Adam haRishon contains this supreme quality.[117]

The significance of this highest quality seems to be the return to nature; that is, raising nature from the profane to the sacred sphere and transforming it into "the steadfast basis of the noblest idealism." In other words, by eliminating the gap separating nature and the holy, nature itself is perceived as holy, and there is no longer any distinction between scared and profane or between good and evil: "to eat from the Tree of Life and to know no evil."[118] The difference between this level and that of the "luminous mirror" is that the latter, in its combination of particularity and generality, preserves the natural, physical dimension whereas in "the divine brightness of Adam haRishon" the body itself is transformed, becoming holy.[119]

We have seen earlier that "divine inspiration," or mystical perception, is described by Rav Kook, apparently following Maimonides,[120] as sudden illuminations, flashes, "intermittent light," and as perception "without articulation or conceptual images." We must emphasize the interesting fact that the nature of this perception as Rav Kook described it is not exclusively cognitive or visual[121] but rather largely acoustical and even musical.[122] He wrote:

> The *zaddik* respects his inclinations, *listens* to their movements, . . . *divine melody always sings in accord with the laws of harmony* within the home of his soul, and the relation of the part to the whole and to the source of all glitters and reveals itself in a myriad of manifestations, intellectual, practical, fixed and acci-

dental, emotional and imaginary, and it is they that establish the *laws of attentiveness* within the pure spirit.[123]

The "divine melody" guided "by the laws of harmony"—this is the unity of existence that listening can grasp, and what Rav Kook called *laws of attentiveness* in the human spirit thus correspond to a similar process occuring in all of nature:

> *Nature and its laws listen,* hear the voice calling; in spiritual awareness lives an inner light of the beginning of thought, and in the spirit of faith all space is sanctified . . . *in speaking to the rock* water will flow forth to give drink to his chosen people; *all listen* intensely, and when he *strikes* it, the shock creates *contradictory images* and warring factions rise to arms. The world is brought low, no longer worthy of its former greatness, of *unending attentiveness*. . . . And the world of the living God will return and gain courage, and the collective listening of all being will arise in its splendor: "thou hast dug open my ears; burnt offering and sin offering has thou not required." (Psalms 40:7)[124]

In one context describing the scale of epistemological levels, mystical perception is formulated in the term the *light of supreme attentiveness*.[125] Thus, even when Rav Kook spoke of vision or hearing, he seems to imply perception of clearly informative significance. Indeed, he affirmed "we listen with general attentiveness, and "we do not hear separate letters and fragments of words,"[126] yet at the same time he also spoke of "listening to complete unity,"[127] and to the world's elevation,[128] whose meaning is certainly informative. The issue is presented explicitly and consciously in the following passage:

> When man accustoms himself to *hearing the voice of God* in everything,[129] his practice reaches the highest essence of the human spirit, i.e., the intellect that, more than any other element, in fact conceals the divine, for he will realize it is a particular power of the mind creating intellectual ideas. But with discipline, by *listening to the voice of God* in everything, he finds *His voice* revealed in the *intellect* as well, and the true revelation of the divine will occur, in fact, in the intellect.[130]

This does not mean that attentiveness is identical with the intellect or even similar to it. On the contrary, "the light of supreme attentiveness" appears as the level of perception beyond body, imagination, emotion, and intelligence,[131] as an inner and penetrating manner of perception.[132] Moreover, "As supreme attentiveness prevails, the individual intelligence can no longer act, and silence begins to reign. When man reaches that stage, normal intellectual occupation, whether profane or holy, lies beneath the level he has reached."[133] Intellectual activity disturbs supreme attentiveness and "silence of thought" is mandatory "in the presence of more concealed, beautiful and exalted thought."[134] In truth, all the energy one devotes to building one's spiritual world is conceived not only in terms of study and meditation but as "the quality of attentiveness."[135] More precisely, we may describe the relation thus: attentiveness is to the intellect as thought is to speech.[136] Speech and the listening bound up in silence are conditions of activity and passivity. The individual who is about to receive divine effulgence is completely passive, that is, silent; when one exerts influence one is active. What is true of the individual also holds true for the intellectual world as a whole:

> The entire intellectual world, along with its branches, . . . is alternately in a state of silent time and speaking time. In readiness to receive divine effulgence, all is silent and speechless. When, on the other hand, each of the receivers is about to influence what is beneath it, at that moment speech begins. This reversal occurs in the human realm as well.[137]

The hierarchical order Rav Kook described—body, imagination, emotion, intellect, and light of supreme attentiveness—this order, in his view, "is true not only of individuals but of the entire nation as well, and holds true despite the various periods in its life."[138] This idea of the development of thought through history is indisputably Hegelian.[139] But Rav Kook's conception is anchored in the well-known midrashic motif: "The Holy One Blessed be He creates worlds and destroys them,"[140] expressed in the idea that the reception of the highest influence requires silence, passivity, and the nullification of previous levels and meaning. This notion is expressed in an illustrative excerpt in which prophecy is presented as characteristic of a particular historical period, that is, Rav Kook's own generation; he called for the annulment of old values, a measure that would allow prophecy to flourish. The passage was published in *Orot haKodesh* with essential changes,[141] and a comparison with the manuscript version emphasizes Rav Kook's true position on this question, which has become clear through our previous examination. Thus, we summarize our discussion with this passage in is published form, with the original version added in parentheses:

The renewal [the annulment] of customary values, as opposed to their previous explanation in matters of holiness and faith, is the cause [are the causes] of positive renewal in the world, and the value of holiness and lucid knowledge of God is thus made vitally active.

This comes about by two qualities in the nature of renewal [change], brought by change [annulment], which is a sort of putrification preceeding the sprouting of the seed and new fertilization, with its promise of great yield. The first quality released by putrification is the life force compressed and hidden in the narrow body of the seed; then the power is set free, giving birth to magnificent fecundation. In the second quality, the preceeding annulment of the external form gives way without limit for creation of the new, more perfect form, no longer needing to suffer the deficiencies accumulated in the first [old] form, and finally the influence of the sublime aspects alone remains, flowing eternally.

Then, it will come to pass in the light of holiness, that the vineyard of the House of Israel will be replanted; if the light of true prophecy is to return in the virtue of the nation, the customary values in the descriptive form they will gain after the end of prophecy must renew themselves [blur themselves] as well by the force of the *chutzpa* of the pre-Messianic age. And from this [And from the force of this putrification] new light shines forth in the efflux of its [his] splendor, as the very heavens for clearness. "And nations shall walk at thy light, and kings at the brightness of thy rising. . . . And thou shalt be called by a new name, which the mouth of the Lord shall express" (Isaiah 60:3, 62:2).[142]

Will and Wisdom—Elements of Reality and Perception

"Will" and "wisdom" are fundamental concepts in Rav Kook's thought, and the epistemological and ontological significance informing them both impels us to consider them in the context of our discussion. The issue mandates a fundamental clarification: although it is no surprise that "will" (*keter*) and "wisdom" (*hokhma*) bear ontological significance as symbols of divine *sefirot*, the epistemological significance, at least of will, is not to be taken for granted.

Indeed, as early as the Middle Ages, will was used as an indispensible instrument in perceiving the fundaments of faith, by means of what is called *willful agreement*.[143] For Rav Kook, however, will was not "agreement" in the common sense, and moreover, in his method the understanding of the epistemological meaning of will is vitally linked to an understanding of will as an ontological category. This, then, is our task: to investigate the issue in all its aspects with the utmost circumspection.

One of the principle problems faced by medieval Jewish thought was the difference between the conception of the divine held by philosophers and the biblical conception, perpetuated by the Sages. The idea of a nonpersonal God, identical with the concept of the "complete" in philosophical understanding, stands in fundamental contrast to the description of God pervading the Bible, with His attributes of will, knowledge, and activity. The godhead of philosophy is completeness that, by definition, knows no change or movement; as ultimate completeness is self-sufficient as well, it needs nothing outside itself. The philosophical conception of the divine negates fundamental elements of Jewish tradition, such as reward and punishment, prayer, and no less grave, it refutes the possibility of the world's creation, thereby not only contradicting explicit sources but also utterly destroying the basis of obligation through *mitzvot*.[144]

The various attempts made by both philosophers and kabbalists to deal with this problem concentrated on a concept that became seminal in Jewish medieval thought: that of "will." Although philosophers and kabbalists differed in their approach and formulation of the problem, these differences remain secondary to our present discussion.

Solomon ibn Gabirol, in *Makor Ḥayyim*, devoted a special and detailed discussion to the element of will, which acquired central importance in his method.[145] S. Pines points out a precedent of ibn Gabirol's doctrine of will in the "parallel" concept of Rav Sa'adya Gaon in his commentary on the *Sefer Yetsirah* and remarks on the resemblance of his doctrine to those common in the Ismaeilia Muslim sect.[146] Yet J. Schlanger claims this parallel can "serve, at best, as a point of origin for a specific teaching about will but cannot constitute such a teaching in and of itself."[147] In any case, even without extensive historiographic investigation of the question, we see that many of the terms appearing in Rav Sa'adya Gaon's works become recurrent motifs, with variations, for Jewish thinkers concerned with the issue.

In the case of ibn Gabirol, we remark that despite his desire to establish a voluntary element, in the form of will, in his conception of reality, he refrained from describing will as a divine attribute, for fear of suggesting God were a changing entity. In addition, he shrank from ascribing change even to will itself, which he presented as an independent element, a divine hypostasis, and relegated change to general matter and created entities alone. This clearly demonstrates ibn Gabirol's wish to introduce the element of freedom in the neo-Platonic view of reality, which claimed necessary emanation, while at the same time absolutely denying all possibility of change and permutation in God himself.[148]

Maimonides perceived the problem in a similar manner. His task was double: "to unite personal understanding of God with the idea of the supreme One which knows no plurality, as well as with the idea of absolute present beyond all movement and change. The first question relates to the very essence of God, the second to his action and the relation of that action to his essence.[149]

The attributes reflecting a view of a personal God according to Maimonides are "able and wise and desiring."[150] Indeed, in keeping with Maimonides's theory of attributes, even the attributes that describe the personal nature of God are no more than qualities of action or negation. In any case, Maimonides did not relinquish the attribute of divine will, but he did distinguish between this will and human will: the latter has an external end whereas divine will is self-sufficient. Just as divine knowledge is intrinsically different from that available to humankind, so divine will is inherently different from human will. "Although 'will' is said of both of them, there is no likeness between the two."[151]

Maimonides's reservations about divine will and his affirmation that it is self-sufficient rather than for an external end are intended to reconcile the personal nature of God with the philosophical postulate of his changelessness. This affirmation is of decisive importance, for it brings Maimonides to identify will with wisdom. "Necessarily and obligatorily the argument must conclude with the answer being given that the final end is: God has wished it so, or: His wisdom has required this to be so."[152] Divine will is not arbitrary but rather identical with the wisdom characterized by the necessity of its values.[153]

The kabbalists grappled with this issue as well. It is usually supposed that in Kabbalah the problem was solved by the duality of *En-sof* and the *sefirot;* that is, the impersonal aspect of God is *En-sof,* and the personal aspect is expressed in the *sefirot.* Closer study reveals this is not at all the case. The development occuring in the conception of will in early Kabbalah discounts the possibility of imbuing the *sefirot* with the qualities of the personal God of the Bible, because the foremost characteristic of the biblical God is willful action, whereas the action of the *sefirot* is primarily motivated by causal and mechanical laws. Nevertheless, one cannot deny a serious attempt was made among the kabbalists of Gerona to deal with this fundamental problem. The earliest endeavor was to include the element of will in the sefirotic system. Its entrance marked a turning-point in Kabbalah.[154] Will is an undeniably personal attribute of God; it expresses divine action as spontaneous and not as a necessary result of his essence. The assertion of will as a quality of God allows his description as an agent with teleological intention, overseeing the world and reacting to the prayers and service of humankind. Yet examination of the writings of some early kabbalists shows a process of retreat from the spontaneous aspect of will, through a change in its status in the system of *sefirot* and by its union with thought.

Will appears for the first time in the works of the pupils of Rav Isaac the Blind and *Sefer haBahir*.[155] Although for Rav Isaac and *Sefer haBahir* thought receives the highest place in the system of *sefirot*, for Rav Azriel, Rav Asher ben David, Rav Ya'akov ben Sheshet, and others will ousts wisdom and supplants it.

In the view of Rav Azriel, will is the ultimate entity, higher than the intellect and wisdom, and in the symbolism of the *sefirot*, will is apparently identified with *En-sof*, the intellect with *keter*, separate from *En-sof* and emanated from it, and only after them is wisdom emanated.[156]

For Rav Asher ben David, a change had already taken place in the status of will. Rav Asher placed the *sefirot* in the following hierarchy: *rom-ma'ala, hokhma, bina*.[157] *Rom-ma'ala* is understood as the *sefira* of *keter*, and unlike Rav Azriel, here it is identical with *En-sof*. *Rom-ma'ala* also contains the will from which all the *sefirot* emanate. Yet *rom-ma'ala* is not called a *sefira* because it is not emanated, and *hokhma* (wisdom) is thus the first *sefira*.[158]

Rav Asher introduces an additional innovation on the position of Rav Azriel: although will is the *sefira* of *rom-ma'ala*, equivalent to *keter* or to *En-sof*, even the *sefira* of *hokhma* can be called *will* due to one of two aspects that characterize it: "will and thought. Will, according to its emanation from the divine will [*keter*]; and thought, which is aroused and brought forth after will."[159] That is, not only because "the blessing drawn from *En-sof* and expanding without cease in *hokhma* makes *hokhma* seem to be the first *sefira*,"[160] but in its essence as well it has something in common with the primary entity, that is, with will, for *hokhma* is a sort of continuation of will taking form in thought. Rav Asher ben David's concept of *hokhma*, with its two elements of will and thought, introduces the identification of will with *hokhma*.

The process initiated by Rav Azriel and continued by Rav Asher ben David was brought to completion by Rav Yosef ben Avraham Gikitilia. For Rav Azriel, will is identified with *En-sof*, and *keter* is differentiated from it and equal to the intelligence between *En-sof* and *hokhma.* Rav Asher ben David equated *keter,* designated as *rom-ma'ala,* with will, and this *sefira* serves, systematically, as *En-sof,* which is never termed as such. At the same time, the *sefira* of *hokhma,* or thought, contains the aspect of will. And here for Gikitilia, *keter* is identified with *En-sof,* though not always definitively.[161] For both Rav Asher ben David and Gikitilia, *hokhma* enjoys a special rapport with *keter* or *En-sof* in the element of infinity informing it. But for Gikitilia, *hokhma* receives the symbolic expression of will and its most important roles in the system although it also serves in the same manner as thought.[162]

The identification of will with thought, as developed in the kabbalistic teaching of Gerona, carries significant theological implications: the symbol of will introduced in kabbalistic symbolism, which implanted the element of freedom in the system of necessary emanation, changes its meaning and unites with thought, characterized by its necessary loyalty to fixed laws.

Clearly, the kabbalists, like Maimonides, *had no peace from the dialectical tension between the claims of rational philosophy,* with its description of divine completeness as a static concept, *and the religious experience* of mutuality and the tradition of the Bible and the Sages concerning the personal nature of God. Gikitilia made open allusion to this tension:

> And those wise men of the ages who feared a change of will, if they had known the source called *will* they would not have feared such a change, for he who knows the nature of will knows it is unchanging; one found worthy, whose prayers reach that source, can attain anything he wishes, as it is written: "For whoever finds me find life, and obtains favour of the Lord" (Proverbs 8:35). That is, he discovers and draws his desire from the source of will, from *En-sof.*[163]

What we find here is an attempt to combine the personal nature of God with the principle of changelessness implied in the philosophical concept of the divine. This is done by developing a conception stating that change occurs within a deterministic framework and should therefore not be seen as real change. Gikitilia explained through a parable: "And he who understands this will have no difficulty accepting natural change and renewal of phenomenon. If, for example, a room contains everything in the world, anyone who has a key can take all he needs, and what change of will is there in that?"[164]

The same problem troubled Rav Moshe Cordovero in the sixteenth century as well, and his *Pardes Rimonim* reflects its history in kabbalistic literature through the centuries preceeding him.[165] A revolutionary step forward in regarding the subject was first taken in Lurianic teaching, as R. Schatz-Uffenheimer wrote: "Lurianic Kabbala represents a vital deviation from the defense of the thesis of changelessness; in contrast, it presents a true dialectical conception built on continual becoming, tending to realism."[166]

Undeniably, on this point at least, Rav Kook did not perpetuate the medieval tradition.[167] As we have said, although he accepted the basic dialectic model of Lurianic teaching, it serves him only as a springboard for dealing with the problems presented by modern European culture and philosophy. During a discussion in "Rav Kook's Circle" ("חוג הראי״ה") that took place in 1934, Rav Zvi Yehuda HaCohen Kook, Rav Kook's son, recalled a conversation between his father and Rav Mordechai Ushminar,[168] who asked Rav Kook, in light of his words, if he had "revelations." Rav Kook's answer was: "In *Tikkune Zohar* there are various aspects of revelation of the prophet Elijah. Some are *intellectual*, some *imaginary*." He added: "Some are also by *will*."[169]

We have already explored at length the idea of intellect and imagination as degrees of perception or types of knowledge; the nature of will as a means of perception now demands our attention. Many passages in Rav Kook's writings are concerned with the mutual dependence of will and intellect, and this relation is powerfully stated: "Intellect raises itself on the basis of the supremacy of will, and becomes clear as will itself is clear."[170] "Weakness of will engenders weakness of knowledge."[171] These two statements point to a manifest connection between the level of intellectual perception and the state of will, yet this does not mean will itself is an instrument of perception or knowledge. The state of will may impede perception or aid it, but it is not a means of perception in the commonly accepted sense.[172]

In contrast, our discussion in Chapter 8 will be concerned with the influence of wisdom of the will "in that it reverses will and the spiritual quality of its students, bringing them closer by drawing all their being to those heights where will itself takes form."[173] At issue, then, is not the one-sided dependence of *hokhma* on will or of will on *hokhma* but rather the mutual kinship between the two that affects the entirety of the personality bearing knowledge or what is designated as "wisdom of the holy." In Rav Kook's words: "Mysteries of the Torah are not revealed by the secular intellect but rather by the holy effluence of divine inspiration, and the glimmer of divine inspiration depends on *purity of spirit* [= completeness of spirit], and purity of spirit, in turn, depends on *the perfection of desire* [= will], which is the inner nature of the soul."[174]

Mystical meaning is therefore not a concept in the normal intellect, and it depends on the *completeness of the spirit*, of which will is certainly one of its most important elements. We have already remarked on the connection between, on the one hand, the nature of mystical understanding that perceives reality in its entirety and unity, and on the other hand, the multidimensionality of the manner of perception, that is, the participation of all the spiritual forces in perception.[175] We see that "the highest perceptions . . . can be achieved only to the same extent that will and intellect are in complete unity,"[176] and "everything [i.e., the level of perception] depends on the measure of unity between practical will and theoretical intellect, which in a wholly unified manner become one only in the ultimate heights of holiness, in the light of the Torah at the root of her root."[177] In other words, supreme perception is possible neither in intellect nor in will alone, but only in the union of those two forces.[178]

To all this Rav Kook introduced a new element. He held that "will becomes complete through acts. And for this reason close attention to deeds and the act of repentance is a vital condition to their serving the mysteries of Torah."[179] This idea of the link between acts and level of perception, beyond its direct moral significance,[180] can be properly understood when we reconsider an issue elucidated previously; that is, the ontological status Rav Kook attributed to thoughts.[181] Because perception is possible only through the union of intellect and will, "everything conceived by the intellect is imprinted deep within will, and in any case it also materializes in life as an active force."[182] Deeds, then, are no mere condition of intelligence, but are in fact its result.[183] This same reasoning leads Rav Kook to identify thought and will with material reality:

> The unity of spirituality joins thought and will within itself. Will is revealed in its true form; only superficially, as it appears to us, does will seem to differ from thought and intellectual conception. This unification leads us to the final unity of all being, until material and spiritual reality become values varying only in their outer garb. Thought, will and all existence are bound together, and as thought becomes more profound and magnified, will is magnified as well, *and the increase of will is the increase of thought, and both are the increase of material reality,* and the increase of material reality is their magnification.[184]

Simply and definitively, Rav Kook affirmed that will and wisdom are not elements different in their very nature but rather "a single matter and essence."[185] In light of this conclusion, more extensive discussion of the ontological aspect of thought and will seems to be in order.

In various passages in Rav Kook's writings, we find two contrary approaches to the status of will. The first sees will as the basic element of reality, and the second perceives it as an element emanated from *hokhma*. Discussion of these two approaches follows; let us begin with a passage presenting the view of will as an emanated entity:

> *The holy in its essence* is *hokhma*, wisdom in itself, the splendor of sublime ideas at their greatest height, *unlimited*, not differentiated even by the most general terms of reality, where all is particular and limited in extent, compared to the breadth and unlimitedness of supreme *hokhma* in its great strength.
>
> *Hokhma* in its magnificent holiness is *above freedom*, beyond the world of freedom, *for all freedom and liberty in the world is emanated from it*. The form of all the worlds and all their ideals, the exultation of their whole being, all the elevation and depth of their lives, the pleasure of their song and gratification of their happiness, even the freedom of their delight—all this is like a prison compared to the holy purity of *hokhma*.
>
> Only when *hokhma* readies itself for ideas, the ideals controlling real values, does the light come into being illuminating the world of freedom. There, *in the world of freedom*, in the *pleasure* of ideas and creation of ideals worthy of descending to the perception of restricted ideals, the fashioners of worlds, makers of life, inventors of souls, renewers of hosts of every kind, by the force of *freedom* the *intelligence* (*bina*) of life eternal in its supreme form, the majesty of *bina* is revealed, the model of pure intelligence perfumed with the scents of song, the melody of loveliness and joyous freedom. The descent to *loveliness* from the holiness beyond all earthly loveliness, that is the emanation of the majesty of *bina* through all the channels of being . . .
>
> Indeed, the original wellspring where absolute being lays hidden is nowhere but in supernal holiness, in the ideals beyond all measure of freedom, whence not even the slightest nuance of servitude can emerge, even after the multitude of lowerings and evolutions.[186]

In this passage "the holy in its essence"—the Prime being, perceived as an infinite and undifferentiated idea—is equated with the *sefira* of *hokhma*, and *keter* is identified with *En-sof*,[187] beyond the sefirotic system and not discussed in this context. In the system of emanation, *hokhma* is "above freedom." Freedom is an element emanated from *hokhma* and dependent on it, identified with the *sefira* of *bina*, also called the *world of freedom, loveliness*, and *pleasure*.[188] Interestingly, the *sefirot* of *hokhma* and *bina* have been raised in function to the level of the *sefira* above each of them, respectively; this is expressed even in such descriptions as "the holy in its essence" in the case of *hokhma* and appropriate, in fact, to a nonemanated element, or "pleasure" in the case of *bina*, whereas for the kabbalists of Gerona it designates *hokhma*.

Freedom is conceived here as the process of emanation itself, whose first differentiation occurs in the *sefira bina*. The transition from undifferentiated holiness, as the primary element of being, to differentiation is in the act of freedom. The creation of the "world of freedom," of dynamic existence, is not an emanating process with any internal order. The emanation occurs after the primary act, which does not occur of necessity: "The circuit from the necessity of reality to its possibility is not gradual, it is rather a violent hurl."[189] The passage from unlimitedness to limitation is "an absolute birth."[190]

We may conclude, then, according to the view presented in the preceding citation, that will is not the prime being; it is emanated from *hokhma* and in its movement calls all reality into being with the vital force contained within it. In Rav Kook's words, "Free will, illuminated from the highest intellect, is the essence of the being revealed in its inwardness, and that is the soul of Adam, the First Man, in its wholeness."[191]

The second approach, which holds will to be a primary element, is expressed in the following passage:

> Being shines forth in *two shades*, limpid and alive, one above the other, light and brillant light, life and the life of life, *the appearance of will*, the worlds and all being in the form of divine intelligence in the brilliance of revelation.
>
> *The spring of faith*, all the secrecy poured with it, flows and bubbles from the edenic source of *will*'s revelation, and the *spring of knowledge*, the seeing of perception and wisdom in all its aspects and worlds, from the highest heights to the deepest depths, all of it gushes and roars, streaming from the living source and revelation in being as divine *wisdom* (*hokhma*). . . . There is no end to the supreme freedom of *keter*, the supernal crown, of the stream of *will* in all its profundity, no need of limitation or confinement; there is no darkness or obscurity, no lack or hindrance, no compulsion and no obstruction of goodness. *Beneath its brilliance hokhma appears*, in a place formerly shrouded in mystery. *Were it not for a restrictive law, hokhma would not become evident;* were it not for advice and understanding of the impediments blocking the advance of ideals, the light of

thought, weighted with reason and causes and the fabric woven from the ways of the world, would not emerge and shine. . . . The source of rationality is in the revelation of the creature as divine wisdom, and the source of mystery is revealed as His will . . . . *Hokhma* is as a body, and will the soul within; *hokhma* comes and plays before will time and again, plays with his earth. . . . Were it not for the light of *hokhma* . . . we would drown, helpless in the miry depths of will, as it is revealed in the creatures on their various levels; and were it not for will, which gives life to all, there would be no association and absolute perfection in being; all hope would be lost and all happiness and treasure would end.[192]

In this text, reality is portrayed as composed of two shades or aspects: will and knowledge (*hokhma*). Of the two, will is clearly granted the higher and primary status, and its identity with the *sefira keter* or *En-sof* is suggested. Rav Kook explains this conception by describing will as the first element, engendering the concept of "boundary" within *En-sof*, itself completely unbounded and undifferentiated. The passage from undifferentiated being to the start of differentiation is not mandated, as we have said, by definition in the concept of *En-sof* and must thus be seen as will, as "an absolute birth." Knowledge is inconceivable in an undifferentiated realm, for no concept can be recognized unless it is differentiated from other concepts. Hence, "the will to draw boundaries" is a precondition of the existence of wisdom. As Rav Kook stated:

Hokhma must be the second emanation, must be ex nihilo, and nothingness (*En*) must preceed it; *hokhma* can only be imagined through limitation [distinction], and *hokhma* arranges a way to defeat all the confines and boundaries, that is, the impediments; as *hokhma* must, as a condition of being, be a party of reality, will must preexist in order to set bounds. And out of boundedness itself God did all he desired, and *hokhma* becomes prominent. But nothingness, the secret of limitation, serving as the foundation of *hokhma*, is surely greater than *hokhma* itself, immeasurably, incomparably greater.[193]

It seems reasonable to surmise that the existence of these two mutually opposed views of will and *hokhma* reflects a certain struggle between two basic intuitions in Rav Kook's world-view. The predominance of will over *hokhma* or of *hokhma* over will implies different manners of perception, different emphases of two aspects of reality: "revelation of will" and "the appearance of *hokhma*." The transposition of will and *hokhma* in the metaphysical hierarchy stems from a view that perceives an aspect of constancy and necessity even in the element of spontaneous and dynamic freedom represented in the concept of "will" and sees an aspect of freedom and movement in the element of aesthetic necessity represented in the concept of "*hokhma*," as the concept of the complete would imply, of which both will and *hokhma* are its manifestations. Embodied in the concept of "*En*" (nothingness), here identified with "will," is the paradox of the unity of infinity and limitedness, freedom and necessity.

Indeed, we have no recourse from distinguishing between will and *hokhma*, for it is impossible to conceive of them, and all the more so to describe them, as a unity. As for the paradox, we can recognize its existence but are unable to understand it. The distinction is founded in error: "Will is flawed by the concealment of radiant *hokhma*, for then will and *hokhma* appear to be two separate matters, though in truth they are a single matter and entity. And just as the highest *hokhma* is limpid *in its truth*, so is it clear in its *goodness*, by grace of the component of will in it."[194]

This position, which bonds will and *hokhma* at their root, is the basis of Rav Kook's criticism of Schopenhauer and his view of blind will:[195]

> Schopenhauer's view of will is not far wrong in and of itself, but his misjudgment is that instead of understanding will as one of the guises of reality, the philosopher mistakes it for all of reality and its very cause. This is a fallacy, based on the contention that "we did not see" is no proof, whereas all those with spiritual awareness do see will, not as blind and deaf, but as full of wisdom and understanding.
>
> The deafness and dumbness of will are the manifestation of the lowest order of creative force in the practical dimension, and there is a higher purpose in leaving it in such a state of dullness, just as there is a purpose in denying animals human intelligence. And in the beginning will is all, containing all, and gradually twisting and turning, diminishing until it is reduced to its fundamental point and substance, solitary will with no other positive attribute . . .
>
> A few thinkers have discovered the *kelipa* of the blind crocodile in all its shades, and the holy of heart must be aware of its presence if they are to defeat it.[196]

Schopenhauer's "offense," in Rav Kook's eyes, is not in his concept itself of "will." The "fundamental point and substance" of will is indeed "will alone with no other positive attribute"—blind will bereft of the aspect of *hokhma*. His failing was in seeing will as all-encompassing, the essence of reality, and not as it should be seen, as "one of the guises of reality." The absence of the aspect of *hokhma* in Schopenhauer's concept of reason leads him to "that malignant, pessimistic, extreme view"[197] that in the end gave birth to the nihilism of Nietzsche.[198] Irrational, purposeless will is inescapably arbitrary. Resting on no rational or moral principle, its freedom is boundless, and its full expression is thus in nihilism.

In contrast to Schopenhauer, Rav Kook could attribute a moral and value dimension to his concept of "will," calling it *good will*,[199] for very reason if its kinship to *hokhma*, seemingly neutralized of all significance as a value. This is because *hokhma* grants direction and aim to will, making room for it in the realm of revelation as well: "Were it not for the light of *hokhma* . . . all would drown, without a foothold in the muddy abyss of will, aware only of its manifestation in various creatures."[200] The elevation of will to this aim is the embodiment of freedom, uninhibited by external forces: "Total freedom, bearing within itself will shielded from all pressure from without—the very essence of life itself is revealed thereby, life that accepts the plan of happy or evil destiny."[201] At the same time, this elevation is the realization of a moral value: "The world contains *goodness* rising ever higher, appearing both in nature and in human will, which was once more wild that it is now."[202] The action of will, the process of development, is the realization of "goodness," for it acts to realize the potential harbored in existence and reveal it, bringing existence to completeness.[203]

Rav Kook's conception of ethics is thus unlike utilitarian, hedonistic moral systems, nor like the Kantian idea of the categorical imperative; it is rather closer to existential conceptions that perceive self-realization as an ethical good, although in his system ethics extends beyond the human domain, encompassing all of being. The concepts "will" and "freedom" for Rav Kook are not only a necessary condition for the existence of morality, as is commonly thought,[204] but are seen as the realization of ethics. Will is the "essential" manifestation, and when it acts without external impediments, it acts in freedom. Even if the "essential" is implied as a given, realized by that being (thus seeming to harm freedom), this very realization itself is freedom.

An interesting point arises from our analysis thus far: the concept of *hokhma* is normally perceived as a symbol of necessity, of fixed and unchanging law, whereas "will" represents freedom and spontaneity. For Rav Kook, on the other hand, *hokhma* grants will the element of freedom. Will alone, devoid of the aspect of *hokhma*, becomes "blind" will. The arbitrariness of blind will carries its freedom to the point of nullifying itself in nihilism. In Rav Kook's system, the aspect of will in and of itself is not yet the principle of freedom. The concept of freedom becomes possible only in the realization of both aspects of being: will and *hokhma*.[205]

We must remark that although Rav Kook distinguishes will and *hokhma* as two ontologically different elements, attributing each, in various places, with the status of primary being, his overall contention is that will is indeed "the fundament of the world."[206] In its complete state, will also includes the dimension of *hokhma* and embodies the unity of freedom and necessity, the notion "more sublime in all than will."[207] In the first stage of emanation, will contains every aspect: "In the beginning will is all, containing all, and gradually twisting and turning, diminishing until it is reduced to its fundamental point and substance, solitary will with no other positive attribute."[208] "Pure will," devoid of *hokhma*, is thus apparent on two extreme levels: the highest of the high, beyond the dimension of *hokhma*, and the lowliest of the low, with its "higher purpose for being left in a state of dullness."[209] On these two polarly opposed levels "pure will" takes on the nature of necessity. On the upper extreme, necessity is, once again, "a matter above all will," whereas on the lower extreme, necessity is the natural law of reality.[210]

Will is thus perceived as an ontological category whose degree of reality increases in direct proportion to the degree of reality of pure will. Because human beings have a large measure of wisdom, they are given a commensurate measure of freedom, whereas animals and living things without intelligence are bound by fixed laws. Yet the power of will as a vital force is greater in lower life forms than in higher ones, according to the lack of intelligence on the one hand and amplification of necessity on the other. We can thus understand the declaration that "in its absolute supremacy, necessity is truth in and of itself."[211] For the degree of absoluteness in being equals the degree of necessity. Freedom is thus no more than a characteristic of will, not identical to it. On the contrary, its attachment to the aspect of *hokhma* is predominant:

> Even the strong, earthly will of animals, whose intellectual prowess is not great, is slightly weakened in vigor and vital force when inhibited [repressed] by that ideal willful element that comes into it; this grain draws all its strength from its attachment to the plant world, which rests undisturbed even by the mildest expression of vitality. The plant world, with all its healthy flow, suffers from its own wandering and from our im-

age of its limitations, and it is healed of its weakness by rooting itself in the inanimate world, by the constant, unchanging and tenacious soul of that world. The culmination of life is in man and is greatly weakened by the freedom in will, gaining its strength through grounding and attaching itself to the animate, material world.

And the various human orders—this rule threads them together; the ideal side, near collapse in an excess of delicacy, is restored by being planted in the material side of being.[212]

How, then, is the principle of freedom expressed? It is "by the elevation of lower necessity to the final perfection of higher necessity," "to be drawn into the body of the King."[213] In all of being, two moments are thus manifestations of freedom: one is in remembering the act of creation; "the passage from the unbounded to bounded" is "an absolute birth,"[214] enacted by the strength of that preexisting will to limit."[215] The second moment of freedom is the dynamic element of ascendence. In light of the unity of existence, these two moments are naturally no more than different aspects of the same will, both of them reflected in reality: "supreme will"[216] and "ascending will."[217]

Inspired by ibn Gabirol, Rav Kook presented the same idea in terms of "matter" and "form."

We strive, through our sciences, to grasp the matter and form of life as one; essential necessity as the matter of life, and the freedom of completion as a form imprinting new character, developing over time, from age to age; the two are joined as necessity is to freedom, darkness to light, thus fundamental reality and improvement proceed in a long, circumscribing line[218] and surround all that exists in the world; being is made full in them by their very segregation as substance and combination in action.[219]

Rav Kook's assertion here is that the two aspects of reality— matter and form, necessity and freedom, basic reality and its perfection—always act together, and one cannot say one action is better than another. Elsewhere, however, Rav Kook tended to see the dynamic principle as the more dominant element of reality: "*Linearity* [ha-yosher] is most fundamental in being, *circles* [ha-'igulim] subordinate; that is, the freedom of life, absolute freedom in the source of being, the freedom in the concept of the divine, whose ethical aspect provides the image of reality, this is all. Thence we know that the ethic of living is what determines life."[220]

The concept of "nature," which designates laws of necessity, has no place in the upper spheres of reality, "where the divine essence shines very, very near." On those levels one can speak of "linearity alone." As distance increases from the source of emanation, "in the influences that have drawn away greatly, like forehead and eyes, there are also circles, that is, spiritual nature which confines, in contrast to free and sublime desire, the fountain of absolute will."[221] Indeed, the idea of the centrality (to the point of exclusivity in a certain area) of the dynamic principle, is expressed throughout Rav Kook's writings.[222] Will is perceived as a force that "flows onward," "rushing and rising, ceaseless breaking in waves and sending forth streams,"[223] and thus all of reality is seen in continuous movement: "Being is always filled with movement, physical and spiritual."[224] "Even inanimate life, which seems to be resting quietly, is really teeming with countless movements in each and every instant."[225]

Yet this continuous movement is not random. "It sends its vitality directly *downward*, from the universal, sublime essences down to humble particularity, and it also moves *upward*, from the particular to the general, from the lower to the upper realms."[226] This, of course, is a patently neo-Platonian notion; beginning with Plotinus, the neo-Platonic philosophers in their scientific, objective portrayal of being preferred to describe emanation as downward movement, from the "One" to the "intellect" and the "soul," down to the physical world. Upward movement, as far as they were concerned, is not relevant to scientific discussion; ascent is part of the striving of the human soul toward purification. Ibn Gabirol adopted the opposite approach, basically Aristotelian: movement is presented and illustrated as a pathway of ascent—not as a subjective spiritual trajectory of the soul but as an objective, scientific approach, deductive and rational.[227]

As usual in holy matters, Rav Kook integrated something from each view, and in his teaching both descent and ascent reflect objective being and subjective spiritual reality at the same time: "An example is in the living organism and the spirit of man, in his very spiritual stature and also in the common link between the body and soul."[228] This is because subjective reality has objective ontological significance, as we saw earlier.[229] Subjective reality is merely the reflection of objective substance.[230]

What, then, is Rav Kook's relationship to modern philosophy? We can recognize two trends, two inclinations in European thought whose imprint is remarkable in his own teaching. Representatives of the first trend are Spinoza, Kant, and Hegel, who set *intelligence* as the highest value. The second trend, whose central figures are Schopenhauer, Nietzsche, and Bergson, is characterized by irrationalism, perhaps even antirationalism. Bridging these two polarly opposed approaches is the figure of Schelling. We are compelled to note that neither Hegel nor Schelling is explicitly mentioned in Rav Kook's writings, yet we cannot ignore the striking similarity between their views, Shelling's in particular, and that of Rav Kook.

Let us outline these two trends.

Spinoza, as we know, carries rational philosophy to its extreme conclusion. His perception of reality is as a complete whole: "Any further unity is utterly inconceivable."[231] Generally, in a monistic conception, multiplicity is at a lower level of being than original unity, and it may lose it resemblance to reality until it appears no more than an illusion. But Spinoza's method is both realistic and nominalistic. Unity, or completeness, is not a reality separate from the world of particularity, and the relation between the two is not merely external. Completeness is no abstract concept but rather the immanent cause of its parts.[232] This connection between generality (the whole) or "substance," in Spinoza's words, and particularity is a logical connection. That is, substance is the cause of the particulars in the sense that their existence is logically drawn from the definition of the essence or "God."[233] As a result, Spinoza wrote in the supplement to his book on Decartes, "if we grasped the entire order of nature in complete clarity, we would find that all is equally necessary, just as all geometrical theorems are necessary." This is a concise and definitive formulation of Spinozian determinism. The conclusion arousing Rav Kook to dispute concerns the static nature of Spinoza's ontology,[234] which the former holds as only one aspect of reality.

If Spinoza's hope was to attain freedom for humankind, he seems to have failed in the attempt.[235] In successive generations, the problem of human freedom grew yet more severe.

> The danger threatening the notion of human freedom no longer lurked in the concept of God but rather in that of the world, which was conceived in the form of causal, mechanical necessity. The idea of mandatory natural law, which evolved into the fundamental principles of physics and the modern world-view, gravely undermined the preconception of human freedom, as well as the personality of religious faith, founded on the basic principle of man's free choice.[236]

Kant's struggle with the problem of freedom bore vital influence on the attempt of philosophy to extract itself from the predicament into which Spinoza had cast it. Kant resolved the contradiction between freedom and necessity by relating causality to the phenomenal world and relegating freedom to a place outside the deterministic system *as the quality of the pure world of intellect and the autonomy of human intelligence.*

This achievement of Kant's was greatly shaken by the burgeoning of idealistic, post-Kantian thought, particularly that of Hegel.

> In this view, reality is seen as a "manifestation" of absolute intelligence embodied within a necessary process. The states of this process of embodiment are fixed by the divine laws of rational and dialectic thought. Hegel indeed saw an expression of true freedom in this gradual embodiment of absolute intelligence, for the process is not bound by external forces but rather is governed by the self-explication of freedom. But in essence, this freedom is identical, as he says, with "the holy necessity" of teleological development, in which each stage develops organically from the stage preceeding it, and all the stages together form a system whose significance is determined by a special aim and order.[237]

This is a return to Spinoza's concept of freedom, though formulated otherwise.[238] The essential difference is in introducing a dynamic element in the concept of "the absolute," a move that allowed other circles to preserve the active, spontaneous nature of the reality, that is, the principle of freedom, within the original concept.[239]

Indeed, in contrast to Hegel's rationalistic method, in which reality is perceived as a manifestation of absolute intelligence, Schelling, for whom the notion of freedom is a central motif, conceived the world as a disclosure of divine will. In his eyes, personality is complete when it succeeds in bringing opposing forces, such as good and evil, will and intellect, to true unification.[240] We have yet to discuss the close affinity between Schelling and Rav Kook, especially on the question of the status of will and intellect and the relation between the two.

Schopenhauer is the earliest representative of the second trend—the nonrationalistic. Unlike the rationalistic approach of Spinoza, Kant, and Hegel, Schopenhauer based the absolute on will[241] and claimed will, in Kant's terms of 'the thing-in-itself' is unknowable.[242] Will is perceived as immediate experience, essentially identical with the body. Science is not the pathway to consciousness of will, because it deals with formal connections alone. It is on this very point that Schopenhauer's doctrine is an antithesis of Decartes and Spinoza. Schopenhauer held that science draws away from the conception of the thing-in-itself; that is, the unique will embodied in manifold phenomena. Within the disorder of nature there is nonetheless a harmony that explains the order and purpose of phenomena to us.[243] It is not a matter of a conscious purpose but rather an instinctual aim implanted in reality.

The purpose Schopenhauer held to be implanted in reality did not lead him, as it did other philosophers, to an optimistic world-view, but the opposite. The nature of will in his conception brings about radical pessimism, for will by nature has no aim. "The individual act of will has a goal, but *ratio* itself has no goal."[244] Will is the force sustaining reality, but it is not a specific will. This will is blind. The polemics between Rav Kook and Schopenhauer's view focus on this issue. As we shall see, Rav Kook did not accept the exclusivity of will in being and claimed a dialectic relationship between will and knowledge; there alone is freedom possible.

Nietzsche, who saw himself as Schopenhauer's heir and successor,[245] carried his teacher's conception to its extreme: nihilism. The most radical form of nihilism is supposed to be the view that *every* belief, every considering-something-true is necessarily false, "because there simply is no *true world*."[246] In Nietzsche's eyes, there is no difference between religious and atheistic philosophy: "Every pure moral value system (that of Buddhism, for example) ends in nihilism: this is to be expected in Europe! One still hopes to get along with a moralism without religious background: but that necessarily leads to nihilism. In religion the constraint is lacking to consider ourselves as value-positing."[247]

Nihilism is thus the result of the lack of correspondence between ethical values and the nature of reality, that is the will of existence: "Everything egoistic has come to disgust us (even though we realize the impossibility of the unegoistic); what is necessary has come to disgust us (even though we realize the impossibility of any *liberum arbitrium* [free will] or 'intelligible freedom')."[248] "Morality is a way of turning one's back on the will to existence."[249] This, then, is the background of the new view: Only what glorifies the "self," existence, is true—the will to power. The new philosophy aspires "*not* to make men 'better', *not* to preach morality to them in any form, as if 'morality in itself' or any ideal kind of man were given; but to *create* conditions that require stronger men."[250] The "good man" is the ideal slave. "He who cannot posit *himself as a goal, not posit any goals for himself whatever*, bestows honor upon selflessness *instinctively*. everything persuades him to this: his prudence, his experience, his vanity. And even faith is a form of selflessness."[251]

It seems that more than the other doctrines we have mentioned, Nietzsche's thought challenges all of theology, especially that based on explicit moral impulses. Karl Jaspers rightly held that it is typical of a theologian to see religion and nihilism as the only two alternatives.[252] Rav Kook answered the challenge. Rather than rejecting Nietzsche's claims, he accepted some of his seemingly fundamental assumptions. Nietzsche's basic interest, the aggrandisement of selfhood, becomes Rav Kook's own, yet he proposed a truly alternative view. We will return to this idea.

The revolutionary spirit inspiring Nietzsche's thought and characteristic, to a great extent, of Rav Kook as well was part and parcel of European intellectual circles of the late nineteenth and early twentieth centuries. In the same period, Switzerland served as the crossroads of forces of the European revolution. Socialists, Zionists, scientists, and artists made her major cities—Zurich, Bern, Basel, and Geneva—the ideological capitols of Europe.[253] Philosophical, antirationalist, and antideterministic ideas began to bear an influence even on natural scientists.[254] One of the figures most prominent in molding the new mentality was Henri Bergson, who in 1912 reached the height of his renown and influence. Rav Kook's relationship to Bergson and the principles he adopted or rejected will be discussed in a later chapter. At this point, though, we may remark Rav Kook's geographical proximity, during his stays in Switzerland and England throughout World War I, to centers of European intellectual activity; in these two countries he composed a good part of his writings, at least half the material in the three volumes of *Orot ha-Kodesh*.[255]

3

Revelation as a Principle

In the history of ideas, the concept of "revelation" has assumed many nuances of meaning, of which two are central: (1) the appearance of God as an occurrence in nature or within humankind, and (2) communication of divine will to humankind.[1] These two meanings of revelation are universal elements of all religions and theologies including, of course, Judaism.

Rav Kook's view of the concept of "revelation" differs from both these meanings. Certain aspects of his view have been discussed by S. Rosenberg in an essay on "perpetual revelation." In his eyes, the *second* connotation of "revelation" is most worthy of attention, for "in all of Jewish thought not disconnected from historical reality, *halacha* is an integral component of its field of discussion."[2]

Rosenberg proceeded to examine Rav Kook's position, writing: "Rav Kook saw the historical development of the Torah and *halacha* not as a major result of a chain of historical events and halachic reactions but as continued prophecy. The source of this revelation is in divine knowledge that reviews all acts and bears witness to a predetermined harmony between the revelation of the concealed Torah and the history of the Jewish people."[3] Another possibility leading to understanding the essence of perpetual revelation, Rosenberg held, is to see it as the invention of a wise man, or Torah sage, granted aid from heaven or from halachic authority founded on the injunction "You shall not turn aside" (Deuteronomy 17:11).[4] In effect, the examples Rosenberg presented from Rav Kook's writings lead him to assert the heritage of the nation is the medium of revelation. Rosenberg indicated the significance and implications of his contention by pointing out its propensity to antinomistic conclusions, for according to it, democratic decision may succeed in altering the foundations of the Torah.[5]

In the following discussion, we shall see that Rav Kook's concept of revelation is founded on both meanings of the concept of "revelation"; that is, all of reality is perceived simultaneously as divine revelation and manifestation of his will, and the radical and antinomistic elements of his method are restrained by other restrictions impeding the possibility of changing the bases of the Torah by "democratic decision."[6] Such change is indeed possible, not by means of democratic decision but through a spontaneous popular process or outburst, which would be considered legitimate only in retrospect.[7] Spontaneity is an element of decisive importance in this context, and we will explore its place in revelation in the course of our discussion.[8] In any case, deeper understanding of Rav Kook's position on the subject demands investigation of his perception of revelation, setting it within the framework of his broader metaphysical view, particularly concerning the concept of "will." This wider outlook reveals that the idea of revelation is a basic principle pervading Rav Kook's thought, implicating a range of views he held on various subjects; implicit in all of them is a tension between revolutionism and conservatism.[9]

Will and the Concept of Revelation

When the term *revelation* is invoked in Rav Kook's writings, it usually does not refer simply to "divine appearance" nor even to a "revelation of content," a transmission of Torah "from heaven" in the widely applied traditional sense. In most cases, the term *revelation* in Rav Kook's writings indicates the ontological realm not to be identified with the essence of God or, in the Kantian expression, the realm of phenomena. In this connection, will plays a central role as the divine element that is *revealed*. As Rav Kook said: "We are aware of the will of the world, the level that is *revealed* as the spirit of life in existence, as active and aspiring will, whose aspects *are revealed* in all orders—inanimate, vegetative, animate, human, in each and every particular, and in all of everything."[10] In another passage: "Free will, illuminated by the supernal intellect, is the quiddity of being revealed within it, and that is the soul of Adam haRishon, the First Man, in all its fullness."[11] Further, "Complete freedom and the will within it, burdened by nothing external, serve to *reveal* the essence of life, that life which acquires the plan of happy or evil fortune."[12]

Yet if we wish to reach the core of the problem, these remarks are not enough. The full expression of the perception of revelation as we have described it is in the assertion that "all manifestations of being are manifestations of the ascending will."[13] It is no longer a question of natural being alone as a revelation of will, but of historical[14] and cultural being, and despite the use of kabbalistic symbols, we remark the tendency toward a spiritualization of the concept of revelation influenced by nineteenth century philosophy.

> The laws of life, laws of heaven and earth, shine with supreme light, light of greatness, light of vitality in all of existence in its highest form, wide and full, the light of everlasting life and source of all life. *All the teachings, statutes, ideas, ethics, naturalness, orders and manners, wisdoms, songs and wills,* the turbulence of life, movements of existence, its progress[15] and grasp on the essence of being, all are but treasure houses filled with riches; the will that rises for our sake in his mighty power (*gevurah*) and the majesty of his lasting endurance (*hod, nezakh*), in the foundation of his magnificence (*yesod, tiferet*) and the sublime desire of his glorious majesty (*malkhut*), this will shall be revealed and visible in them in full brillance; from the lowest movement, things proceed in order and without interruption to the highest heavens.[16]

Rav Kook thus saw all of culture and its manifestations as a revelation of the holy. Although there are different degrees in the intensity and quality of revelation, these differences are not crucial, as we will see later. Rav Kook made explicit mention of many events and cultural phenomena, which he saw as revelations of the holy. Even the political system, in his eyes, numbers among them:

> The *tikkun* [improvement, restoration] of the state in general and the body in particular takes place through the appearance of supreme holiness, whose very sublimity prevents it from being illuminated openly in the light of reason, with its evident holy form; rather the light is stretched out in it and with it like a garment, and the fringes emanating from these practical details for the sake of national and societal improvement, in the form of *mitzvot*—they are like the *tzitzit* [fringes], while all of culture is like the *tallit* [prayer shawl]. The *tzitzit* reveal all the light concealed in the entire *tallit* in its manifold appearance, and the acts of *mitzvah* and holiness signified in all human actions for the

improvement of his life in general and in particular—these *mitz-vot* activate the light hidden in the depths of human culture, leading its manifestations to a place worthy of it, to unveil the light of eternal life that gives life to all, even to the fleeting moment.[17]

Although this conception of revelation requires a rigorously monistic attitude like that of Rav Kook, it also allows the pantheistic, acosmic nature of reality to be bounded and confined, for all of creation is perceived as "revelation"—a concept that assumes a distinction between the divine and the world. The domain of revelation is the reflection of the divine in reality, a sort of path or gateway to the inner chamber:

> The way to enter the inner chamber—through the gate—must be made evident. This gate is the divine revealed in the world, the world in all its beauty and splendor, in every spirit and soul, each animal and creeping thing, every plant and flower, all peoples and kingdoms, in the sea and its waves, in the canopy of heaven and the glory of the sun and moon, in the words of every conversation and the ideas of every writer, the images of every poet, the meditations of every thinker, the feelings of all that feels and the surge of valor in every hero.[18]

Because all of creation is an aspect of revelation, it is natural to see the thoughts of all thinkers and works of every artist as manners of revelation. The realm of revelation is in fact broader than all that exists in actuality, for "the *possible* speculations in the realm of the holy are the most sublime poems, and the truth they harbor and reveal is higher still,"[19] because of the infinite nature of the divine.

It must be noted that in his perception of revelation as a manifestation of divine-cosmic "will," Rav Kook used the term in both its aspects: *will* or freedom, and *wisdom* or determinism as one.[20] In his understanding, the complexity of reality reflects the paradoxical nature of will:

> When we are asked: what is the essence of life and the source of existence, and whence is life revealed as the quality of complex forces carving their mark together in an inner and original spirit?—And the answer: the hand striving to closeness with God, which is revealed in all of being as a necessary element of general aspiration, holding within it full freedom in all its courses—this hand does it all. Thus it sets all of being in motion

in its every stage, directing the progress of reality toward revelation by compounding necessity and freedom in various forms, both the smallest of the small [*ze'ir*] in the children of being, and the very longest [*arich*] among them.[21]

This phenomenon itself, "the revelation of two apparently contradictory visions," can be seen not only in being as a whole but in the human soul as well:

> The proper unification of these two general visions is that which gives life to their entire field of action. . . . We see the fruit of this correspondence and unity everywhere we look, in social, cultural, economic and political life, as well as the practical and spiritual life of every individual.[22]

> The miracle of human reason can only be understood as a single spark . . . of the larger will that invests all of being.[23]

Human life is therefore a further *revelation of the two cosmic principles in their dialectical relationship.* Rav Kook took care to explain that our reason and will, like everything in existence, is "a spark from the All" and "from the All it emerges,"[24] for human and cosmic will are bound by ties of mutual dependence: "The universal moment of mercy in the world and the moment of spiritual mercy within the individual depend on each other in various ways."[25] On the one hand, all aspects of the human spirit, "every aesthetic order of life, every endeavor to arouse man's aesthetic sense," as well as "all the visions and ideas, the desires and imaginings," inasmuch as they are manifestations of divine will, "are much more influenced by those constant emanations [of will] than from the pragmatic value of the deeds of men."[26] On the other hand, the very same manifestations serve as instruments preparing "paths to the appearance of divine lights from the divine spiritual treasurehouse, which flow without cease and will become evident in every place able to contain them."[27] Yet even here there are varying degrees: good moral attributes are a better means to the revelation of the most holy than are pleasant modes of life and the aesthetic sense, and superior to them are other ascending degrees of importance: "the practical commandments, and even more the Torah, and the inwardness of the Torah higher still, and the divine *yikhudim* [mystical intentions] in their purity when all the ancient preparations are complete."[28] As far as human consciousness is concerned, this conception embodies two aspects of the divine spirit: one is passive (i.e., the human spirit as an instance of the divine spirit); and the second active (i.e., the human spirit as a creative force), forging the countenance of reality by serving as the instrument that makes the world ready to receive the revelation of the general will.

From here it is only a short stride to Rav Kook's contention that "all honest and common views flow from the source of inner brightness of divine wisdom."[29] This contention comes as no suprise in the context of a view that, as we have seen, considered the wholeness of reality as an aspect of revelation. What is interesting is the emphasis on the special status of "common" views by grace of their simplicity. We have already spoken[30] of Rav Kook's inclination to accredit the more primitive levels of existence with a greater measure of authenticity, considering them nearer to the source, to the essence of being. The same view carries to the creations of the human spirit: "The more honest the masses, the more their views and tendencies are enrooted in the source of divine knowledge, the more there is to learn from them. The masses feel their natural bond to higher knowledge in its inwardness and they carry it, wrapped in thinner or coarser husks according to their state."[31] Indeed, "if the views of the masses in their purity . . . originate in the highest of metaphysical orders, all the more so for the view of those of pure heart, accomplished and learned, concerned with living a life of Torah and developing it with the toil of their souls."[32] Clearly, then, the advantage of the simple masses is evident—the less sophisticated the mind, the more "natural" and "healthy" it can be, as Rav Kook described it:

> The intelligensia thinks it can rise above the masses, enabling it to be more healthy of spirit, more noble of thought. This is a fundamental error, an error out of ignorance to the healthy side of natural awareness and senses, imperfect yet unspoiled by cultural influences. The healthy aspect of integrity is more prevalent in coarse people than it is in learned, ethical, thoughtful people. The learned are more outstanding in various aspects of morality, its laws and details, but the essence of this feeling is found in healthy and natural people, simple and common. Not only in their fundamental moral sense are the masses superior to the elite but in their faith, their sense of divine greatness, beauty, sensuality, all that is part of a life of integrity, not filtered through channels filled with the melancholic rewards of knowledge and wisdom, all this is healthier and purer in the masses. Yet the simple man cannot retain his strength and purity himself, he cannot connect his thoughts, he does not know how to fight when conflicting consciousness and feelings struggle within his soul or out in the external world. For this he needs

help from those of greater insight, who can straighten the paths of his world before him. But just as advice and insight are bestowed upon him, so he grants them a life of health. The element shared between the noble of spirit and the masses is the force that maintains both sides of their pleasant nature, preserving them from decay and degeneration, both moral and material.[33]

In fact simplicity, the absence of the sophistications and fashionings of culture, assures the authenticity of revelation. In this sense, Rav Kook preferred emotion over intellect[34] and held instinct in high regard.[35] Such a preference would seem to ensure the authenticity of revelation, but it also harbors the threat of complete anarchy. Rav Kook thus took care to include remarks clearly delimiting the bounds of what is possible or legitimate in terms of human action: "As long as we are concerned with Torah and wisdom, with charity and social welfare, with love of humanity and proper conduct, we need not fear an outburst of our worst imaginings."

This reservation is no mere external element of Rav Kook's thinking, which he was forced to include out of obligation in another area. These two elements, the undertone of reservation regarding the dangers concealed even in authentic revelations and his conviction of the necessity of the *mitzvot* and ethics as the ultimate instruments of revelation, both are inherent to his method:

> The spiritual light in our every concern, whether in practice or in study, emerges from a plane higher than that level revealed in each separate fact, and the soul ascends according to the degree of spirituality revealed in each in its own manner. And sometimes the light of life rises so high that from the source of sources, most sublime and distant, the spirit emerges and penetrates both fact and study. Such a moment of favor glows with the radiance of the divine countenance.[37]

Through our discussion we will realize how much Rav Kook's concept of revelation is founded on a paradoxical combination of radical elements and conservative reservations. On this point, in any case, we must stress his clear recognition that the honest views of the masses are an authentic expression of revelation, and he boldly proclaimed as legitimate other realms of revelation that seem removed or even opposed to the holy: "great souls," "the genuine" reveal the living light of the most holy even with "secular wisdom, with foreign things, magic, strange and impure beliefs."[38]

Relativity of Views and Deeds

In light of the preceding, Rav Kook's relativistic position toward the value and status of faith and heresy, and of beliefs and opinions in general, is clear. An outlook that sees all aspects of being as an expression of divine revelation and claims that "all the wonderful aptitudes possessed by living creatures . . . the light of their lives, are shards of the highest, the divine soul filled with wisdom and aptitude, which was divided into many parts"[39]—such an outlook must see all manifestations of the human spirit as an aspect of revelation and, further, as we have seen,[40] must accede their truth. In recognition of the divine source of these thoughts, Rav Kook adds: "All thoughts are reasonable, and their links systematic . . . and in any case we know no thought in the world is vain."[41]

However, it is impossible as well as undesireable to ignore the distinctions among levels of revelation. As Rav Kook said, "The differences between sacred and profane are facts; to disguise them would be disastrous,"[42] yet at the same time one must remember these differences are really only an epistemological problem, without ontological substance. The "facts" of which Rav Kook spoke have no relevance outside the ken of human awareness:

> As for the distinction between spirituality and materiality, the essence of the difference is only in relation to our mental and sensual perception; in and of itself, and all the more so in relation of God's wisdom, no such distinction could possibly exist. When we want to explain things we say that in spirituality we perceive a more evident part of appearances, while in worldliness—it is a more hidden [contradictory] and secret part, and in the divine source everything, both great and small, exists in completeness, reality revealing itself as it can be received. What is revealed is being itself, yet it is only a single spark of the whole; in it we perceive all that is missing, what we usually call "materiality." It is not true, but in any case it is the truth conceived by men, augmenting continually.[43]

Thus, in Rav Kook's eyes, one can make "no absolute division between elements, but only a division of degrees."[44] This notion is in keeping with Rav Kook's basic metaphysical structure, according to which all the affairs of the world are in ascending movement, and the differences in degree between upper and lower are no more than relative. "Every individual becomes the base for his neighbor, and the highest neighbor of all makes him center, soul, and light";[45] from this we learn that "worthy" thoughts as well as "fallen" thoughts need to be raised.[46]

Without a doubt, despite his many reservations about atheism,[47] the legitimacy he attributed it as a basically positive phenomenon, as a catalyst to the nationalist revival[48] and as something supposed to purify the concepts of faith itself[49]—this legitimacy issues from Rav Kook's view of atheism as a certain degree of revelation:

> Compared to sublime divine truth, *there is absolutely no difference between imagined faith and unbelief, for neither contains the truth,* but of the two, faith approaches truth whereas unbelief approaches falsehood, and in any case the good and the bad are drawn from these two opposites; the righteous will go in their path and the apostates stumble in theirs, and the whole world, with all its material and spiritual values, all is relative to our worth, and the truth is revealed in faith, the source of good, whereas falsehood and unbelief are the source of evil; but in the light of the infinite all are equal, *and even unbelief is a revelation of life force.* For the living light of the divine splendor burns within it, and the valiant in spirit draw sparks from it, and turn its bitterness to sweetness.[50]

Clearly, then, the source of atheism is in holiness, and this grants both moral and ideological validity to the battle waged by unbelief, in the person of the "free" (*hofshi'im*) against the "enslaved" (*meshu'abadim*), or the observant:

> The war is fierce, and both camps are justified in their fight and their defense; the free ones fight for the sparks of good in their desire not to suffer needless bondage . . . , and the enslaved, who remember the past and love it in all its glory, defend their bondage, that the noblest edifice of the world not be destroyed by the contaminated parts of will. Great souls are needed to mediate peace between the combatants by showing each of them the boundary which is true for him.[51]

One may well be amazed at Rav Kook's analysis and description of the two fighting camps, as if from the perspective of someone personally removed from the conflict. It is not mere objectivity that guides him; his words are an expression of the sense of freedom that, more than anything else, characterized his thought. He measured the orthodox, limited way of thinking by the same standard of freedom and did not spare it the rod of criticism:

> Smallness of faith makes it appear that every means by which people are eager to improve their status, to combat the views that agitate the world, to gain knowledge, strength, beauty, order—all these things are external to what is holy in the world, and many people thus regard the world with a narrow eye; in their view, they alone apprehend the divine fundament, the progress of the world; they hate culture, the sciences, political machinations among Jews and other nations, but all this is a great error and lack of faith. Pure knowledge sees *the divine manifest in every aspect of life*, individual and collective, spiritual and material, it measures things according to the benefit or damage they bring, and to this extent there will never be a completely negative movement, when it attempts to create something, whether material or spiritual; the thing can have disadvantages, but all in all it is a divine creation, in constant action; "He did not create [the earth] a waste land, he formed it to be inhabited" (Isaiah 45:18).[52]

This passage demonstrates Rav Kook's highly positive attitude, from the start, toward culture in the widest sense. The concept of "culture," prevalent in the writings of his contemporaries in Eretz Israel, received a truly metaphysical connotation in Rav Kook's own thought. He repudiated fanaticism, claiming even the wisdom of the nations deserves respect and the truth should be accepted for its own sake. He wrote:

> I do not understand the necessity of this excessive fanaticism, for if all the paths of human intelligence are forbidden to Israel then where is the beauty of Yephet in the tents of Shem, and where is the joining of the divine image, invested by the Holy One in man, by which we honor what is wise and honest in every person, and accept the truth from whomever utters it; in our tradition, he who speaks wisely, even from among the nations, is called a wise man.[53]

Rav Kook's fundamentally positive view extended not only to cultural creations of a neutral nature but also to faiths other than his own, Christianity in particular.[54] Yet he was never indifferent to qualitative differences and did not ignore their virtues and limitations,[55] for what view or deed has no disadvantages? Rav Kook appears to found his view of faith and heresy on the assumption both are incomplete. To him, faith and heresy are interdependent, each in need of the other, and they join together in building the world of spirit and of human creativity in the broadest sense:

> They are to be praised, all the thoughts and ideas of fear of Heaven uttered with a pure heart out of perfect awareness and feeling. However, when thought does not emerge from a broader awareness it restricts life, saps energy, ruins physical forces and spiritual prowess—this is the source of feebleness. At this point the quality of opposition makes its appearance, spread by books and newspapers and influences; the destruction and vulgarity grow and grow, until their stench becomes unbearable. Yet an essence of might and valor can be extracted from them, strength of will, coming as a quality to restore the vitality of life, and it is diluted by the naive influence of God-fearingness, ungraced with clear perception. These two forces together will establish the world and a nation as well, bringing redemption and eternal help to the House of Israel and to all life.[56]

Rav Kook understood modern atheism, in the context of the philosophical developments of the modern era, as a legitimate demand for a reasonable explanation of reality:[57] "The insolence preceeding the coming of the Messiah [*hachutzpa de-ikveta demeshicha*][58] occurs because the world is so ready that it demands to understand how all the details are related to the whole. No detail, unconnected to the greater wholeness, can satisfy this desire."[59] During the Enlightenment the world reached the level of seeking the rationality of life. This demand for a rational explanation of reality is tantamount to an attempt to abstract and generalize the myriad details of the world into principles or rules. An act is considered rational if it fits a general principle.[60] In the modern age, the injunctions of the Torah seem irrational, for we do not see how the details are connected to the whole. When modern individuals fail to understand the principle that serves as the basis and unifying force of individual ideas and acts, they seem meaningless to them.

The claim of rationalism at the root of this idea of "insolence," justified in and of itself, becomes doubly valid by being an impetus hastening the reparation of "the terrible destruction" with the "divine remedy" that is "added strength in the spiritual aptitude" and whose ultimate purpose is to intensify "the understanding and accompanying feeling of how all details of the Torah are beloved with holy love, and how the universal light, full of life and giving life to the world flows to each and every detail";[61] that is, the understanding of a revelation of will or the divine in all particularity.

The Jewish People as a Revelation of Divine Will

We have spoken of various levels in intensity of revelation and different degrees of authenticity. Let us turn our attention now to a particular organism of revelation: the people of Israel. The process of revelation of divine will in all of being is most fully expressed in the way of life and works of the Israeli nation:[62]

> [The higher forces] . . . glitter in the appearance of the holy, passing through the pure channel of holiness, of heavenly ascent, of manifestation of the divine in the world and life, in science and in emotion, in creating and giving birth. Life is charged with laws, and these laws are enacted from all of being, from the ultimate source, passing through all stages of formation, reaching all the way to the collective, to the people itself, acting deep within them and giving each what it is able to accept, until the impression is formed of the special separateness of *Knesset Israel* [the Assembly of Israel], which is an extraordinary creation, complex and solidly unified, and this people has the living Torah, which fills everything around it, surrounding and penetrating, restoring and establishing in particular detail.[63]

As we have remarked, all manifestations of being are revelations of the ascending will. Clearly, Israel's uniqueness in the organism of revelation is that "all the desires . . . native to the universal soul are in the form of *Knesset Israel*."[64] In other words, all the aspirations that are manifestations of divine will are concentrated in the people of Israel as the "essence of being." "The soul of Israel" is "the root of divine revelation and the desire for unity of being in the world."[65]

This description of *Knesset Israel* as the "essence of existence" is related to the highest aspect of the nation, represented in the world of the *sefirot* by *malkhut* [sovereignty], but for this very reason, the same quality can be attributed to the actual people of Israel:

> *Knesset Israel* is the essence of all being, and in this world, this essence is emanated *in the actual Israeli nation in its materiality and spirituality*, in its annals and its faith, and Israelite history is the ideal essence of universal history. There is no movement in the world, among all the nations, whose elements are not found

in Israel, and hers is the most precious essence of all faiths and the source emanating all the goodness and the ideals of all faiths, as well as the force controlling all concepts of belief, eventually bringing them to the level of clear speech to call on the Name of God, Holy of Israel, Lord of the world.[66]

Rav Kook attempted to clarify this idea and make it seem reasonable, for he sensed its potentially shocking nature, and explains: "*Knesset Israel* is the highest spiritual revelation of human experience; just as we should not wonder at what is in the brain or heart, there are such manifestations of life whose like we do not find in the entire body . . . it is impossible to think in any other way."[67] However, the explanation is not yet complete. Rav Kook's perception of the uniqueness of Israel as an aspect of revelation, concentrating and focusing all the forces as they are revealed, is rooted in the connotations of the concept *Knesset Israel* in Jewish mysticism.[68] In a paragraph rich with kabbalistic associations he wrote:

He who is of the attribute of *malkhut* has nothing whatever of himself; in this attribute deficiency and virtue are joined together as one. Such a man can absorb everything into himself, and when he turns to the good and realizes that nothing is truly his own, he is willing to be filled to abundance, for all the attributes, all qualities and aspects, contain no contradictions. *His selfhood is so profound* that whatever he receives becomes a part of him, because he has no *essence that is restricted to him alone.* It is beneath him to do useless things and to sink into sleep, he must guard himself as much as he can from the taste of death;[69] his connection and link to Eretz Israel is intrinsic,[70] and he senses that anyone who lives outside of the Land is like a person without God, "for they have driven me out this day from being joined to the inheritance of the Lord, saying, Go, serve other gods" (I Samuel 26:19), and his soul pines with deepest desire for love of the holiness of the Land and awaits salvation.

This attribute is at the essence of Knesset Israel, the essential nature of the Israeli nation, for they are continually diminished and sense how small they are, aware that all that fills them is not their own, *that they are only a vessel* receiving the light and overflowing blessing of the Most High, and all they receive is emanated.[71]

Knesset Israel is thus perceived as a receptacle into which sublime effluence flows, divine will in its various aspects. "The souls of Israel" are like a "channel . . . in which the element of divine will and free-

dom of choice rests in their consciousness and rational inclination."[72]
This is the source of holiness in Israel as a whole[73] and in the individual Jew specifically.[74] What is this "aptitude" of holiness? Schazt-
Uffenheimer saw in the "holy" "an ability to shape the profane, the
capability of observing and understanding how being is a transformation of something else,"[75] or in Rav Kook's words, "how universal
light, full of life and bringing life to the world, disperses to each and
every particular."[76] Yet, here this aptitude is a formative ability, observation, and understanding, and through our discussion the source of
this aptitude becomes clear: the nation of Israel is an instrument of
revelation, the embodiment of supreme powers, or the point where
they break through from concealment to manifestation.[77]

We can thus understand Rav Kook's desire, throughout his writings, to legitimize all instances of Jewish creativity, even those seemingly in opposition to all notion of holiness: "each and every scattered
spark of life will somehow be rejoined to life, and everything of the
scent of Lebanon from the fountain of Israel will blossom; whether
driven out unintentionally or deliberately,[78] in plenty or in bitter disobedience, the highest light, light of mercy to Abraham is spread over
all, and within all it penetrates and descends."[79]

If this can be said of Jewish creativity on the periphery of Judaism, the same is true, to a much greater extent, of creativity entirely in
the realm of the holy. The creativity of the Israel nation differs fundamentally from all other human creation, not only because of the "essence" it contains, but because of its unique creative force. Although
general human creativity does not actually create but merely describes, orders, and preserves, Jewish creativity innovates experience, creates in the true sense of the term. Rav Kook wrote:

> Divine intellect is *creative intellect,* fully and completely ac-
> tive, whereas the intellect of creatures is *descriptive intellect,* capa-
> ble only of representing to itself what it perceives.
>
> God's closeness grants created beings the quality of the
> divine intellect, *and the greater His divine closeness, the greater is his
> creative power.* Even simple intellectual conception has a large
> measure of the holy sap of divine closeness. And as this quality
> of closeness widens, expanding [spreading] and deepening, its
> similarity to the creative intellect becomes ever more evi-
> dent. . . . *The essential difference between Israel and the nations,* in
> their inmost soul, is that the human intellect as a whole is mere-
> ly descriptive, imagining existence and realizing it in actions, in
> all sorts of arts, all the peoples on earth adapting themselves to
> it, but the *divine attribute of creative intellect*—this is the mar-
> vellous gift of Israel.[80]

As we have said, creative power increases in proportion to divine closeness, and when that closeness becomes identification—in the *sefira* in which *Knesset Israel* is a divine attribute—this creative force appears at the acme of its intensity. From this perspective, it can be said that "Israel has no symbols that are merely factors of thought and feeling, but rather *mitzvot* and teachings: ardently living, true and pleasant for ever and ever, their curse is a curse and their blessing a blessing."[81] That is, the deeds of Israel, particularly fulfillment of *mitzvot*, have more than mere symbolic significance; they do not designate nor allude to any particular reality, but rather innovate and establish reality. Again, we speak of the level at which divine closeness turns into identity and embodiment: *Knesset Israel* herself is *"the inheritance that Moshe received on Sinai"* [קבלה למשה מסיני] and the Oral teaching[82] in that both are embodied in the *sefira* of *malkhut*.[83] This identifying *Knesset Israel* with the concept of Oral teaching is indeed a radical step and illustrates Rav Kook's conviction that consensus of the nation is the source of halachic authority:

> Know that we gladly maintain Jewish customs in full awareness they were not commanded to us by any prophecy; we do so out of affection for our nation, for its love and honor is dear to us with the affection of supernal divine holiness. All the *mitzvot of the rabbis* we fulfill, as well; their basic element is acceptance by the "entire people," which is the honor of the nation and its historical, eternal, divine, and beloved influence that, the more it deepens the more beloved it becomes, revealing within it more and more the will and common character of the entire nation. And even though the rabbis based it on "Do not stray" (Berachot 19), in any case the clear foundation is the *acceptance of the nation*, because agreement is needed (Avoda Zara 26b), that is, when it spreads to most of the Jewish community. According to Nahmanides ("Shoresh rishon," Maimonides's *Sefer ha-mitzvot*), the negative element of "Do not stray" does not actually refer to the words of the Sages; nonetheless, these words are pleasant to Israel and are performed with love. And those who discern the power of this love with all their hearts, they are the *foundation of the nation forever*, though perhaps few in number, "And among the remnant those whom the Lord shall call (Joel 3:5)." . . . Ignorance of the center of gravity of the nation's heritage to all generations, its kinship to the Oral teaching, has caused many mistakes in research. Many of those who thought the vital element of fulfilling Oral law is only what is traditional in the nation from the stature and holiness of the rabbis; pursuing a familiar aspiration, they became insolent and

critical, full of impudence and extremist tendencies, attacking the leaders and forefathers of the generations, *hoping the normative, obliging power of the practical halacha would be thus weakened.* They did not know that the greatness and holy superiority of the Sages is absolutely true, and that it can also add relish, enhancing and improving the inclination to walk in their path, but the everlasting basis remains *the nation's acceptance for all generations in all facets of its life. . . .* And the fulfillment in deed of the Written law is certainly no less mandatory, as a national fundament, than Oral law and rabbinic teachings, . . . whose basis is the divine significance within that nation, more unique and wondrous in these aspects than all other peoples, *the oral aspect of the written Torah* is spread before us, that is, the whole nation's acceptance and the divine character, unmistakeable to every eye in all its history and activity. This stops the mouth of every unbeliever and destroyer, even those who rashly oppose the Holy Scriptures with their deluded criticism.[84]

In sum, we can conclude with the following formulation: the people of Israel is an instrument of the revelation of divine will, and its creativity is the authentic expression of this revelation. The Israeli nation is also identified with the Torah, both oral and written,[85] thus allowing it to become a source of halachic authority.

The Perception of Torah and Status of the Commandments

In our discussion of the people of Israel as an aspect of revelation and the identification of the nation with the Torah, we mentioned the connection of this perception to kabbalistic teachings. This kinship is expressed in utterances such as, "The entire Torah is names of the Holy One, blessed be He,"[86] or statements ascribing the *mitzvot* not only symbolic significance but actual power as well,[87] as they appear in Rav Kook's chrystallized theories. Even Torah learning, in his opinion, is not learning in the normal sense:

The world is renewed through novel interpretations of Torah. This is simply because the innovation revealed to us in limited form comes to us as an infinitely diminished essence after the tremendous spiritual waves have flooded and flowed away, rolled from one world to another, becoming every more constricted and diminished, until they at last appear before us in the form of some innovation.

At its source, this innovation is not a private lightning flash of intellect but rather the renewal of a new land, all according to the nature of what is renewed.[88]

Just as Torah learning and regeneration is a creative force, renewing being, that is, divine power, so too "in practical matters we must understood that they are all segments and garments of *Or ha-Yosher* [God's will],[89] and within all the particulars is the divine soul of the world's perfection, and the descending light also penetrates each and every particular."[90] Often in Rav Kook's writings, even the *mitzvot* are described as instruments and expressions of revelation: "All actions, all *mitzvot*, all customs, are no more than manifold instruments, each containing within itself a few sparks of the supreme light."[91] Fulfillment of the *mitzvot* is "the revelation of thought, divine animation in the practical sense,"[92] and they originate "in the same *sefira* beyond any limited realm."[93]

Yet Rav Kook was not content with this representation of Torah and *mitzvot;* he extended the possibilities presented by this conception to their furthest limits.[94] If indeed "the entire Torah is the names of the Holy One, blessed be He," then

> every positive attribute and manner of living is part of the Torah, and every wisdom originates in Torah, and every good quality in man and community shines with the name of God, but there is a *difference between he who knows* that all is light sparkling with the name of God and *he who does not know.* Yet this difference in knowledge is only a matter of degree, and really depends on the inward point of will, to what extent it is verified to the good.[95]

This perception immeasurably expands the meaning of *Torah.*[96] In Rav Kook's view,

> Constriction in the concept of Torah does nothing but evil. At first, out of pettiness the Torah is conceived superficially, and sublime, inspired thought grows alien to its nature; it sinks deeper and deeper until it can no longer raise itself . . . and can no longer guide itself and the world with concepts of the holy worthy of conquering a higher place in the future life of the world.[97]

The fact that the Torah is not usually grasped in its wider sense is due to incomprehension of the idea of revelation as Rav Kook understood it. Yet in his eyes, unawareness of the phenomenon of revelation cannot alter the basic fact of the concept of "Torah" in the widest sense, dependent not on perception but on the element of will.

The classic belief in *"Torah min haShamayim,"* bestowed from Heaven, undergoes a fundamental transformation from its original meaning. Once again, at issue is not the giving of the Torah from the hand of God as a unique historical act nor of "receiving the Torah" as a temporal event. The Torah is perceived as divine power "from heaven," which extends through reality and is particularly revealed in the character of the nation, completely suited to the ethical nature of being, that is the aspiration of ascent: "The Torah of Israel must be from heaven, and it spreads throughout the earth, the inner quality of the nation, like that heavenly light whose every ray follows in the footsteps of the actualization of sublime morality beyond all limitation, spreading to complete wholeness."[98] On this point, Rav Kook explains his view with astonishing daring:

> There is unbelief that is like acknowledgment and ac-
> knowledgment that is like unbelief. How can that be? A man
> may admit the Torah is from heaven, but he conceives those
> heavens in such a strange manner that they retain not a single
> element of the true faith. And how can unbelief be aknowledg-
> ment? A man denies the Torah is from heaven, but his denial is
> based solely on that same perception of heaven imagined by
> minds filled with vanity and emptiness, and he says the Torah
> must have a higher source than that. He begins to search for its
> root in human spirituality, in the profundity of his ethics and
> higher wisdom; although he has not yet reached the heart of
> truth, this atheism as acknowledgment is important, and it
> draws closer and closer to the recognition of true faith. Such a
> generation of upheavals must be understood to its credit. Torah
> from heaven is a model of each and every aspect of belief. Rela-
> tive to their expression, their inner essence, it is the principle of
> faith so earnestly sought.[99]

Against the background of similar processes in Jewish thought of the nineteenth century, Rav Kook's conception embraced a spiritualization of the concept of revelation. This is a primary and essential component in his works, which seek to propose a reinterpretation of religion and reality. In the following chapters we will discuss the aims and implications of this revolutionary course of interpretation.

PART THREE

Religion and Freedom

4

The Concept of "Freedom" and the Category of "Self"

The history of the idea of "freedom" is almost as old as that of Jewish thought.[1] Nearly every thinker concerned with ethics has regarded liberty as equivalent to happiness and good, describing it as nature or as reality, as a manifestation of reason or as experience. More than 200 connotations of the term *freedom* have been suggested by scholars of the history of ideas.[2] In most cases it is perceived as a quality or situation attributed to a subject. Freedom is distinguishable in practice in social and political activity, in works of art as well as in independent thought. In all its manifestations, freedom can be seen as an ability or as autonomy. This autonomy may be realized either as "internal freedom" or as "external freedom." As "internal freedom" it is perceived as becoming determined for action out of natural necessity alone[3] or as a response to the autonomous moral imperative.[4] "External freedom" was understood as liberation from external forces, that is, from ethical or religious norms, or from political forces.[5] In Jewish thought and tradition, the idea of freedom as an aspect of choice and decision was a basic and accepted assumption, as Maimonides phrased it: "No one in our nation or of our faith was heard to challenge it."[6]

Consciousness of the question of freedom is one of the predominant characteristics of Rav Kook's works. It is represented both as a mystical ideal and as a central idea in his theoretical teaching.[7] Yet the concept of "freedom" in his doctrine differs significantly from the usual conception. Rav Kook indeed described freedom as the best of ideals, as the "aspiration of man's soul"[8] and as an idea "whose standard our nation bears,"[9] but all this is insufficient in illustrating his attitude on the subject.

The thesis we would like to propose states that freedom, in Rav Kook's perception, is not a quality or condition related to a subject, freedom is a subject in and of itself; or in the words of Jean-Paul Sartre: "Because human freedom is not a quality like other qualities— clearly every man himself *is* freedom."[10] The metaphysical elements discussed previously[11] lead us to the conclusion that freedom can be seen as a *process of personal actualization*. The measure of self-realization is commensurate with the measure of freedom. In our discussion that follows we will see that, in Rav Kook's opinion, freedom is not to be viewed as an aspect attributed to any particular "self," for it is completely identical with the "self." This idea holds for both instances of freedom, human and divine. It is our task to clarify the relationship between these two instances of self-actualization.

In Jewish theological thought, this relationship is usually perceived as problematic, yet accepted as a paradox, whether necessary or illusory. In any case, one pillar of faith[12] remained: "All is foreseen but freedom of choice is given."[13] Nonetheless, in a monistic-pantheistic world-view, the question may become senseless. Such a view strives toward complete or nearly complete identification of the human personality with the divine. It is no longer a matter of *devekut* (devotion, adherence) in the sense of "And you shall walk in His paths—just as He is merciful so you are merciful, etc." or of the intellectual devotion of philosophers, but rather of a mystical way to *devekut* through ecstacy[14] or the quietistic path of crushing the ego.[15] The meaning of *freedom* in this view differs radically from the usual sense. And in effect, although Rav Kook's metaphysical view can be seen as monistic, the concept of freedom and its relation to the concept of self are overshadowed by the tension between the two aspects of transcendence and immanence. We will focus on the question of the status of the human self versus the divine self, and a clarification of the precise connotation of the concept of freedom in Rav Kook's thought, its implications and ethical significance.

Freedom of Thought, Free Choice, and the Concept of "Self"

In a short essay, Rav Kook analyzed the difference between the conditions of freedom and slavery, not as a contrast between liberty and compulsion but rather as a difference between a state of complete harmony in one's internal world and a state in which no such correspondence exists:

> The difference between the slave and the free man is not only one of status, in this case that the first is enslaved to anoth-

er, whereas the second is not enslaved. We could find an educated slave enjoying boundless freedom as well as the opposite, a free man with the spirit of a slave. The freedom to be unique is that same elevated spirit which uplifts man and the entire people, to be *true to his inner* self, to the spiritual quality of God's image within him, and in such a quality he can consider his life as worthy and purposeful. This is not so for one who has the attitude of a slave; the content of his life and feelings never correspond with his own spiritual qualities but only by what is beautiful and good in the other who rules over him in any way at all, whether officially or morally—with what this other sees as beautiful and good.[16]

Freedom is defined here as "that same exalted spirit" of loyalty to the inner self, to the quality of the divine likeness. In contrast, the "spirit of slavery" means the absence of this loyalty or lack of correspondence between the content of life and feeling and the quality of one's "essential spirit." Freedom here is not a matter of capability, free choice, or creativity. All these will be examined later, but they are perceived by Rav Kook as expressions of freedom rather than as freedom itself. In this passage, freedom is seen as a spirit of loyalty to selfhood. The nature of this selfhood is not yet clear, but will be taken up presently. On this point we merely indicate the close connection between the concepts of "freedom" and "self." This connection is drawn unambiguously in another passage, which describes freedom as a measure of affirmation of selfhood, bound up with the absence of jealously:

> Highest freedom in its luminousness is connected to divine *hesed* [loving kindness], and the two visit this world only in the purity of the highest attributes; this purity consumes all envy from the heart, . . . and thus it is untainted by jealousy, and is content with itself, and does not move from its inner attribute; he envies neither his neighbor's externality nor his inwardness, and his own selfhood can thus exist.[17]

Through self-affirmation, one confirms one's existence and actualizes one's freedom. Although in certain instances the term *freedom* is used to refer to an aspect or quality, what is meant is only manifestations of freedom. Rav Kook truly believed freedom is no single manifestation of life but rather the essence of life itself. Indeed, this life—in its vitality or in its freedom—must be expressed in various forms of thought, creativity, and action:

The intrinsic inwardness of the soul, thinking, living a true spiritual life, must have absolute inner freedom. Her freedom is *her life*, gained through *her original thought* that is her inward glimmer, enkindled and burning by study and reflection, but this essential spark is the basic element of idea and thought. And if this intrinsic glimmer is not given room to appear in its full light, nothing external can be of any help.[18]

Man, by definition, is free. His freedom lies in his humanity. This freedom must be expressed in original thought, for original thought alone reflects the personality. It requires daring, as a certain risk is indeed involved, yet one must see that as a condition of human existence.

He whose soul does not wander far and wide, who does not seek the light of truth and good with all his heart, does not suffer spiritual ruin, but neither does he build anything of substance. He finds haven in the shade of natural structures, like rabbits who take refuge among the rocks. But man, *possessed of a human soul*—his soul can find shelter only in structures he himself builds with his own spiritual toil, and he never ceases from his zealous labor.[19]

Yet original thought is not the sole reflection of personality. In Rav Kook's eyes, there are two authentic manifestations of personality: will and thought. "Will tells more about he who wills than action tells about the agent, and likewise, all thought tells more of the thinker than what any deed shows about the doer."[20] It is no accident that the divine itself is also revealed in the two aspects of will and *hokhma*, as we have seen earlier. The similarity is more than coincidental; it betrays a real link between the human personality and the divine, and we will consider the matter further in the course of our discussion.

Let us examine the two main branches of freedom: freedom of choice and original thought. Just as these two branches faithfully reflect human personality, they mirror the relation between God and the world as cosmic forces: "Simple observation shows us that the spiritual connection between the world and God, the forces of will and awareness in being, is more evident than the material connection visible in active and mechanical forces. And what is observable in the world is even more visible in man."[21] The nature of this parallel between being as a whole and the human being is explored at length in a letter Rav Kook wrote to Moshe Zeidel:

Divine observation[22] is concerned with creating being, its most essential quality worthy of that name, according to its highest point, to fullest reality, *and full reality* is that which is filled with the revelation of essence. And this essential revelation, in its chasmic depths, in fact occurs according to the *measure to which free choice reveals its substance.* This is the wealth of divine science (knowledge) [מדע], whose standard is borne by our nation, to declare the absolute freedom in absolute and supreme reality, "Whatever the Lord wishes, he has done in heaven and on earth" (Psalms 135:6), not continuous cause and effect like the image of light from the sun,[23] nor in the image of secondary ideas from axioms.[24] We seek a total reality, whose absolute power makes it ten times more desireable than any conditional reality; and this exaltation springs from the sublime revelation of being, *in the living image of a free spirit of choice. "Image of God."* Thus, the basis of the ideal of reality is *absolute essence,* which is *revealed in freedom of choice;* and this freedom of choice is imaginable only when there is good and evil. Then the good is intrinsic and essential and the evil, intrinsic and essentially evil; and destiny is good for those absolutely good, and bad for the evil commensurate to the essential character of the good—this is the goal of contriving a reality of character, complete in its highest being. This is my wish in saying: "Because we realize that complete freedom and the will contained within it, burdened by nothing external, serve to *reveal the very essence* of life, that life which accepts the plan of good or evil fortune." My concern here is not with psychic questions, to distinguish the true essence of life, revealed by free will. Though the character of its "private owners," in your words, my friend, be revealed and made visible by free will, the two are separate essences: intrinsic being on the one hand and free will on the other, or *perhaps free will itself is the essence of life—for us they are one entity.*[25] We desire only to envision innocence and guilt as a mighty law, corresponding to the wisdom of being and eternal justice, not superficial but profound . . . and whether the perfection of being to its essential point depends on its inner nature or on some means we call *free choice,* whose quality is to emphasize and reveal being in its deepest self, as far as we are concerned, there is no difference. We naturally tend toward the unity of things, and we have no need to attribute essence to anything aside from free will.[26]

Here Rav Kook explains the connection between freedom and reality: the substantive existence of "fullest reality"; that is, real existence is commensurate with the degree of the revelation of its absolute essence. And the degree of essence corresponds with the degree of freedom of choice. Thus freedom of choice is what determines the reality of humankind and world. The relationship between God and the world is not based on a deterministic principle in the sense formulated by Plotinus or Spinoza, but rather on the principle of freedom, inherent in ultimate reality. The absoluteness of this principle, by grace of its absoluteness, not only permits but necessitates the existence of nonabsolute freedom ("conditional reality"). Hence his understanding of the concept of "absolute" or "perfect" (complete) as inherently contradictory, containing its opposite within itself.[27]

"Conditional reality," then, is fashioned in the image of "total reality," absolute in the sense that the principle of its existence, like that of absolute reality, is identical with free choice or with the concept of "freedom." This, in Rav Kook's eyes, is the true meaning of the notion of "God's image"; the resemblance between the divine and the human is as the relation between freedom and existence. Yet, in its realization, this connection removes the human from the realm of "conditional reality," for "conditional reality is guided toward its elevation, toward the heights of absolute reality." The realization of human freedom is thus a process of the human's elevation and departure from conditional to absolute being.[28]

The formulation he offered of the manifestation of selfhood is restricted by free will, as he had no interest in insisting on definitive distinctions on the metaphysical level. His chief concern was not in knowledge for its own sake but rather in the ethical significance of knowledge: "We desire only to envision innocence and guilt as a mighty law, corresponding to the wisdom of being and eternal justice"; that is, to see the phenomenon of ethics as a "natural law," as a cosmic phenomenon. Thus his inconsistent formulations do not distort the fundamental and predominant tone, which perceives freedom as the essence of being and human selfhood: "Of course, we incline more to the unity of things, and we have no need to ascribe essential being to anything other than free will."

At first sight, the said resemblance between the two freedoms, divine and human, seems to exist in principle alone rather than in particularity. Yet this is not the case. Rav Kook affirmed there are two sorts of choice: "*Concealed* choice is the basis of all law and justice, and it orders all of reality at its various levels, from the greatest to the smallest. And *revealed* choice, embodied in man, made visible by evident justice is no more than a drop in the sea compare to that secret choice, which is the controlling power behind the entire law and order of being."[29] Rav Kook marked the difference between these two kinds of choice: "Concealed choice functions not according to moral and evident meaning, but to the supreme ideal of highest expectation, beyond the conditions of actual reality."[30] In other words, revealed choice in the normal sense is seen as an ability to select and choose between alternatives. Concealed choice, in contrast, is not an ability to chose but rather a power of existence, "engendering being."[31]

The distinction between revealed and concealed choice is thus not a differentiation between humankind and being, for the distinction is perceptible even in the individual: "There is revealed will within the soul, the will of the heart, and there is hidden will in the body as a whole. When the will of the heart is revealed for good, its light draws the will hidden in all of life from potentiality to actuality, and a wondrous spiritual fusion is created."[32]

This view, which perceives free choice as a reflection of the "self," is what determines its moral significance:

> In true justice we always associate innocence with choice. When a person choses the good and his deeds succeed in accordance with his ways, this situation pleases the sense of justice in us . . . because we realize that total freedom, which contains within it will unburdened by no external pressure, serves to reveal the very essence of life, that life which acquires the plan of good or evil fortune. Thus, essential revelation alone should determine whether good or evil is drawn to the person who must bear it in life.[33]

This moral vision of the success of someone who has chosen good "pleases the sense of justice in us." Rav Kook's evaluation is aesthetic, that is, pleasure comes from seeing the beauty of the similarity between the authentic good, revealed in free choice, an expression of divine will, and moral good, or the ethical nature of God, evident in the success of the chooser.[34] Nonetheless, the main importance of free choice is not in the pleasure engendered by the occurrence of a moral vision, but rather in the responsibility it imposes on one:

> One of the elements of repentance in human thought is man's recognition of his responsibility for his actions, born of his belief in free choice. The same is true of the act of confession accompanying the *mitzvah* of repentance, in which man admits no agent can be blamed for his sin and its results aside from he himself. In this he realizes his own freedom of will and his

tremendous control over his way of life and deeds, thus clearing his own path to return to God.[35]

In Rav Kook's view, no peace can be made with anarchistic tendencies, born of modern psychology, that seek to deprive the individual of moral responsibility: "Modern science has become aware of certain innate natural tendencies in man, and they wish to uproot the element of moral outrage in this, but "'the word of our God shall stand forever' (Isaiah 40:8)."[36] Nonetheless, Rav Kook did admit the difficulty of refuting deterministic claims by means of what could be seen as manifestations of freedom in reality. Absolute freedom in all its purity is not yet apparent in the world, but this by no means refutes its existence:

> From the beginning of creation, from its lowest to highest stage, natures increasingly *differentiate* from one another in the quality of *their own freedom, which is their freedom of will.* "The wondrous works of him who is perfect in knowledge" (Job 37:16)—all of creation is redeemed from the prison of slavery, from the bonds of necessity and lack of free choice, all according to its internal lack of differentiation. In the human realm, that same quality of freedom is much wider, yet still incomplete. True freedom has not yet come into the world; the world is not yet delivered from its chains of servitude, but new stages are reached as each personality comes to gain, through its positive tendencies, deeds, and aspirations, its own choice and ultimate freedom. This is more characteristic among the nations; in their general conception, they are more hindered by the bonds of necessity than are individuals, and the quality of slavery in each individual gradually combines to cast an iron yoke on the neck of the collective.[37]

We have remarked that, in Rav Kook's eyes, there are two authentic manifestations of personality: will and thought. Now that we have explored the aspect of will expressed in free choice, let us turn to the question of thought. The demand of freedom of thought, "which every thinking person requires of himself,"[38] is not a luxury but rather, as we have said, a condition of human existence.[39] We have already discussed at length the status of original thought as a form of revelation,[40] as well as Rav Kook's perception of free, Jewish thought as "secrets of the Torah."[41] He phrased his idea as a definition, affirming: "Mystical thought is the freedom of Israel, of the Israelite soul."[42] The comparison is thus trifold: mystical thought is identified with the freedom of Israel, defined as the Jewish soul. Kabbalah, then, is not a doctrine or school, for because secrets of the Torah reflect the freedom of each individual, one's own "self," even the contents of one's thought, and of these, the "secrets" themselves are exclusive and original. Everyone's faith is intimately connected with his or her personal uniqueness and unity of belief is thus inconceivable. In Rav Kook's own words:

> Hidden knowledge is unique in every individual. It is bound up with his selfhood, is unrepeatable, and transmitted by no sound or explanation. "They shall be yours only" (Proverbs 5:17). A righteous man shall live by his own, his very own, faith. And from this luminous faith, which forms a separate Eden-paradise for him, he goes forth to walk in the gardens of the Lord, bounded as public domain, where his mind intermingles with that of his fellows. "So will thy spring be dispersed abroad, and streams of water will flow in the broad places" (Proverbs 5:16).[43]

All this is true not only of original thought but even of modes of expression, language, and style.[44] Commonly accepted terms and symbols, Rav Kook claimed, must not impair free creativity: "Gaze upon the lights in their inwardness. Your soul will not be swallowed up by the names, the phrases, and the letters; they are delivered into your hand, and not you into theirs."[45] The resources at the disposal of the thinker are like clay in the hands of a sculptor. The free soul is a creative soul,[46] and its creativity cannot be limited.[47] Spiritual creation is free, compromising with no external influence, and it creates as its inner spirit directs it. And as its faith in itself mounts, it ascends ever closer to truth.[48]

Rav Kook saw the importance of separating external influence from personal spiritual creativity, thus guarding the uniqueness of the individual's path toward God:

> What one soul receives from the influence of another, even though it may benefit it in some way, imparting some knowledge or good feeling, helping it occasionally, it harms the soul as well by *mixing an alien element in its essence,* and the world can become complete only through the negation of foreign influence; *"man shall no longer teach his neighbor, nor every man his brother, saying, Know the Lord: for they shall all know me"* (Jeremiah 31:33), young and old. The process of eliminating the alien influences threatening every individual, though seemingly destruc-

tive, is the contradiction that leads to a more enduring and perfect building, the sole gateway to the world to come, *for God makes a separate Eden for each and every individual;* as it is written, "drink of the river of thy pleasures [Edens]"—His Edens and not His Eden (Psalms 36:9).[49]

Self-Awareness and Intensification of Will

We said earlier that self-affirmation is a condition of freedom or, more precisely, is tantamount to freedom and existence themselves. Self-affirmation implies the absence of envy of the other, neither of another's external nor internal being. Self-awareness means satisfaction with one's existence in and of itself; loss of this awareness is paramount to a sin of losing oneself. This is true alienation—in dissatisfaction with oneself, jealousy, striving toward goals external to the action itself, every desire for what is beyond the existing or practically attainable—all these are attempts to magnify the self, to aggrandize and improve it. In effect, though, they lead to the antithesis of this goal. A loss of self takes place. This, in Rav Kook's eyes, is the meaning of estrangement:

> "And I am among the exiles [in the midst of the exile]" (Ezekiel 1:1), the inner, essential *I* of each person and of the community is truly revealed not only according to its holiness and purity, its supreme might, consumed in the pure illumination of sublime brightness burning within it. We have sinned as our fathers have, the sin of Adam, the first Man, who was *estranged from his essence,* who heeded the snake and *lost himself,* could offer no clear answer to the question, "Where art thou?" because he did not know his own mind, because he had lost his true *I-ness* by his sin of bowing down to an alien god. Israel sinned—it went whoring after strange gods, deserted its own essence; Israel neglected the good. The Land sinned, denied her *selfhood,* sapped her own strength, pursuing aims and ends, did not devote all her hidden virtue to making the taste of the tree be as the taste of its fruit.[50] She cast her eye outside of herself, taken up with fortunes and careers. She cursed the moon, lost her inner orbit, her contentment with her lot, began to dream of glorifying foreign kings. And thus the world *sinks ever deeper in loss of self,* of each and every individual and of the whole.
>
> Learned educators come along, caught up with externality, they too are distracted from the *self* and add fuel to the fire,

offering vinegar to the thirsty, cramming minds and hearts with everything other, everything outside of themselves, *and the self is gradually forgotten, because if "I" am not, neither is "he" and, moreover, neither are "thou."* "The breath of our nostrils, the annoited of the Lord" (Lamentations 4:20). That valor and might *is not external to us, it is our own breath, the Lord our God and David our King whom we shall seek,* we stand in awe before the Lord and before His goodness. *We shall seek our "I," our selves, and we shall find us.* Cast off all alien gods, remove every stranger and *mamzer,* "And know that I am the Lord your God, who brings you out from the land of Egypt to be your God, I am the Lord."[51]

In this passage, *self-awareness* is indeed defined as self-affirmation, as finding sense and meaning in oneself rather than in the other. This definition suits the "I-ness" both of the individual and the community, as well as that of cosmic entities such as the moon and earth. Yet the question of essence stubbornly remains; that is, when all is said and done, what is this "I" spoken of so adamantly? A response is offered in the preceding passage. Rav Kook hinted at the identification of the human self with the divine self, or at least a correspondence between the quest for the human "self" and for God: "We shall seek the Lord our God and David our King . . . we shall seek our selves."

It is transparently clear that the phrases "David our King" and "the breath of our nostrils, the annoited of the Lord" allude to the messianic longing, the "hope for redemption," linked both to the human "I" and to the divine itself. This idea and our conclusion that the concept of "freedom" refers to the category of the self correspond completely with another formulation Rav Kook offered, comparing freedom with the "longing for God's nearness," on the one hand, and with the "essential nature of life," on the other: "The freedom of the human spirit demands the rights[52] to long for God's nearness in all aspects of life, for in all the might of its perfection, aspiration alone ascends to the zenith of the grand ideal of freedom."[53] Rav Kook added:

> Life itself, all of life, its very essence cannot possibly be anything other than the elemental longing to be close to God. Thus it fulfills the unique *connotation* of *human life,* composed of the desire for a sense of self—shared by all creatures—along with a striving for completeness. . . . In this it is a true shadow of the absolute, unconditional life of the absolute divine, "in the image of God He created him."[54]

What Rav Kook described is a principle by which freedom is identified with existence on three planes: the divine, the cosmic, and the human. This, as we have said, is the meaning of the concept of "God's image,"[55] the *continuous* "*exodus from Egypt*" in echo of the verse Rav Kook introduced there, "And you shall know that I am the Lord your God, who *brings* you out from the land of Egypt to be your God, I am the Lord" (Leviticus 22:33);[56] in other words, the perpetual process of realization of supreme freedom.

But it is impossible really to define freedom and the essential nature of humankind. In a fundamental and highly characteristic comment, Rav Kook marked the limitations of every conceivable definition and sets the boundaries of discussion:

> No man can *know* the *essential nature*, even of himself, not to mention the other; neither of an individual nor of a nation. We circle about the point of knowledge, occupying ourselves with *speculations* and assessments, orienting ourselves by events we can perceive, most of which are really also hidden from us, particularly their complicated causes, and on the basis of such sources of information we speak of a unique character and a distinctive soul. We must realize our knowledge hangs upon nothingness, and "the judgment is God's" (Deuteronomy 1:17).[57]

The human self is understood as "the thing-in-itself" and hence unknowable.[58] Only one entity is "something in and of itself", and that is God. This sends us back to his assertion of the identification of the human self with the divine:

> Only the holy, personal and universal, has an essential nature and living being from its original, inward essence. But the profane, and certainly evil and sin have no essential nature, no essential longing, no real essential will, but only an external drive inciting material and spiritual actions. And the source of desire, lust, character, selfhood is in the holy, and all who cleave to Him receive His influence—"And you who cleave to the Lord your God, all of you are alive this day."[59]

The absolute "I" is thus the holy, and the more the human self cleaves to the holy, the greater is its strength. In effect, it is imprecise to speak of the human "self," for there is no such thing as human essence. One possesses selfhood as an instrument of the revelation of the divine "self." Clearly, this essence is identical with the absolute

"I," the divine, that is revealed in humankind. This idea is particularly true of the nation of Israel that, according to Rav Kook, was favored with a large measure of freedom:

> He who is of the attribute of *malkhut* [the divine dimension of sovereignty] has nothing whatever of himself, and in this attribute, deficiency and virtue are joined as one. Such a man can absorb everything into himself, and when he turns to the good and realizes that nothing is truly his own, he is ready to be filled to abundance, for all the attributes, all qualities, and aspects contain no contradictions. His selfhood is so profound that whatever he receives becomes a part of him, because *he has no essence* that is particular and restricted to himself. . . . This attribute is at the essence of *Knesset Israel*, the essential naturalness of the Israeli nation, for they are continually diminished and sense how small they are, aware that all that fills them is not their own, that they are a mere vessel receiving the light and overflowing blessing of the Most High, and all they receive is emanated.[60]

The freedom of Israel, then, is paradoxically expressed by a lack of self-awareness in the conventional sense. It consists in the people's constant self-effacement, sensitivity to their insignificance, awareness that all that fills them is not part of their essence. At the same time, they serve as a receptacle for divine "will"; their freedom is actualized as this will materializes and strengthens. Manifestations of will in the activities of the Jewish nation are, as we have seen, manifestations of divine will. The humility demonstrated by this diminution of essence (self-effacement) makes way for another sort of self-awareness: the sense of having a share in the absolute. Self-abnegation and humility become self-affirmation, realization of one's selfhood:[61] "Man is destined to rise to recognition of his will, to self-consciousness, to the highest perception of happiness in doing his own will as the will of his Maker, *for his will is none other than his Maker's will.* And the more penetrating this recognition, the more it embodies its being."[62]

At issue here is not *annihilatio,* or self-annihilation, the logical conclusion of pantheism.[63] Nor is this a summons to "abnegate our will before His will" but rather the opposite: self-affirmation is mandated, the intensification and reinforcement of human will. Indeed, this view is informed with a recognition that human will is but "a single spark of the blazing flame of the great Will in all of being, the manifestation of the will of the Master of the World, blessed be He,"[64] and should by no means be understood as a demand for annullment of the self. If a quietistic undertone occasionally seems audible in Rav Kook's words, it is an error of hearing. The question concerning him is not the annullment of life but rather its expansion:

> The supreme holiness is the holiness of silence, of being, when man *recognizes* himself as nonexistent in his individual inwardness, *and lives a collective life*, the life of all, experiencing the vitality of the inanimate, the vegetative and the animal, the life of all being, of all speaking creatures, of each and every man, the life of all, recognizing, attaining, feeling everything.[65]

It must be emphasized that self-annullment is a matter of consciousness and not of will. "One sees oneself as if without existence." There is an awareness of the insubstantiality of border lines, of what is particular and what general, and the mistake of seeing them as real is thus eliminated. Will, in contrast, is far from annulled. Rather the opposite: the fortification of will is an everpresent undertaking:

> When a person senses his will is listless, he must make an effort to strengthen it by every means, to enable him to actualize every positive thing suited to his nature. And it is better to work toward increasing the power of will than to deal with the details of moral improvement.
>
> Certainly, while will is being strengthened, its purity and refinement must not be forgotten, nor should the process of elevating will toward the holy. But the main occupation of the weak-willed must be in *fortifying the essence* of will through various devices—natural, ethical, intellectual, Torah—and they must not dismiss any suggestion that could further the highest purpose of fortification of all of will.[66]

Will is not strengthened through abstinence and mortification, whose true aim is to crush it, but rather through full involvement in natural life.[67] Man "is not made holy, differentiated, set apart"— instead "he lives." Moreover, "all his life is holy of holies."[68] For "the holy man of silence" as well,

> normal life is not emptied of its quality, its usual human concerns, individual physical life, social life, manners and honor— these are not blurred but rather idealized. The meaning of life is transfigured, its purpose sanctified. The desire for a superior good, whole and all-encompassing yet private and pervasive as

well, is expressed more and more vitally in practical embodiment.[69]

In light of his view of will as an element of life, Rav Kook spoke
of a conscious effort to develop and fortify human will and self-
awareness and rejected every approach potentially weakening to it.[70]
A series of remarks reveals that Rav Kook saw religion itself as a
palpable threat to human freedom, and he did not hesitate to warn of
this danger:

> Will is a basic element of life, and it must pulse through
> life. Ethics, Torah, all holy and sublime light must act upon it
> and straighten it, but must not obscure its power. The enfeeble-
> ment of will by worrisome burdens, *even though, according to
> man's knowledge, they may originate in a supreme and holy place,*
> impoverishes the highest form of human splendor. The light of
> the holy is revealed in the might and freedom of will, in its
> flourishing splendor. "For thou has not called upon me, O Jacob;
> but thou has been weary of me, O Israel" (Isaiah 43:21). *And the
> easing of hindrances is one of the purposes of the divine Torah;* it sets
> out a path of life, a straight way for all the force of will to flow
> from the fountainhead, from the source of life.[71]

The Torah, in Rav Kook's eyes, aims to perpetuate human freedom, to "ease the burden,"[72] but religion, as people perceive it, "im-
poverishes the highest form of human splendor." What is more,
"Even the acceptance of the yoke of the Kingdom of heaven familiar
to human beings is an enslavement of flesh and blood, because the
kingdom of heaven itself has been dishonored and diminished by the
darkness imposed by human beings to obscure its light."[73] Thus
"those possessed of highest vision" can be bound by no servitude,
not even the acceptance of the yoke of the kingdom of heaven in the
usual sense, for "all servitude is the invention of flesh and blood."[74]

He enumerated the deficiencies of fear of heaven inconsistent
with the true aim of the Torah and says that "fear of heaven is replaced with fear of thought," and man is thus deprived of "the light of
his soul; his strength wavers, his spirit is beclouded."[75] Such fear of
heaven brings man to "boredom and idleness, he loses his will and
his own essential self, . . . until he is drained of vitality, and society is
stricken as well, neither force nor desire strives toward perfection,
toward the improvement of social life."[76] "Man is reduced to a creep-
ing, idle thing by fear of heaven bereft of understanding."[77]

Nevertheless, courageously facing the truth and admitting the deficiencies of fear of heaven does not imply its negation or unimportance. For after all, "this feeling of fear of God is everything, all of life and all good."[78] When one recognizes this,

> He will not forsake his treasure, and no matter how much he suffers, whether physical or spiritual afflictions, no matter how much it seems he will not be able to resist modern freedom, the mighty cultural striving of temporal existence, the bewitching beauty, the noisy ferment of life, or even natural morality and honesty, to overcome them time and again and beat them into the form of God-fearingness in life, as he understands it— all these will never summon enough force to cut the thread of life and the strength of approval, for only in fear of God does man have safe refuge.[79]

The way fear of God is expressed in life seems opposed to the modern concept of freedom, unsuited to the grand cultural aspiration of temporal life, and may even contradict moral values and conscience, but none of this warrants its rejection, for these deficiencies are merely the products of the "external aspects" of fear of God; in its essence, it is the motive power of life, "it is everything, all of life and all of good."

What is more, the element of servitude bound up with fear of heaven, with the acceptance of the yoke of the kingdom of heaven, in its pure form, adds a deeper dimension to freedom itself. The freely made decision implicit in the acceptance of the yoke of the kingdom of heaven is a more complete freedom, for here one's freedom grants one reign over freedom itself. This is the true significance of the responsibility that emerges from freedom: the ability to draw the bounds even of freedom itself. "Total freedom—when man is so free that in his absolute freedom he can subjugate himself in a proper manner, can be a slave in such a way that his slavery is true freedom."[80] "A truly free man is one who rules over the greatest of forces, which is freedom itself."[81]

Yet the acceptance of the yoke of the kingdom of heaven is perceived not only as an expression of freedom's ability to contain itself; religious aspiration or, as Rav Kook put it, "the striving toward closeness to God" is described as the

> culmination of the great ideal of freedom, the object of yearning held dear by the best of men, for which the human soul and

social life in its every shade so earnestly long. 'Unto the utmost bounds of the everlasting hills, the world of the Jubilee, the world of freedom.'[82] Thus, the ultimate goal and direction of all the man's spiritual labors—is it not to complete that same inclination, all-encompassing and pulsating ceaselessly within him, concentrating his whole being?[83]

This led Rav Kook to consider the nature and task of education:

> We are brought to recognition of the naturalness of education on the basis of the aspiration toward divine intimacy, since education is the sole legacy promised to humanity . . . for we do not hold education as the creator of new things in the soul of the pupil, but rather as a supervisor, drawing from obscurity to openness, from potentiality to actuality, what is hidden within the student, revealed as the universal and central character of humanity and its groups, both historical and national. *And the correspondence between the individual and general culture* at its most profound—this is the natural progression and the success of education.[84]

Rav Kook believed the task of education is not to teach and sculpt the personality of the pupil, but rather to help one uncover and discover one's own "I," hidden in one's soul[85] and to lay bare the correspondence between the pupil's inwardness and the profoundest nature of general culture. In this sense, education plays a central role in the manifestation of freedom and the strengthening of self-awareness. Because freedom is perceived as "self-affirmation," even as the definition of human life itself, lack of self-awareness or, in Rav Kook's words "he knows not his name,"[86] is compared to the death of personality: "And we are 'as the slain lying in graves' (Psalms 88:6).[87] One's aspiration to freedom actually reflects one's dread in the face of death: "Individual selfhood is terrified of being robbed of its essence."[88]

Before us is a very interesting view of the concept of "death," which aids in dealing with the human horror of death. Death is already present in human life in the form of negation of freedom, denial of selfhood. Yet Rav Kook suggests a way in which "we can reach that freedom for which we live."[89] The path is by "elevating the will"[90] and self-awareness: "the soul's making itself known to man in any and every way is itself a small corner of redemption."[91] Rav Kook demanded a deeper contemplation of being and a greater sense of self-awareness, enabling one to achieve freedom and control over one's destiny and condition; his demand is phrased as a dramatic challenge:

> If you wish, O Man, regard the light of the *Shekhinah* in all of existence, see the Eden of heavenly life, how it penetrates to every corner of life, both spiritual and material, before your very eyes and the eyes of your spirit.
> Contemplate in amazement Creation in its divine anima-tion, not as some dark form, brought to you from afar, but rather know the reality in which you live. Know yourself, your world, know the meditations of your heart, and of every thinker. Find the source of life within you, beyond you, around you, find the glory and splendor of the life in which you live.[92]

Individualism and Moral Relation to Society

The unique importance Rav Kook ascribed to individual inde-pendence and the nurturing of self-awareness, on the one hand, and his metaphysical-monistic approach, on the other, give birth to an original and individualistic outlook. In a letter written in 5668 (1908) to Rav Shmuel Alexandrov, Rav Kook reacted to the question concern-ing the element of liberal anarchism in Judaism, writing:

> His honor finds indications of liberal moral anarchism in Judaism. Indeed, all ideas can be found in a source of truth. Truth cannot be partial, it must encompass all, but its virtue is in transforming everything to its own true shining light. Not only the anarchy contained in liberalism will find its source in Juda-ism, in the light of Israel, but material, individual anarchism as well, but it too will be purified in reaching the pure border. The highest awareness of unity, when it isolates itself in its superi-ority, must come to the conclusion that the entire process of details is a delusion, a too-narrow field of vision. Our limbs are joined together organically in such a way that when one is in-jured all feel it, and thus *we have an anarchic self-love*, abstract as well, "Skin covers skin" (Job 2:4)[93] by means of the same chan-nels that convey feeling from one to another. Such relationships exist in a spiritual, experimental sense between souls joined in love, out of which the family is founded, until—if only we can struggle free of habit—we will set no great importance on the difference between that spreading feeling and pleasure or pain,

whether between one limb and another or between son and father or lover and beloved. When the channels grow very wide, the feelings become more flowing, more tangible and evident. And when the organism of the nation is at its fullest and most complete, it too weaves itself in the form of family. Development must only widen the channels, and *individual unity extends to the borders of the nation.* It is but a stride from the nation to humanity; from humanity to all of life yet one more step. Between interest in filling a single globe and the inward and momentous interest in filling reality in all its breadth there is a certain distance, indeed a great distance, but eternity is in no hurry. And the matter comes ever closer to the *individual elevation of all of existence.* Thus, we have need only of anarchy, great and large self-love, mighty and developed. The paths on which this love will come are ways of life originating in the source of unity, the One, life of the universe, that is Judaism.[94]

Rav Kook's words contain a positive tension between a metaphysical, monistic view and a strong existential tendency. We might expect any monistic outlook to produce a quietistic moral doctrine dedicated to self-annullment. If this is what Rav Kook had wanted, he would have found himself a rabbinic authority to support him,[95] yet he chose instead the path of self-affirmation. Indeed, the early kabbalists already triumphed the idea of individual-mystical redemption,[96] and Hassidism spoke of ending the exile of the spirit by expansion of the "self."[97] Rav Kook also attested here that "individual unity is expanding," yet the emphasis of the individual had no implications in the direction of ending the actual, national exile but rather in the sense of religious individualism that becomes possible solely within the framework of a community of "keepers of the faith."[98]

When Rav Kook spoke of "the individual elevation of all of existence" he removed the meaning of individualism from its common connotation. His teaching is individualistic by grace of its monism, for the true individuum is exclusively "the One, life of the universe." Such an interpretation of the concept of the "individuum" could preclude the anarchistic connotations concealed in an individualistic outlook as well as the existential prominence of self-consciousness. But that was not Rav Kook's way. He did indeed claim that "the paths leading to anarchy are ways of life stemming from the source of unity of the One, life of the universe, that is Judaism." Yet we must not forget that anarchy was not rejected out of hand; as we shall see,[99] it is permitted, with limitations, to individuals within the framework of a religious community. Rav Kook's approach on this question is existential; it relates the individual personality's demand for freedom, yet recognizes the dangers lurking at the doorway of freedom unbounded by consideration of the particular, spiritual-cultural existential demand of the community, of which the individual person is but a component. His position is a sort of "golden mean" between an extreme individualistic attitude and its polar negation. The following words elucidate his view:

> Science is now rebelling against morality as well, its childhood friend, but it will not gain glory in that way; though the coin be turned over and over, it will always retain its own character; science rebels against societal morality, in the name of the *private demand*, which is a *moral demand* as well—here, at last, we must reach the heart of the psychic vision.
>
> *The private demand that knows enslavement to no principle,* which establishes anarchy in its most terrible form, flows, as well, from the highest inner, moral, and scientific drive, which does not acknowledge the principle of distinction between workers and slaves, between agents and subjects. Ideal morality in its greatest purity has no wish to recognize a particular personality; pleasure and pain is equally felt wherever it may be in all the endlessly wide space of reality, and thus *absolute individuality alone remains.* When this feeling itself is humbled, it must destroy all normative morality that comes from the refining of outer elements. Truly, the two extremes are only the boundaries of the "orchard" where the spirit of life and knowledge wanders, and they will never be reached, neither at the acme of negation of details before the universal stream, nor at the low point of universal obscurity in the face of the reality of immediate and tangible details.[100]

In this matter as well, the question of fostering the individual, Rav Kook saw religion and morality as erecting obstacles in the positive path of general culture. Culture, "when it finds all that religion and morality has suppressed, sets forth to combat and eventually defeats them. After the war, religion and morality make their own discovery, finding their light themselves, until this personal freedom, along with its natural, positive demands, is recognized as a part of religion and morality themselves."[101]

Thus, when it becomes clear that personal freedom is one of the foundations of religion and morality themselves, Jewish ethics can be defined as "individual morality": "Jewish ethics are none other than individual morality, as well as familial and national, and also universally human, even though everything is contained in it, it is essentially divine, the Torah of God, creator of the world, a teaching that perpetuates the process of creation, no less."[102]

Jewish ethics can be individual morality because in actuality it is not morality at all or, in any case, not human morality. Human morality sees the individualistic approach as an undermining of its foundations, for morality provides guidelines, founded on concession, of suitable behavior and of forming interpersonal relationships. Divine morality, in contrast, is founded on the ideal of holiness; that is, an unbounded drive toward perfection. Holiness is completeness, or all-encompassing unity,[103] and divine morality, as a process of perfection or elevation to holiness, has an intensified inclination toward self-affirmation. The emphasis on self-awareness in accordance with divine morality does not harm the demands of human morality, for it is accompanied by a ceaseless drive toward expanding the individuum; this drive eliminates the sense of compromise characteristic of human morality.

It was Friedrich Nietzsche who laid bare the contradiction secreted in human morality and averred that "morality is a way of turning one's back on the will to existence" and that "as long as we continue to believe in morality, we continue to pass judgement on existence." For this reason, in his opinion, morality is completely impossible: "Everything egoistic has come to disgust us, even though we realize the impossibility of the unegoistic."[104] As we will see, Rav Kook adopted Nietzsche's basic position on this issue, and his following words suggest an alternative to Nietzsche's rejection of morality:

> The ultimate goal of life is holiness. Holiness is supreme unity, which contains nothing of the *weakness of morality*. Holiness does not fight against the self-love embedded deep within the soul of every living being, but rather it sets man in such a superior state that the more he *loves himself*, the more the good within him will spread over all, all around him, over the whole world, all of being.
>
> The nature of a social group by no means contains the *possibility* of the inclination of *weakening self-love*; it holds only moral destruction, if the chance comes, and internal decay, all-consuming.
>
> Thus it is *completely impossible to demand there be a moral nation in the world*, but only a holy nation: as it *strengthens itself*, as it rises in internal and external value, so will the light and

good in the world rise and strengthen. And we find that the best essence of morality is already there in holiness, in most splendid form, full of beauty and delight.[105]

This "self-love" triumphed by Rav Kook is not egoism in the narrow sense. The aspiration to expand the "I" implicit in "self-love" is at the same time the broadening of love itself:

> The great thought of the oneness of being *eliminates the question of love itself,* a question considered by some as the root of sin and by others as the basis of morality. There is only love of all, which is truly self-love, enlightened and sublime. False self love, which loves the small spark, visible to bleary eyes, and hates the clarifying selfhood—this is blindness, as foolish as it is wicked.[106]

The affirmation of self, consciousness of the "I," is a condition for affirming the selfhood of the other, and when there is no *I,* there is no *he,* and there certainly is no *thou.*[107]

The meaning of this individualistic outlook is evident in the emphasis on the uniqueness of each individual and legitimization of personal and original ways:

> Every man must know he is summoned to serve according to his own understanding and feeling, according to the root of his soul.[108]

> The spiritual world builds *each and every person* within himself. The quality of attentiveness itself serves only to make ready the eternal and essential *structure of the individual;* the Torah is centered about the verse containing His own Name. This is all the weight of judgment, all the depth of the question, all threat of responsibility, all punishment after death.[109]

Such a view imposes all "threat of responsibility," which is the aspiration to fuse with "spiritual and practical form of the whole,"[110] despite the autonomous position one must develop. This is especially true in light of the tremendous space before the free individual as someone who determines his or her own values:

> Happiness is founded on intellectual love of truth, love of integrity in life, love of the beauty of emotion, love of the good in action. *In all values, every man builds himself truth, integrity,*

beauty and good in and of itself according to his ability. And all these
attributes of each and every human being gathered in one united
whole; all of truth, integrity, beauty and goodness are drawn
together in harmony. The path of knowing God is thus reached,
an enlightened path, full of holiness, limpid fear of God.[111]

We have already remarked that, for Rav Kook, freedom is no
mere philosophical-theological question, but rather an existential trial. Without awareness of this fact, one cannot hope to appreciate the
incredible daring of many of his formulations. In this context, let us
consider a characteristic passage, written in a very personal tone, that
describes the experience of freedom in no uncertain terms:

I must find my happiness deep within myself, not in *the
consensus of society*, nor in any career whatsoever. The better I
come to know myself and the more I allow myself to be original
and to stand on my own feet in inner awareness combining
knowledge, awareness, emotion, and song [poetry], the more
God's light will illumine my way, and the greater my forces will
grow to be a blessing to myself and the world.[112]

Unconcern with the opinion of society and the drive toward independence, and originality is guided by the faith that
originality is a guarantee of truth, as it is an aspect of revelation.
"With all the peace and honor the righteous summon to guide
the masses, they will return to the Lord who continually *appears*
to them from their own *personal* windows, through their lat-
tices."[113] The individual is vouchsafed revelation through deal-
ings with himself; not only is this revelation divine truth, but it is
also identical with "the source of Torah," and the meditations of
the individual are thus tantamount to words of Torah themselves: "If you strive to the source of Torah, rise and take heart
as you approach that supremacy which pulses within your spirit, with all your thoughts, with all the spiritual and physical load
you bear, take courage, and gaze toward the light shining to you
through the lattice."[115]

Yet all this is only one aspect of the dialectical relationship between the individual and the collective in Rav Kook's system. The
emphasis on the qualitative advantage of the individual personality[116]
and its priority due to the objects of awareness challenging both spiritual and intellectual effort,[117] as well as the dependence of the whole
on its members,[118] is reflected in the case of the priority of the whole
in those very same aspects.[119] The contradiction seems severe, yet in

fact this paradox bears much fruit; the measure of freedom, in spirit
and in thought, each individual takes for himself is commensurate
with his spiritual connection and active loyalty to society:

> We will be safe from all delusion, all wickedness and false-
> hood our imagination could invent to affront us, if we hold fast
> to the tree of life of the Torah of our fathers, to its pleasant ethic,
> to its commandments and precepts in all ways of life, to *our loyal
> bond with every man*, to *family and nation*, to life and all its wishes.
> *We must in no way be bound* in societal chains, which strangle the
> sublimely free spirit, profane the holy that descends from the
> upper worlds, the world of freedom, where liberty was granted
> the seraphim, utter freedom to all striving, complete freedom to
> the inclinations of will, and to creativity. *And holiness will grow
> along with freedom*, and life will be exalted.
>   . . . Each person shall imagine, in truth and honesty, what
> his soul shows him, and will draw forth his spiritual harvest
> without deceit, and these sparks of light will gather in torches,
> illuminating all the world in their glory; from these inward
> splinters of truth, the great truth will appear.[120]

The Concept of "Sin" and Idea of Repentance

The conviction Rav Kook held about the affirmation of selfhood
was voiced as well in his perception of the concept of "sin" and the
idea of *teshuvah* (repentance). This pair of concepts are the theological
expression of the idea of freedom. *Sin* usually signifies nonfulfillment
of an obligation, disobedience to a norm, and an implicit offence
against the body that imposed the obligation or created the norm.
Teshuvah means turning back from the "sin" to the straight path, to
fulfillment of the obligation, hence return to faith in He who imposed
the obligation—"Turn to me and I shall return to you" (Zecharaiah
1:3). In any case, the concepts of "sin" and "*teshuvah*" (literally, "return") hold freedom as a given fact. Philosophically, it is freedom that
makes sin possible; although in itself a neutral entity, it gives meaning
either to "sin" or to "repentance."

In Rav Kook's teaching, the concepts of "sin" and "repentence"
receive a fundamentally different meaning from the usual framework, limited to the realm of relations between God and human. In
his system, the concepts are related to the category of the self—sin is
first and foremost against the "self," and repentance is a return to
self, to the "I." Moreover, in his method, the concepts of sin and

repentance represent cosmic processes in which the individual plays a central role. Thus human actions themselves receive importance beyond the well-known complex of obedience or disobedience—human action becomes creative in the sense that not only does it discover the meaning of human deeds and all of existence, but also contributes significantly to the determination and creation of this meaning.

Let us begin, then, with the concept of "repentance." Rav Kook devoted a separate book to this idea, *Orot ha-Teshuvah,* although he broached the subject in other contexts as well. In *Orot ha-Teshuvah* we find a general yet clear definition of the concept of repentance: "*Teshuvah* is fundamentally a movement of return to originality, to the source of life and highest being in their wholeness."[121] This general definition applies on various levels, cited in detail:

> When we forget the essence of our soul itself, when we are distracted from introspection, from the content of inner life, everything becomes confused and doubtful. The beginning of repentance which immediately illumines the darkness is *that man return to himself, to the root of his soul, and he will at once return to God,* to the soul of all souls, and will stride ever higher in holiness and purity. This is true for the individual and for the entire nation, for all of humanity, for the perfection of existence as a whole; its ruin always comes when *it forgets itself.* And if you claim it [existence] desires to return to God, but does not summon itself to gather its exiles—this *repentance is a lie,* invoking God's name in vain. Only in the great truth of *return to himself* will man and the nation repent, the world and all the worlds, all of being to their Maker, to the indwelling light of life. This is the secret of the Messiah's light, the appearance of the soul of the world, in whose brightness the world will return to the root of being, and the light of the Lord will shine upon him. And man will draw life of holiness of true *teshuvah* from this great source of repentance.[122]

One's return to oneself, one's faith in oneself and one's abilities,[123] are simultaneously a return to God. Our discussion in previous pages dealt with the identification between the human "I" and the divine. The act of *teshuvah* engenders this identification, whereas sin, on the other hand, is seen as a force engendering disunion between human and God.[124] Repentance is parallel to freedom in its role of increasing self-awareness, whereas sin, as an act of division, of constricting the self by obscuring its dimension of divine infiniteness is perceived as slavery.[125] The statement can also be formulated in the opposite direction; that is, all slavery, in a certain sense, is sin. Becoming fixed in a rigid framework in practical life and in an inflexible position on the speculative and spiritual plane can be thought of a sin in its negation of human freedom:

> This obstinancy in insisting on a single view and concentrating upon it, bound by the ropes of sins that have become habit, whether in the form of deeds or views, is a sickness caused by sinking into slavery so cruel that the light of freedom offered by repentance cannot shine forth in its strength; for repentence aspires to true and original freedom, divine freedom that knows no slavery.[126]

We spoke earlier of the identification of freedom with existence; let us now add that Rav Kook perceived repentence as "renewal of life,"[127] and the freedom of choice implicit in it is possible as long as "the spark of life burns."[128] The victory over death harbored in freedom exists in repentance as well: "as repentance becomes more profound, fear of death diminishes until it is extinguished completely."[129] Repentance is the "absolute essence of the soul,"[130] and "the greater is repentance, the greater its measure of freedom."[131]

Nonetheless, just as the concepts of "freedom" and "necessity" are different aspects of a single reality, so repentance and sin are interwoven. Repentance is part of reality itself, and sin is likewise an expression of that essence:

> Repentance preceded the world and is thus a fundament of the world. Life becomes complete as its essential nature is revealed. And because nature, in and of itself, does not have the property of seeing and distinguishing [that is, has no freedom of choice], *sin dominates*, "for there is not a just man upon the earth who does good and sins not" (Ecclesiastes 7:20). *Vitiating the naturalness of life to keep man free of sin, that in itself is the gravest sin,* "And make atonement for him, that he sinned by the dead" (Numbers 6:11; see TB: Nedarim 10a). Thus repentance *repairs* the damage and returns the world and life to its source, precisely by revealing the *highest fundament of their essence,* the *world of freedom,* and hence we call the name of the Lord 'the living God [or the God of Life]'."[132]

We realize once again that, in Rav Kook's eyes, the diversity and infinity of reality cannot be exhausted in a simple definition, and this multidimensionality must appear to the human mind as a paradox. That paradox enables us to understand his claim regarding the ability of the human will to form not only the future but the past as well. The idea of "evil deeds turned to virtue" is explained by the fact that evil does not need a "new creation" to change its essence but rather "the revelation of its originality."[133] That is, the element of virtue hidden within evil deeds is brought to light. Because disconnectedness is not a part of reality and life rather, has a certain continuity which determines the relation of all acts to the essence of life, to their source, for that reason "desire can cast a unique impression on all past actions."[134] The ability, revealed in freedom, to change the past implies insistence on the fundamental unity of various aspects of reality, making evident the positive merit even of evil deeds.

5

Man and the Origin of the Religious Phenomenon

"Human culture as a whole can be described as a process of man's gradual liberation."[1] With these words Ernst Cassirer concludes his book *Essay on Man*. Language, art, religion, and science are, in his view, stages in this process. Rav Kook would probably have agreed with the basis of such a statement, with one significant modification: for him, religion is not a component of culture and thus is not a stage in that process of development. In fact, the relationship is inverted: culture is one stage in a process whose most internal workings can be understood solely in terms belonging to the realm of religion. This fundamental inversion is a clear expression of the message audible throughout Rav Kook's work, which seeks to confront the vital philosophical challenges of his generation by a phenomenological evaluation of human nature and which offers a religious interpretation of myriad processes—psychological, historical, and cultural.

Rav Kook believed dealing with metaphysical questions served more than critical or even moral aims.[2] In his eyes, metaphysical study itself is nothing more than an expression of one of the basic human spiritual needs.[3] Metaphysical contemplation, perhaps the highest form of cultural creativity, as well as all cultural manifestations at their various levels, reflect, in his eyes, a fundamental psychological quality in man: the sense of uneasiness or even fear in the face of impermanence, of the incomprehensibility of life and reality, and of incompleteness. Rav Kook recognized the aspiration to immortality as the base on which all of human cultural creativity is built, or as he said: "Infinity is the mighty foundation of all cultural life in

127

every aspect. The striving to glorify infinity conquers death and wipes tears from all faces."[4]

In Rav Kook's view, this aspiration to immortality is fundamentally religious. He perceived it as inherent to human nature, discernible from birth, "as long as his soul has not yet been sullied by the evil inclination [literally, "leaven in the dough")[5] in the turmoil of life." Religious striving is, in his opinion, the central and dominant impetus in human life, as he wrote: "We must decide the most ardent striving to be close to God is the sole and central element of all drives, all desires and aspirations of the human soul; all of them flow from it and return to it. This is so in general, in the universal, collective human soul and individually as well—in the soul of each and every human being."[6]

Rav Kook proceeded to describe processes of development and rationalization undergone by culture, and the demand for "ordered life" as motivated by the striving toward closeness to God.[7] He saw religious aspiration as emerging from "natural, internal, essential necessity" and as the primal element of all spiritual striving. In this perception, the "ethic of self-actualization," developed similarly by Rav Kook's contemporary Aaron David Gordon, finds clear expression.[8] We must point out that this psychological phenomenon is, for Rav Kook, merely the tip of the iceberg; the same quality characterizes all of being, and he described it as a natural law, "unchanging for the many or the few, for great or small."[9]

We must remember Rav Kook was not so naive as to think all people, in all their deeds, are motivated by the force of religious and spiritual striving, at least on a conscious level. Rather, he believed other aspirations—social justice and equality, for meaning and significance, for knowledge and wisdom, and above all for freedom—all these objectives can be explained in anthropological, psychological, sociological terms, but their essence can be understood only in terms of religious perception. All aspirations are united by totality, the striving toward completeness and the absolute, which can be nothing other than a religious hope. The concern with social improvement, political and economic accomplishments in and of themselves cannot fulfill the needs of the human soul. "That is not her rest and disposition."[10] In his opinion, "it is impossible to live without the sacred influence of faith," because *human thought is too narrow to clarify the depths of being.*"[11]

In other words, Rav Kook claimed that the human search for the meaning of existence will inevitably lead to what is beyond concrete existence:

When we are asked what the goal of social life is, that life itself gives us no answer; our only recourse is to aspire toward a world grander and more sublime than it . . . and this helps us realize that no human aspiration can be completely immersed only in social life; it is necessarily so, for if social life were to cease nursing from the breast of that life superior to itself, which makes its very being meaningful and purposeful, its own vitality would be greatly diminished, and grave faults would appear within it, until its own worth would diminish. The *perfection of the world thus demands anticipation of redemption* from deep within the supreme wells of redemption. The eternal hope of Israel for *the light of the Messiah,* divine light in His world, that is the world's very fundament, the foundation of all its conditions, and of the social world as well in its every part.[12]

The messianic idea and hope are thus vital to the world's existence and are the very essence of the religious phenomenon, for the meaning and purpose of any enterprise must necessarily exceed the realization of the undertaking itself.[13] If they do not, its fulfilment is doomed to be immediately succeeded by deterioration and decline. The existence and indispensibility of the enterprise itself require its meaning to be understood in terms borrowed from the realm of eternity or the absolute; that is, in religious terms. We must know

an exclusively practical view is impossible. [And likewise for] the pragmatic world in and of itself, even when it will be arranged and ordered to the utmost perfection, to be a source of life for man, whose soul rises high above all those boundaries confining the contents of deeds. Man must be joined by a constant link with the upper planes of existence, with the highest of spirituality.[14]

Rav Kook then clarified his own use of psychological and other secular terms in explaining these phenomena: his sole purpose was "to make his words as comprehensible as possible," for didactic reasons. In his eyes, the striving to draw close to God is not just one of many aspirations, nor even a central and essential striving. This aspiration is in truth "the essence, being and fundament of the soul's existence, . . . its most inherent vitality."[15] We can now understand this statement in light of our discussion of Rav Kook's entire metaphysical conception, and particularly in the concept of "will" in his method. In his view, humankind's uniqueness is not in being an

Animal rationale or *Homo sapiens*, nor even in his being a creator of symbols (*Animal symbolicum*), in Cassirer's definition. Humankind's humanness for Rav Kook is in our *religiosity*, engendering a new technical term: *Homo religiosus*.

The preceding statements could leave the impression that applying religious categories to the description and analysis of human nature and the motivations of culture blurs distinctions between domains and obscures the theoretical discussion of the religious phenomenon itself. Yet even if Rav Kook rejected such a distinction between religion and culture in their essence, he did not ignore the fact of their appearance as specific and separate manifestations in the history of humankind. What is more, he even related to the distinction commonly made in comparative religious studies between natural religions, or "religious sentiment," and institutional-traditional religion and spoke of the connection between the two:

> faith becomes complete when *its body and soul* are linked closely together . . . these signs may sometimes grow so faint that *tradition* and *natural faith* grow apart, and an illness of faith then appears. Its danger is very great. . . . And sometimes, in its vast flood of light of internal faith, it rises above traditional belief. This too, though it comes about through spiritual elevation, is a defect and enfeeblement; a healthy state requires coordination, so that as spiritual faith ascends, traditional faith rises with it, . . . and in the Jewish people, this connection and union is the internal request of the practical content of each mitzvah.[16]

It is not surprising that Rav Kook demanded an accord between natural faith and the religious-traditional framework and saw any disharmony as illness, as an unhealthy state. Interestingly, when he criticized Christianity on this point, he portrayed natural faith as inferior in worth, though in the preceding quotation it is perceived as the "soul" of tradition. He wrote:

> Apostasy grasped the content of natural faith, but its evil was in separating itself from all above it, thus "cutting all the shoots" [in the garden of faith]; natural belief is most basically a worthy vessel to contain and hold the sublime lights shining higher than all law and nature, and thus natural faith rises and refines, and human nature, along with the entire world, ascends and becomes pure, soon joining with the completeness of its ideal form.[17]

In any case, the very distinction Rav Kook made and the attention he devoted both to natural faith and traditional religion demonstrates his awareness, to which his own words attest, of the real tension between the two. Rav Kook leaves no room for doubt that perhaps the *mitzvot* need not be fulfilled, and in response to the view claiming that the *mitzvot* will be annulled in the days to come, he declared that "before the new world will arrive . . . when it will be relevant to speak of annullment of the *mitzvot*," there will be "a renaissance of Torah and *mitzvot*, perfect in all its splendid majesty, complete in loving repentance that encompasses the whole nation, affecting all the world as well."[18]

How is this "renaissance of Torah and *mitzvot*" to come about? Rav Kook's answer—in the same way all of human culture acts and marks its impression on human nature:

> The *mitzvot* will develop human nature, until they themselves become man's permanent nature, and just as the culture of humanity endeavors to have what it learns become part of its nature, so *divine culture* rises far beyond in striving to renew human nature and elevate it to God's supreme state, which makes an internal demand on the entire Torah, and virtue is its own reward.[19]

Rav Kook's position on the status of the practical commandments will be discussed more extensively in Chapter 9. Here, in any case, we must stress one point: the natural character of religion. Rav Kook fundamentally believed in the essential identity between natural religion and the content and norms of traditional religion. In an ideal state, humankind would have no need for commandments and statutes, for these exist as natural acts or actions demanded by common sense:

> When all shines with its full light, there is no need of any special guidance by laws and ordinances. The absolute good of action is drawn after the light of the intellect and all of life's obstacles resolve themselves. Statutes and ordinances no longer exist as commandments, but rather as natural movements, as subjects overcome by the mind's brightness.
> Good and evil and all their values . . . came into being after the intellect diminished its light; that light was replaced by emotion, excitement, and depression of the senses following the Primal Sin—eating the fruit from the Tree of knowledge of good and evil.[20]

The idea that the intellect mandates the religious command-ments necessarily implies that religion is rational, at least in the sense that its details accord with an inclusive principle on which it is based. Indeed, Rav Kook held one of the causes of atheism in the modern era is the fact that no such logical connection between the elements of religion and any general principle seems evident, whereas "the world is already able enough to demand *understanding* of how all the parts are connected to the whole."[21]

Yet, despite the world's insistence on rational understanding of religion, Rav Kook contended such understanding cannot be gained intellectually, "for the intellect must work to find a relation between the *essence* acceptable to the heart, according to its understanding, and the distant branches of *individual processes*, and it always fails, exhausted, on the paths of life. And the limited intellect and all its considerations will be unable to light its way."[22] In other words, an-other, superrational strength is needed to understand the rationality of religion, and "if the world were concerned with the light of Torah to such an extent that the *spiritual soul* grew to realize the appropriate connection between the details and the spiritual principles, *teshuvah* [repentance] and the world's *tikkun* [restoration, perfection] would become an actuality."[23]

Rav Kook himself did not think this analysis exhausted the causes of religious crisis nor the elements leading to reparation. When we speak of the crisis of religion or its decline, we must distinguish between the universal crisis and that which gripped Judaism, for in Rav Kook's mind, the crisis in Israel has its roots in completely differ-ent soil than that of the nations. "The mistaken assumption must be uprooted that the collapse of religion in the world as a whole, and the downfall that has harmed Israel as well, are equivalent; and that just as this downfall in the general world is engendered by cultural devel-opment, the same is true for Judaism. According to this erroneous view, the wound seems unhealable. . ."[24]

Rav Kook disputed the theory, commonly accepted in his time by historians of religion, that religion is no more than an anachro-nism, a "remnant" of the past, a way of thinking that enlightened humanity has managed to overcome.[25] Regarding the peoples of the world, however, he did accept this theory, for in his view, the pagan elements of Western religions were in fact splintering in the face of "the fortification of the intellect and human development in general," and the idolatrous element itself, so inherent to these religions, was bringing them to a state of collapse.[26] But, in the case of Israel, the basis of Judaism is not interwoven with pagan elements, and nothing thus impedes its acceptance even on the advanced level of intellectual development of the modern era.

The roots of the religious crisis in Judaism, then, are isolated in a single cause: the limiting and depressing image acquired by religiosity through the years. In Rav Kook's words:

> God-fearingness is deficient in its external aspect, in that it *softens* the heart too much, subduing man's innate strength so that he falls powerless at its side. In the way, God-fearingness, even if it is divine, issuing from a tradition pure at its very essence, *prevents the improvement of the world and perfection of the human image.* And when this state is reached, when the quality of God-fearingness grows filled with great bitterness, when its influence increases and threatens to *depress* the heart too much, when the spirit surrenders to it too much, then humanity begins to call it by a different name, *a spirit of nihilism,* which comes to counteract the venom of external God-fearingness. When these two *external* dispositions begin to struggle against each other, the world is as if drunken, dust rises to the Heavenly Seat, *feebleness, extremism, hypocrisy,* on the one hand, and *great evils, insolence, competitiveness, lawlessness, empty spirituality* on the other[27] fell many a mighty warrior. And the people continue to dissolve, until that time when the light of justice will shine, and supreme divine knowledge will appear in all its glory, bearing on its wings a healing remedy.[28]

Secularization and nihilism are thus seen as a reaction to a long period of repression of the human spirit and natural aspirations by religion. "The need for this revolt comes from a tendency to materialism that must violently emerge in the nation after so many years in which it was neither necessary nor possible to occupy oneself with material concerns."[29] And when "the profane is cruelly treated by the holy, until matter becomes impoverished," then, Rav Kook claimed, a period is reached "when matter demands justice in its own cause, and the creditor is urgent, and the profane takes its debt from the holy with interest, and insolence increases."[30]

The outcome of the struggle between these two distorted spiritual movements is thus that the element of truth and authenticity in both is lost. Weakness, fanaticism, hypocrisy, and cruelty rule the religious camp; disrespect, lawlessness, and emptiness characterize the nonreligious camp. Rav Kook's neutral approach in describing and examining the process of secularization within the Jewish people is founded on the metaphysical principles just discussed.[31] The fact that not only faith but even heresy is seen as a revelation of life force, in which "the living light of divine luminousness is clothed"[32]—this fact allows us to perceive its positive aspects as well and to discern the positive role it plays:

> The entire negative element was created in order to cleanse the soul of man and of the world from that terrible and morbid deterrent, the fear of punishment. And the poison of crude atheism destroying the world is founded on the same base *as a counterpoison* against the restrictive force of fear of punishment; as it spreads, it cuts itself off from the light of the Torah, from higher awe, from the true love that comes from fear.[33]

This tolerant attitude not only characterized Rav Kook's approach to the phenomenon of secularization, it was in fact his profoundly religious world-view that enabled Rav Kook to see what was useful and even true in other religions and beliefs. Thus he wrote: "And because the connection between human thought and feelings and the divine, unlimited and highest light *must be of many and varied shades*, for this reason each and every people has its own distinctive spiritual life."[34] That is, the particular form taken by every nation, culture, and religion is no more than one revelation of divine light; and this is its truth.

The question of tolerance is above all an ethical question.[35] Rav Kook was indeed well aware of the problematic nature of tolerance from the religious point of view.[36] He was convinced tolerance was fundamentally opposed to natural faith, and the more daring faith becomes, the more fanatical it becomes as well. "Normal theology holds," he claimed, "that religions must unavoidably be opposed to each other."[37] The religious position, however, is motivated by more than the natural feeling of religiosity. Rationality is an intrinsic element of faith,[38] and from the point of view of religious *awareness*, tolerance is the clearest expression of understanding of divine revelation in all its variegated forms. In Rav Kook's words:

> Faith is composed of many elements—nature, consciousness, knowledge. The natural component is full of power and glowing fire, tolerating no opposition, and not only would it destroy what opposes its essence but even what is contrary to its private way, its special style; this is why different faiths cannot live together and intermingle without causing each of them natural damage. And the more glorious and sound, the more im-

portant and immense the faith, the more its natural power grows, and the greater its envy and demand for purity. *The component of consciousness* in faith is filled with *broadminded knowledge* and crowned with mercy and *great tolerance*, and the consciousness of faith makes it know that the inner spirit of the divine longing and highest completion it yearns for are also so richly variegated, and that spirit can clothe itself in many different guises, even in contrary descriptions; it transcends all contradiction, it is higher than any opposition.[39]

The idea does not remain on the theoretical level, a phenomenological observation without practical value. On the contrary, Rav Kook, with great daring, drew pragmatic conclusions from that same essential position:

we must study all the wisdom of the world, all the views of life, all the different cultures and ethics *and the religion of every nation*, and with great broadmindedness must understand how to refine them all.[40]

Despite differences of opinion among religions and faiths, among races and climes, we should try to comprehend the world's peoples to the best of our ability, to learn their nature and their attributes, so that we can know how to build human love upon the most real elements possible.

. . . And narrow-mindedness, which causes one to see all that is outside the pale of the unique nation, even outside the bounds of Israel, as no more than ugliness and impurity, that is one of the worst kinds of darkness, which mindlessly destroys the whole structure of spiritual good to whose light every noble soul yearns.[41]

We must emphasize that Rav Kook's pluralistic view does not imply indifference to the variances in level and value of other religions and faiths. Although he believed "all dimensions of the spirit are an organic whole" he did not ignore distinctions "between essential and incidental, high and low, holy in a greater or lesser degree, and between these and the secular."[42] Rav Kook added, moreover:

And so we rise above the decadence in which the nations are sunken, and it is to that vital thought of their more distinguished scientists concerning the difference between the Semitic spirit and the Aryan (sic). We glorify in the Lord of the Universe who created all of man in His image, in the image of God He created him. Each branch grows its own way, this one to the right and that to the left, some higher, some lower, but in their essence all will rise to a single place, all will transcend, to reform the world in the majesty of God, and all flesh will call on You.[43]

This rejection of all distinctions and difference in the domain of the spirit caused by racial or national factors is of great interest. Rav Kook's formulation of his view in this passage is particularly surprising in light of his apprehension of the metaphysical-mystical essence of the Jewish people;[44] the difficulty of striking a harmony between these two ideas is obvious and can be achieved only if both are accepted with reservation, as Rav Kook himself did in regard to differences in the value and uses of the limbs of that organic body.[45]

How, then, are the distinctions between Judaism and other religions expressed? Clearly, they vary in spiritual and ethical *orientation*, rather than in metaphysical *insight:* "The difference is not merely in saying that divine unity contains metaphysical truth, for that can be said of any people or faith, but rather in the internal, divine quality of love of equity and justice and the valiant striving toward these divine ideals in their great strength."[46]

It is impossible to overlook the clear relation between the Jewish metaphysical conception, which Rav Kook understood as monistic, and the spiritual and moral orientation of Judaism, which he understood as a unifying tendency. In various contexts, Rav Kook described the nature of the spiritual-ethical tendencies that characterize other religions. He distinguished four basic aspirations of the human soul: (1) the striving to the reign of absolute evil in all spheres of life, a tendency basic to idolatry; (2) the striving to annihilation, grounded on the acceptance of the total reign of evil in reality, characteristic of Buddhism; (3) the striving attributed to Christianity, described as "half-way to despair," that is, despair of the material world and deliverance of it to the reign of evil, and wish only for the soul's salvation; (4) the striving characteristic to Judaism, to hope "to save all of man . . . body as well as soul . . . evil itself just as good . . . to raise the world and all within it, with all its dimensions and manners."[47]

The most prominent deficiency cited by Rav Kook in idolatry and Christianity is the schism they impose on reality. "The heathen world," he wrote, "strives to be joined to nature as it is," and sees in it "its own final aim."[48] Christianity, on the other hand, distanced itself from nature, denying it completely and, by seeing every aspect of natural life as contrary to religion, "empoisoned the aggadic [theoretical-spiritual] dimension and set it in opposition to the mighty statues of halacha."[49] In other words, Christianity's denial of life induced the Church to reject the commandments.

These varying tendencies indelibly mark the religious consciousness of the faithful of all four religions, naturally influencing their ritual as well.[50] Rav Kook believed the differences originate in the vastly disparate basic religious experience of each. In every other religion, he claimed, the source of religious worship is in the experience of "horror and shock,"[51] a clearly negative sensation. The experience that is the life blood of Judaism, on the other hand, is described as "love" and "the bold aspiration toward divine ideals,"[52] a clearly positive sensation.

Religious consciousness formed by negative experience is by nature dependent and servile, as Rav Kook said, "the service of a slave";[53] in contrast, "enlightened divine service" is founded on positive feeling, creative and constructive awareness.

"And it transforms the divine ideals, cultivating them, perfecting them, striving to exalt them, to glorify them among the people, in man and in the world."[54] He opposed consciousness of servility, the legacy of primitive belief, to the religion of freedom,[55] the aim in the battle against alien worship (*avoda zara*):

> When devotion to God is distorted, misdirected away from the Lord of truth . . . when appeal to the divine is directed toward something other than God, then the evolution of creation is impeded . . . the world's freedom and its flight aloft depend on the radical *extirpation* of all alien worship from thought, language, deed, emotion, attitude, and inclination, from national, religious, and psychic design. This is the aspiration of *Knesset Israel*, "And on that day the Lord alone shall be exalted, and the idols shall be utterly abolished" (Isaiah 2:17–18)[56]

Rav Kook thus perceived Judaism as the realization of freedom—of the individual, of the nation, and of the world.

6

The Purpose of Man and Existence

"To be or not to be, that is the question." This existential quest for meaning is usually seen as a fundamental motivating force in all religious thought. It is often said that, in contrast to philosophy and science, which answer questions of "what" and "how," religion responds to questions of "why"; that is, of purpose. Indeed, Rav Kook himself made a similar characterization of the elements central to religion, on the one hand, and to science, on the other: "Faith offers the ultimate goal of being, and science the ways it is recognized and understood."[1]

The stand taken on this basic question doubtless depends on how earlier questions concerning human essence and being were treated and the possibilities available to each.[2] At this stage in our discussion, after having explained matters of essence and knowledge and before examining the influence of Rav Kook's views regarding praxis in his method, we must devote our attention to his conception on the question of purpose.

Rav Kook's discussion on this subject focuses on three classic motifs: fear of God, love, and *devekut* (devotion or mystical adhesion to God). Each bears diverse connotations in his writings, depending on context and his aim in each place where it appears. Yet all three are intertwined, and we may say they are actually perceived as various aspects of a single issue; that is, the ideal of *devekut*. Throughout the history of Jewish mysticism, *devekut* has been a central concept:[3] both in kabbalistic literature and in Hassidism, *devekut* is held as an ideal of religious and mystical life,[4] whether perceived as a most sublime ideal to be realized only by a chosen few or as a starting point relevant

to each individual.[5] The ideal of *devekut*, which implies intimate connection to God,[6] has been perceived at times in rationalistic-
intellectual terms, that is, the intellect's cleaving to its source, reached
in the process of enlightenment; at other times in experiential-
emotional and irrational terms, such as love, longing, or suprain-
tellectual revelation.[7] In any case, in both kabbalistic and Hassidic
literature, *devekut* is perceived as a religious challenge posed to one as
an individual. In Rav Kook's oeuvre, in contrast, these classic elements are evoked within the larger context of his thought, acquiring a
new dimension whose significance passes beyond the realm of relations between the individual and his or her God.

Let us begin our discussion with the concept of fear of God,
which in its general form represents natural religiosity, meaningful to
humankind as created "in God's image": "The internal form, the essential content[8] of man, is revealed solely by the image of God within
him, latent in the inward point of *fear of God*, the quality of the people
of Israel."[9] *Awe of God* [יראת ה] or *fear of heaven* [יראת שמים] translates in
life to "fear of sin"; that is, the effort to avoid sin, accompanied by fear
of the sin itself. For Rav Kook, fear of sin does indeed express the
basic religious position, "great faith in the unity of being."[10] Yet this
fear of heaven, as we mentioned earlier,[11] contains negative aspects
as well, for in its primitive form it can depress one, repress one's
freedom of thought and creativity, and hinder one's elevation. Supreme effort is thus needed, Rav Kook believed, to guard against that
primitive anxiety: "We must be awed with a higher fear, not a lower
one, which only impedes the broadening of that more sublime awe,
the fundament of life and good, truth and light."[12]

Despite the deficiencies of primitive fear, it is important to stress
Rav Kook's awareness of its positive role, which he would by no
means reject: "Although fear of punishment is very great, as it becomes more dominant, itself incurring pain and suffering, it also
purifies, and contains a higher benefit, which *becomes the basis* of
supreme awe."[13] Thus, Rav Kook said, "we shall not uproot the gross
element of fear of punishment from our spiritual thought, although it
sits in the abject pit of our spiritual order, and that is the only place for
it; yet that yeast ferments to become the choicest wine by remaining
there in the depths.[14] In other words, the task of primitive religiosity
is to arouse and strengthen religious feeling on a more sophisticated
plane.

On that higher level, religiosity is customarily not formulated in
terms bearing such negative connotations as "fear," but rather in the
positive term of "love." The human connection to existence in its

fullness, including the higher *sefirot*, is described most primarily as an intensely emotional experience: "How the heart yearns to love every-thing, all of creation, all actions, all creatures, all the myriad acts of the Creator, the roots of deeds, all of life, might and force, exalted splendor, *hokhma, bina* and *da'at, tiferet, netsah* and *hod, yesod,* and *malkhut.*"[15]

Yet all this is clearly no mere emotional activity.[16] Love must necessarily exist, because it expresses powers extending beyond the individual. The individual is no more than a channel through which the cosmic or divine stream of love can flow. He wrote:

I love everything, I cannot but love all of humanity, all peoples. . . . Truly, I have no need to suppress this feeling of love, it *flows straight from the holy source of wisdom, of the divine soul.*[17] Men great in spirit cannot remain separate from the all-embracing wholeness; their only desire and striving is forever the good of all . . . *they draw the love of all of being . . . from su-preme love of God,* from love of the absolute and complete whole-ness of the First Cause, who created and gave life to all. When love descends from the world of *atsilut* [the world of emanation and of the divinity] to the world of *beriah* [that of Creation], it decomposes into minute details, opposites and contradictions demanded by the *tsimtsum* [contraction] and diminishment of the quality of love.[18]

We see, then, that love is a cosmic dynamic, a process of emana-tion in and of itself, revealed in the love of the righteous—this love has a double nature. On the one hand, love is directed to all elements of being; "the great *zaddikim* are full of love . . . everything in the world receives their love."[19] Yet, on the other hand, the love of these holy men is so great that "it cannot be filled by any thing. For every-thing of this world is small compared to their sense of love. It can be fulfilled but by the divine."[20] This great love, which flows from the world of emanation, aspires to surround and affect absolute whole-ness, for "the loving soul is always greater and more enduring than the soul of the beloved. And sometimes love must spread to include a number of souls, so great is his loving and all-embracing soul . . . and the supreme model is divine love for all the worlds, all actions, all creatures, those emanated and those created, and all their desires.[21]

If love of particulars is possible despite the propensity toward love of entirety alone, this is due solely to a view of all particularity as manifestations of the divine wholeness: "For the abundant light of

God shines in everything, and all is a revelation of the delight and pleasantness of God, His mercy fills all the earth"[22] and "for all are the issue of divine light."[23]

Indeed, according to the model of divine movement, described as two contrary directions, downward and upward,[24] love as well is described, on the one hand, as we have seen, as descending from the world of *atsilut* and disintegrating into particulars, yet on the other, its ascent is also described: "The exalted *zaddikim*, God's valiant, their natural love of family rises to expand over all of Israel, the nation, *Knesset Israel*, and from its light they grow with lucid love for all of creation, love that becomes one with complete love, filled with pleasures of holiness and purity in God's high and secret place, the source of all life."[25]

Yet not only the *natural* feeling of love acquires mystical significance; mystical contemplation itself is portrayed as love and, on the contrary, love in its essence is the optimal means to supreme, universal love: "The exalted *zaddikim* know they love union through their souls . . . and in this love they reach supreme love."[26] We have already spoken[27] of the nature of love in its essence, revealing itself as love for the Other and for the whole. Yet we must recall such a view becomes possible when all of reality is seen as the revelation of the divine dimension, a revelation expressed in the human:

> All the worlds are embodied in the soul, and the deeper we delve toward inward knowledge of the contents of the soul, the more we understand the All, and the source of the world and the original light of all life becomes ever clearer. The world's manifestation ever grows within the soul's inwardness itself, until the light of God shines upon man, so great is his introspection into his own soul.[28]

This notion of the identification of the human with existence, or at least the continuity between them, is the source of the human metaphysical ability. As we have seen, Rav Kook viewed human will not only as an aspiring force, but as an agent with certain power. "Man in his sublime spirituality is the greatest active force in all of being."[29] In the course of our discussion, we distinguished various elements in Rav Kook's writings that sketch an image of reality characterized by continuity and unity among its components. The individual, in such an existential picture, appears related in many ways to all that surrounds him or her.[30] In this conception, reality is perceived as an organic body, and the connections between the limbs of this body naturally reach the root of their life, in their very essence:

When we say man is not only influenced by the whole world but influences it in turn, and this influence is formidable, general and spiritually positive, that is, not mere partial influence, we discern in his harnessing natural forces to do his will—smoke, fire, water, electricity—for all this is one limited and superficial aspect, but rather the *essence* of the world in all its fullness and extent relates to it, and the relationship is one of servitude and acceptance of influence, as mystical teaching would hold—when we say such a thing, we have decided there is an essential fusion between the soulfulness that acts in the world and the soulfulness of man.[31]

In other words, humankind not only reigns over forces of nature, but its influence can also be discerned over the very essence of reality. Humankind is perceived as more than a limb like other limbs; it is rather the center and epitome of all the life forces in being,[32] thus making its influence on the world so absolute and extensive: "When man's will rises, all of creation rises with it, and when it is brought low, all are degraded."[33] Rav Kook believed the significance of this idea is in the moral *responsibility* it imposes and the concomitant increase in motivation to act:

The knowledge that man is the central content of all of being enlarges his moral responsibility and arouses his desire to do great deeds. If the material form of the world is widened by the multitude of revelations, science sets before us *free control in the form of man*, and his revelation is the highest and essential center of being [= i.e., man is the expression of the cosmic force of freedom], and life is surely *the epitome of unfeeling reality*, and the *epitome of life* is the *reign of desire*, which rises to its greatest strength by uniting with absolute good and appearing in actuality in its most likely form.[34]

The individual is perceived as the representative of the principle of freedom in being, and because the principle of cosmic freedom is manifest in one, the ascent of one's will implies the ascent of all of being. The human relationship to the whole of existence, or to *ha-Adam ha-Elion* (literally, "Uebermensch"] in Rav Kook's kabbalistic term, is not allegorical in the sense of the relation between microcosm and macrocosm in neo-Platonic philosophy.[35] The microcosm here is the continuous manifestation of the principle of life and freedom significant to the macrocosm:

The axis of the world is in free will, which ascends and becomes in all its freedom, its own noble [refined] attribute, mighty and constant in its action toward steady good, rising ever higher. This entity is the human figure, whose entire soul sends out its lines in every place and manner that has a vessel suited to its light. And the expansion of the soul of this "Uebermensch" fills all the worlds, for in all of them man is limited, sketched in the unique traces of that central light.[36]

The question of one's status as a microcosm in the framework of a neo-Platonian world-view is problematic due to two opposing intuitions on which it is based: the notion of emanation and the idea of parallelism between "micro" and "macro."[37] If we accept the theory of emanation, according to which reality originates and is drawn from a single source in a continual process extending from that supreme source to the lowest level, there is no place for an analogy proposing two parallel worlds, one large and one small. Yet we will see Rav Kook mitigated this apparent contradiction, for in his system one is no more than an instrument in the revelation of divine will.[38] Moreover, one is the instrument that concentrates all the life forces of being and brings them to their full manifestation. The importance of the individual as the center of being is in the weight one's acts have and the supremecy of one's will over the development of all of being. One plays a central role in one aspect of the two-way movement of being: the aspect of ascent or repentance. Rav Kook described reality, as we know, according to the metaphysical neo-Platonian model of gradual emanation and of return and ascent to the source of emanation.[39] He called this return *teshuvah*, and it is supposed to redeem the "sin" of "fallen will." This reparation is the "unique and unending mission" to which we are summoned.

The terms *breaking, falling,* and *sin* might seem to allude to abnormal events and deviation from the order of reality, but this was not Rav Kook's intention. We have already spoken of the fact that both sin and repentance are integral parts of reality.[40] Rav Kook's view focused not on the development of crises and catastrophes but rather on continuity and constant becoming, in which aspects of sin and repentance are implicit.[41] Human action and its contribution to redemption is also a continuous process of being, an undying drive to achieve "the unique and unending task" designated to us.[42] This longing is a manifestation of the superior working of the human will: "That ideal has never been absent from the Jewish people, the *constant ascent of the Shekhinah,* to whom we turn each day in our worship, the ascent of human will until it attains the place meant for it in the will of being, and the will of all being, the light of will in absolute divine appearance revealed to him."[43] The identification of the ascent of the human will with the ascent of the *Shekhinah* is consistent with Rav Kook's conception of the connection between the human self and the divine, as we have seen.[44] The particular formulation of the connection between *zaddik* and Shekhinah comes to the fore in a few contexts,[45] and emphasized as "the *Shekhinah* herself [השכי נה ממש]." Here are two examples:

> When every *zaddik* senses his devotion to God has diminished, leaving his great thirst unslaked, his every limb breaks from grief and the longing of his soul, and he has no rest in the pleasures and comforts of the world—and this is truly *the anguish of the Shekhinah herself*; the content of life of all the worlds yearns for the supreme divine completeness to be revealed in it.[46]

> The thirst for God and the delight conjoined in it, along with the anguish of divine lovesickness when it bursts forth and floods the souls of *zaddikim*, fill them with boundless greatness. . .
> And at such an hour of favor, happy is he who meets these holy ones while they are taken up with the exalted light of God's mercy, and *all who greet them, it is as if they receive the very presence of the Shekhinah herself.*[47]

We have spoken of the fact that intensification of will is a necessary condition if the individual's freedom is to increase. An additional aspect of this idea now becomes clear. *The magnification of will is one's designated "labor,"* and the redemption of the entire world depends on it: "The real labor is the revival of will and strengthening of the divine soul, in man and in the world, through good deeds and true thoughts,"[48] "and it all depends on our will, our desire to rise to the highest heights of holiness, with a constant and original demand, the mighty sanctification of flesh and spirit, to resemble God by walking in his paths."[49]

This *union* of human will with divine will is the *ultimate aim of human action.* That is, the human aspiration to self-realization is a yearning for total correspondence with all-encompassing being, with entirety: "All of science serves to *make us suited* to true being, and because the basis of being is the will of existence, the *correspondence* to the will of being is the most supreme height."[50] Yet Rav Kook immediately qualified his words and said will is also only one aspect of reality:

Yet the highest understanding must ascend still higher, and justifiably declare the attribute of will is one of the attributes of greatness we seek, a restricted emanation of the light of *En sof*. And the highest *keter* [supernal crown; i.e., will], though it is brilliant and shining light, is darkness compared to the Cause of Causes. Not in impiety do we say this but in purity and strength, perfect wisdom and truth. Even if we describe every-thing in will, we feel compelled to say that all visions external to will are included, and all the *content of life* is for the sake of *correspondence* to supreme and universal will, will whose every tendency become active. And this is truly one of the insights through which the moral will of the element of the holy is re-vealed.[51]

The desired correspondence with cosmic and divine unity[52] is thus not gained solely by the elevation of will, but by the elevation of the intellect as well, and Rav Kook spoke of the existence of two paths: "The first is the way of pure science, and the second is scien-tific and ethical."[53] The active force in the second path is will, which aspires to *total cleaving* [*devekut*] or in Rav Kook's words: "The aspira-tion that raises all can be nothing other than to be drawn into the body of the King, the supreme longing of *devekut*, which leaves *noth-ing divisive* in its wake, for 'In You is the source of life and by your light do we see light' (Psalms 36:10)."[54] At issue here is not only human will but cosmic will as well: "The tremendous desire to be drawn into the body of the King, to return to the highest and purest source of reality, free and mighty, the source of *En sof*, which is plant-ed in all of existence and creation, that is the elemental force setting all of being in motion."[55]

The active impetus in the first, the "purely scientific" path, is the power of the cognizant intellect, and "the more knowledge increases, the closer man and the world come to God's greatness, and in his highest elevation and complete awareness, man realizes that *every-thing is contained in God*. And the private essence of each and every detail of being is none other than revelation of the divine."[56] "The realization of the yearning for *devekut* or [its] correspondence thus signifies broadening of consciousness[57] and its elevation to the high-est plan of perception. Hence the clarification of knowledge and forti-fication of the spirit are enough to turn everything to good,"[58] and "what is needed is not the expulsion of evil but rather the *elevation of thought and will*."[79] *Devekut*, according to the "scientific path" depends on *awareness* that all of reality is in fact revelation:

And all the world's toil and raising of its qualities serves only to bring about the highest age of science to be revealed in the outflowing of its source of truth; all of morality, both general and specific and all the improvement of ways of life, of justice and honesty in individual and collective life, all depends and imminently reaches the place of its integrity through the *recognition* made by consciousness of its originality, that it rises ever higher as the splendor of the light of life in the source of holiness is *laid bare;* that is the brilliance of truth, the light of God engenders all.[60]

There is thus a difference "between he who knows that all is light sparkling with the name of the Holy One, blessed by He, and one who does not know it, but this difference from lack of knowledge is only a matter of degree."[61]

Our discussion leads us to understand the ultimate goal is not restricted to a definition in strictly intellectual terms, such as *awareness, insight,* and *perception.* It seems on this subject, as throughout his writings, Rav Kook wished to make peace between two opposing approaches, expressed in the intellect and in will both as cosmic principles and as human inclinations. Therefore he wrote: "The ultimate purpose of creation is *knowledge* according to philosophy, and this is by no means refuted by the *feelings of the heart,* which wishes to discover the aim of every particular."[62] Contrary to philosophy and its interest in knowledge alone, "the spirit of man, elevated by lucid *awareness* and the ascent of *will* in purity and completeness . . . that [elevation] is the *propensity toward divine devotion.*"[63]

Devekut, both as cosmic movement and as the aim of religious and mystical life, signifies the unity of will and the intellect: "the religious aspiration in the mystical sense is a combination of intellect and will."[64] As Rav Kook said: "The supreme unification is in the conjoining of man's intellect and will with all of existence, in general and in its every part."[65] The distinction between the cosmic and the human plane becomes indistinct, and Rav Kook identified the cosmic movement with human yearning: "The aspiration of reality is no different from the aspiration of personal being."[66] Because the two elements of intellect and will are various aspects of reality as a whole, which can be seen as different aspects of human work to repair the universe,[67] beginning with one's personal world and leading to the perfection of the world in a wider sense: "All the world's purification, all depends on the clarity of will and intellect, and as soon as one ascends, he brings the light of the Messiah into his world; redeemed, he brings redemption to the world."[68] Hence, the "highest service of all of individual humanity is to raise the natural life forces of will, that they be in harmony with the forces of thought and intellect."[69]

The broadening of awareness,[70] as an act of repairing the world, is impossible when not supported by will. It is completely dependent on the intensity of will, and in that sense will can be seen as the basis of progress and ascent, whereas consciousness of will, that is, "the broadening of awareness," is its manifestation. The two elements of will and intellect are mutually dependent, for without the real action of will, awareness would have no object to grasp. And without awareness, the action of will would remain unknown and thus meaningless to humanity:

> When the effulgence of intellect appears, yet the trait of morality latent within it contains seeds inferior to the quality of the thinker, illuminated by the light of intellect, then the whole takes on a nebulous and mystical cast. But when moral will, which pulsates through the supreme and shining intellect, is completely equal to the very essential will of he who deals with those supreme aspects, then the illumination acquires the form of a luminous mirror and perceptions become clear recognition, vitally alive, standing in all stations of life, an eternal inheritance.[71]

One of the channels through which will and intellect flow is prayer."[72] Prayer is a definitive expression of will, as well as a tangible, active force.[73] Its influence, however, is noticeable and possible only when consciousness perceives the human will expressed in prayer as a manifestation of the universal divine will, thus engendering, in essence, the identification between the two wills and their union, the very goal of prayer. Human will is realized in accordance with its kinship and resemblance to the will of God:

> The element of prayer is the elevation of will and its manifestation. If what man requests, what fulfills his will, is expressed in conjunction with the idea and desire for God, will rises to its highest worth. It unites with the general will, universal will, the light of eternal life, in which all lights are contained. And when the individual will phrases its request in a private matter, the life of will activates the request according to the way the universal will comprehends the necessary detail in measure with its clearest individuality.

When desire ascends to the highest planes of knowledge, it becomes clear that no creation of will is separate from the universal and divine will, revealed in the light of all life, in all beings. And the greater knowledge becomes, the more it recognizes the great truth of the ocean of life as it spills into all the rivers of will, collective and personal, and the more intense grows the mighty influence of the request and its consequences.[74]

Clearly, in Rav Kook's view, the significance of prayer reaches far beyond the dimension of ritual. He perceives it not merely as "divine worship" in the normal sense, nor even as "worship of the heart" alone. The concept of prayer is linked to other concepts of general significance in his teaching, such as "unity," "development," "repentence," "*devekut,*" "faith," and "freedom," which represent being as a process of ascent and longing toward the source of life, toward the divine. Rav Kook believed that "the continual prayer of the soul strives endlessly to emerge from oblivion and become manifest" and stated that "the soul always prays . . . she soars and nestles against her beloved without cease; during prayer alone she reveals herself in actuality."[75] Prayer, then, is a constant spiritual-psychological reality, expressed primarily "in practice" yet in all "activities man invests with spiritual content as well."[76]

No mere psychological event, prayer is thus in fact a concealed cosmic phenomenon, made manifest in human prayer. The human will expressed in prayer as a desire for intimacy with God is actually the appearance of cosmic will aspiring to its source.

For us and for the whole world, prayer is total necessity . . . prayer is the ideal of all the worlds. The whole of being yearns for the source of its life, every plant and flower, every grain of sand and clod of earth . . . all languishes and longs, thirsts and clamors for the precious completeness of its supreme source . . . and the age comes when all these supreme desires in prayer are revealed . . . man elevates all creatures with his prayer, uniting all of being with himself . . . to the source of blessing and the source of life.[77]

The theological problem inherent in the possibility divine will may change, which disturbed the peace of mind of medieval thinkers and kabbalists,[78] loses its severity in Rav Kook's conception. For it is not a question of the human influence on divine will but rather of human will as a *manifestation* of divine and cosmic will; by directing oneself to the source and ascending there in one's prayer, one alters the conditions and status of reality.

> Prayer desires to change nothing in the divine, which is the source of eternity and unmutable—rather to ascend along with all the changes that overtake the soul and the whole world . . . it speaks of the divine, toward which it longs . . . in great freedom. . . . Prayer speaks to God as if to a ruling king who may change his mind, as if to a father open to changes . . . for when she desires to rise to the divine, her will ascends at once, and her will is all her essential being.[79]

To conclude this chapter of our discussion, I believe we can state the idea of correspondence of cosmic and divine unity constitutes, in Rav Kook's view, the major role of religion. He held that religious level is commensurate with the extent the concept of God is understood. When the divine is not perceived in its widest and most profound sense, religion is seen as the "servitude of a slave."[80] In a more broadminded view, on the other hand, religion is perceived as an aspiration to draw closer to "the unlimited completeness of divine ideals in the forms of life themselves, of being, of the collective, of deeds, of desire and idea—this is enlightened worship of God."[81] Morality and religion are not confined to human freedom. On the contrary, they are an opportunity for its realization. They demand the absolute response from every individual of self-realization, that is, correspondence to the essence of being as a whole:

> For *all of man* must be taught, guided to *adapt to universal being* and its originality. No place of education can be founded for the spark of a man, for one drop from his sea of life; rather every individual must be brought to the heights of his yearning. All of man, all his qualities, in his life full with material and spiritual being, temporal and eternal. All of man, he and he alone can absorb within himself the complete and favorable solution of the *enigma of the world and of life*, which stabs and pains so cruelly.[82]

7

The Way of the Holy

Rav Kook's bequest to us contains no moral code as such.[1] Those of his books that do discuss moral issues directly were not intentionally written as systematic doctrines on morality. Yet even on this subject, and perhaps particularly here, certain conclusions can be drawn; as we shall see, his theoretical fundamental stance clearly yields practical halachic guidelines.

What is the nature of the ethics mandated by Rav Kook's theoretical discussion? It is no accident that Rav Kook left no detailed *Shulkhan Arukh* of conduct or specific actions incumbent upon the servant of God beyond the formalized halacha collected and summarized in Jewish halachic texts. This absence is due primarily to his belief in the individual nature of religious worship. "Every man must know," Rav Kook affirmed, "he is summoned to worship in accord with his own understanding and feeling, with the root of his own soul, . . . every one must say, 'The world was created for my sake' (TB Sanhedrin 37a)."[2] Yet, at the same time Rav Kook sketched a general outline of clarifying the domain of religious worship, its objective and its ways. We must point out that the numerous passages relating to divine worship or the "way of the holy" clearly demonstrate that many aspects—its realm, objectives and means—extend far beyond the definition customary in research of the *via mystica* in the literal sense; that is, as a particular technique to attain mystical intimacy. This fact reflects a certain difficulty in Rav Kook's view of mysticism and reinforces, once again, the conjecture at the base of our investigation of the tension between rational elements and mystical tendencies in his thought.

This tension is remarkable in various formulations in Rav Kook's writings that relate to the nature of "supreme worship." Frequent passages speak of creating a synthesis between the intellect and will as the goal of religious worship. "The supreme worship of the individual personality," Rav Kook said, "is to elevate all the natural and willful forces of life, that they become fused in their nature with forces of thought and intellect."[3] The desired balance between intellect and emotion or will is no distant aim whose attainment is a mere dream. Rav Kook saw this balance as an existential necessity, and its absence inflicting humankind with serious flaws:

> Man cannot live with intellect alone, nor with emotion alone; intellect and emotion must forever be joined together.
> If he wishes to burst beyond his own level, he will lose his ability to feel, and his flaws and deficiencies will be myriad despite the strength of his intellect. And needless to say, if he sinks into unmitigated emotion, he will fall to the depths of foolishness, which lead to all weakness and sin. Only the quality of equilibrium, *which balances intellect with emotion* can deliver him completely.[4]

Rav Kook's assumptions concerning the necessity of balance and his presentation of it as the goal of religious worship lead him to comparable conclusions about the goals of education; that is, "In education of the individual, as well as that of the collective, the nation and of humanity, we must be aware of spiritual unity; that is, that the intellect exerts a direct influence upon feeling, and feeling upon imagination, and imagination upon actions."[5]

Will, however, is not mentioned in this passage, and the citations just presented could create the impression that the tension between intellect and will is easily resolved and brought to a state of harmony. Yet it is difficult to ignore paragraphs in which neither intellect nor will appear and that suggest no balance between the two. Certain passages stress the central and exclusive role of will in the perfection of humankind and the world, stating that "real worship is instilling will with life,"[6] by means of "good deeds and true minds," and that "all depends on our will, on the desire to ascend to the supernal heights of holiness."[7] In contrast, other contexts emphasize the role of the intellect in navigating religious life: "Enlightened souls must draw their holy light from the heights of the intellect, not from flights of the spirit, nor the excitement of imagination, nor from simple faith alone."[8]

Indeed, as we have seen,[9] Rav Kook's every invocation of the term *intellect* does not necessarily refer to the rational intellect; often his intention is "intellect" in the kabbalistic sense, that is, the *sefira* of *hokhma* or of *bina* emanated from it. But undoubtedly, in the context of this discussion, Rav Kook stressed the status and role of the rational, or "natural" intellect. This interpretation is supported by another passage in which Rav Kook stated the nature of the relationship between the rational intellect and the superior, mystical intellect, whose source is on the cosmic or divine level. He wrote:

> The highest emanated intellect, in the form of appearance of the holy, cannot take the place of the natural intellect; the two are conjoined as body is to soul. And man must continually fulfill the intellectual measure of the natural intellect in all his qualities, that his spirituality may be sustained as well—that is a healthy soul in a healthy body, the *holy spirit,* shining and open *within the intellect.*[10]

In light of the indispensibility of the intellect in the human attainment of spiritual balance, Rav Kook stressed the need to guard against repressing and nullifying the intellect even though spiritual effort may be focused on strengthening faith and mystical intentions.[11] The fact that, in various contexts, the intellect or will are alternately emphasized as of vital importance clearly expresses the internal struggle in Rav Kook's world, but this conflict still does not blur the tempering stance he took in numerous other instances: in this view, balance is vital not only to human spiritual health, but to the process of cosmic *tikkun* (reparation, perfection) as well: "The refinement of the world, all depends on the lucidity of the *will* and the *intellect,* and he who ascends immediately, brings the light of the Messiah in his own lifetime; he is redeemed and brings redemption to the world."[12]

Through our discussion, and in many other statements Rav Kook made, an additional aspect of the issue becomes increasingly clear: the question of the relationship between spiritual, intellectual, and emotional activity, on the one hand, and physical action, on the other, in the framework of religious worship. Our remarks to this point may give the impression that religious devotion is primarily an internal spiritual activity, implying the elevation of the intellect and will and their fusion in harmonious unity. Indeed, we find many instances in which the essence of worship is explicitly defined as a spiritual, cognitive, or emotional activity: "The fundamental meaning of worship . . . is to show the world and man how sublime is the connection between the world and its Creator, and following that, between man and his Maker."[13] And, in another passage, "Internal worship has some sort of arrangement of thoughts in it, which is the essence of the contemplative life, and an arrangement of feelings, which is the life of poetry and song, and also the links between these two qualities."[14]

Even when actual deeds are mentioned, they are described as mere instruments, as means rather than as the main object of worship: "The substance of worship has two elements; there is imaginary and real worship. The imaginary is dedicated to draw man's emotions to greater matters . . . but *real worship is truly the renewal of will* and the fortification of the divine soul, in man and the world by means of good deeds and true thoughts, and everything that is holy and true."[15]

The centrality of the motif of spirituality in religious worship is founded on the very interesting idea that divine creation as a whole is absolutely complete, and the human soul alone requires perfection. The defective state of the soul in and of itself constitutes a deficiency in all of being, and the repair of the soul thus engenders restoration of all the worlds. These are Rav Kook's words:

> The creative force directing the world acted in absolute wholeness, and all that God has done, it is very good; only one very small part is incomplete, though it seems insignificant compared to the great things the Lord has made, yet the perfection of all of creation depends on its completion. That small part is the *human soul* in the form of *will*, caught up in the imitation of divine spirituality. It is man's task to repair this part, thus bringing all of creation to completeness.[16]

The perfection of the soul, that is, the intellect and emotion as one, is an integrally systematic effort, not to be left to accident or to chance intellectual illuminations or spontaneous emotional arousal:

> Whether in wisdom or in cunning we must fight against all impulses that do not lead to *orderly thought, perfect reason, and particular feelings*. Those other impulses are the husks (*kelipot*) of the world of chaos, which languish for destruction and waste, both spiritual and material; the *builders of the world* must overcome them, must direct thought and spiritual ideas in all their aspects, in a *constructive and arranged plan*, that the soul may come to resemble her Creator, building ever more perfect worlds, full of strength and courage, beauty and splendor.[17]

On this point we must emphasize that despite all the preceding, Rav Kook's view is not to be seen as spiritualistic, or at least not radically so. Rav Kook held true to the goal of balance and remained loyal to it even on this issue. The spiritualist motif in his vision of the pathway to the holy is quite evident and may even be seen as central, yet at the same time, in several places he adamantly stated that spiritual worship is not only insufficient but contains a fundamental falsehood, for religious action disconnected from divine ideals—even when it expresses some moral content—is inherently defective. These are his words:

> When man's metaphysical thought elevates itself to describe the universal good and endeavors to desire it for itself and for the whole world, it cannot be complete unless it looks for the possibility of such a way of life that would found the world on elements able to mend it socially, demanding improvement of private life as well, both in its external and internal aspect. . . . Every thought that renounces the mending of the world and its political orders, a merely spiritual imagining that boasts of mending souls and causing their success—such thoughts are founded on groundless lies, and any thought estranged from higher eternity, which deals only with material orders of life and their improvement, even if it has moral content and values of justice and honesty, will eventually be befouled.[18]

An exaggerated increase in spiritual merits at the cost of disassociation from the real world leads, in Rav Kook's eyes, to decline and crisis. We have already borne witness to his awareness of this danger and seen his offer of two remedies, diametrically opposed: descent to the material world,[19] or such spiritual ascent that would make the severance from this world a permanent state.[20] Yet extreme solutions are not usually acceptable for Rav Kook. He preferred to limit and restrain mystical tendencies and anchor himself in rationality and actions in the real world.

Rav Kook was conscious of the problematic nature of the intrinsic paradox he saw between mysticism and rationality. On the one hand, mystical insight rejects reason, yet on the other, denial of mystical truths also causes logical distortion.[21] To the same extent, when the physical and the spiritual world support each the other, the two become interconnected:

> The more the spiritual ideas in man and in all thinkers maintain affinity with his material ideas, depending on his level, the more solid they become, growing and fortifying themselves, constructing even their physical being with beauty, but when

spiritual ideas draw too far from the material, the boundless from the bounded, their influence falls and breaks asunder.[22]

The practical conclusion to be drawn, in Rav Kook's view, attests once again to the way of balance: "Thus it is better for man not to sink too deeply into bonding with the real mystical experience, but only enough to understand that such a connection must not make his direct bond to the real world less conceivable; he lives in that world, in all its naturalness and order. 'Dwell in the land and enjoy security' (Psalms 37:3)."[23] Attention should be given not only to the spiritual dimension but also to the active aspect of serving God; that is, the importance of the practical commandments.

As we have said, a priori and in principle, Rav Kook considered every letter of the *mitzvot* to be an obligation, unequivocally and without restriction. In his opinion "temporal *mitzvot* raise the individual human soul to the treasure house of the whole,"[24] and yielding on the question of fulfilling the *mitzvot* is thus inconceivable, even on constructive grounds. Rav Kook defined the attempt to ascend spiritually without connection to performing the commandments as "the sin of Nadav and Avihu [who brought alien fire before the altar], separating the divine elements of father and mother."[25] He spoke of the need of performing the commandments in happiness[26] and believed the time would come in which "all of Israel will cleave in the love of every heart, in the essential divine nature within them, and in the greatness of their love and desire will be enjoined with the holiness of all the *mitzvot*."[27] In his view, this era would preceed the utopia in which all *mitzvot* would be annulled; it is clear, however, that Rav Kook's affection is with the era of *mitzvot*.

Human commitment on the active level is mandated first and foremost from a moral point of view, "for the only true redemption is when the redeemed bring it about *with the work of their own hands*. That is the element of *justice* in human labor, gaining forces and ordering them for the more holy and sanctified purposes of life."[28] At the same time, Rav Kook spoke of two sources of the inclination toward the minute details of religious laws:

Pedantic observance originates in two sources. It may be drawn from the lower place of fear of punishment, greatly encouraged by the imagination . . . , or the inspiration to extreme strictness in action may come with the abundant light of life at the source of perception, in the clarity of the idea of the holiness of the *mitzvot* and the unity of the natural spirit of Israel with the King, . . . and with pleasant love and sublime desire, limpid and lucid, sacred and lofty . . . and he, full of love and mercy, appears in the light of pardon and loving kindness and great knowledge.[29]

Indeed, in a few instances Rav Kook suggested reasons that may even be seen as pragmatic or beneficial in the sense that they protect human spiritual health:

> This spiritual greatness, which yearns for the highest holiness and for all that is sublime and great, must also care for the improvement of the attributes and actions, and *sometimes* to descend into the abyss of practical life and to pierce to their minutest details, to mend them and direct them in paths of justice and law, according to Torah and halacha, and to penetrate to the depths of the spiritual attributes, to remove all evil and distortion from them.
>
> And if attention is given only to ascent, and not to the lower purity and sanctity, all of that sublime light threatens to break apart and become an impediment. Greatness of the soul could turn into alien pride, and thirst for knowledge of powerful mysteries into imagination presumptuous in its myriad colors. The force of the spirit, which elevates the appearance of life, can elevate the stormy desires of the body as well, desire for gain, honor, and sensual pleasures could burst all boundaries. And the most disastrous fall could be from the mighty heights of the supreme aspiration to be as angels.[30]

The fact that Rav Kook qualified his claim with the word *sometimes* when he spoke of the need "to descend into the abyss of practical life" is of great significance and will be discussed later. In any case, it is clear Rav Kook had no reservations regarding the question of the *mitzvot* and participation in practical life. On the contrary, the *mitzvot* and actions are even included within the Lurianic idea of "raising the fallen holy sparks."[31] Rav Kook employed the terms *raising sparks,*[32] *distinctions,* and *raising worlds;*[33] his position on this subject is unique in the equal status he gave to the intellect and will in the process of restoration, in the *tikkun* of reality; he is thus not to be seen as continuing the view taught by Chabad or that of the Maggid of Mezeritch in the framework of Hassidic interpretation of Lurianic Kabbalah.[34]

In Rav Kook's perception of absolute identification in reality, the value of spiritual worship is essentially predominant, for "there is no need to banish evil but rather to elevate thought and will."[35] That is, in the broadening of consciousness and strengthening of will, the

unity of being is purified and realized, and real action seems superfluous. Yet Rav Kook stressed that although he saw real worship in
spiritual deeds ("the revival of will"), aid is needed as well, and may
appear in the form of "good deeds."[36] All kinds of worship are actually means to achieving cosmic *devekut* (attachment, devotion): "All
worship, all of Torah, all wisdom, all ethics, all actions performed in
the world are preparations to raise the entire world and man as a
whole, to the level of divine *devekut.*"[37]

In this context, we can fully grasp expressions spurred by enthusiasm for immersion in Torah and *mitzvot* "with great love and
ardent diligence . . . in completeness and elevated thought, which
together lead to closeness to God, with the deepest happiness of its
expanse."[38] Indeed, the goal of worship is to attain this devotion and
intimacy, "and Torah, prayer, worship and the *mitzvot* are the ultimate."[39] The Torah itself is granted special status in that sense, for

> as the Torah, in all its details, flows from the rich and mighty
> spiritual source of all the worlds, he who learns Torah for its
> own sake is joined and perfected with all the life and purity of
> being in all the wide worlds. . . . He gradually *struggles free of the
> chains* of bondage cast upon him by the human intellect and
> moral flaws,[40] born of his restriction, and he becomes a pious
> and holy man, honest and faithful.[41]

Despite all this, we have yet to exhaust Rav Kook's ideas on the
issue. The body of his comments on the question of the practical
mitzvot leaves the impression it was difficult for him to determine
their precise significance. He vascillated between enthusiastic praise
of their importance, stressing a profound and positive emotional link
described with the words *happiness* and *love,* and seeing them as a
burden and stumbling block in the *zaddik*'s path to spiritual completeness, an idea to be explored in the following pages. We must not
forget that, in any case, we have also found remarks of a pragmatic
nature concerning the vitality of the practical commandments to preserve spiritual health and the soul's equilibrium.

The common understanding of the concepts "Torah" and "*mitzvot*" seems too narrow to encompass Rav Kook's sweeping perception. We have already discussed[42] the meaning of Torah in his system
and have seen how much broader it became. Just as the concept of
"Torah" was widened, the domain of the *mitzvot* is extended as well:

> The early kabbalists called those who engaged in mystical con-
> templation "masters of worship." . . . Their lives are lives of

worship; their *mitzvot* are not symbols but rather polished [shining] facts, raising, improving and verifying all, and *the mitzvot are unlimited for them; all is mitzvah*, in all your paths, know—let all your acts be in the name of Heaven . . . and they are never free from the *mitzvot*, ever and eternally.[43]

The commandments spoken of here are not simply the 613 commandments enumerated in the Torah. "All is *mitzvah*," every deed done "in the name of Heaven" is considered a *mitzvah*, and in this sense, the "secret watchers" are "eternally bound by the *mitzvot*"; that is, they are never exempt from the demand that all their acts be for the sake of Heaven. An act is thought of as *mitzvah* not because it is perceived as a divine precept, as a law and statute, but rather because in doing it, one directs oneself to the divine,[44] to raise, improve, and perfect all of reality. The normative element of the *mitzvot* is entirely absent here. Statutes and ordinances in their normative sense are of completely functional importance:

> When the intellect shines in its full light, there is *no longer need of any special guidance of laws and ordinances*. The absolute good of action is drawn after the light of the intellect, and all the impediments of life resolve themselves. Statutes and ordinances exist not as precepts but as natural movements, subjects bright with the illumination of the intellect.
>
> Good and evil and all their values, their division and the great labor devoted to navigating the average way, neither adding nor omitting, all these came about after the intellect lost its light, and feeling, contentment and the depression of the senses took its place in the wake of the primal sin of eating from the Tree of knowledge of good and evil.[45]

In the ideal state, before that fateful act, that is, in a state that knows no distinction between good and evil,[46] there is no need for laws, precepts, and prohibitions.

Unbounded freedom is possible, for one acts naturally, guided by internal inclination and the light of intellect, choosing good."[47] However, in a reality in which the light of the intellect has been eclipsed through that sin, laws are intended to prevent the blurring of values, anarchy, and nihilism. All this is true of *zaddikim*, men great in spirit; even they must "sometimes descend" to practical life, to the minutest details, to act according to Torah and halacha.[48] *Zaddikim* risk harming themselves in their descent to deal with "the revealed Torah and the practical commandments" and "they must provide themselves defenses against injury incurred by being removed from their natural level."[49] All this is possible even though the Torah "emerges from the illumination of the highest truth, which knows no difference between man's inwardness and worldliness at its very source."[50] That is, there is a correspondence between the Torah with its *mitzvot* and the human inward being, as both share a common origin. Yet this correspondence does not guarantee there will be no spiritual damage to *zaddikim* who descend to deal with the practical commandments. For at that low level, the fundamental correspondence is not evident. The soul of the *zaddik*, "the holy man of silence," is fundamentally unsuited to "narrow, restricted worship," for

> if the holy man of silence lowers himself to limited worship, to prayer, Torah, confined morality, pedantic observation of details, he will suffer and be oppressed, will feel his soul, full of all being, is gripped in tongs forcing it into the narrow prison of measures, plotting one particular path, while in truth all the paths are open before him, each of them full of light, each a treasurehouse of life.[51]

Because, in Rav Kook's view, "great *zaddikim* . . . are sometimes able to occupy themselves neither with Torah nor with prayer nor *mitzvot* since the supreme holiness appearing over them demands its expansion,"[52] he thus wished to create some meaning that would grant legitimacy to that anarchic way of life as well, as he said: "*Their every utterance* [= of *zaddikim*] *is truly Torah, every desire and yearning of their hearts is prayer, each of their movements is mitzvah.*"[53]

This lack of correspondence between the practical commandments and the personality of the individual is a crisis caused by time. "The insolence preceeding the coming of the Messiah [*hakhutzpah de'ikveta demeshikha*] occurs because the world is so ready that it demands to understand how all the details are related to the whole."[54] It is a crisis of both understanding and experience and can be resolved by strengthening "spiritual aptitude."[55] The goal and principle of learning Torah for its own sake is to close this gap: "The essence of learning Torah for its own sake can only be accrued by this confirmation [validation, הכשר] of understanding and its accompanying sense of all the details of the Torah are beloved with holiness, and how the all-encompassing light, full of life, brings life to the world, pervading each and every detail."[56]

Fundamentally, Rav Kook saw complete correspondence between *Knesset Israel*, or the Community of Israel, and the Torah in its duality: the Oral teaching, like *Knesset Israel*, is identified with the *sefira* of *malkhut;* and the Written teaching, perceived as of supreme origin, was meant to correspond to the character of the Israelite nation—this character thus determined the content and nature of the Torah itself.[57] The Oral teaching can therefore be seen as the fruit of the nation's spirit. The correspondence between the Torah and the people of Israel is expressed first and foremost in the authority the nation has to interpret what is written in it, and this interpretation, even when it is clearly innovative, is on the order of revelation:

> Understanding from one's own insight is the highest point of spiritual elevation. All that is learned is received from without, and its character is inferior relative to meditation within the inmost soul. All that is learned serves as no more than a design of how to draw from the hidden places of the heart, from the depths of the soul, the inner meaning of knowledge.
>
> Knowledge flows onward, creating and acting. *The supreme renewer does not innovate but reproduce,* bringing new and living lights from a sublime original source to a place no one has ever been, a place unknown by birds of prey and that the falcon's eye has not seen [re. Job 28:7], a place untraveled, where no man has settled. *And in that great and personal revelation, the loyal ear is created, the attentive heart, saying nothing he did not hear from the lips of his rabbi,* prophets true and right; God's word of truth is in their mouths.[58]

"The supreme renewer does not innovate but reproduce" implies that the personal interpretation of the Torah scholar is "the great personal revelation." This paradoxical statement actually grants original and innovative creativity the validity of revelation. In light of our detailed discussion of the concept of "will" and conception of revelation, it can be understood as one simple implication of Rav Kook's wider metaphysical view. According to that conception, as we remember, the beliefs and opinions of every individual—one's thoughts and suppositions, one's study of Torah and innovations—are all in the realm of revelation. Hence, laws and ordinances are no more than confining limitations, because the true *mitzvot* are the entirety of human actions done for the sake of Heaven, from free and inward desire. *The normative element is completely absent.* Obedience attains new meaning: "To hearken to God's voice" in Rav Kook's method implies "attentiveness," awareness of the process of life, the emergence of all particulars from the source of divine wisdom. This awareness is hearkening to the voice of God, hearing commandment and guidance. As Rav Kook put it:

The essence of attentiveness to God's voice is in listening to the whole procession of the paths of life in all their details toward the various larger groups, each individual in his own way, in the whole and highest wisdom, which lives and revives all of being. The more the particulars emerge from sublime and all-embracing spiritual life, the wisdom of the divine spirit in the world in its purest form, the more clearly man hears and hearkens to the voice of God speaking to him, teaching and truly commanding him, "I am the Lord, who teaches you for your benefit, who leads you by the way you should go" (Isaiah 48:17).[59]

This injunction is, of course, neither specific nor detailed. Although there is a voice, there are no distinct words; it is a general guidance to do good, audible to one whenever one "listens," that is, becomes aware of "the entire procession of all paths of life." We have already spoken of the mystical connotations of "attentiveness";[60] if existential terms may be used in this context, I would say: the moment of meeting between the individual and being is a moment invested with revelation containing attentiveness to the voice of God, a moment of commandedness.[61]

One fundamental question must now be clarified. When Rav Kook spoke of the worship practiced by "the most holy *zaddikim*" or "the holy man of silence," to whom does he refer? The intention seems to be not to every human being but rather people of particular virtue. Yet at the same time, Rav Kook's statements in many passages make it difficult to set up precise criteria defining who is pious and who evil. His discussions create the impression the distinction between the holy and the evil is not one between "good" and "bad" people. There is neither unbounded approval for *zaddikim* nor uncensured condemnation of evildoers. More precisely, there is almost no condemnation of "bad people" beyond what is hinted in the terms themselves. On the contrary, Rav Kook clearly tried to diminish the essential differences between the holy and the evil and to present them as dissimilar in role and designation, differences likewise destined to become obsolete.[62]

Who, then, are the *zaddikim* and who are the wicked? It is clear beyond any doubt that the *zaddikim* are not necessarily the *haredi* community as a whole. Rav Kook makes explicit distinctions among them. He believes that for the sake of redemption, there is need of the worship of the *zaddikim*, yet also for the traditional and conservative masses "who anxiously respect every written line."[63] Traditionalism and conservatism and anxiety about every word are characteristics of the masses, yet not necessarily of *zaddikim*. On the contrary, the latter are distinguished in that "their path of worship is not at all like the paths of other men, always caught up in the limitations of this world, their own desires, the prison of their body and all its drives." Thus when they are seen doing peculiar things, they should not be doubted, for all their ways flow from the highest source of holiness."[64] This general mention of "peculiar things" in the actions of *zaddikim* however, is insufficient, and he explained further: "There are such *zaddikim* who do not need to study nor to pray, on their level, more than occasionally, like Rav Yehuda, and they must not crush their own attributes; rather, they allow their needs and inclinations to expand and broaden, and all their desire is done."[65] In this statement we find a daring recognition of the legitimacy of a path of worship not marked by strict observance of particular acts:

> Neither the surroundings nor individual actions are the foundations on which spiritual happiness is built in its internal storehouse, but rather greatness of the soul, inward, holy and pure, the strength of will and power of thought. Surroundings and actions are subdued before spiritual power when it arises. Thus, the main concern of great *zaddikim* is with internal greatness. Naturally, they are careful in their actions, strive to purify their surroundings, but all this is a result of the inner cause of the supreme light shining in the soul . . . and they will not denegrate themselves to be continually stuck in the narrowness of precise observance of details without end, which weary the spirit in its ascent.[66]

These *zaddikim* absorbed in holiness and internal purity suffer a severe and painful depression when they are forced to "fall to constricted worship," and as we have seen, not only did Rav Kook understand their situation, but granted it legitimacy as well.[67]

Who is a *zaddik* according to this definition? And is a person's piety measured by his strictness and precision in fulfilling *mitzvot*? Is he distinguished by enormous diligence in learning Torah or by vast knowledge? No such external measure can be used to recognize just who are *zaddikim*. The *zaddik* is a person great in spirit, of immense spiritual aspirations and unique sensitivity: "He feels the vitality of the inanimate, the plant and the animal, the collective life of all speaking creatures, of every man of the human race, the life of every intellect and every conscience, of all that perceives and feels."[68] These attributes are not necessarily the exclusive possession of an elite of eminent individuals. There are degrees of piety, and as "the *zaddik* bears the sin of his generation," thus "each and every Jew suffers in his own way from the sins of his time. And as the soul becomes cleaner and more refined, this pain becomes infused with love."[69] In essence, Rav Kook held, "no one in the world is completely devoid of righteousness."[70]

Thus we find no spiritualistic idealization of the image of the *zaddik*. "True *zaddikim* must be natural people, for whom all the natural characteristics of body and soul are qualities of life and health."[71] A life of holiness, in Rav Kook's eyes, does not mean denial of the world.[72] Rather the opposite: "normal life *is not altered;* normal human dialogue, singular physical life and social life, manners and honor are not blurred [obscured], but they ascend to an ideal plane. Life in its essence is elevated, its *purpose* sanctified."[73] Rav Kook repudiated fasting and mortification as a means to attain "exalted aims" and claimed that, in our time, strengthening *will* and the *body* are worth as much as "the fasts and self-imposed afflictions of earlier generations."[74] The *zaddik*, then, is a person of intensive spiritual experience, whose existential concern is indisputable, and he has within him a shadow of anarchy though rooted in practical, social and cultural life.

As we have said, there are various degrees of piety, ranging from "the preeminent *zaddikim*"[75] down to the level of those called *wicked*, who actually serve as a lower link of well-known service in the hierarchy of *zaddikim* building the world:

> The element of righteousness of the *zaddikim* is founded on the evil of the wicked, who are *really not wicked at all* as long as they remain devoted in their hearts to the nation as a whole. "And your people, *all of them are righteous*" (Isaiah 60:21). Their external wickedness serves to strengthen the *zaddikim* as fermenting improves wine, and by illusory disunion the holy itself is undermined, deeds of Amalek are done, the hindmost feeble in the rear are smote, refugees of the cloud, "he has put forth his hands against those at peace with him: he has broken the covenant!" (Deuteronomy 25:18; Psalms 55:22).[76]

Not only did Rav Kook affirm that the wicked "are not really evil at all," he went so far as to esteem their level by comparing them to the most eminent *zaddikim:* "The impudence before the advent of the Messiah comes from an innmost desire for the sublime holiness of silence,"[77] the holiness that characterizes the most supreme *zaddikim*.[78]

The principle merit of the wicked allowing them to be included among the righteous is, as we have said, in their being "attached in their heart's desire to the nation as a whole." Their spiritual connection to the Jewish people is of such value that it removes them from the category of the wicked: "Before the coming of the Messiah, all who join themselves in the inclination of their heart to the salvation of Israel have the soul of a *holy zaddik,* who cannot be assessed by normal measures."[79] The messianic dimension of this era before his advent, of course, is not to be ignored, as it justifies the term "holy *zaddik*" in the preceding passage.[80] Yet this justification is not disconnected from the context of Rav Kook's metaphysical world-view and particularly not from his conception of will and revelation, which permit a certain relativistic attitude, according to which "Just as praise of the Holy One blessed be He rises from *zaddikim,* so it rises from the wicked as well."[81]

Those "great of soul," the "upright," even when they deal "with profane wisdom, alien things, magic, foreign and contaminated beliefs"—they know "to stand in the breach and immure themselves."[82] The wicked, on the other hand, "the impudent," although they are *"pathbreakers and breachers of fences,"*[83] will bear sons who will be "prophets of the highest caliber, on the level of Moses our teacher and the supreme luminousness of Adam haRishon, the first Man. The Tree of Life in its profound goodness will be revealed in them and by their hand."[84] Thus "deeds of Amalek" should not be done, and people must abstain from contact even with sinners of Israel, and the contention that such contact may harm *zaddikim* spiritually is to be rejected as well. Love of Israel and positive regard for the laborers pave the way for unimpeded spiritual ascent.[85]

One essential difference Rav Kook sees between "sinners of Israel" and "Jews of complete faith" (i.e., observant Jews) now deserves our attention:

> The *soul [nefesh]* of sinners of Israel in the era before the advent of the Messiah, those individuals who join themselves with love with the interests of the community of Israel, to the Land of Israel and the rebirth of the nation, is *more perfect* than the soul of Jews of complete faith, who lack the merit of that essential sense for the good of the whole and construction of the nation and the land, but the spirit [רוח] of the God-fearing, observant of Torah and *mitzvot,* is much more perfect.
> . . . And the soul of the God-fearing preservers of the Torah will be repaired through the wholeness of soul of *sinners* who are *good* in their relation to the collective material and spiritual laws of human awareness and feeling, while the spirit of the sinners will be repaired and made complete through the influ-

ence of the God fearing. . . . And the highest *zaddikim* . . . will
be the channels uniting the two.[86]

At least in formulation, a modicum of balance is preserved in
Rav Kook's view of the observant and the sinners of Israel. Similarly,
"Jews of complete faith" are not equated with "the highest *zaddikim,*"
who transcend distinctions and differences. They unify the various
parts of the nation. Expressed here is a conception of the virtues of
both the "sinners of Israel" and "Jews of complete faith." Indeed, the
merit of "sinners of Israel" is in the "soul," one's lower component,
which gives life to the body and fulfills one's needs,[87] among those
needs are the "material and spiritual hopes in human awareness and
feeling."[88] In contrast, the merit of the observant is in the spirit, the
higher component in one,[89] which houses aspiration in the realm of
Torah learning and fulfilling commandment. These differences naturally reflect the variant approach of these two groups to the external
project of building a Jewish social system, state, and culture in Eretz
Israel. Yet, in Rav Kook's perception of the *zaddik,* can the dam of the
obligation to observance be burst under any condition and without
waver? In general we can say that Rav Kook appropriated almost
unlimited freedom in the realm of thought, yet adopted a very conservative approach in the realm of halacha and action. At the same time
this freedom could not possibly fail to leave its mark on his position
toward halacha and action, as he himself affirmed.[90]

The great freedom Rav Kook invested in the realm of thought is
rooted in the conviction that every opinion and assumption has a
measure of holiness commensurate with the measure of divine revelation embodied in it. "Indeed, in *practice* no human being can reach
that measure by which the Torah drew eternal boundaries. But as for
thought, ten handbreadths do not confine it; the adversary and evil
hindrance cannot touch it."[91] On the practical level, we are confined
by the limits set by the Torah; they apply to everything, never to be
annulled. Breaching the boundaries poses danger. Thought, though,
has no confines, and limitless freedom poses no potential danger in
that realm:

> Every idea and thought that comes from *search and criticism*
> alone, *in the purity of its freedom* will have no touch of evil, neither
> in the general faith shared by all the wise and upright in heart of
> the human race, with their knowledge of God and the victory
> of justice and morality as a whole, including eternal life and that
> of all generations, nor in the fundament of the Israel, the eternal

nation, and its connection to the Lord of their fathers and His holy covenant with Torah and *mitzvot*, as it is written, "No weapon that is formed against thee shall prosper; and every tongue that shall rise against thee in judgment thou shalt condemn" (Isaiah 54:17). Only the evil heart . . . causes all the turmoil and deficiency[92] in Israel and in man.[93]

Unencumbered thought and investigation in the name of the search for truth, in and of themselves, are altogether harmless. The danger comes from dogmatic and unobjective investigation, guided by "the evil heart" alone. Rav Kook believed a priori in the power of the Jewish faith to come out on top in all ideological battles. This is the source of his claim for intensive study, for it is superficiality that gives birth to narrowness of thought:

> Superficial study may constrict thought, obscuring it from the moment it is born. And accustoming oneself to assiduous study, with systematic constancy, is just what intensifies that illness of narrowness of thought. We must endeavor to save ourselves from this with all our strength, to liberate our soul from the pressure of its chains [מִצְרִים], to free it from Egypt [מִצְרַיִם], from the house of bondage.[94]

As we have seen, Rav Kook was aware that one of the causes of superficiality and narrowness of thought is in fact stupid "fear of Heaven," and in arousing anxiety at the suggestion of free thought, this "God-fearingness" diminishes the human spiritual stature.[95] Moreover, in faith itself, the human perception of God does not profit from this foolish fear, for the level of faith is always equal with the level of understanding. "When understanding of the divine is small, the way we imagine God is small as well, and when the divine content makes clear the infinite diminutiveness of man relative to it, *man is inconceivably demeaned and made ineffectual by fear of Heaven devoid of understanding*."[96]

We need not emphasize that Rav Kook shrank from narrow apologetic thought.[97] The uncompromising search for truth does not demand adopting one particular view or opinion, rejecting absolutely all other views or denying the very legitimacy of the existence of differing views. On the contrary, the identity of the "truth" with the "existing" implies that just as existence is not one dimensional, truth is many faceted as well.[98] The notion that all views are expressions of divine revelation undeniably demands appropriate respect of all aspects of human creativity: "He who thinks of divine matters in their purity cannot hate or demean a single creation or ability in the world, as the divine cause is revealed in all, in His eminence and power."[99]

Yet it would be a mistake to assume freedom of thought has no bounds. Rav Kook named at least three reasons such freedom should be limited. The first states that the principle of freedom of thought is of ethical value only in undertaking research, perusal, and study dedicated to the search for truth. In such a case, freedom is positive and meaningful. But the concept of "freedom of ideas" is senseless when such freedom does not actively exist; that is, amidst the masses guided by their imagination and swayed by every wind.[100] The other two reasons are related to the danger of nihilism and the destruction of the status and existence of the nation, which may emerge from unlimited freedom. "There is not a single attribute in the world," Rav Kook said, "that would not be harmed by extremism."[101] He declared the axiom demanding freedom of ideas does not apply to any opinion threatening to throw off "the yoke of all agreed-upon morality" or leading, in its brazenness, to the ruin of "the world's existence."[102] Yet at the same time he was aware of the difficulty of fixing the precise boundaries of freedom, especially in light of the relativity of moral conventions:

> We learn there is a limit to freedom of ideas, but the difficulty is in defining the boundary. And it becomes apparent the limitations cannot be the same in every human society; for example, a certain heartfelt agreement there is nothing wrong with walking around naked—a person who feels this way and encourages such behavior in our society commits a sin, and it should be seen so. But among the natives on the islands of New Guinea, for instance, that is no sin at all. And because there is unavoidable distance between one society and another, this difference does not stand still, but rather moves and divides itself among the myriad circumstances.[103]

In certain cases, the difficulty in determining clear boundaries and the confrontation or "conflict of interests" between the aspiration to freedom and practical considerations create an oppressive problem and sense of guilt. The individual who contemplates without restraint recognizes the fact that one's free thought has implications on the practical level within the realm of sin, and this recognition engenders an effort to bridge the gap between "the higher plane of life" and "the way of limitation"; that is, the path of *mitzvot* and actions leading to that higher plane.[104] Many passages discussing the tension between the striving for freedom and the yoke of the *mitzvot* that weighs like a millstone on the neck of the individual, the *zaddik* or the "holy man of silence," clearly reflect Rav Kook's reservations in relation to the practical commandments. Let us be reminded once again: Rav Kook does not perceive any specific law, or halacha as a whole, as superfluous, at least not in our own time. We recognize[105] his connection, emotional as well as fundamental, to the *mitzvot,* yet at the same time we cannot ignore his assertion that in the end of time, "in the utopic future," a revolutionary change will occur:

> The eternity of the Torah in the form of material action—the obligation of the commandments—remains only as long as this world exists . . . we must say that the *purpose of life* in the future will *not be worship and fulfilling the commandments,* but rather the great pleasure and eternal happiness that "no eye has seen another Lord beside You," of the recompense of *mitzvot* we fulfill in complete faith.[106]

Rav Kook naturally stressed "these conclusions need not exert an actual influence,"[107] yet there is certainly the hint of a measure of difficulty, as our discussion has shown.

Rav Kook distinguished between two degrees of religious experience: "שיר" (poetry) and "שיח" (speech).[108] The first embodies the attributes of intellect, ability, and will (the initials of these three words in Hebrew form the word שיר), and it is opposed to the second element, שיח, which represents intellect, ability, and life (their initials forming the Hebrew word). "*Shir*" (i.e., the intellect and ability expressed in *will*) is "the element of revelation of the holiness of Israel"; that is, the element of religious life entrenched in revelation. In contrast, "*Siakh*" (i.e., the intellect and ability expressed in *life*) implies a life of completeness. Life based on Torah is not whole, although it may be compelled by reality. Will, the basis of revelation, "is no more than a tiny branch of *the entire tree of life* and the future strides toward *life in its completeness* coming into being."[109] Thus it is no accident that Rav Kook sets the concepts of "Torah" and "life" as opposites: "For now I give you Torah; in the time to come I give you life."[110] In other words, for now limitations and boundaries; in the hereafter, freedom.[111] Indeed, there are no shortcuts to that utopic religious experience: "The guide to that exalted level is in *guarding* the path that prepares and distinguishes between good and evil";[112] that is, keeping the commandments.

The fact that "sometimes it is impossible to busy oneself only with Torah, excluding any other activity, *mitzvah*, or worldly concern, for the will is devoted to connection with the supreme image of the delight of endless light"—this is not a general command, yet undoubtedly the very recognition of this fact testifies, at the very least, to consideration of the existential problems and religious experience of the individual. Such statements in and of themselves show great daring. Indeed, in a broader context, on the halachic and practical level, there is almost no expression of this revolutionary view.

Indeed, in Rav Kook's famous ruling on the issue of *shmitah* (releasing the Jews living in Eretz Israel from agricultural restrictions related to the sabbatical year) we find clear expression of his metaphysical and ideological view. The major principles supporting his decision were definitively nonhalachic.[114] (1) The settlements could not preserve their existence and observe the *mitzvot* of *shmitah*. (2) The restrictions of *shmitah* will prevent observant Jews from making *aliyah* due to the impossibility of keeping the sabbatical year halachically, and this will accelerate the process of secularization already occurring in Erez Israel. (3) Easing the restrictions would prove the land could be rebuilt in loyalty to halacha, and this would encourage obedience to rabbinic authority on other issues as well. (4) The unconditional prohibition of all agricultural activity would define every undertaking of the settlements as illegitimate religiously, a fact that would utterly contradict Rav Kook's entire world-view.[115]

And yet his ruling easing the restrictions of *shmita* is a unique example of Rav Kook's conservative approach in the realm of halacha. The disparity between his incredible daring on the contemplative and personal level and his immovable conservatism on the halachic-public level is quite obvious and demands explanation. This fact, when placed against the background of his conception of revelation, described earlier,[116] seems easily understandable, as we see in the following passage:

> At times, when change is needed in a matter related to Torah and no one of the generation can show the way, the matter could explode, and it is always better to reach such a state inadvertently, based on the principle that unintentional sin is less severe than intentional; the situation can be remedied only when the people of Israel are graced with prophecy, through emergency instructions in the form of easing restrictions and commandment revealed to all. But when the light of prophecy has been obstructed, this *repair* is effected through a *long period of*

revolt, which grieves the heart *externally* and gladdens it *inwardly.*[117]

In this paragraph, the radical elements of Rav Kook's method are intertwined with the conservative. He is aware of the fact that change is sometimes imperative in matters of Torah, yet, bereft of prophecy, the *posek* or halachic expert lacks authority to ease restrictions, and there is no one to guide the generation. The urgency and severity of the *need* for change is not diminished here. Its fulfillment, in Rav Kook's eyes, amounts to a *tikkun,* the repair of an imperfect state, and in the absence of halachic authority this improvement is reached through social "eruption," which distresses the heart because it contradicts the Torah, yet at the same time it is a cause for inward happiness, because the repair it effects is truly necessary. A priori, we have no authority to initiate changes in matters of Torah, making halachic reform impossible.[118] Yet when a *spontaneous* transfer on a matter of Torah actually takes place, it becomes legitimate a posteriori, in that it, like any other authentic expression of the nation, is a form of revelation, and as such a cause for happiness.

The authority the public possesses, enabling it to determine halacha in its spontaneous life, can also annul earlier rulings,[119] yet this fact does not lessen the stature of the halachic authorities throughout the generations. In another context, but based on the same principle, Rav Kook made the following comment:

> Yet the greatness of previous generations is not hidden from us, nor our insignificance compared to them, and we say, "If they are as angels, then we are as men."[120]
> In any case the account is settled, *that our weakness relative to them does not invalidate our exalted strivings,* our attempt to overcome spiritual idolatry, which gathered false gods from amidst all those who dwell above. And we, we raise ourselves proudly and proclaim, Whom have I in heaven? *Only the absolute truth, greatness alone, nothing but originality* itself, divine power—that is all we demand and all we shall seek.
> Similarly, in other accounts our predecessors will not impede us. Though we may reach a goal *precluded to them for some reason,* whether intellective or moral, national or a destination of faith, and despite their honor and greatness and our smallness and significance, *we will not cease* striving toward it, for our soul longs for it, and the hand of *time* teaches us we are capable of attaining it. We call on the name of God in the *the revelation of life*

and spirit in each and every generation. The verse prefers the honor
of the *zaddik* in his grave before the honor of the living *zaddik.*[121]
. . . The words of our forefathers, our inheritance and traditions are truly imprinted with the stamp of divine completeness, and we need never waver from them. That is the watch-
word distinguishing between the essence of the Oral teaching,
which the nation knows is a fundamental obligation, and the
judgments of individual wise men of all the generations.[122]

In all humility, and despite the awareness we must not deviate
from the words of the sages who "bear the stamp of divine completeness," Rav Kook perceived self-annulment before them as "spiritual
idolatry." In his view, one must consider the direction "given to us by
the times," setting the "absolute truth" alone before one's eyes. Nonetheless, the way to the holy is not strewn with roses. It is paved with
uncertainty and suffering engendered by opposing forces, and the
servant of God must bridge the gap between them: the conflict between will to *devekut* and mystical contemplation, on the one hand,
and the demands of the intellect for a rational formulation of religious
life, on the other; the sense of tension and heaviness related to observing the *mitzvot* and view of them as means to an end, opposed to
love of the *mitzvot* as self-sufficient principles; anarchic individualism,
on the one hand, and deep connection to the known public, on the
other. The highest goal on the path to the holy is the unification of all
opposites, "lessening the burdens," and liberation from all distress,
all bonds and fears, foremost among them the fear of death.[123] All
these can be concentrated in a single word, which in Rav Kook's
opinion defines our religious destiny: "*To this we are summoned,* and in
its name we *fight,* and all our defeats do not discourage us from the
highest goal, borne in our hearts, we strive toward it, passing through
all the many and twisting stages, and we shall reach that *freedom* for
which we live."[124]

PART FOUR

Between Rationalism and Mysticism

8

The Dynamic of Rationalism and Mysticism in Rav Kook's Thought

Rationalism and Mysticism—A Definition of Terms

In philosophical literature, the two concepts of "mysticism" and "philosophy" are often held as polarly opposed,[1] yet this polarity is unnecessary and certainly not essential. It stems from understanding rationalism and mysticism in a narrow sense, disregarding changes that occurred in various periods and systems of thought in the concepts of "rationalism" and "rationality" and ignoring the spectrum of meanings and contents of the mystical phenomenon. Let us, then, devote a few words to clarifying the use of these concepts in our discussion in light of their transformations and variety of senses.

Rationalism and *rationality* are derived from the Latin word *ratio*, which means "reason."[2] *Rationalism* usually signifies a particular philosophical outlook, or a class of philosophical views, that see reason as the major source and distinguishing characteristic of perception[3] and claim the world is governed by an order, structure, and set of laws that the human intellect alone can recognize. *Rationality*, in contrast, is a characteristic or quality attributed to or used to describe specific views or actions. We usually say a certain act is rational if there are good and sufficient reasons for doing it, and a conjecture is considered rational if it can be based on good and sufficient grounds. A sufficient reason, in this context, is a practical inference or claim valid in a logical sense.

Thus we can say *rationality* is a methodological principle; that is, the principle that determines the paths and progression of thought.

175

Rationalism, on the other hand, as a philosophic method, may be founded completely upon rationality, its significance primarily methodological, or it may seek to claim something regarding the order of reality, bearing ontological significance.[4] Indeed, A. N. Whitehead opposed such a restricted definition; he spoke of speculative reason, affirming that its very essence precludes its limitation by method.[5] Whitehead, we hasten to add, was by no means the sole spokesman of this approach. Reason is increasingly recognized as a system far from pure and unique, revealed and explainable once and for all. It is rather a subjective and dynamic activity, its nature interested and inquisitive, and it cannot be exhausted or enclosed in any final system.[6]

In that case, rationality can naturally be seen as important to philosophy in and of itself, whether we perceive reason as "the ability of highest intellect itself," as Kant defined it in broad terms embracing the opposition between understanding (*Verstand*) and reason (*Vernunft*) in their specific sense;[7] or whether we see rationality as the expression, conceptualized and formulated, of the various aspects of experience, as Whitehead held it to be. In Whitehead's view, the concern of philosophy is to overcome the fragmentary nature of human experience by seeking to give formulated, and therefore rational, expression to all the sides that the discontinuity of experience cannot encompass. Speculative reason is motivated by the ultimate faith that each and every fact can be understood as examplifying the general principle of its nature and its status amidst other details.[9]

Rationality, then, is the heart of formulated, conceptual expression, and in that sense is philosophy itself. Philosophical thought, as opposed to thought that is not philosophical, is distinguished by being conscious knowledge; that is, a conceptual formulation of knowledge that was previously unformulated or nonconceptual.[10]

This sense of the notion of rationality, that is, the conceptual expression of knowledge whose essence is not conceptual, is akin to the sense employed in the field of comparative religion when describing processes of abstraction and rationalization that occur in the development of religions.[11] *Rationalization*, in this context, implies not only a process of abstraction but the creation of principles, order, and method in ways of life and perceptions of material being.

Rudolf Otto, in his classic work concerning "the Holy,"[12] claimed the striving to grasp and characterize God by using descriptions in the form of clear and distinguished concepts is central to all theistic world-views. Yet Otto also believed rational concepts are insufficient in describing the religious phenomenon, for the irrational element of faith, the "numinous," is what determines the uniqueness of religion.[13] Nonetheless, in Otto's view, not only must the irrational be discussed rationally, but even religious belief itself becomes possible through conceptual expression, and through such expression alone can it be called *"faith* as opposed to simple emotion."[14] As a result the "holy," which defines the boundaries of the religious realm, is a synthesis of the rational and the irrational elements of religion.[15]

We can, then, summarize, rationality or rationalism cannot be defined precisely and exhaustively. We can speak of analytical, speculative, or dialectic reason, and of rationalism in various senses, for the concept of rationality appears in various contexts; in philosophy it is theory bound in the doctrine of decision making;[16] we find it in the social sciences as well,[17] in anthropology and comparative religions. Perhaps, then, rationalism should be qualified by describing the major forms in which it appears; in light of our discussion, we can distinguish three. First, *rationalism is an ontological contention,* which conceives reason as a metaphysical entity or sees material being as having rational structure, or acting according to some rational order. Second, *rationalism is a methodological principle,* which sees rationality as a principle guiding thought, paths of inquiry, and human activity in general (n.b. rationality is not necessarily a logical deduction). Third, *rationalism is a trend toward abstraction and conceptualization,* which relates primarily to nonconceptual domains and leads irrational intuitions to conceptual formulation and to the development of abstract and inclusive theories according to which each separate fact can be understood as an example of the general principle of its nature and place among other particulars.

In our study of Rav Kook's thought we make use of all three senses of the concept "rationalism." When we speak of a general characterization of his thought as belonging to the rationalistic tendency in Jewish mystical tradition, we mean rationalism in the third sense. When Rav Kook himself spoke of rationalism, his intention was usually in the second sense, and at times, during discussion of his metaphysical views, elements of partial rationalism in the ontological sense are employed. This rationalism is inherently incomplete, for as we have seen, in Rav Kook's outlook reason is only one of the dual aspect of reality.

To characterize mysticism is an easier task. Two schools of mystical thought are prominent in religious studies: the first distrusts and ultimately rejects the normal information gathered by way of the senses and by reason, whereas the second accepts what is perceived by the senses and by reason as a partial manifestation of the spiritual.[18] Only the second school, of course, is able to and interested in developing a philosophy. And indeed, a good part of mystical literature deals not only with experience, or at least not only with emotional experiences, but with knowledge that is principally informational and cognitive and with theosophic, cosmological, and anthropologic theories not necessarily irrational.[19] Nonetheless, mysticism, like religion, has one vital element without which it could not be seen as a unique category. When rationalism and mysticism are juxtaposed as contrary forces, the intent is not usually to a realm in which they may or do overlap but rather to those polar tendencies they are said to represent; that is, the view that distinguishes laws of logic in reason against the view of mysticism as an intense emotional trial that cannot be described or translated into conceptual terms.[20]

Our major concern in this study is not with these two opposing approaches, but rather with the continuum between them, which may be termed *mystical philosophy*.[21] This domain, extending between rationalism and mysticism is not "philosophy" if that term implies a crystallized ideological framework, systematic from its inception, that justifies and substantiates each of its conclusions; nor is it "mysticism" if that term implies experiencing what "can be clearly expressed only through concrete contact."[22]

We do not seek the impossible, to propose an exhaustive characterization or definition of *mysticism*.[23] Yet we must make clear that, in our eyes, a mystic is not only a person who has had an immediate and real experience in the eyes of the divine, of absolute being, nor even one who consciously strives to reach such experience.[24]

It is usually difficult to distinguish between mystical experience and what can be seen as intensive religious experience. In the view of Rudolf Otto, there is no essential difference between mysticism and religion. Both recognize the element of the irrational; mysticism, though, emphasizes it immeasurably more, becoming a sort of maximum and exaggerated amplification of the irrational and emotive elements in religion at the expense of the intellectual element.[25] But how can the nature of this exaggeration be measured exactly?

William James viewed religion from the opposite direction. The root and center of the personal experience of faith, in his eyes, is in mystical states of consciousness.[26] In such a state of awareness, James stated, "the finite self rejoins the absolute self, for it was always one with God and identical with the soul of the world."[27] Psychologists speak of the blurred consciousness of self in childhood, and of lack of distinction between the child's self and his or her environment as mystical states.[28] Therefore, if the *unio mystica* alone were seen as a mystical experience, it is doubtful whether we could speak of such a thing as Jewish mysticism at all. Mystical union with God is generally not set as an ideal in Kabbalah, for if it were, it would be difficult to harmonize with the monotheistic faith to which Judiasm is bound.[29]

Without committing ourselves to generalization outside the realm of Rav Kook's thought, the framework of our discussion can integrate the definition given by R. C. Zaehner, who saw mysticism as a "constant and unshaken phenomenon of universal longing of the human spirit for union with God."[30] Within the context of Jewish tradition, this same striving to become one with God receives the sense of the aspiration to *devekut*, a special intimacy with God implying a certain commonality between human and God and simultaneous awareness of the substantial duality and distance separating God from the human, perceived as "the wholly Other" [*"das ganz Andere"*].[31]

Research often tends to distinguish between *mysticism*, which serves to characterize God and his manifestation in the world in living symbols and myths, and *philosophy*, which penetrates to the pure concept of "God" in the attempt to free it and distance it from all esoteric and anthropomorphic language.[32] Gershom Scholem, in his essay *Kabbala and Myth*,[33] pointed out that Judaism through the ages has been caught in the tension between these two forces;[34] in the movement of the Kabbalah, particularly between the twelfth and seventeenth centuries, both found expression in the mystical streams within Judaism.

Yet the Kabbalah itself, a many-faceted and diverse ideological movement, was certainly not spared this tension, and alongside the mystical and mythic propensity, characterized by figurative-symbolic thought, is another, rationalistic tendency, characterized by a conceptual-discursive thought process.[36] Such seminal kabbalists as Rabbi Azriel of Gerona, Rabbi Avraham Abulafia of Saragossa, and Rabbi Moshe Cordovero in Safed belonged to the rationalistic trend in Kabbalah although they were driven by a purely mystical impulse.

On the basis of this historical distinction, it seems Rav Kook can be seen as a descendent and follower of the rationalistic kabbalists, even though he is not a kabbalist in the usual sense of the word. This contention does not imply Rav Kook's thought is devoid of the dialectic tension between rationalism and mysticism. On the contrary, this tension is a constant companion throughout and, as we shall see, is anchored in the basic concepts of his teaching: "will" and "intellect" (or *hokhma*).

Domains of Rationalism and Mysticism

Rav Kook was not oblivious to the tension between the mystical and the rationalistic approaches that combine in his thought. In many of his works he approached the question of the nature of rationalism and mysticism and examined the relation between the two from various perspectives.

At first glance, mysticism seems to receive undeniable preference in his writings, whereas his relationship to philosophy and intellectual insight seems more ambivalent. But closer scrutiny reveals the subject must be considered on many levels and in several aspects, and the terms *rational* and *mystical* do not have one single, constant meaning.

We will not treat all the questions related to the subject and branching from it, as some of the points to be mentioned will be treated in depth in the next chapters. Our discussion here will focus on two aspects of Rav Kook's view of rationalism and mysticism and the connection between them: (1) rationalism and mysticism as separate fields of knowledge or awareness; and (2) the relation between intuition or mystical experience and discursive thought.

Kabbalists, for the most part, considered the Kabbalah superior to science and philosophy in its knowledge of the truth.[37] In that sense, Rav Kook's affirmation that the understanding grasped by philosophy "does not reach even a thousandth part of the truth, compared to the deep understanding of the world and all of being which comes from the holy,"[38] is characteristic of the thinker loyal to kabbalistic tradition. Yet at the same time, Rav Kook recognized and greatly esteemed the virtue of rational thought in terms of clarity of perception, and he even used the term *mystical* to signify obscurity and lack of clarity in thought. Mysticism, he believed, needs the "protection" of rational thought to keep it from deteriorating into imaginings.[39] Optimally, with proper ethical preparation and a healthy, balanced life,[40] one could, in his eyes, reach a level of clarity tantamount to rational, even in the domain of mystical conception. This approach, it seemed to Rav Kook, makes the task of delimiting the absolute boundaries separating rationalism and mysticism highly problematic, rendering all such limitations completely relative.[41] He wrote:

> When the effulgence of the intellect appears and the moral attribute harbored within it holds grains unequal to the essence of the thinker, who is illuminated by the light of that intellect, then the matter appears *obscure and mystical*. But when the moral will pulsing in the supreme and glowing intellect is completely equal to the essential will of he who occupies himself with those sublime aspects, then the brightness is transformed to a luminous mirror, and his perceptions become pure insights, vital and alive, upright in all paths of life and the inheritance of all generations.

Thus, man must not hasten to pass judgment about which phenomena or ideas are in the class of mysteries, because it all depends on his own moral state. Innumerable matters will seem obscure as long as one is morally unready. Yet when one is elevated, they will shine before him, brillant as the sky, and he will recognize them in the same way a normal, learned man understands the rational thoughts of scientific theory and ethics.[42]

Rav Kook did not usually attack philosophy in and of itself,[43] nor did he reject rational thought and the gains of science. Yet despite the legitimacy of philosophy, mysticism in his eyes remains superior both in stature and value in a multitude of respects. The difference between philosophy and mysticism lies first and foremost in the separate realms to which they are directed, a fact that naturally influences their nature and the importance of their philosophical or mystical perceptions. The domain of philosophy is limited, in Rav Kook's view, to knowledge of the world and the cosmos,[44] and thus, "as for the pure and tremendous being at the divine source," all that philosophy can grasp is no more than a "mere specter," "dark shadows," "solitary colors," "external knowledge."[45] Mysticism, on the other hand, is directed toward the infinite.[46] The object of mystical perception, "the holy of holies" or the "fundament of fundaments," is not in the realm of rational knowledge. "It is beyond all name, description and designation, elevated above all logic, even of the holy, in that very infinity it is higher than all profane, and in its lofty and profound gaze, the holy and the profane become equally important elements of reality."[47]

Indeed, the difference between the two domains is significant and implies rational philosophy cannot recognize the principle uniting all the details of reality, characterized by the "analytic quality";[48] that is, distinction and separation. "The gift of understanding how all views, feelings, and inclinations, great and small, are interconnected, and how they act on each other, how disparate worlds join together— this it cannot imagine."[49] Mysticism, in contrast, "perceives the unity in all that is, in its bodily form and its spirituality, in its greatness and smallness, inward knowledge."[50]

These words are not to be taken literally, for Rav Kook was undoubtedly familiar[51] with seminal and well-known philosophical theories in which the principle of unification, the "absolute spiritual" or the "One," was of central interest. Yet he most likely did not intend to make an overly simplistic distinction between rational philosophy and mysticism, and in another text, his full view of the question becomes clear. Rav Kook stated that the rational approach, in relating to the plane of entirety, disregards the details. "It swallows the fine, precise points and lines within the broader light, enabling it to ascend to more general expanses."[52] This is because logical thought cannot tolerate seeing oppositions and contradictions as real and still accept the description of reality as unity.[53] Mysticism, on the other hand, can take such a paradoxical stand, and in any case, it does not stop examining details[54] though it seeks the "unity in all of being." In other words, the aim of esoteric teaching is to discover the principle of unity in the particulars most of all, in each and every detail of reality:

> To show the entire world there is truly supreme greatness even in the smallest of beings. There is no loftiness before God and no degredation, for all is high and mighty, and all is humble and low; all is lofty in its source of life, the Everlasting light that flows through all; and all is base and humble as long as it imagines it is alone, bereft of the source of light—then all the *sefirot* are darkened.[55]

In other words, insistence on the principle of the unity among particulars themselves means that seeing reality as a collection of opposing principles depends on the perspective of the observer and does not reflect reality as it truly is; that is, as absolute unity.[56]

At the same time, however, Rav Kook held mystics must sometimes adopt a rational approach; that is, one that looks away from the details to grasp the unity. This "compromise" he makes in favor of rationality, in spite of its measure of superficiality, is based in his consciousness of the possibility that extreme concern for details may cause one to sink into narrowness and triviality, losing sight of the ultimate goal of mysticism: the perception of unity.[57] Thus Rav Kook's affirmation about the urgency of the path of rationality, of the "analytic" becomes clear, alongside the "synthetic" approach for the sake of "the construction and perfection of the spiritual world." He wrote:

> The analytic quality, after it has completed its examination to clarify the nature of each discipline, must leave room for the synthetic quality to appear in the light of the unifying soul, the mind of the sciences; all the spiritual faculties in their varied hues will be made visible by it as the many limbs of one body, shapely and vital, where a single soul, shapely vital and alive, of great power, shines within.[58]

Moreover, in another passage Rav Kook compared philosophy and mysticism in terms of their sources and claimed philosophy and prophecy are separate realms in which "the divine spirit" is manifest.[59]

The fact that mysticism preceives reality in its wholeness and unity seems to be related to the multidimensionality and immediacy of its manner of perception. "In perceptions of the holy . . . all revelation is embraced in each and every force: life, which contains all action, feeling, imagination, and intellect, all are gathered in a single unity."[60] Mysticism, or in Rav Kook's words, *secretness*, "penetrates the depths of all thoughts, of all feelings, of all tendencies, of all strivings, of all the worlds from beginning to end. It knows the unity of all being, in its materiality and its spirit, in its greatness and diminution, inward knowledge."[61]

Yet all that is not enough. Rav Kook described esoteric knowledge, "חכמת הקודש" as having a wide-reaching psychological influence, "in that it transforms the will and spiritual character of those who study it, advancing them by drawing their very essence to that same elevation in which it itself is substantiated.[62] Moreover, although the various sciences only "describe and present . . . what is in reality," mysticism can create a new reality, "bring endless creation into existence. Plant heavens and found the earth, even carving in relief a new form upon the meditating soul."[63]

Yet in this context, "esoteric knowledge" does not mean mystical contemplation alone. Rather it is the Torah in the broader sense, including its various domains and the many ways it can be learned. In any case, it is perceived as having unique qualities, as "wisdom above all wisdom"[64] from the perspective of the mystical hermeneutics and world-view. The reasoning is based explicitly on ideological elements of kabbalistic teaching: "this is because all matters of the holy come from the source of life, from the basic and vital element that brings all into being."[65] What is interesting is that, in Rav Kook's view, the roots not only of mysticism are in the sublime, but those of rationality as well,[66] and in the course of our discussion we will return to this point.

In sum, then, the major differences Rav Kook cited between rational thought and mystical perception are these: (1) mysticism is directed to a realm of supreme reality, whereas rational philosophy is directed to natural reality;[67] (2) mysticism comprehends the principle of unity even when it is occupied with details, something that "analytic" philosophy cannot do; (3) the mystical manner of perception is multidimensional and immediate, making use of all the forces of the personality at the same time, the same is not true of rational thought; (4) the influence of mystical thought on human will and actual events in the realm of the spirit is revolutionary, whereas rational cognition only reflects and documents an existing state of affairs.

Thus far, we have dealt primarily with the differences among the various realms of perception and the possibilities they contain. Now let us consider Rav Kook's view of mystical perception and knowledge of God. We begin with a passage from an unpublished manuscript, which reads:

> That supreme conception of spiritual perception is not limited to the logical intellect. No knowledge in the world can limit it, and all the force of its being and inspiration on man comes from the *holy power of its faith*,[68] the brillance of life is the light of faith, the sense of divine faith, in all its heroic might, this life is true life,[69] of which death has no part.[70]

In another passage, Rav Kook continued:

> Mystical teaching alone is the soul of faith, the soul of Torah, and the vigor of its life gives life to all that is fixed, all that is grasped by the mind, and all that is done in action. The open oneness of mystery embraces all creations, all conditions of thought and feeling, all manners of poetry and prose, all inclinations of life, aspirations, and hopes, all aims and ideals, from their utmost depths to their most soaring heights.[71]

That is to say, the holy force of faith is what enables the highest perception of the "secret" or of mystery." Yet, on the other hand, "the secret is the soul of faith"; that is, that element which makes faith possible is itself the essence of faith. What, then, is faith? Is it perception or intuition? Is it identical with the Torah, as implied in the repetition "the soul of faith, the soul of Torah"?[72] In the first citation, Rav Kook equated faith with "the brilliance of life," "true life . . . of which death has no part." Elsewhere he said: "Faith is neither intellect nor emotion but rather the most basic manifestation of the soul's essence."[73] "And the expressions 'sense of faith' or 'feeling of faith', not to mention 'science of faith' or 'rationality of faith' are no more than metaphorical, because faith itself has nothing to do with them, as it is beyond them all."[74] He continued, "the unique insight of faith, is itself, in its essence an aspect of God, it is the light of prophecy; in descending to a lower level it becomes the abundance of divine inspiration, for these at times descend as well and become one with the intellect and feeling as they are manifest." Faith thus designates or describes that basic power that brings life and reality into being, which, in other places in his writings he called *will* or *repentance* or *striving to closeness with God*.[75] In any case, faith, though perceived as divine force, a manifestation of the soul's essence, also designates a manner of relating to reality, a "unique perception" in his words, which characterizes prophecy, divine inspiration, and even lower degress of perception. Yet in a broader perspective, as we have said, mystical perception, like all levels of perception inferior to it, reflects the basic force causing reality to exist. It is seen as one of the manifestations of that force.[76]

May we, then, suppose the difference between faith and intellect is the difference between mysticism and reason and that all the many distinctions just recognized are only steps and stages on the path leading to perception of God? Here as well there seems to be no simple answer. In the previous passage, the intellect and emotions are indeed described as a lower level on the continuum whose summit is prophecy. Yet the term *intellect* appears in Rav Kook's writings in various senses: "natural intellect" as opposed to "the divine emanated intellect,"[77] and "secular intellect" compared to "holy intellect,"[78] and so forth. We soon realize what is called *divine emanated intellect* or *holy intellect* actually designates mystical perception. In our earlier discussion concerning epistemology, we considered the precise place of the intellect in its various connotations within the hierarchy of states of perception. Now we would like to stress that, despite the differences in value and importance between the "divine emanated intellect" and the "natural intellect," Rav Kook's relation to the latter, that is, to rational thought, is indisputably positive, seen as an irreplaceable and advantageous element:

> The divine emanated intellect, as a manifestation of the holy, cannot take the place of the natural intellect, which stands in relation to it as body to soul. And man must always fulfill the intellectual attribute of the natural intellect in all his qualities so that, in his spiritual dimension as well, a healthy soul will inhabit a healthy body; that is, the *holy spirit,* shining and whole *within the intellect, enlightened, limpid and clear.*[79]

We have already remarked on Rav Kook's desire to reveal the rational dimension[80] on the sublime level as well, and his very use of the term *intellect* to speak of mystical insight may itself bear witness to this tendency,[81] which reflects his true regard for the advantages of rational thought.

The roots of this insight can be traced to Rav Kook's metaphysical world-view and his consideration of *hokhma* and will as ontological elements and aspects of reality, a view based on the metaphysical plan of kabbalistic thought, according to which will [= *keter*] and *hokhma* stand at the apex of the system of the *sefirot*.[82] He spoke of the matter directly: "The source of rationality is by the revelation of the creature as divine *hokhma*, and the source of mystery is by its revelation as His will."[83] The nature of the relation between will and *hokhma* on the sublime level is naturally what determines the dynamic between rationalism and mysticism and their interrelation on the human level as well.[84]

This tendency is also expressed in passages written in programmatic, instructive style, such as this one: "Great enlightened men must draw their holy light from the heights of the intellect and not from the soul's excitement or an inflamed imagination, or from simple faith alone, but rather from the illumination of all these."[85] We find the same in passages that speak of the need to educate toward a balance of intellect and emotion[86] and encourage a way of life guided by such balance.[87]

Hence, along with the demand "to diminish the sovereignty of the human intellect over man's spirit to make room for the supreme rule of divine light over it," Rav Kook warned against thus harming "his divine and supreme side," for "all our intention is only to the outer shell of the human mind . . . but its purest point is God's light itself, a spark of the *Shekhina*."[88] Diminishing the dominion of the intellect is an "intellectual self-affliction" Rav Kook believed "man must use from time to time to free his conceptions from the relentless bondage of the human intellect, whose stupidity exceeds its wisdom."[89] And yet, "we must continually guard," said Rav Kook, "that the influence of faith [not lead] to extinguishing the light of the intellect,"[90] adding: "Faith without the consent of the intellect arouses anger and cruelty *for the most sublime aspect of man, the intellect*, is made miserable because of it."[91]

At this juncture, we must clarify that, even when Rav Kook spoke of mysticism as a realm or path to divine insights, he did not believe knowledge of the root of being, or in his words *the source of sources*, is possible. Moreover, most people are unable to grasp even "the general order of the world," that is, the laws by which reality exists, and Rav Kook emphasized: "Not only [the order] of the whole world, a divine secret entirely beyond the human mind, but also the order of their own [human] regions."[92] And if the order of the world is a divine secret beyond human grasp, at least that of most people, the root of being cannot be discussed at all: "We do not speak of and do not contemplate the source of sources, but even in not rejecting it, all lives on forever."[93]

Nonetheless, in Rav Kook's view the assumption of existence is evident,[94] and his writings thus contain no ontological proof, neither in the Kantian sense[95] nor in the manner of Anselm, Descartes, or

Spinoza.[96] Indeed, in contrast to Spinoza, in Rav Kook's view, the object of human investigation can never be absolute being in and of itself; that is, God. "After rational, favored knowledge, man has no knowledge of essences, neither of divine law nor of any concept whatsoever."[97] Discussion forever remains in the realm of relations between God and human and the world; that is, in the realm of phenomena. "The everlasting element of knowledge of God is the divinity beyond all reason, sealed within reason and emotion by the stamp of humility and the impossibility of its attainment."[98]

Rav Kook's harsh criticism of Spinoza's approach is concentrated in this point. Spinoza claimed the possibility of complete knowledge of being, of the "essence," and saw the concept of God and the concept of nature as completely identical (*Deus sive Natura*).[99] If Rav Kook rejected the possibility of perceiving essence or being out of hand, what, then, is the primary ontological element of which he spoke? It is "the holy."

"The holy in its essence is *hokhma*, awareness in itself, the brilliance of the supreme ideas, in their highest sublimity, unlimited, devoid of all particular character, even the most general traits of reality. For all is particular and limited relative to the breadth and boundlessness of supreme *hokhma* in its great glory."[100] This "essential holy," then, is in some way the fundamental basis of reality. Various terms are used to describe it: *hokhma, awareness, the brillance of supreme ideas,* and a few lines later, *the form of all the worlds.* All these terms, borrowed from different methods of thought, are directed toward a primary metaphysical element. His meaning is clear: reality is founded on an infinite idea that contains, undifferentiated, all of being. In other words, "all of existence is gathered in a single point."[101] The concept of the holy serves here in the sense of all-inclusive unity.[102]

At this point, however, we must attend to the testimony of the editor of *Orot ha-Kodesh;* in the introduction of the book he recorded that when Rav Kook was asked to define *the holy,* he answered: "what is revealed through the Torah, which is the supreme will." Rav Kook refused to speak of the concept of the "holy" in and of itself and described it according to its revelation, or in Kantian terms, according to its phenomena. Clearly, Rav Kook's words here reveal more than they conceal, for by identifying the "holy" with *hokhma* or with "supreme will" no small window is opened to an understanding of the matter; its fuller explanation is found in the fourth chapter.

In any case, Rav Kook clearly delineated the realm which even the highest perceptions cannot reach. Hence that the idea setting knowledge of God as man's religious ideal cannot be understood at face value:

Certainly, teleological knowledge is in no way in the same
realm as rational, moral knowledge. . . . And we suppose we
thus complete some plan, and at once the mind within us, and
our desiring spirit tells us we only yearn for the ideal of knowledge, yearn for the desire so great we cannot even meditate on
it. This desire, in any case *in and of itself* is that attribute of
knowing God and serving Him which we see as the ultimate goal.
The secret of Israel is most simply darkened *walking*, gradually
purifying itself, patiently and slowly, with calm and unending
diligence. . . . And identifying the teleological knowledge of
God with regular knowledge, intellectual or moral, constricts
and understates its meaning.[103]

In the chapter concerning epistemology, we discussed in depth
the epistemological views and system of reasons Rav Kook offered to
support his statement that there can be no true knowledge of the
object of religious consciousness. Here, in any case, in full awareness
of this problem, Rav Kook based the religious ideal not on knowledge
of God in and of itself, which after all is impossible, but rather on the
aspiration toward knowledge of God.[104] In his eyes, the consciousness
of this aspiration is itself an aspect of "knowing God and serving
God."[105] This helps us understand the tendency in his view to define
Jewish mysticism not as a certain level of perception, nor as a realm of
perceptions or experiences with clearly defined boundaries, but rather as a process of self-refinement, of purifying one's thought out of
yearning for divine knowledge.[106]

Mysticism and Reason—Experience and Interpretation

When we speak of the relationship between mystical experience
and the theoretical idea accompanying it, we must distinguish between the term *mystical interpretation*, in which W. T. Stace includes
theories developed by mystics or philosophers on the basis of mystical experiences, and the term *philosophical mysticism*, which we prefer
for several reasons.[107] The term *mystical interpretation* naturally assumes that mystical experience is the object of theory, which interprets
and formulates it conceptually. Use of the term does not necessarily
imply one-directional movement from experience to interpretation.
Mystical philosophy can include varied trends and directions: from
esoteric experience to rational understanding, from discursive, logical
thought to mystical intuition or experience.[108]

In a few contexts, Rav Kook spoke clearly of these two trends,
and he did not seem to favor one over the other. I say this with

reservation, for in the course of our discussion we will see Rav Kook considered the first trend a miracle so rare that it could not be deemed a recommended path toward grasping the truth. Let us consider the matter more closely.

"There are two ways to perception—" Rav Kook wrote, "from above downward—אור ישר ["direct light"], and from beneath upward—אור חוזר ["reflected light"]."[109] Interestingly, in his method, the kabbalistic terms *or yashar* and *or hozer*[110] designate the two approaches characteristic of mystical philosophy.[111] Rav Kook explained the matter at various opportunities, first presenting passages showing interpretation of mystical experience through rational thought: "When we gaze at the pure secrets of the Torah with a faithful heart, although the spiritual things are conceived by the imagination, they are then *interpreted* by all the means of the intellect, and become equal to all the ways of lucid reason."[112]

Nonetheless, Rav Kook averred, rational thought cannot exhaust the full dimensions of mystical experience: clearly, "even though all the depth and the height, all the life and originality in the abundance of divine inspiration cannot be contained in the framework of logical analysis, however much can be contained in those vessels, however much of the affluence of the supreme soul can inspire life in those bodies, is very very good, and does a great deal to elevate the essence of humanness."[113] And in any case ["spiritual things" = mystical experience] are more numerous and greater than all the interpretations, and will be the spring that enriches all the rivers flowing from it with glory and greatness."[114]

In another instance Rav Kook pointed to the intuitive nature of mystical perception and defined the talk of rational thought that follows in its wake: "Sublime contents are revealed in the spirit in a *surprising revelation*, with no systematic order, with no apparent cause, and afterwards *reason* comes and clarifies, ordering the branches of awareness, examining everything in its related causes."[115] And in yet another passage:

> We listen with general attentiveness, and we hear a speaking voice. Although articulated *letters and separate words*[116] are not audible, all our labor in Torah and science is only to discern, in that sublime voice that ever sounds in our inward ear, as many clear things as we can, that we may present them before ourselves and others, in a way leading to action, to ordered and careful study.[117]

Mystical philosophy is represented here as something that clarifies and describes the undifferentiated substance of mystical experience. Discursive thought does not have the power to grasp the truth. Rav Kook claimed explicitly that "Truth is not revealed to man bit by bit, but in a total appearance all at once."[118] By the sparkling of divine inspiration, great orders of wisdom are perceived all at once, without toil; they harbor delight, beauty, holiness, blessing, love, valor, and reach the lower worlds through emanation as they are revealed in the soul hewn from all of them.[119]

On the one hand, truth is perceived only by the strength of intuition,[120] but on the other, Rav Kook spoke of the role of discursive thought to empower one "to that general appearance."[121] Science in general contributes to this empowerment in that by grace of its accomplishments in exploring nature, "the wisdom of *the act of Creation* becomes more and more a revealed knowledge publicly explained," and thus even "divine truths . . . increasingly become *things equal to every soul,* until it is no longer possible to explain simple faith to average people except by broadly presenting sublime truths standing high above the world before them. And the open gateways of the *act of Creation* themselves cause the gates of the act of the *Divine Chariot* to be opened."[122] In these words and in his previous statement concerning "רז ישראל", the secret of Israel, which essentially means "going toward" and "longing" that will never be completely realized as some "program," the utopian undertone is unmistakable. Particularly interesting is the role and status attributed to science as a vital factor in the process of realizing the utopia. What is remarkable in this perception is that the redemption is considered the very process of perfection of the human consciousness, a process that will end only in the messianic age.[123]

Yet beyond this general preparation Rav Kook saw philosophy as a legitimate and promising path and claimed that perhaps "the real divine revelation will in fact be through the intellect, and the more examination and philosophizing, the more holy faith and devotion there will be, and the more illumination of the holy spirit."[124] Moreover, conceptual, discursive thought is a vital precondition to the attainment of truths, and without it we would find nothing of what we desire of spiritual insights."[125]

How, then, can Rav Kook's other statement be understood, that true perception comes only through mystical intuition, and that it is the task of philosophy to interpret it? These two versions may be resolved in the following explanation, in which Rav Kook held that mystical intuition is a rare instance of revelation, tantamount to a miracle, and not the normal and suggested path to sublime perceptions. He wrote: "As an exception, some crack may form in the walls of the cave,[126] which blocks out the divine luminousness, and the hidden light suddenly flashes, unlike the gradual way of revealed knowledge; such miracles must be accepted with joy, but one should not count on miracles, and the customary order is to go from the revealed to the concealed, from the detail to the general,"[127] and thus Rav Kook concluded, "better a wise man than a prophet."[128]

In any case, even the recognition of the indispensibility of discursive thought does not mean raising it to the level of sublime mystical knowledge, and with great consistency Rav Kook went on to state that "all knowledge coming from research is no more than a means to attaining that highest knowledge."[129]

Our discussion clearly uncovers the tension everpresent in Rav Kook's world, and in his view, such tension exists in the world of all mystics: "Those whose spirit shines, their soul forever does two interconnected spiritual actions. Manifold emanations of sublime images are ceaselessly conceived in them, coming from above downward, and intellectual compositions of *bina* [understanding] are put together from down below upward, and the forces kick at each other."[130] This tension between the mystical and the rational tendency originates, as well, from the exhaustion and weakness ensuing from intensive mystical experiences, weariness that causes the desired perceptions themselves to be blurred,[131] but primarily from the awareness that mysticism and rational knowledge are two legitimate paths, and the advantages and disadvantages of each balance the other.[132]

9

Mystical Language, Myth, and Symbol

Expression and Concealment

In the previous chapter, we spoke of the relationship between mystical experience and rational thought. Our discussion here will circumscribe the means available to speak of this experience or, more exactly, the question of Rav Kook's mystical language. It is usually said that mysticism is a kind of knowledge that can be expressed only symbolically;[1] the English scholar W. R. Inge even presented a view claiming a fundamental link between mysticism and symbolism in which mysticism is a way of viewing reality as the symbolic expression of something else beyond the symbol.[2] The question finds concrete manifestation in Rav Kook's idiosyncratic writing style, whose strangeness was probed in the introduction of this book.[3] The stylistic element deserves exploration, as it reflects a significant and characteristic theme in his thinking. One has the impression Rav Kook developed a new mystical language that is neither symbolic nor mythic.

In an essay devoted to the question, A. Steinsaltz wrote that the gap between kabbalistic content and nonkabbalistic language is what engenders Rav Kook's obscure style. Steinsaltz added that the impetus for Rav Kook's choice is "the desire to express the contents of the Kabbalah in such a way that it is accessible to anyone, even if he is unable or unwilling to enter the Kabbalah, into all the intimidating technical difficulties involved in its study."[4] This explanation, however, is at odds with Rav Kook's own words and does not correspond with the basic assumptions underlying his teaching.

193

Did Rav Kook indeed wish "to make the Kabbalah and its conclusions more popular and clear to every Jew" in Steinsatz's words?
Rav Kook's own words do not confirm such a thing. He wrote:

> Knowledge of the highest secret matters is not meant to
> spread through the world in a great expansion, that many may
> know of them, for it is impossible. And if many know of them in
> their external aspect, they will know nothing of their internal
> content, and all this will do more harm than good. Indeed, this
> knowledge must penetrate to all secrets that contain a divine
> element of supreme contemplation. And those individuals
> unique in their spiritual height, raise the world from its deg-
> redation by their very existence and not by their tangible in-
> fluence.[5]

Moreover, not only does Rav Kook have no interest in spreading
the contents of the Kabbalah and see such a thing as harmful, its
translation "to language meaningful beyond the bounds of the Kabbalah," in Steintaltz's expression, is both undesireable and impossible
in his eyes: "Concealed matters must be explained and understood
through concealment, and not by revealed means. This system in
gematria is 'תרדמה' [literally, 'slumber']. The hidden through the hidden becomes clear; in the myriad parts of the mystery each illumi-
nates another, and from this mystery comes forth light."[6] In another
place Rav Kook added more strongly:

> The language of mystery is the sublime language, which
> speaks the absolute truth without retreating. And this clear
> speech needs to be guarded, that the light of faith not fall from
> its great height, from that place where the primal light dwells in
> its natural state, *and all that linguistic connection is bound to it in
> deepest truth*, to that lowly place of the practical world, where
> only the *tongue of falsehood* is spoken, and lies become acceptable,
> and truth is naturally affected. And by this same *falsehood* of
> deceitful human beings stealing away in the garb of truth, if
> those utterances of the sublime language of the source of truth
> would weigh things using that false plummet, they would *de-
> stroy the world*.[7]

These passages indicate the Kabbalah is not to be translated, since
kabbalistic language is intrinsically bound to kabbalistic content, or as
Rav Kook said, "all that linguistic connection is bound to it in deepest

truth." Thus, any translation, in Rav Kook's eyes, amounts to falsehood, counterfeit, and destruction.

Two questions, however, remain. The first is related to an indisputable fact; that is, Rav Kook's thought indeed contains theoretical elements originating in the metaphysical world-view of the Kabbalah, although his language is not recognizably kabbalistic. The second question is related to Rav Kook's view that the achievements of science turn "divine truths . . . to things equal to every soul, until even simple faith can be explained to average people only by broadly presenting sublime truths before them, truths that stand beyond this world."[8]

If Rav Kook did indeed reject translation of kabbalistic language, why did he not normally use the technical language of kabbalistic teaching, and how does his opposition to the dissemination of the Kabbalah coexist with his belief that his generation is indeed ready to understand the secrets of the Torah? In searching for a solution to these questions, we must consider three factors: (a) Rav Kook's relativistic stance on epistemology, which, as we have seen in Chapter 2, permits no dogmatic and consistent bond to any single kabbalistic method. This helps us understand the fact, already outlined by R. Schatz[9] that the dimensions of Rav Kook's thought are not enclosed in the method or conceptual system of medieval philosophy, nor is it a continuation and simple conclusion of Lurianic Kabbalah. (b) Rav Kook's belief that the Kabbalah is not only a tradition of mystical knowledge handed down from time immemorial but also the original ideas of the individual Jew, creations of his free spirit, considered "mysteries of the Torah," "*whether spoken in the same language and style that other masters of mysteries used, or spoken in another style and another literary form.*"[10] (c) Consciousness of the originality of his work, as he himself bears witness: "I am not a learned man . . . but I have been favoured by God with an *original gift*."[11] While Rav Kook believed the secrets of the Kabbalah should be transmitted only in kabbalistic language, since he saw his thought as original he had no need for classical kabbalistic symbolism, thus he used language freely.[12] He himself explains his unique style:

> My thoughts are wider than the seas; to express them in prosaic words I cannot, for I am unwillingly forced to be a poet, yet one who is free. I could not be bound in the fetters of meter and rhyme. I flee from simple prose, from its heaviness, its constriction, and I could not put myself in other confines, perhaps even bigger and more depressing than the weight of the prose from which I flee.[13]

The abstruseness and awkwardness of his style, then, do not come from the desire to communicate kabbalistic themes in nonkabbalistic language, but rather from the personal and original nature of his thinking, which cannot be transmitted with precision in kabbalistic symbolic language, yet finds no other language able to express its creative and free spirit. Rav Kook was aware of the subjective character of the mystical intuition at the basis of his thought, and that is the source, in his eyes, of the difficulty inherent in its expression. He wrote:

> Mystical knowledge is unique in every individual. It is bound up with his selfhood, is unrepeatable and transmitted by no *sound or explanation*. "They shall be yours only" (Proverbs 5:17). A righteous man shall live by his own, his very own faith. And from this luminous faith, which forms a separate Eden-paradise for him, he goes forth to walk in the gardens of the Lord, bounded as public domain, where his mind intermingles with that of his fellows.[14]

This theoretical reasoning expresses the existential experience of "spiritual muteness," and many passages reflect this terrible distress. An example:

> We feel this "spiritual muteness," alas, how much we have to say, how great is the light of justice and wisdom illuminating us in the depth of our souls, but how shall we discover it, how clarify it, how will we utter and bring forth even the tiniest edge of that sublime brightness, for that, the gates are shut before us. In prayer we approach them, with supplication we knock, in joy and praise we raise our voices, offering allegory and thoughts, keeping watch by the doors, perhaps they will open a crack, only a needle's breadth before us, and words will stream from our mouths, and our tongues will be as flowing streams, rivers of honey and butter.[15]

Rav Kook held that even when he spoke of clear and understandable things, whenever he said something original, from the "depths of his soul," his words held sublime truths "beyond the normal ken of sense and logic," making them difficult to explain in normal language. That, in his eyes, was "a trustworthy key to difficult elements in my words, and those of all who speak in this manner, ancient and modern."[16]

In any case, although Rav Kook was aware of the limitations of his words, he did not abandon his aspiration to express,[17] "even stuttering" the message he believed to be divine revelation. Therefore he wrote: "And our words shall be as refining fire and an anvil breaking rocks asunder, *for they are the word of God,* and they stream from the source of holy and life-granting light; happy is he who harkens to me."[18] This is no mere fulfillment of the spiritual need for self-expression but rather a feeling of responsibility that compels Rav Kook to elucidate in a reasonable, acceptable way "this long process of study [toward knowledge of values of the holy and profane], for resolution of all the difficult questions of our private and collective lives depends on this knowledge, and we must examine it over and over again, in literature and in life, without cease, neglecting it not for a single moment."[19]

As for the second question—Rav Kook's opposition to the dissemination of the Kabbalah, on the one hand, and his belief that his generation is in fact ready to comprehend the secrets of the Torah, on the other—the explanation is related not only to his view of the contribution made by scientific advances, for that reason itself is connected to Rav Kook's messianic vision and his belief our age is in the grips of awakening powers and abilities that can lead us to discoveries and transcendence inaccessible in the past: "Without the impudence that comes before the advent of the Messiah the secrets of the Torah could not be completely revealed. Only with the coarsening of the emotions caused by impudence can the highest intellectual lights be taken in, and at last all will return to perfect completion."[20] Rav Kook's implication is that in fact "impudence," that is, the atheism of the new generation, of the Zionist pioneers and the Maskilim—this very atheism is paradoxically what enables a spiritual ascent that would not be possible without it. Rav Kook went even further, saying: "The impudent sons, who destroy all paths and boundaries, shall become of the highest order, the level of Moses our rabbi and the supreme luminousness of Adam haRishon. The entire tree of life to the depths of its goodness will be revealed in them and by their hand."[21]

At the level of "the supreme brightness of Adam haRishon" nature itself is perceived as holy; in other words, it becomes clear "nothing in the world is absolutely profane"[22] and to this end, among others, are the secrets of the Torah revealed in the world.[23] "The Tree of Life" as something that will be revealed in and by "the sons of the impudent" designates the *sefira* of *tiferet,* an aspect of the Written teaching and identified with the nation of Israel,[24] in contrast to the "Tree of Life" that indicates freedom, the Torah in its mystical sense rather than its historical manifestation.[25] Indeed, in the Kabbalah, the perception of the Torah as a historical manifestation is only one of the diverse ways it is revealed in various times,[26] and thus we understand why the freedom evidenced in the atheism of the "sons of the impudent" corresponds to the mystical meaning of the Torah that, in the Messianic era, will be the manner in which divine truth is revealed.

In sum, we can state Rav Kook's thought contains almost no esoteric content for its own sake. That is, he makes no effort to hide things by writing in a certain way, nor does he wish to reveal kabbalistic secrets by translating them to nonkabbalistic language. His writing is spontaneous, imbued with a spirit of freedom and sense of creativity and originality, and if there are stylistic enigmas and obscurities in the course of generally clear prose passages, they can be attributed to two causes: the mystic element of his thought, which resists all endeavors to reveal it,[27] and his aspiration to formulate his views in conceptual and logical terms. Awareness of the individual, innovative nature of his thought and of all that distinguishes him from classic Kabbalah induced him to create a mystical language suited to his personal experience and his own contemplation. This language is not poetry, nor should it be seen as common prose, and it is above all not an outshoot of classic kabbalistic symbolism.

Myth and Symbol

The conclusions we have reached up to this point by no means preclude the fact that Rav Kook's language abounds with allusions to Jewish literature, the inheritance of generations, and many of these associations point the reader to kabbalistic works. This fact demands consideration of Rav Kook's use of kabbalistic symbols and even, at times, of myths. Such examination is also critical to avoid two widespread beliefs: one, the claim Rav Kook was "more a poet than a systematic thinker,"[28] giving birth to doubts whether Rav Kook indeed had a philosophic method; and the second, that the metaphysical schema found in classic kabbalistic symbolism is the key to reconstructing his theological views.[29] Rav Kook's works do provide some support to proponents of these beliefs, but their undue exaggeration impedes a comprehensive view of the real picture.

As we have seen earlier, Rav Kook's thought represents an all-embracing world-view, within internal structure and order; its parts become clear in light of their underlying principles, for in that sense, what we have before us is a philosophic method we are obliged to uncover from beneath the cloak of unsystematic formulation. Yet the systematic root of this thought is not expressed in consistent use of terminology and symbols with defined theological connotations. On the contrary, it can be deciphered in spite of the absence of a clear conceptual code.

Rav Kook saw kabbalistic symbols as somewhat technical terms designating no more than the external aspect of reality, and in his view, poetic style is best equipped to express the internal dimension. This idea is reflected in the following:

> Just as psychology speaks of the nature of the soul from the point of view of inward observation of its depths in song and the poetic internal insight, and science speaks of the phenomena of revealed life, so divine emanation, as the soul of being, speaks of the poetic contemplation of divine inspiration, of the inner light; and in the case of divine science, in the phenomena of orders, actions and visions *in the vessels*. The essential spirit rises beyond the revealed laws of psychology and divine emanation is above creation.[30]

Elsewhere, Rav Kook continued: "Gaze upon the lights in their inwardness. Your soul will not be swallowed up by the names, the phrases, and the letters; they are delivered into your hand and not you into theirs."[31]

At the same time, Rav Kook defended the right of the Kabbalah to express itself in symbolic, even mythic, language. He rejected all rationalistic criticism on the issue,[32] and even dismissed the assumption "there is mythological imagination here" and that, at least in this case, the Kabbalah is "foreign born."[33] He held that "worldly allegories do not harm the pure unity of the Godhead," for "the divine, in its attribute of unity, is above the common image of unity, and it truly transcends unity to the same extent that it transcends multiplicity."[34] This view, that in truth it makes no difference whether the divinity is spoken of in terms of unity or multiplicity because the concept of divine unity is superior to both of them, is very characteristic of Rav Kook's teaching[35] and demonstrates the relativity of his method compared to all other conceptual systems and to any particular image of the world.

Rav Kook's own use of kabbalistic myths and symbols was not the same in all cases. At times, kabbalistic symbolism served as an illustration or turn of phrase emerging in the flow of writing, and expressions like "holy and bright light," "pure light full of brightness"[36] and so forth cannot always be given precise and definitive interpretation. Sometimes the symbols of the *sefirot* are used to describe unified being in the widest, most encompassing sense and sometimes in its various aspects, spiritual and material, but not necessarily with adhesion to the original, defined essence of the symbols.[37]

Consider, for example, a symbol of outstanding mythic nature: *Shi'ur Komah*, which in Kabbalah embodies the mystical figure of the godhead.[38] It is easy to see how a conceptualization of this important symbol takes place; these are Rav Kook's words: "When organic understanding augments, bringing all of being to one great mystical figure of the godhead, the great connection the world has to its details, its events and instances, its ways and all its degrees to the existing upper and lofty worlds. . ."[39] In this context, *Shi'ur Komah* points to the idea of all-inclusive unity, the result of increased "organic understanding"; that is, a level of perception that sees reality as an entire organism. Rav Kook seems to have summoned concepts borrowed from two very different cultural systems, because both kabbalistic terms and modern philosophical terms are equally insufficient, in and of themselves, to express his ideas with as much precision as he would like. the truth Rav Kook wished to express is too enormous and profound for both the expression and the symbol. Clearly, though, the role and status of the symbol are different here than in the Kabbalah. Although it arouses an association with the sources of his metaphysical model, at the same time, its connection to the concept of "organism" bears witness to its changed significance in Rav Kook's own perception.[40]

In another instance, Rav Kook used a different formulation of the symbol, explaining it from another perspective as well. He wrote:

> The *mitzvot* themselves are the universal "Uebermensch" himself; that is, the qualitative essence of the entire form of spiritual being in supreme morality in its most exalted aim. The image of life that comes into being through the fulfillment of the commandments is an ideal life, not only for man as an individual and social being—that life is an ideal for all of existence.[41]

Here the "Uebermensch," "האדם העליון" identified in Kabbalah with *Shi'ur Komah* represents, according to Rav Kook's own interpretation, the essence of being, the teleological ideal all of being seeks to realize. Fulfillment of the *mitzvot*, thus, is a realization of the principle of divine and cosmic life within the life of the individual person.[42]

The same symbol undergoes yet a third transformation in another passage: "The free will, illuminated by the supreme intellect, is the essence of the being that is revealed in its inwardness, and that is the spirit of Adam haRishon in all its wholeness."[43] Here as well an abstract concept, "the essence of being," is combined with the kabbalistic symbol "Adam haRishon" as a sort of abstract interpretation of a particular kabbalistic theory expressed in mythic, symbolic language. We must, of course, remember Rav Kook sometimes described the interrelations among the *sefirot* themselves, and in that case the symbols usually bore specific theological meaning, though he might expand their presence to the realm of psychology or epistemology.[44]

Rav Kook might discuss a certain subject on two levels, the symbolic and the revealed, and one does not know which has precedence in his mind, for both could stand alone; and in any case there is no evidence of artful translation from kabbalistic language to any other manner of speech. Examples of these phenomena are found throughout this book in numerous discussions, but I would like to show their relevance in the case of two mutually related subjects: the Torah and *Knesset Israel*. As these subjects will be treated in another context, here I will be brief. In our present discussion, we must consider not only content but style as well, and particularly the use of symbols. Here, then, are Rav Kook's words, first of all concerning Torah:

> We receive the Written teaching through the highest and most comprehensive image of our soul. From within we feel the flash of splendor [*tiferet*] in the living, general light of all existence. We reach, through it, beyond all reason and intellect, we sense the spirit of the Lord supreme hovering [fluttering] above us, touching and not touching, flying just above life and casting His light upon it. The light flashes, sparkles, penetrates all, embracing everything under the heavens. It is *not the spirit of the nation* that gave birth to this great light—rather the divine spirit creates all creatures, this Torah of life, the root when all the world is created.
>
> In the Oral teaching, we descend into life . . . we sense that the *spirit of the nation,* fused, like flame to ember, to the light of the Torah of truth—this spirit, by its special nature, caused the oral law to be created in the unique form it was, and the *human Torah* is surely contained in that divine Torah.[45]

We remark that the entire passage, in its poetic style as well as content, seems to reflect a mystical experience, and except for one allusion in the word *tiferet,* employs no kabbalistic symbols. Yet this single symbol, invoked more as a turn of phrase than as a technical term, is enough to hint that Rav Kook's view of the relation of the written to the Oral Torah corresponds to the kabbalistic model that identifies the former to the *sefira* of *tiferet* and the latter to the *sefira* of *malkhut,*[46] the lowest of all the *sefirot.*

In another passage, also formulated in nonkabbalistic language, Rav Kook held that the Written teaching is superior to the Oral teaching on the level of revelation alone, whereas "in its internal form, was the Torah not given to Israel by grace of its highest internal quality; that hidden virtue of its character induced the heavenly Torah to appear before it *and the Oral Teaching in its essence is higher than the Written teaching*—the words of the Sages are more beloved than words of the Torah."[47]

There is a basis in kabbalistic literature for the idea that all we have in our world is the Oral teaching and that the Written Torah is a mystical concept,[48] yet this idea does not change the superiority of the Written Torah as a matter of principle. Yet Rav Kook's claim is much more far-reaching: it is in fact in our revealed world that the Written teaching is perceived as superior to the Oral teaching, whereas on the fundamental internal plane, in its most supreme "root," the Oral teaching is higher than the written. The argument Rav Kook introduced to support this idea comes not from the Kabbalah but from the Rabbis: "the words of the Sages are more beloved than words of the Torah."[49]

This idea coincides with Rav Kook's view that "acceptance by the entire people" or "the nation's agreement" is the source of the authority of Torah and halacha, and he develops it in another context[50] with no overt link to any particular kabbalistic theory. Indeed, Rav Kook's perception of the essential nature of the Jewish people is clearly related to the kabbalistic belief identifying *Knesset Israel* with the *sefira malkhut*,[51] and thus he can even speak of a parallel between *Knesset Israel* and the Oral teaching. This fact elucidates the theological background that makes Rav Kook's stance *possible* regarding "the nation's agreement" as the source of halachic authority,[52] as well as the depiction of original metaphysical speculations made by a chosen few Jews as "secrets of the Torah."[53] Yet as we saw in the passages introduced earlier, Rav Kook went much further. The development of his views on those and other subjects is the fruit of a synthesis of all his knowledge and personal experience. His thoughts on many issues did not stem directly from kabbalistic theories and are thus not completely dependent on them, although some of them can be seen as extracting fundamental elements buried in kabbalistic theories or in their underlying principles.

What is true of kabbalistic theories and symbolism holds all the more so in the case of kabbalistic myth. Rav Kook's voluminous works contain almost no mythic elements, and there are naturally no allusions to mythic belief. In isolated instances we may find some phrases with mythic-dramatic tinges[54] or allusions to myths appearing in Midrash and the Kabbalah, and in all these cases the mythic formulation is no more than an illustration of an abstract idea. A few examples follow. In one of his letters[55] Rav Kook spoke of the difference between spirituality and corporeality and asserted that in truth there is no difference whatsoever between the two concepts because "the essence of that difference is only in our own level of perception." Our impression of lack or of materiality is, in Rav Kook's eyes, "the truth cast to earth and growing, ever growing." These words allude to a midrash recounting a conference held by the Holy One blessed be He with the angels before man was created, following which God cast truth down to the earth and created man despite the opposition of truth (personified).[56] In the course of his discussion, Rav Kook offered an innovative interpretation of the midrash: the truth cast down to earth signifies the opacity (nontransparency) of reality, which obscures the absolute truth from the human gaze. The truth cast down grows along with the development of human awareness until it reaches the level at which the unity of reality will be perceived and it will become evident that "materiality" has no real existence.[57]

In another passage, Rav Kook undertook a polemic against the German philosopher Schopenhauer and countered his view of "blind will." In his conclusion Rav Kook said: "In the work of a few thinkers, the *kelipah* [shell] of the blind crocodile is revealed in all its aspects and the holy of heart must recognize it in order to defeat it."[58] The *tannin* or "blind crocodile" is a very ancient symbol, appearing throughout kabbalistic literature, and its connotations are undeniably mythological.[59] Here, once again, Rav Kook's use of the term serves as a fascinating and original manner of interpretation: *blind crocodile* designates the philosophic stance that rejects the theory of teleological evolution and sees reality as the caprice of blind will.

One last example will conclude our discussion. In a text contemplative as a diary entry, found in a manuscript, Rav Kook spoke in the first person of his love of God flowing from thought and observation of the world and being. The thirst for more sublime insights induces the appearance of ideas and thought that cannot endure because they do not correspond with being in its present state. This account, founded on personal mystical experience, describes a conscious process by means of the kabbalistic myth of "the death of the Kings."[60] The myth, in this case, is no more than a literary framework for presenting Rav Kook's own ideas and experiences. He wrote:

> I am filled with love for God. I know that what I ask, what I love, has no name. How can something have a name that is more than everything, more than goodness, more than the Essence, more than existence; I love, and I say I love God. The light of *En-sof* dwells in the expression of the Name, in expres-

sion of the Lord, and in all the names and appelations in the heart of thinking, teaching man, as his soul ascends higher and higher.

I cannot satisfy my soul with the love that comes from reason, from the search for God's light by the world, by the being that penetrates within the eyes.

In our souls, divine lights are born to us, divine powers [אלקים רבים] for the sense in our spirit of the one true God. And before one man, God in His deepest truth appears, masters us, conquers all our spirit, the spirit of all existence. In every place there is idea, feeling, thought, and will, everywhere there is noble spiritual life, *divine light reigns*, rules, and conquers, sparkles in splendor, glorifying and praising, enlivening, raising, all in the brightness of the light of being. *Reigns and dies*, the kingdom is finite as long as it is part of the world and of existence.

Sometimes the light grows stronger. Desire longs for more delicate light, more internal, more true in itself, more powerful in its inward essence; the light appears over the vessel, thought over being—this state cannot exist. The content does not suit. *The vessels shatter, the kings die*, the gods die, their soul flees away, from the skies to the distant heavens, the bodies fall down to the world of separation; being is left naked, alone, torn, scattered. And within it, hidden and secret, is an endless desire for supreme light, everlasting mercy placed His sparks of light in the broken vessels. In every movement of every realm of life, in every essence there is a spark. The glimmer of a spark, smaller, fainter than faint.

The inner light, light of the supreme God, building and establishing, gathers the scattered, repairs worlds without end, orders and joins. The reign of all the worlds is revealed, the light of *En-sof* in the inward soul, from God to the world new light is born, the brillant glory of the Lord's countenance.[61]

Conclusion

Before we turn, in the next chapter, to an examination of Rav Kook's teaching from a phenomenological point of view, let us sketch a rough outline of the methodological elements we have considered and crystallize the thesis we have proposed as a framework for understanding his views.

In Rav Kook's thought, rationality is not only a method used to express truths discovered along mystical paths nor a mere means of communication, but rather an adequate expression able to unite aspects of being; it is thus essential to mysticism to create a complete conception of reality in all its dimensions. The dialectical relationship between mysticism and rationality reflects a dialectic of ontological significance—at one pole "will" and at the other "wisdom," *hokhma*.

Yet, in Rav Kook's monistic outlook, the fundamental concepts of "will" and *hokhma* and the tension between them bear more than ontological significance alone. They are the central pillars supporting all three major realms of interest: the ontological, the epistemological, and the anthropological or ethical. Rav Kook's relativistic, pragmatic views in the epistemological realm preclude a dogmatic stance in the realm of ontology, and the focus of attention is therefore transferred to the anthropological-ethical realm.

The tension between rational and mystical elements is vital to the primary interest of his thought, an interest that can be formulated in existential terms: "self-realization"[62] or "completeness of self."[63] Only when both approaches exist, the rational and the mystical, can all one's qualities be realized, the diverse aspects of one's being. The same dialectical principle acts not only in humankind but in all of existence. The individual, like the entirety of reality on a lower level, is actually a manifestation of the divine on a high level, becoming clearer and clearer, more and more revealed as consciousness grows clearer and will intensifies.

The idea of self-realization carries no existential connotations in Rav Kook's thought, although the existential dimension of his personal experience cannot be ignored. When all is said and done, the idea is identified with the mystical aspiration, thus rendering it an undeniably mystical idea. Self-realization or completeness of self are achieved by the very existence of the mystical aspiration in human beings, an aspiration seen as the tip of the iceberg of a cosmic dynamic toward completeness and harmony. This yearning is described in various terms in Rav Kook's writings. It is identified with the concept of *teshuvah* (repentance), with the ideal of *devekut* (cleaving, adhesion) or the desire for intimacy with God, it underlies the will to know the secret of unity, and it is no less the very essence of the will to freedom and the idea of freedom itself that runs like a scarlet thread throughout Rav Kook's oeuvre. Freedom, for Rav Kook, is an existential interest because he held it as a theoretical challenge. The thirst for freedom, the longing for space and unlimitedness, is linked, for him, to the mystical aspiration to expand the self, to expand knowledge, to break the bounds of logic and conceptual expression. Freedom, too, is realized only through the existence of a dialectical relationship between will and wisdom, the mystical and the rational.

10

Before the Secret of Existence

The philosopher Harold Hoffding remarked that the history of thought, contains two types of thinkers:[1] the first searches for unity, connections, continuity, gradual transitions in reality; whereas the second looks for seminal innovations, sharp transitions, revolutionary changes, defined boundaries. Both are universal psychological traits present in human spiritual life as a whole.

The first attitude described here is probably similar in spirit to the mystical type; but in contrast to the thinker who *searches* for unity, connections, and continuity in reality, the mystic type has *already found* them. It is not a question of fundamental and evident assumptions, the bequest of generations of philosophers, but rather *basic experiences* that indelibly mark the mystic's view of reality.

Now that we have presented and examined the basic principles underlying Rav Kook's thought, the time has come to consider some aspects of his sense of reality from a phenomenological point of view, those basic experiences that determine the mystical nature of his thought. By *mystical nature* I mean mysticism as an a priori spiritual attitude, a unique approach to reality that is no mere mood or idiosyncratic orientation but rather a manner of experiencing reality bound up with a feeling of unshakeable certainty.

Our discussion will concentrate on three points of Rav Kook's general experience: (1) the experience of identity; (2) the experience of metaphysical ability; and (3) the mystical aspiration. The three are connected; regarding Rav Kook's meditative works, they reflect the mystical nature of his attitude in the presence of the secret of being, on the one hand, and his unwillingness, on the other, to resort exclusively to the mystical path either in contemplation or action.

207

The Experience of Encompassing Unity

The experience of being united with the whole and the conception of all of reality as absolute unity is generally accepted as one
summary of the mystical experience.[2] We have already mentioned
that mysticism is perceived as a discipline directed to the absolute,
whose objective is complete fusion with the supreme power.[3] We also
pointed out such a perception of mysticism does not reflect the
unique nature of Jewish mystical thought. Nonetheless, despite careful avoidance of formulations suggesting absolute unification with
God, we cannot ignore the fact that seeing reality as an organism, or
as an absolute unity bond by no clear limits, whose details are merely
illusory, is a dominant and seminal force in Jewish mysticism as well;
in the speculative trend in particular, we find formulations clearly
tinged with pantheism and panatheism.[4]

For Rav Kook, in any case, all-embracing unity is a primary
intuition, as he said: "All of being is contained in a single point."[5]
This is the origin of his metaphysical outlook as well as its aim; that is,
the aspiration of reality to be gathered into harmonic unity. All the
epistemological and ontological theories Rav Kook developed in response to various considerations, perhaps blurring the imprint of his
basic sense of identity do not negate it as a focal point of his awareness, and the experiential power of that sense stimulates its appearance over and over again in diverse theoretical formulations. Numerous passages speak of all-embracing unity and the identicalness of all
the particulars. The following paragraph expresses this intuition
without justification or explanation and with no philosophical statement. Its style and rising enthusiasm betray, beyond any doubt, its
roots in an intense experience of identification:

> You are He in this world, and you are He in the world to
> come, the worlds will not be torn asunder, and the details will
> not be rent from the whole, the divine attributes will be neither
> torn nor separated from each other, and none will be discon-
> nected from *En-sof*, and the light of *En-sof* will not be stripped
> from all the individual *tikkunim*, the minutest of details; *all is
> entwined together*, all is blessed unto eternity, "Blessed be the
> Lord, the God of Israel from everlasting and to everlasting,"
> "And let them bless thy glorious name, which is exalted above
> all blessing and praise" (Psalms 41:14; Nehemiah 9:5).[6]

The sense of all-embracing unity does not imply unconscious-
ness of differences and changes; rather, such differences are perceived as illusory:

We must understand that just as time has no being relative to infinity, and in any case, all temporal reality is surely present in infinity in greater completeness, so there is no change relative to supreme equalness and in any case all processes of change exist equally in supreme completeness; moreover, all *we sense as change in being only seems so to us*, but in truth, is everything not infinitely more divine than it is differentiated?[7] Thus all *the changes are not changes* but rather *equal and constant realities*.[8]

Rav Kook believed mystics, or as he called them "those who gaze within," need not be disturbed by the discrepancy between the world as it is perceived through normal contemplation and the "inner" truth they have grasped, for the intuition of identity actually reflects the "great truth," whereas the contradictions, differences, and changes are no more than a product of limited, narrow observation. Mystics, very characteristically, have *certain knowledge* of the "great truth." Thus he wrote:

> Those who gaze within *are not at all disturbed* in their meditations by the superficial manner of seeing, which does not suit their own ways, *they know their world is a world of certainty*, and the contradictions coming from another world mean nothing to them at all. The absolute truth is clear to them, that all the contradictions are due to the conditions of the limited intellect, which is negligible compared to the great truth in its essential absoluteness.[9]

The sense of certainty described here stands in sharp opposition to the relativistic conception Rav Kook developed in his epistemological teaching. Yet the intuition of identification is what underlies many theories central to his view of reality. Let us consider a few examples. We have seen that one aspect of Rav Kook's monotheism is the principle of parallelism; that is, "All that happens to an individual and his soul . . . the same happens on a larger scale in all of creation, in all the worlds, and what happens to all the worlds happens to every man as well."[10] The principle of parallelism is no more than one theoretical formulation of the sense of identification. The idea of revelation in his teaching can also be understood as based on the experience of absolute identity, for seeing all of reality, including human culture, as an emanation of the divine[11] is a conclusion of a monistic outlook and paves the way for some of Rav Kook's most daring conclusions on a variety of issues: the epistemological value and ontological status of metaphysical assumptions,[12] the blurring of differences between contradictory thoughts or opposing values (for example, faith versus atheism) when viewed in the light of absolute truth,[13] one's place before God,[14] and human metaphysical ability, as we shall see later.

Another intuition of decisive importance in Rav Kook's perception of reality is that of constant movement: "The phenomenon that allows man to sense creation not as something finished and completed but as something continually becoming, ascending, developing and raising itself . . . "[15] The awareness of this movement, in which "all flows, trembles, and desires"[16] is founded on the principle of parallelism. Through his own experience, Rav Kook perceived the dynamic nature of reality with the spiritual excitement that was his nature. He wrote: "Being is constantly filled with movement, material and spiritual. . . . We see this in the living organism, in the human spirit, in man's spirituality itself, and in the mutual relationship between body and spirit."[17]

A graphic and highly sensual testimony of the dynamic nature of Rav Kook's internal world is found in a passage describing mystical contemplation:

> Thought must be greatly expanded, in length and in breadth, in depth and height, in extent and in size . . . *and one goes* from large to small, from small to large, from particularity to generalness, from generalness to particularity ever and ever again.
>
> *One flies* from *atsilut* [the world of emanation and the divinity], from ideality to manifestation, to materiality, practicality, and returns and rises from practicality to *atsilut*, to ideality, *forever in movement*, filled with life, *leading and bringing, raising and lowering*.
>
> Such living is joyful and holy, in the majesty of God's Name. *We yearn to express the Name, desire to interpret*[18] the sublime light, grow full with supreme thirst, overflowing with delight, that our mouths may fill with praises for the Lord of Lords, and in our great and pure homage, the intensity of awesome reverence, *we return to silence*.[19]
>
> Separated entities are rejoined in holiness, sublime unions, in exultation and in holiness, in song, gaeity, and purity, in fear and trembling, in happiness.
>
> And all their essence will shout with joy, and the kingdom of heaven ascends, the supreme majesty rising. Their soul strides mightily, and they fill with praise and song; heaven and earth rejoice in their happiness, and all judgments are sweetened, and seraphs and angels sing with them, and the minister-

ing angels gather as if at a wedding. All utters His glory, blessed be the Lord from his holy place, blessed be He and his great Name, hidden from all living things, concealed from all being, magnified and exalted over all, Selah.[20]

What Rav Kook described here is an experience composed entirely of movement, suffused with the desire "to express the Name," "to interpret the sublime light"; that is, to express the ineffable in words. One has no recourse but silence. Yet this return to silence, to passivity, is clearly alien to the dynamic, excited rhythm of the passage as a whole. Silence is a still point, a temporary pause between the movement preceeding it and resuming after it.

The centrality of the experiences of identification and movement in Rav Kook's conception of reality cannot be overemphasized, although he himself often restricted the conclusions to be drawn from them. Thus, for example, he stated "the idea that all of being concerns the divine alone, and there is nothing else at all aside from God"; although "He delights the heart very much"[21]—this idea must be kept from becoming a pragmatic consideration, for "the world of practical action cannot choose its course according to it."[22] In fact, such restrictions are inherent in the dialectical structure of Rav Kook's world-view; thus the idea of movement, development, or growing completeness, that is, the principle of freedom, is qualified by the idea of absolute, static completeness, that is, necessity. Hence concepts such as "will" and "wisdom" or "circles" [עגולים] and "straightness" [יושר] are the supporting pillars of Rav Kook's metaphysical teaching, set in a dialectical relation, and reflecting, whether conceptually or symbolically, an unmediated sense of reality.

The Experience of Metaphysical Ability

Rav Kook's self-awareness and belief was graced with unusual powers, combined with a certain withdrawal and weariness from the spiritual intensivity involved in that sense of strength, were a constant source of tension and agitation in his inner world. It seemed to him that "spiritual fatigue,"[23] the feeling of internal pressure,[24] and the states of depression that sometimes grip the *zaddik* come about when his faith in his own ability and strength is shaken:

When the tremendous faith a sublime soul has in the power of his innermost self is diminished, he is plunged into melancholy and grows desolate. And with him all the world and its light are darkened. But when he returns in full repentance and the beauty of faith in his own supreme strength pulses in him without cease, returns to him, then his spirit will revive and shine. . .[25]

Zaddikim, he averred, must know they are unlike "the common masses," and "the nature of their souls is a completely other and *exalted* quality."[26] When Rav Kook said in the third person, "There are great *zaddikim*, who have supreme qualities deep in their souls,"[27] he seems to refer, first of all, to himself.[28] He said explicitly that "for such *zaddikim*, an inward yearning for mysteries of the Torah and all the wisdom of holy knowledge cleaves to their nature,"[29] and the passion of those words points clearly to their author. He even summoned his soul and urged it to recognize its elevation and worth: "Awaken, my soul, awaken in your divine greatness, do not belittle yourself. Do not weep [30] before the proud rebels, who cannot touch your state of mind and the fineness of your soul in its pure imaginings and in its highest longing for noble exaltation, divine exaltation, for true honesty and revered purity. Know your worth and ascend.[31]

What is the nature and source of this sense of strength? Clearly, Rav Kook's view is theoretically bound to kabbalistic and Hassidic teachings about humankind and the figure of the *zaddik*,[32] but there are significant differences and emphases as well. In any case, the sense of capability is linked experientially to the sense of identification described previously. Because reality is unified and all its parts identical with the whole, the individual is perceived as one with the entirety of existence, and "we declare the essential fusion between the soulfulness that acts in all the world and the soulfulness of man."[33] Thus, everything happening in one, both in one's internal world and in one's deeds, actually occurs in reality as well; and this is the secret of one's power:

> Man is the essence of everything, belongs to everything, how can he not act on everything.[34]
> We grasp an idea of man's greatness, an idea that concetrates being in man's existence, his value, the striving of his will, brave and holy. The body and its powers are of completely earthly essence, and the spirit with all its powers are of heavenly essence. . .
> The transcendence of the body and the spirit is the ascent of a central part, and by its elevation, all that surrounds it rises as well.[35]

For Rav Kook, this is no mere theory. He averred that the *zaddik*, or "the holy man of silence," has a sense of total unity with all that surrounds him. He *"lives a universal life,* the life of all. He *feels* the vitality of the inanimate, the vegetative, and the animal, the whole common life of all speaking creatures, of every single human being, of every intelligent and conscious entity, all that perceives and feels, and being as a whole ascends with him to its source."[36] Rav Kook adds:

> Man can reach such a state in which he discovers the cen-
> trality of all of existence within himself. Then *he will feel in his*
> *spirit all that excites, all that is done . . . and all that moves in the*
> *fullness of being at each and every one of its stages.* For the Lord God
> did nothing but reveal his secret to his servants the prophets.[37]
> That inward revelation of what is concentrated in the human
> soul brings its truly hidden elements from potentiality to actu-
> ality.[38]

This highly significant relationship between humankind and the All, compared to the relation between a center[39] and what surrounds it (the two linked by identification), essentially dictates the absolute dependence of existence on humankind. Rav Kook did not speak of an ability to perform miracles and change the orders of nature, but rather of one's adhesion to being as a whole, in other words, to God.[40] As he puts it: "Great common ability and strength, tremen-dous and sublime, appears in the soul of the holy man who cleaves to God, the Everlasting."[41] This adhesion is the source of one's essence; one's actions are none other than the acts of God himself:

> Godly ability is connected to *His desire,* and human capa-
> bility is designed to reach that divine attribute, to be bound to
> his *desire.* I said *you are Gods* (Psalms 82:6). Thus, man is never
> denied that impression of the *ability to desire,* and it grows ever
> more noticeable, until it reaches the degree of "You shall decree
> a thing, and it shall be established unto you" (Job 22:28). That is
> the character of the *zaddikim,* and in his uprightness man resem-
> bles his Creator, Make of all with his utterance.[42]

Ability is attributed here to will. Thus, when devotion (*devekut*) to God is complete, it exists in both its aspects of manifestation; that is, in will and in *hokhma.*[43] Spiritual adhesion, as the goal of "secret knowledge" is characterized by "developing *spiritual strength* until it reaches its inner strength to *draw from its source* without any need of mediated study, and this phenomenon leads all of being to *recognize* itself, and out of this inward recognition flows abundant life, *in the union of intellect and will,* unbroken by boundaries and particularity."[44]

Rav Kook was consistently inconsistent in presenting his system, which reflects the dialect tension between intellect and will. As in his epistemological teaching, in one context he declared the precedence of will and in another the precedence of *hokhma*.[45] In a certain passage we saw that "ability is bound to his desire," yet in another it seems that thought is the source of human ability and influence:

> It takes great experience to be able to *feel* the force of life and being in *the power of thinking*, to recognize the *might of the idea* and the ruling power exerted by life, and the *rich reality of thought*, and to learn from this recognition that the more sublime, refined, and pure thought becomes, the more man and the world also rise, growing ever more refined and pure. And the ascent and descent of all aspects of reality, forever inferior to the power of thought, *are dependent on the ascent and descent of man's thinking power*, and this will lead man to awareness of the great happiness he brings himself and the world through the godliness of thought. Thought bound to the divine image is the finest, most glorious, sublime and mighty thought in the world, and its validity gives strength and power to all deeds, movements, being and life. All learning and education in the world only grant the means to fortify the power of thought, enabling its constant actualization at the ultimate level, in the divine image.[46]

Humankind's all-embracing influence becomes clear when one is exposed to the congruence and correspondence between the Torah and the soul of every individual, and between these two and the whole, the world and being in the widest sense:

> First, the essence of the entire Torah in all its expansiveness is found in the individual soul, in its perfected aspects and its flaws, in its ascents and descents, and after that, the individual soul is found interwoven with the whole; then the essence of the whole, in the entire world and in being is recognized as dependent on the perfection of each individual's moral behavior and knowledge of Torah; each person must say, "The world was created for my sake," and "When will my deeds reach those of Abraham, Isaac, and Jacob, our fathers?"[47]

Consciousness of ability exists on various levels, developing from the stage of potentiality to the level at which "the *tzaddik* ordains and the Holy One blessed be He fulfills": "Just as ability and *gevurah* is first described in the image of the holy, it rises and ascends in the intellect, becomes actualized until the stage of 'You shall decree a thing and it shall be established unto you' (Job 22:28)."[48]

Thought and will, then, are perceived as creative forces that alter the order of being itself. Yet they are not alone. The human resemblance to God, "Creator of all with His utterance," also affirms speech as a creative power, "You shall decree a thing and it shall be established unto you": "The virtue of speech will be manifest in the world as well as the virtue of will and thought, the quality of simple speech, in which a blessing is a blessing and a curse a curse, *which says that the decree must be established.*[49]

Thus the *zaddik* is the active force of being, determining its object, for through him the soul of being is revealed, the cosmic powers of intellect and will. The *zaddik* senses his power and is aware of his metaphysical influence:

> The world lacks all object as long as no higher soul shines within it. And when that soul comes and illumines with its precious light, the world becomes more perfect . . . the upright of heart, the highest *zaddikim, know* that they themselves are the channels drawing the abundance of life down to all of existence; they *feel* the waves of influence of the good emanated upon them and through them down to the world . . . the vision of the *zaddik,* pillar of the world, is enrooted in this truth.[50]

Another aspect of the sense of ability is the experience of an immediate link with God, including certain prophetic dimensions. The aim of mystical teaching, in Rav Kook's eyes, is the development of the human soul's ability "to draw from its source with no need of mediated learning."[51] He perceived the ability to feel "in his spirit all that storms, all that is done,"[52] as prophetic ability; this is hinted in a context in which he introduced the verse "Surely the Lord God will do nothing without revealing his secret to his *servants the prophets"* (Amos 3:7).[53] In other words, the experience or sense of reality is an aspect of divine revelation visited on the prophet. All this seems to demonstrate Rav Kook's conviction he himself had been given prophetic ability. He nearly professed as much: "Let our words be as a refining fire (Malachi 3:2) and like a hammer that breaks the rock in pieces (Jeremiah 23:29), *for they are the word of God* and they issue and flow from the source of holy light giving life to all; happy is he who harkens to me."[54] Rav Kook saw the era of national rebirth as an age in which the spirit of prophecy returns and awakens, and in his opinion, this arousal must be encouraged as something natural to the Jewish people. He wrote:

As for the Israeli nation, now, at this moment it has begun to flower, we must arouse the striving to the highest spiritual aim, which is the attribute of divine inspiration. . .

In truth, the absence of divine inspiration in the nation of Israel is not a lack of completeness, but rather a flaw and illness in the Land of Israel, a painful illness that must be cured. "For I the Lord will heal you."[55]

In another instance he wrote: "To the foundation of prophecy we are called, parched with thirst, but a fountain of gardens, a well of living waters *is before us* . . . from the spirit of the Messiah winds begin to stream and blow, and they come to us."[56] Yet Rav Kook believed the spirit of prophecy was actually stirring in his own days, and his revealing expression of this conviction was partially censored by his editor: "these outgrowths of prophecy spring forth, and the sons of prophets awaken, the spirit of prophecy roams about the land, seeking refuge, demanding heroes, valiant and holy, who will be able to marshall their words, to speak the truth, who will recount how God's word was revealed to them, without lies or flattery, expending their spirit in faith."[57]

Mystical Striving

The earliest studies of mysticism were founded on the assumption that all mystical experiences are identical.[58] Although this assumption need not be rejected out of hand, as some universal elements do characterize mystical experience, it tends to ignore the particular and individual manner in which the mystical aspiration is perceived by the mystic; this manner is what ultimately determines the nature and significance of any individual mystical experience.[59]

To appraise the essence of a mystical experience, then, we need the account of the mystic, as well as knowledge of the conception at the basis of his or her experience. Rav Kook recorded very few accounts or confessions enabling us to probe beneath the level of abstract examination, allowing us to glimpse the living reality of intensive religious experience. Yet even on the basis of the sparse biographical material at our disposal, combined with the theoretical courses, we can appreciate the unique nature of Rav Kook's mystical striving and arrive at some important conclusions. Many of the theoretical passages are written in the third person, yet as we have said, the vast majority of them in fact reflect Rav Kook's own experience. They are distinguished by penetrating self-awareness and self-observation, and a number of them develop phenomenological premises of no minor significance. In our assessment of Rav Kook's mystical striving,[60] let us begin with a rare testimony made by Rav Ya'akov Moshe Charlop ז״ל, who accompanied Rav Kook on his trip in the Galilee in the winter of 1916. Rav Charlop recounted:

> I awoke in the middle of the night and saw the Rav carried in a storm wind from one side of the room to the other. I was terrified and I raised myself up, and he came over to me and seized me, his hands were cold as ice and his face burned-shone like flames, and from his mouth burst forth words of fire: "Rabbi Ya'akov-Moshe, ich wer verbrennt fon ahavat-haShem!" [I am burning with love for God].[61]

This fascinating record offers a highly vivid description of the excitement and the force of Rav Kook's religious experience, yet it reflects only one side of his situation. Rav Kook was aware of the full uniqueness of his position, of the tension between the mystical tendency on the one hand and the rationalistic on the other. In his eyes, occupation with either mysticism or revealed essences depended on various psychological inclinations.[62] These two tendecies are usually mutually opposed, but Rav Kook believed that fundamentally even those who deal with revealed truths enjoy some inward "mystical wealth." In fact, their excess of mystical richness even brings them beyond satiety, driving them to reject it and yearn for particular knowledge and concrete action.[63] Just as these individuals are adept at understanding nature and searching its every detail, so they "lack that divine longing as a deep and primal request, and all the more so they lack the profound raising of thought in the secret heights of the world through its divine resolution."[64] In contrast, people of the mystical disposition, the "godly," "do not have the same strength and the same thirst to search to the depths of realistic phenomena [investigation of nature] as that thirst typical of the valiant scientists of nature."[65] Instead, they "feel a terrible hunger and mighty thirst for concealed, recondite images, and the questions of highest value that rise to the heights of mystery grant them no rest."[66]

How did Rav Kook characterize himself between these two profiles? He seems to have placed himself in a third group, which he described as a complex personality:

> It is a rare vision to see a man in whom *the demand for the revealed and the concealed as one exists in wholeness;* there is always some opposition between the two. Only if man is drawn after

his surroundings *and sees the good* and the splendor that *both sides obtained* in their labor, a feeling of intense rivalry comes upon him, and *he desires* to satiate himself with *both attributes;* in most cases he confronts *obstacles* in his path, and he strives everywhere to overcome them.

Such people are forever weighted with a great burden, of *painful knowledge,* but they always bring much good to the world; after all, by the fruits of their spirit they *create a new world where heaven and earth meet and kiss.* And after they draw this *complex vision* from potentiality to actuality, others can finally receive what they have created and a permanent spiritual creation comes into being, throughout generations, able to grasp these separate and contradictory realms as a unity—then a *double creative power* is truly revealed.[67]

Rav Kook's respect for the value of the rational approach made him reluctant to forego it and underlies the tension he alluded to in speaking of the "obstacles" he must overcome and of "painful knowledge." Numerous passages in his writings express delight and desire in the same breath with suffering and spiritual affliction, and they reflect the fundamental tension in his inner world. Therefore he wrote: "Who can describe and tell of the tremendous fire of great thirst *zaddikim* have for God."[68] Indeed, when "the divine adhesion demanded from the depths of the heart, spirit, and soul" [רוח, נשמה, לב, נפש] is not attained commensurate with the thirst and desire, "the pain is unbearable, the penetrating wound awful."[69]

The *zaddik's* suffering reflects more than a mere psychological state. It is in fact the same as the sorrow of the *Shekhinah;* that is, with cosmic suffering, or the cosmic longing for completeness:

> The great suffering every *zaddik* feels in himself for his own lack of devotion [*devekut*] to God, leaving his great thirst unquenched and wracking all his limbs with pain and yearning, granting him no rest from any pleasure or comfort in the world, *this is truly the anguish of the Shekhinah;* the inward life of all the worlds pines for the highest divine completeness to be revealed in it.[70]

Yet in effect, the psychic distress engendered by the distance between the desired adhesion and the extent to which it is actually attained merely expresses a certain duality between various aspects of the human psyche, the aspect of individuality opposing the sense of belonging to the whole:

My heart shall not retreat from any sorrow in the world, for I know it contains some revelation of the seed within all levels of the soul, whether in its *individual* part or its *relation to the whole*, and all my sorrows will lead me to the source of the pain, that they may be repaired and filled with light, by action and intellect, by idea and image; and all the paths are open as God's kindness is very great; "For great is your steadfast love towards me: and you have delivered my soul from the depths of *She'ol*" (Psalms 86:13).[71]

This realization serves in some way as consolation for sufferings by giving them meaning. In Rav Kook's view, "One whose soul is expansive endures great afflictions from the confinement of thought in isolated details. But he must overcome and endure these afflictions with love, for they themselves lead him to an even greater happiness."[72] This willing acceptance of suffering brings Rav Kook to consider pain not only as an impetus toward attaining greater blessing but as a positive experience in and of itself: "When the heart is continually agitated, yearning and longing, the soul thirsts for God. *The pain itself is glorious*. This affliction is the torments of love, the faithful wounds of a lover (Proverbs 27:6)."[73]

Suffering contains another meaning as well, enrooted in the sense of mission it entails. As we saw earlier, Rav Kook believed those personalities who contain both the inclination to the revealed and to the concealed "bring goodness to the world" and "engender a new world in the fruit of their spirit"—such people found a sort of spiritual school in which the dissociated and contrary disciplines are perceived as joined." He said moreover:

The inward torments the *zaddikim* suffer because the sense of holiness is not pure in them as their heart desires and their soul longs—they *cleanse the filth of the entire world*, and he should bear in silence all the pricks of the thorns surrounding the holy rose, that these inward torments may sweeten all the bitterness of life and *increase the spirit of holiness, peace and happiness in the world*.[74]

Rav Kook expressed his certainty that the suffering of *zaddikim* will eventually bear fruit, "and in the end the great honor will arrive, the gates will open . . . the world will unite, the revealed and the concealed converge, the body will be joined to the soul, the lights and the vessels will meet."[75] Yet Rav Kook's relation to the details, whether in *theory* or in *practice*, remains problematic. On the one hand, he was interested in the real union of both tendencies: the all-inclusive view and attention to particulars. Yet, on the other hand, dealing with particularity seems to him to harm the supremacy of the *zaddik*, as he wrote:

> When a great man involves himself too much with details, whether by studying them or by anxiety about them, he is diminished and his stature lessened; he must return and repent with love, with greatness of soul, and bind the contents of his spiritual life with great and sublime ideas. Certainly, he must not slight any detail, and always expend force and holiness in his deeds as well.[76]

Despite the caution against disregard for details, they are clearly described here as lowering the eminence of great men. Indeed, in another passage Rav Kook expressed the repulsion he felt from dealing with details as a weakness and an inferior quality. There, he graphically described the heights his free soul yearns to reach, compared to the attention to details that comes upon him as a sort of "assault," and the myriad details as beleaguering his soul:

> How great is the war within me, my heart is filled with longing, high and wide; I wish divine tenderness to spread throughout my being. Not for the pleasure of it but because it must be so, because that is the nature of reality, the meaning of life.
>
> And I continually yearn, roar with my inward essence, with a great voice, Give me divine light, the delight of the living God and His pleasure, the great revelation of allowing me to contemplate the Temple of the eternal King, the God of my father; with all my heart I am given to love for him. Awe for Him elevates me.
>
> And my *soul* rises higher and higher, transcending all *degradation*, pettiness, and *limitations* on which nature, the body, surroundings, and agreement confine it, gripping it in tongs, locking it in stocks. *Then comes a flood of obligations,* purposeless study and pedantry, tangles of ideas, generating casuistry focused on letters and words, it comes *and surrounds my pure, free soul,* light as an angel, clear as the sky itself, floating as a sea of light. *I have not yet reached that level,* to gaze from beginning to end, to understand the pleasantness of every single halacha, *to feel the sweetness of strictness,* to see by the light within the world's darkness. So am I filled with pain, and I hope for salvation and

illumination, for highest elevation, for the appearance of insight and brightness, drops of the dew of life, even in those narrow channels from which I suckle to repletion. I will delight in the beauty of God, will know the purity of the ideal will, the sublime and secret force filling every letter and every crown, all being and argumentation, and I will delight in Your commandments that I love and will speak of Your laws.[77]

The aspiration to the complete unification of these two opposing tendencies thus suggests a certain promised destiny whose realization seems remote. In any case, we must emphasize that despite all the difficulties involved in living such an intense spiritual life, Rav Kook saw no escape from bearing that burden. On the contrary, he enthusiastically encouraged every flash of mystical propensity:

The thirst for God that blazes and flames with fiery might in the heart must not be extinguished. Just as whoever puts out an ember from the altar of the Temple violates the commandment that "The fire shall ever be burning upon the altar; it shall never go out" (Leviticus 6:6), so must one never put out one of the supreme spiritual embers from the altar of the soul, filled with holy life, the soul of the Israelite.[78]

Even more, Rav Kook claimed that for the "highest *zaddik*" the mystical path is the only possible path:

All the desires in the world, all the scholarly competitiveness in the world, and all the attributes of Torah and wisdom in the world *will not move the highest zaddik from the root of constant devotion to God*, which is his life's success, the light of the entire world and the source of all life. Many waters cannot quench this love, nor can the floods drown it (Song of Songs 8:7).[79]

All this is not said of some anonymous "highest *zaddik*." What Rav Kook described here is his own internal world, and in another passage, he used the same terms in speaking of himself:

I cannot move from devotion to God, and thus I must endeavor to see the divine light and its beauty in all words, all speech, act and movement, whether my own or others', and all the more so must I feel the appearance of supreme light through the channels of truth and justice, in the Torah itself, even in its simple sense, and in halachic disputes and argumentation. This is why I tend to support debate—for its logical reasoning and its sensitivity as well.[80]

It is interesting to realize that this continual demand for ever-intensified religious experience caused Rav Kook to see himself as obliged to broaden the realm of religious experience, to infuse all dimensions of life with religious-mystical meaning, and to avoid an excessive concentration of mystical energy on the spiritual level alone. This fact shows he was not unaware of the dangers lurking in the mystical path. In a few contexts he reveals particular awareness and sensitiveness to three major kinds of danger: the first is related to the conflict between mystical life and the values and norms of religious tradition,[81] the second concerns the mystic's disregard of the needs of practical life, and the third is the possibility that the mystic's spiritual equilibrium might be upset.

The conflict with the values of tradition and the needs of everyday life, stemming from the mystic's sense of boundless freedom, arouses dilemmas, pangs of conscience, and even depression. The crisis can be resolved by investing even day-to-day actions with "highest holy" meaning. Rav Kook wrote:

> The insight that bursts forth to rise above and beyond the bounds of human imaginings—there the *differences* between good and bad, between pure and impure are *obscured*, and even though this comes about from an abundance of light and highest holiness; there are truly returns to the good and the holy, there is no adversary and no evil hindrance. But in our own limited lives, evil and sin is plentiful and we must be immersed in recognition of its ugliness and hatred, just as we must be bound with love for the good, the pure, and the holy, and recognition of his honor and glory.
>
> Thus people with such *overflowing thought* feel a somber sadness within themselves at all times, like the pangs of conscience borne for sins, because *the freedom of their thought* and its highest holiness does truly *sin* against practical values. And they recover their holy spiritual state, continually joyful in the light of the Lord, by grace of what they draw from the source of the highest holy, not only a state of the soul's expanding and supreme inclusion, but also the *narrow path, the unique essence* through which the highest state of life can be reached.[82]

Rav Kook pointed to yet another danger related to the state that develops, with no appropriate preparation, following mystical ecstacy:

Sometimes, when great effort is expended to cleave with supreme spirituality, all the powers of spiritual life rise to the world of highest thought, and the body is abandoned behind, and destructive qualities rule over it. Later, when contemplation has ended and the life force returns to its normal state, the soul finds the body broken, its character ruined, and a very dangerous internal battle begins.[83]

In other instances, Rav Kook alluded once again to the nature of the danger inherent in this internal battle and its accompanying spiritual effort. He wrote: "At times, thirst for God grows so fierce that it exceeds the limits of all the vessels, until the *spiritual order is destroyed.*"[84] And elsewhere: "Sometimes acute *spiritual illnesses* develop from the mere distress of unslated spiritual thirst."[85] The implication is undeniably a case of psychic instability, of psychic illnesses that may result from inordinate spiritual efforts expended on the mystical path. Rav Kook's apprehension of this and worse dangers was manifest, as we learn from the account of Rav Charlop ז"ל:

In the summer of 1921, the Rav went on holiday to Har Tov; and I went to visit him there and we continued to speak of mysteries until late into the night. In the morning, I sensed the Rav was late in his prayers and, quite unlike his practice to do nothing else before praying, I saw him approach the innkeeper and begin to speak with him about horticulture and which fruit trees could be grown in the area, and only afterwards did he go to pray. The delay and the conversation astounded me, and I made so bold as to ask the Rav what it all meant. His answer was: "This morning a flaming thirst for the living God blazed in my heart, making me fear my soul would be consumed in prayer, and I was forced to diminish the fire of holy feeling by lowering my thought to tangible, practical matters."[86]

This awareness of dangers brought Rav Kook to the conclusion that moral preparation, repentance and refining of one's nature must preceed[87] "contemplative ascent," thus preventing a complete disconnection from the body in the soul's "ultimate elevation."[88] Yet Rav Kook was less than consistent in this conclusion, and his diverse remarks on the subject show his doubts remained unresolved. The following paragraph loudly echoes the dilemma he faced; nonetheless, in contrast to the previous passage, it demonstrates his unhesitating preference for the mystical path, even without preparation:

Even though one must make a great effort to improve one's qualities, that moral purification must not delay him, *Heaven forbid,* [from elevating himself to greater spirituality and meditation. On the other hand, moral attributes cannot become pure without great spiritual elevation. A person sometimes reaches such a state that he must draw everything from his understanding, and he need not consider the attributes, for it is a promise, and in the elevation of knowledge all ascend, and in his purity they are made pure.[89]

Rav Kook went even further: "Instead of combatting the illnesses that have already come into being, it is better to fight against the primary cause of all illness and to alleviate the unquenched thirst, satiating yearning souls."[90] Rav Kook seems unwilling to forego mystical contemplation despite his awareness that even a temporary remission from it, combined with attention to quotidian matters, actually strengthen the *zaddik,* in that sense even gaining an aspect of holiness. He asserts that "It cannot be done a priori [mystical contemplation avoided], for it is on the same plane as the *mitzvah* of the forgotten sheaf—a pious man brings a thanksgiving sacrifice for it."[91] In other words, such a pause from contemplation, like the commandment of "forgetting" (Deuteronomy 25:9) is viewed with favor and acquires meaning as a *mitzvah* only after the fact, when it occurs without having been planned.

We thus have no choice but to conclude Rav Kook's attitude on the question is far from definitive, reflecting the internal ambivalence of a torn personality that can reach no decision. The humanness and honesty of the following passages bear witness to that spiritual longing and Rav Kook's own conscious repression of it at certain times:

My soul cries aloud in protest that I do not allow my thinking power to expand in all its goodness. It is a great cruelty, the trouble of humanity, that man does not want to ascend, to expand upward. So he sinks in the mud. Two things cause this—external, coarse, crude fear, full of stupidity and foolish imaginings, and material [. . .] that draws whatever it can seize to decadence and lowliness; and we must overcome all of this, forbearance of thought, refinement of will, force of life, all in the fullness of its highest strength.[92]

Man must not make his soul a lie, must not falsify his inner feelings because of the stormy impulse of common opinion, and if he feels exultation and the holiness of reason in a special discipline, he should always take care to nourish himself with [the abundance[93] of] sublime delights from the place of his desire. And I, who am so filled with the solace of God in my study of the mysteries of the Torah, *even when I feel myself so abstract,* I am not disheartened [literally, "my hands grow not slack"] [. . .] I must hang on even though it is impossible not to give practical tasks what they demand, whether in their practical aspect or in the very law of the Torah and apprehension of it in all the disciplines.[94]

The first of the two passages is very surprising in its apparent expression of deep feelings of guilt, and inhibiting intellectual abilities from expanding is seen as irredeemably negative. In the second passage, the elements obstructing mystical ascent are adaptation to social norms and the need to function in practical life and in the performance of the commandments of the Torah—an inescapable imperative.

Clearly, the mystical impetus overcomes all barriers, and Rav Kook saw it as the most ontological manifestation of human essence: "A man knows in his soul, when divine longing grasps his very heart, that his spirit is revealed within him."[95] Thus the mystical path helps achieve self-actualization, in Rav Kook's words: "Directed to the source of the soul, handling it in a manner worthy of it."[96] Here as well, complete actualization is in the union of two aspects of being: "In the innermost heart, there is a tendency to shed light on that point in which *feeling and intellect* and all the force of life join together."[97]

The mystical impulse and the response to it are thus perceived as an expression of freedom: "Because the light of the soul bursts forth immediately, it must be given *its freedom* to grow broader, imagine, muse, learn and attain, aspire, that man may reach the heighest heights, his source and root, his soul's life, the light of the soul of all the world, of the supreme God, His goodness and glory."[98]

Rav Kook's choice to describe the mystical striving and experience throughout his writings in terms of freedom and human liberation leaves no doubt of the decisive influence exerted by the prevailing Zeitgeist.[99] "To liberate man," Rav Kook said, "that is our aim."[100] It is the goal of mysticism as well, and is attained by mystical effort: "Through his ascent, his elevation, the revelation of all his *inner* abilities . . . that the inwardness of things is the divine goal of being, the object of man's hidden longing."[101]

In the same direction, Rav Kook honed his formulation until mystical thought became completely equivalent to freedom and the essence of the soul. These are his words: "Mystical thought is the freedom of Israel, of the Israelite soul. . . . When this freedom rises to its zenith, when the soul no longer suffers the burden or yoke of conventional opinion whose source is not in Judaism, then the ideas continually created by that pure holiness are themselves mysteries of the Torah."[102] He added: "Concealed learning . . . is joined with the essence."[103]

Nevertheless, Rav Kook spoke of two kinds of "intellectual tasks," and the difference between them is described as constriction as opposed to freedom and space. The first task is the rational, which "turns to bring in and to clothe the abundance of divine inspiration in the garments of human intellect and reasoning," whereas the second is the mystical task, whose aim is to bring "the rational systems of the heart . . . out of narrow and confined life, for they exist throughout it, and into the world of most exalted freedom."[104]

Thus, not only is the mystical path seen as the expression and realization of freedom; freedom itself, or in Rav Kook's terms, *freedom of ideas*, is the essential precondition to reaching adhesion to God, or *devekut*:

> The outward, lying imagination makes it seem to man as if freedom of ideas and divine devotion are mutually contradictory, but when man rises to the heights of refining his ideas to purity he will reach the understanding that *total freedom of ideas alone can lead to adhesion* to God in its purest intellectual state. And this *devekut in freedom* will elevate his insight until he raises his whole will with it, and the essence of his being, his nature and his striving.[105]

We devoted a separate chapter to the systematic examination of Rav Kook's conception of freedom. Thus, the experiential side of the kinship between mystical experience and the sense of freedom is particularly relevant to our present discussion. We will conclude, then, with some of Rav Kook's remarks on the subject:

> Masters of supreme contemplation sense that highest freedom, and they cannot be enslaved in any bondage, for all bondage is imposed by flesh and blood alone. Even the common acceptance of the yoke of heaven by human beings is enslavement of flesh and blood . . . *and the striving to absolute freedom is the ultimate repentance* [תשובה].[106]

> He whose spirit is filled with the appearance of the light of *En-sof*—all manner of finite thoughts press upon his heart, yet

he finds no satisfaction from them. His soul must therefore be gladdened with the supreme, unbounded pleasure of the world of freedom.[107]

As inward divine emanation [*atzilut*] intensifies within him . . . the spirit of freedom grows within him as well . . . and he is granted liberty from all his enslavement.[108]

Our heart . . . is open to all pure feeling, and longs with all its might for every noble sensation, filled with freedom.[109]

These words surely portray the spirit suffusing every page of Rav Kook's writings. Our author was no mystic in the normal sense of the word. Although he was drawn to the mystical path, he recoiled from the dangerous excesses lurking in it. Mysticism, as a world-view and discipline of thought, provided him with the *Lebensraum* so essential to one who ceaselessly strives to understand the secret of being and whose sense of freedom demands not only that the yoke of societal constraints and narrow-minded religious views be thrown off, but also that one must be freed from the chains of inflexible rationalistic thought unable to answer the riddle of existence and unable to fulfill the utopic destiny to which one calls.

The tension, whether dialectical, theoretical, or experiential, omnipresent in his writings between mystical and rationalistic tendencies reflects the sense and the awareness that all of reality is too complex and rich to be grasped, described, and exhausted by any single discipline and certainly not to be formulated by any one metaphysical method. This fact gives birth to far-reaching ideological openness and corresponds to the basic principle uniting Rav Kook's oeuvre; that is, the element of freedom. We do not mean the freedom Rav Kook allowed himself on various issues and subjects but rather his consciousness of the question of freedom—consciousness that transformed freedom to *the ideal of the mystical path*, creating a theoretical-speculative way of thinking in which *the idea of freedom* is vitally important.

Afterword

The paths of inquiry and analysis we have traveled in our discussion lead us, I believe, to some conclusions and new understanding of Rav Kook's thought and its significance, as well as his contribution to religious thought in general and Jewish thought in particular.

If we were to characterize the essential nature of his thought, its central element would be his refusal to be content with the ordinary, his untiring search for what is beyond, and his awareness that whatever is perceived is only one aspect of manifold reality, multidimensional and limitless. This quality finds expression through our discussion and creates the dialectical nature of his thought. It is reflected in his relationship to mysticism and rational philosophy and his unwillingness to forego either of them, from his understanding that no restricted approach to reality can satisfy the undefatigable demand for completeness. The same quality reappears in our consideration of the question of perception and being, when Rav Kook asserted the relative and subjective value of all metaphysical views and called for openness to the infinite aspects of reality, impossible to circumscribe by any single theory. What, then, is the nature of this attitude? What impulses engender and direct it?

Many of the linguistic building blocks fundamental to Rav Kook's oeuvre are clearly hewn from classic sources of Jewish tradition at its various strata: the Bible, Midrash, philosophy, and Kabbalah. Yet his central views and his understanding of the nature of reality and human essence and destiny were undeniably chiseled and developed in the quarry of the ideological and social revolutions of his own era. From the perspective of religious thought, the challenges posed by his times were unprecedented in scope and seriousness. Violent protest from all directions and levels began to fissure the most basic religious beliefs, confronting all it wished to express. Idealistic

229

philosophy, which could be seen as corresponding to the "true" content of religion,[1] began to lose its luster, and the seeds it bore were Marxism and existentialism. These two ideological trends saw Hegelian philosophy in the way it indeed wished to be seen: "as the ultimate expression of the classical concept of truth based on the principles of generality and objectivity."[2] Both trends rebeled against that concept, each after its own heart but following a single impulse: to free the individual subject from its absolute neglect by idealistic philosophy.

Although in the end Marx returned to the same principle of generality he had originally rejected so utterly, the appearance of materialism as a philosophical trend gradually winning its place in public consciousness served to deepen and intensify the already critical damage caused by the process of secularization. The challenger and opponent now confronting theology was no longer any one scientific discipline or philosophical method, but rather a total and all-embracing world-view that interpreted reality in material and mechanistic terms. It was a comprehensive weltanschauung, and in its understanding of reality, with its laws and processes, there was no place for God or the human spirit and its freedom.[3]

Existentialist philosophy, for its part—concerned mainly with the individual, one's lack of essence and freedom, and existential problems—was no easier for conservative theologians to digest because of its rejection of the absolute or fixed dimension of reality and its view of all of being as becoming. Reality was no longer "essence" but rather "existence"; that is, it has no defined content but instead was open to all possibilities, to endless human creativity.[4] The "concept" was replaced by the human being as the preeminent object of philosophy. Humankind was the starting point and center of all discourse, the criteria used to measure truth and good, and in Nietzsche's revolutionary teaching, even created its own worth. Needless to say, in this view religion was bereft of all glory and savor. Barren and naked, it was portrayed as meaningless, numbing humanity and estranging it from the dynamism and creativity of human nature; in Nietzsche's thought, morality itself was held as the spoiled fruit of religion and must be exchanged for new norms reflecting the new concept of humanity.

The very doorposts of the house of Judaism were shaken as well. The nationalistic renaissance and flourishing of the New Yishuv in Eretz Israel generated by young idealists, lovers of their people and their land yet rebels against the yoke of the commandments—this development presented a challenge demanding theology to respond. In the spirit of modern philosophy, the Jews of the Second Aliyah, pioneers in the settlement of the Land of Israel, wished to prove the Jew could control his or her destiny and bring redemption without divine aid—indeed proclaiming his or her rejection of the kingdom of heaven.[5] In Rav Kook's eyes, the secular Zionist undertaking was to be neither ignored nor discounted; it mandated confrontation with the attitudes and philosophical methods pervading contemporary literature and setting the wheels of that generation's social and scientific revolutions in motion. Rav Kook could not but remark the progress, the blessing, and the promise brought by these events. In his eyes, the sincerity, search for truth and hatred of fraud expressed in the great rebellion of his era were commendable, and he shared the sense of freedom that characterized it. He felt compelled to find religious meaning for the central processes and spiritual cultural phenomena that deemed religion, at the very least, to be superfluous and completely irrelevant.

Against this background, Rav Kook's thought is revolutionary as well in the realm of Jewish religious thought, as a general philosophy seeking to propose an alternative to all existing systems by reinterpreting reality, human nature, and religion itself. Historical and social reality yields no direct revelation of the religious meaning it contains, and even the classical sources of religious literature do not speak in a language disclosing their "true" meaning in modern concepts. Both reality and religion, therefore, must be interpreted if they are to be understood, enabling one to respond to the divine summons issuing from them. If the most virulent contention of Nietzsche's thought consists in his biting criticism of morality, with its hypocrisy and falsehood, in order to build a new morality on its ruins, we can say Rav Kook sought to wage war against the religiosity of his age, against the hypocrisy and lies infecting it, not to create a new religion but rather to develop *renewed understand of the meaning of religion.* Only through a reinterpretation of religion—tantamount, in his eyes, to a reinterpretation of all of reality—could one combat on the battlefield of general culture and theology and emerge victorious. What is mandated is by no means a mere apologetics but rather an essential reorientation. His message was addressed first and foremost to observant Jews and to the Jewish people as a whole, and only afterward was it meant to spread further.

If we were to speak in the terms of hermeneutics, we could say Rav Kook's approach to religious texts was a clear "hermeneutics of demythologization." His path, guided by midrashic and kabbalistic sources, was completely abstract and devoid of all mythic content. Moreover, Rav Kook opened all of reality to interpretation[6] following the same spiritualistic impetus. It would be an offense and a basic misunderstanding of his teaching to see the essence of his message in his nationalistic outlook, his positive regard for the Zionist undertaking, and the concretization of the idea of redemption. Although the utopic element is the lifeblood of his thought, in its wake the very concepts of redemption and messianism are given new interpretation suited to his conception as a whole.[7]

In opposition to the materialistic-mechanical weltanschauung, Rav Kook proposed a spiritualistic image of reality. The world is portrayed as suffused with spirit and soul. Matter itself, physical events, not to mention historical, cultural, and social ones, conceal spiritual processes.[8] In Rav Kook's view, the development that characterizes nature and culture is but the realization of the will to completeness pulsing through all of being just as it pulses in humankind. Cosmic movement as a whole harbors moral significance and moral direction. All that distinguishes between the individual and being is self-consciousness; one is aware of oneself as an expression of the powers of consciousness and will. The rebeliousness and restlessness that characterize modern individuals declare one's aspiration, religious at its very heart, though not expressed as such—the striving for wholeness.

Yet in Rav Kook's teaching, completeness is not a defined concept that can actually be attained, realized in practical terms, or even grasped by human perception. This completeness is beyond all that exists, open to all possibilities, a sort of continual creativity, or as Heidegger would say, completeness is "existence." This is the definition of the Jew or *Knesset Israel* as a whole. Neither exists in and of itself. *"Knesset Israel* has nothing of its own" [לית לה מגרמה כלום]; for very reason of its openness and unlimitedness, it is an expression of true completeness. Nonetheless, completeness is not to be seen as mere potential but rather as undeniable, concrete being. Clearly, any attempt to understand the concept of completeness through logical thinking leads only to paradox. In Rav Kook's opinion, great *freedom* is needed to struggle away from the narrow confines of rational thought and to *open oneself to the mystical dimension* of reality. Only with such openness can one penetrate to the heart of hearts of being and grasp its hidden meaning. The utopic age, in which human horizons stretch ever wider, is informed with such openness to the mystical dimensions of reality; and in our day, thanks to the enormous gains in the natural sciences, it no longer seems unreasonable. On the contrary, an extreme, stubborn rationalistic attitude has ceased to be convincing. Rav Kook fought for the legitimacy of a mystical world-view by elucidating its reasonability to common sense and by showing its moral and religious value. In his eyes, a mystical-spiritualistic view of the nature of reality and human essence demands great responsibility because it endows one with powers and influence of unfathomable proportions.

This sort of spiritualistic conception imposes more than responsibility. It awards all of human creation with tremendous validity and even holiness. Reality as a whole, including human culture in all its variety—thought, literature, art, even its diverse religions—is perceived as a revelation of the divine. A distinction must indeed be made between partial revelations as they are expressed in general culture and religions, on the one hand, and manifestations of the principle of completeness or unity itself as it finds expression in the Jewish people and its creations; nonetheless, every element of human creativity is of value. Rav Kook's pluralistic, tolerant attitude on this subject did not originate in some liberal outlook but rather in a deeply religious position that refuses to chain the divine in the fetters of constrictive religious thought. God reveals himself in multifarious forms of being, culture, creation; the mission of Judaism is not to combat religions and general culture in order to negate them, but rather to uncover the principle that unites their diverse aspects and details and determines their significance as partial revelations of the inexhaustable source of life.

In exacting the meaning of kabbalistic ideas concerning divine emanation, the essence of the Torah and *Knesset Israel*, Rav Kook initiated a revolutionary change in our understanding of the concept of "revelation." Divine revelation is no longer perceived as a miraculous, supernatural event or as an intellectual abundance emanated from above, directed downward to human consciousness, as it was held to be in medieval thought. Henceforth, revelation is to be perceived as the transcendent dimension of existence;[9] that is, the divine is revealed in nature and in culture, in creation by human hands, and by the nation of Israel in particular. The metaphysical assumptions conceived by Jews in spiritual freedom are seen as "secrets of the Torah"; when a community of observant Jews spontaneously bursts the boundaries imposed by halacha, this in retrospect proves to have been an authentic revelation of divine will; and the pioneering undertaking of the people of the Second Aliyah, heretical and "impudent," is actually an expression of the universal process of repentance including the entire Jewish nation and the world as a whole. The concept "Torah from heaven" [תורה מן השמים] becomes exceedingly broad, representing the infinity of the Torah in terms of its source and meaning, as well as the dynamic nature of its revelation throughout history. The realm of the commandments expands accordingly, and humankind is summoned to hear "the voice of God" [קול ה'] in each of His myriad manifestations.

The influence of existentialist philosophy in Rav Kook's writings is unmistakable. His use of kabbalistic symbols only emphasizes their modern significance. His internalization of some of the fundaments of modern philosophy allowed him to reformulate traditional religious conceptual systems in contemporary terms. The centrality of the individual in existentialist thought was mirrored in Rav Kook's own world-view. For him, as well, "individual essence" is of primary importance, and freedom is seen not only as a basic right or challenge but as intrinsic to one by one's very being. Rav Kook claimed, as did Nietzsche, that "in all values, every man constructs truth, equity, beauty and good for himself according to his nature," and he too believed that morality is contrary to human nature. Yet, whereas for the existentialists the concept of "man" was drained of content in its individual disconnection from all "completeness" to be maintained by "existence" alone[10] and morality gave way to nihilism, in Rav Kook's conception the existence of the individuum is a possibility only in relation to universal wholeness. That is the source and meaning of one's life. The individual must not be swallowed up by the whole, and one is charged with nurturing one's essence and freedom in disregard of "societal approval." One must know, however, that one's uniqueness has significance only in its connection to the "collective individuum," that is, Knesset Israel, and in a wider sense to the "absolute individuum," that is, the unity of being or the divine itself.

Rav Kook's distinct advantage both over idealistic philosophy and the existentialists is that, in contrast to Hegel, he managed to stress essentiality and portray humankind in its individual existence without falling into the net that entrapped the existentialists, leading them to void the individual of all meaning. To affirm the significance of the detail in his relationship to the whole is affirmative and binding. Indeed, normal morality is no longer possible, for morality is bound up with willingness to compromise on being. In opposition to this morality, Rav Kook posed holiness. According to the "morality of the holy," one's love of oneself is identical with one's love for the collective individuum, the absolute, and every one of its expressions; that is, love of all, benefiting all. The "morality of the holy" implies the realization of human essence and at the same time justifies and establishes the link between existence and transcendence.[11] "Morality will not be without its source," Rav Kook affirmed; the metaphysical outlook is thus indispensibile as an ideological model providing a moral challenge.

In our evaluation of Rav Kook's teaching, we must remember he never made explicit claim to propose an exhaustive philosophy, with definitive concepts and a systematic framework; and his writings indeed testify to the lack of any such intent. Nonetheless, his works do reflect a broad world-view anchored in a number of fundamental concepts; in their interrelationship and connection to his position on particular subjects, these principles form an inclusive philosophical method. This method is not free of contradictions and the claim could be made that if some kind of system does in fact exist, that is its greatest drawback. Two responses are possible: first, philosophies, even the most rational and consistent, that contain no contradictions are extremely rare, and despite their contradictions they remain systems. It is natural for a philosopher to develop a comprehensive view based on various intuitions, and that in and of itself ensures the presence of contradictions. Second, Rav Kook, as we have said, made no pretention to offer a consistent, unambivalent system; on the contrary, in his teaching, contradictions themselves acquire the status of system in their reflection of the manifold nature of reality.

Does the lack of crystallized concepts and incomplete system render Rav Kook's teaching abstruse, bordering on meaningless? Undeniably, Rav Kook did not stand up to the rationalistic demand for clear and precise concepts, and this fact indeed makes his world-view more difficult to comprehend, yet at the same time it reveals a message of vital importance: the very nature of rational thought and its worth as an instrument in the perception of reality compared to other disciplines become the object of critical discussion. Although Rav Kook was interested in appealing to common sense and presenting his outlook as reasonable, logical requirements do not bind him as they do other philosophers, for his primary interest remains in what is beyond the grasp and the language of logical tools. It would thus be neither just nor constructive to measure his thinking with the yardstick of logical thought in the strictest sense of the term. Nonetheless, certain questions demand response, and we must examine his conception on the basis of his own concepts and demands, with an eye to their contribution and meaning for us today.

If we accept the assumptions of a dialectic and harmonistic conception such as that of Rav Kook, it becomes very difficult to criticize, because within its framework even contradictions are part of its system. Yet beyond the contradictions, ambivalent formulations and dialectic inquiry, the troubling question of how Rav Kook really wished his words to be understood still persists. How can his view of the relativity and subjectivy of all perception be reconciled with his triumphing of the right to take a stand on metaphysical problems? How can openness to mysticism be encouraged while avoiding the dangers posed by that openness? What practical halacha can be gleaned from his contradictory remarks about the mitzvot? Can a person, if he has reached the level of *zaddik,* hasid or "holy man of silence" consider himself exempt from the commandments, and under what circumstances? Is there any element built into Rav Kook's conception to guard against deterioration into total religious anarchy?

Other questions demand an answer as well: What resolution is reached in his writings among the highly developed consciousness of freedom, the elevation of the concept of "freedom" to the central focus of interest and a deterministic view of processes occuring in reality, man, history, and in culture? Does that deterministic element of his thought not hide the seeds portending the development of false messianism? And more: how is his view of individuality related to his estimation of the nation as a vital entity and to the ties binding him to the normative system of halacha and its values? Can ethics be founded on the basis of such an abstract idea of morality and such extreme individualism in which every person sets values for him or herself?

Throughout our treatment of these matters here, we sought to respond to these and other questions. Now, in conclusion, let us review some central theses.

Indeed, the anarchistic implications contained in Rav Kook's thought cannot be overlooked; and this was clear both to his most vociferous opponents of the Old Yishuv and to those who wished to draw practical instruction from it beyond his own intent, as for example, Rav Shmuel Alexandrov. But that was not Rav Kook's way. Throughout his oeuvre, the interest of ethics is preeminent. Despite the spiritualistic elements of his thinkings, Rav Kook was no spiritualist. He mandated action and fought for the place and standing of the commandments as the sole discipline by which to attain completeness. The *mitzvot* are seen as the ultimate revelation of God's will; they reflect divine qualities concealed in reality. Fulfillment of the *mitzvot* integrates the individual in cosmic-divine movement and conforms one's world and values to "divine ideas" inherent in all of being. In Rav Kook's eyes, progress toward the utopic destiny of broadened awareness and recognition of all-embracing unity must cause a revolutionary change in public mentality, a kind of "Torah rivival," a renaissance of fulfilling *mitzvot* and arousal of religious feeling. There is indeed a measure of ambivalence in Rav Kook's relationship to the practical commandments, both in the existential burden involved in their observance and in their essential value in future days. The contention is present in Rav Kook's writings that the *mitzvot* will be annulled in days to come, and they are not to be seen as the felicity and aim of human existence. This view, however, can be understood in light of what he wrote in another context: although the *mitzvot*, as a reflection of divine values, will not be annulled, they will no longer have normative validity. In the utopic age, the *mitzvot* will be understood as natural acts performed out of freedom, for the sake of human self-actualization. Further, just as the significance of Torah and *mitzvot* is broadened, the concepts of "sin" and "repentance" acquire wider meaning as well. These concepts no longer represent a violation and restoration of formal halacha, but rather the directions offered one in making one's existential decision: on the one hand, self-affirmation or alienation; and on the other, their mystical significance as cosmic-divine processes.

The conclusion seems inescapable that despite the ethical objective of his oeuvre, no ethics are to be found in all of Rav Kook's writings. He did not map clear boundaries between holy and profane, between good and evil, between pious and wicked, between *mitzvah* and transgression. On the contrary, he destroyed commonly accepted, agreed-upon boundaries, and the evident danger involved in religious acts achieved through transgressions impels us to emphasize that he remained absolutely faithful to halacha. This must be realized beyond any doubt: even though Rav Kook did not delineate formal, objective boundaries, the entirety of his writings yield a principle enrooted in the dialectical nature of his thought, and by that precept each individual sets his or her own boundaries: *the principle of balance*. Rav Kook utterly rejected all extremism and stridently claimed "there is not a single quality in our world that would not be harmed by fanaticism."[12] In Rav Kook's teaching, as in his personality, there is great potential for extremist tendencies. Again and again, though, throughout his writings, he called for balance and control, and his way of life inspired practical halacha. Any attempt to take up one aspect of his teaching while ignoring others only distorts it, for its dialectic nature is of the essence, determining its uniqueness. The demand for a balanced life has metaphysical significance, as well as ontological and ethical. It expresses Rav Kook's perception of the need to discover the right balance among various disciplines, as it mirrors the dialectic nature of reality itself. The whole of one's religious and moral problems must be judged in light of this principle, as well as questions of resurrection and redemption.

I am continually confronted with a troubling question, posed by students and colleagues alike: Rav Kook's teaching, charged as it is with messianic tension, interwoven with deterministic elements, offering a mystical interpretation of historical and cultural processes— do its dangers not outweigh its benefits? And the shadows it reveals, do they not obfuscate its lights? It seems vaguely heretical, does it not contain hints of "false messianism"? As our discussion draws to a close, I am impelled to clarify my own position on this urgent issue.

Since the dawn of its appearance in the Jewish world, the messianic idea has left an indelible mark on Jewish history, shaping it to such an extent that each manifestation of messianism has ultimately been drawn ad absurdum. Messianic awareness contains irresoluble dialectic tension. The nobility of the messianic idea, its vision of an ideal world order and human image is an emanated entity, transforming redemption into a utopia. Here, then, lies the danger: on the one hand, if one abandons the idea of redemption a priori, one's life is stripped of all sense and meaning, and nothing more can motivate one to improve the world. On the other hand, if one anticipates the end of days and begins to clear the path for redemption within one's own concrete world, one will be driven from society and accused of a purveyor of "false messianism."

Yet the historical force and contribution of the messianic idea in Judaism stem, in fact, from the tension created by its dialectical nature. Any attempt to release this tension actually threatens to sever the vital link between the real and the utopian, for the moment the utopia is "realized," light will be eclipsed by the dark shadows of reality, and utopia it will be no more. Yet if the vision is lost and no one seeks it, if one does not long to build the earthly Jerusalem in the image of the heavenly Jerusalem, then every undertaking is bound to perish in its infancy, "and the pit cannot be filled from its own digging" [by digging more earth out of it].

The question is whether something in Rav Kook's teaching does upset this delicate balance. Did he wish to resolve or eliminate the dialectical tension inherent in the relationship between heaven and earth, between spirit and matter, between vision and action? Our discussion, I believe, leads us to one fundamental conclusion: nothing characterizes Rav A. I. HaCohen Kook's thought more than its dialectical nature. The guilt of those who violate that complex nature in selective interpretation must not be cast on the shoulders of that vital nature. It is when the messianic idea is made concrete in flagrant disregard of that dialectic nature and its manifestations on all levels of reality—in history, culture, and human consciousness—then and only then does it bear sour fruit.

Does the danger of false messianism compel us to abandon the concept of "messianism" itself? As far as Rav Kook was concerned, the meaning of any undertaking lies beyond it, and the strength to endure is drawn from the infinite aspiration toward an inexhaustible goal; that is, the messianic hope. Messianism, then, is the lifebreath of the Israelite nation, the secret of its force and eternity.

Does the principle of balance contain any assurance that balance will actually be maintained? Clearly, this question cannot be answered affirmatively. Then, does the very fulfillment of the moral teaching ensure morality will be realized in life?

It is on this point that Rav Kook's teaching presents the challenge that the person of faith must ceaselessly confront in the modern era.[13] That teaching strives to free one from the chains and constraints of societal consent and narrowminded religious ideas, yet at the same time it imposes a heavy burden on one, exacting self-control; the ability to limit oneself is seen as the most inalienable expression of freedom. The Jewish people are summoned to greatness: to think "in monumental terms," for they must be pioneers striding before humanity toward new planes of awareness, toward recognition of the unity of being and understanding the secret of life. Whereas, for Heidegger, humankind stands before death, its reality coldly palpable, Rav Kook challenges death. Human existence means the intensity of life, progress toward life with no shadow of death, "life ever after."

It is difficult to say just how aware Rav Kook was of the grave dangers concealed in his world-view. In his eyes, in any case, the dangers latent in simplistic and petrified religiosity were no less threatening, and he chose the path of constructive and creative daring; that way alone offered the hope of renewing the vitality of religion and rescuing it from its distress.[14]

NOTES

Preface

1. Joseph Klauzner, *Philosophiya ve -Hogey De'ot*, vol. 2 (Tel Aviv and Jerusalem, 1941), p. 158.

2. Ibid.

3. G. Scholem, *Devarim be-Go* (Tel Aviv, 1976), p. 76.

4. R. Schatz-Uffenheimer, "'Utopiya U-Meshihiyut be-Torat ha-Rav Kook" ("Utopia and Messianism in the Teachings of Rav Kook") (November 1978): 15.

5. *Igrot Harayah (IG"R)*, vol. 1 (Jerusalem, 1962), p. 128.

6. See R. Schatz-Uffenheimer, "Reyshit ha-Masa' neged ha-Rav Kook" ("The First Campaign against Rav Kook"), *Molad* (new series) (1974): 251–262; Menachem Friedman, *Society and Religion: The Non-Zionist Orthodox in Eretz-Israel 1918–1936* (Jerusalem, 1978), pp. 87–109; David Canaani, *Ha-ʿAliyah ha-Shenia ha-Ovedet ve-Yahasah la-Dat ve-la-Masoret* (Tel Aviv, 1977), pp. 118–121.

7. The studies are of three essential types: monographs and historical studies, articles about specific problems in his philosophy, and summary articles. Collections and anthologies of excerpts from his writings also exist interspersed with comments by the compiling editors, but these are not studies in the accepted sense of the wrod. A partial bibliographical list is found at the end of this book. I intend to compile an exhaustive bibliographical study in the framework of a book to be published by the New York University Press, edited by Lawrence Kaplan and David Schatz.

8. Scholem, *Devarim be-Go*.

9. All italics are mine, also further on, except where noted.

10. A Steinsaltz, "Ha-Baʿayatiyut be-ʿOrot ha-kodesh," *Kovetz ha-Rayah* (Jerusalem, 1966), p. 2102. The question of Rav Kook's terminology is an essential one that will be discussed in detail in Chapter 9.

241

11. Hillel Zeitlin, *Safran shel Yehidim* (Jerusalem, 1979), p. 235.

12. S. H. Bergman, "Torat ha-Hitpatchut be-Mishnato shel ha-Rav Kook," in the anthology *Shitato Shel ha-Rav Kook*, (Jerusalem, 1963), p. 69.

13. Schatz, "Utopiya."

14. The objection to viewing Rav Kook's thought as systematical is reminiscent of the debate on a similar question regarding the philosophy of F. Nietzsche; Ron Sigad establishes that Neitzsche's philosophy is, in fact, systematic. See his *Existentialism* (Jerusalem, 1982), p. 73.

15. These remarks were based on the testimony of the author Alexander Ziskind Rabinowitz in the book *Ha-Mahshava ha-Yisra'elit*, ed. A. Kalmenson (Jerusalem, 1920), p. 13, and cited in Z. Yaron, *Mishnato shel ha-Rav Kook* (Jerusalem, 1974), p. 106.

1. In the Grip of Contradiction

1. The letter, dated 29 Tishrei 5667 (1907), was sent from Jaffa. It is currently held by the Genazim archive in Tel Aviv.

2. On the life story of Rav Kook, see Y. L. Ha-Cohen Fishman, *Ha-Re'ayah* (Jerusalem, 1965); also J. B. Agus, *Banner of Jerusalem* (New York, 1964).

3. See Y. L. Ha-Cohen Fishman, "Toldot Ha-Rav," *Azkarah* (Jerusalem, 1936–38), pp. 47, 48.

4. Rivka Schatz-Uffenheimer has already remarked that Rav Kook must be viewed as a contemporary writer. See her "Utopiya," p. 15. See also E. Goldman, "Zikato Shel ha-Rav Kook la-Mahshavah ha'Eyropeyit" ("Rabbi Kook's Involvement with European Philosophy"), in *Yovel 'rot, Haguto shel ha-Rav A. Y. Ha-Cohen Kook*, ed. B. Ish-Shalom and S. Rosenberg (Jerusalem, 1988), pp. 115–122.

In this article Goldman argues that a comparison of phraseology and wording clearly points to Fabius Meises's book *Korot ha-Philosophiya ha-Hadasha* (Leipzig, 1887) as an important source of Rav Kook's philosophical knowledge. This book may indeed have been a source; but Rav Kook may also never have seen it. Linguistic and technical similarities do not suffice to prove a link to any particular source, for a similar style was common in the Hebrew journals of the period, in which various articles on philosophers and their theories were published. Rav Kook himself was published in these journals and no doubt read them as well. For example, in the booklet *Yizra'el*, a literary collection edited by A. Z. Rabinowitz that appeared in Jaffa in 1913, Rav Kook wrote (under the pseudonym "Rab'ai") thoughts entitled "Perurim Me-Shulhan Gavoha." In the same booklet, adjacent to "Perurim," an anonymous article on Goethe (signed A. S.) was published; the ideas and phraseology bear striking resemblance to those of Rav Kook. This article as well as

David Neimark's articles in *Hashiloah* on "religious philosophy" (vol. 7) and on "modern philosophy" (starting from vol. 8 in installments), as well as Hermann Cohen's lecture on "The Founding of Departments in Ethics and Religious Philosophy in Rabbinical Seminaries" (*Hashiloah* 13 Cracow, 1904, p. 356) are but examples of texts available to Rav Kook. (Also see Rav Zvi Yehuda Kook's letter to Brenner in which he mentions his lecture as a source that influenced Rav Kook's writing in his book *Ikve Hatzon* [note 1]). More, Rav Kook's writings reflect references not only to philosophical sources but also to Kabbalah and all of Jewish thought. For example, in the aforementioned article in *Yizra'el* Goethe is quoted (in Hebrew translation) as follows: "I cannot divide life, not what is within it nor what is outside of it. Everything together must yiueld the whole" (*Yizra'el*, p. 55). Rav Kook remarks elsewhere: "I cannot distinguish absolutely between parts of reality. Rather, the totality of existence reveals itself to me in gradual distinction" (*'Arpalei Tohar*, p. 33). In the next words of the sentence Rav Kook reverts to kabbalistic symbolism: "From the smallest creatures to the most spiritual phenomenon full of great might (*gevura*) and glory (*tiferet*), crowned by the crown of wisdom, understanding and knowledge (*keter, hokhma, bina ve-da'at*) . . . lays the foundation for everything . . . and their presence combines in the royal order (*yesod*) . . . and God is king (*malkhut*)." The topic requires further discussion. See also note 17.

5. Of interest in this context are the remarks of the Danish philosopher Harold Hoffding, a contemporary of Rav Kook: "A philosopher cannot help but be (a product) of his time and of his people. Even in his most independent moments he is often guided by a desire to express singular qualities and biases of whch he is not at all aware." See H. Hoffding, "Philosophy and Life," *International Journal of Ethics*, 12 (January 1902): 138, 140, 143. Quoted in L. B. Feuer, *Einstein* (Tel Aviv, 1979), p. 107. Karl Mannheim also commented on the relationship between the visions and feelings of the genius and the historical experiences of the group to which one belongs: "Underlying even the profound insight of the genius are the collective historical experiences of a group." K. Mannheim, *Ideology and Utopia* (New York, 1936), p. 269.

Rav Kook himself relates to this matter, writing: "We all realize that in our era, with its division into separate nations, no one can receive spiritual influences without donning the distinctive garb of his own people" *'Arpalei Tohar* (Jaffa, 1904), p. 78. "Great scholars, despite all their superior knowledge must receive the good and healthy substance of their ideas from the honesty of the masses, must interpret and elevate that simple honesty and present it in refined form; those who do so are joyful thinkers, and they bring blessing to the nations" (ibid., p. 24).

6. See T. Ross, "Musag ha-Elohut Shel ha-Rav Kook ("Rav Kook's Concept of God"), *Da'at* (Winter 1982): 109 ff.

7. H. Zeitlin, *Safran Shel Yehidim* (Jerusalem, 1979), pp. 235–237.

8. *Kivunim* 1 November 1978.

9. Ross, "Musag Ha-Elohut," pp. 123–124.

10. Eliezer Goldman, "Ziyonut Hilonit, Te'udat Yisra'el ve-Takhlit ha-Torah" ("Secular Zionism, the Vacation of Israel and the Telos of the Torah: Rabbi Kook's Articles Published in Ha'Peless Between 1901–1904"), *Da'at* (Summer 1983): 125.

11. See *Ha-Shiloah* [Crackow] 13 (January–July 1904). Dr. Yossef Klauzner and Haim Nahman Bialik, Eds., pp. 356–367. The lecture on "The Founding of Departments in Ethics and Religious Philosophy in Rabbinical Seminaries" was delivered by Hermann Cohen on January 6, 1904 at a general meeting of the members of "the society for the promotion of Jewish Wisdom" which took place in Berlin. This lecture was translated into Hebrew and published under the name of a man who signed himself *Sofer*. Thus, despite its great importance, it was not included among the other writings of Hermann Cohen. (My thanks to Binyamin Lehman, a student at Yeshivat Merkaz ha-Rav, for graciously providing me with a copy of Rav Zvi Yehuda's letter.)

12. Goldman, "Ziyonut Hilonit," p. 103. A substantial portion of Rav Kook's writings still exist only in manuscript form and await a "redeeming hand." On the controversy surrounding the manuscripts, see C. Segal, "Orot Be-'Ofel," *Nekudah* 113 (September 1987): 16–27. Responses to this article appear in subsequent volumes.

13. Ibid., p. 125.

14. From the booklet *Li-Shlosha be'Elul* (Jerusalem, 1947), p. 5.

15. *Ha-Rayah*, p. 62.

16. See Kook, "'Al Bamoteynu Halalim," *Sinai*, 17: pp. 1–5.

17. Therefore, in contrast to Goldman's approach in "Ziyonut Hilonit," it appears that the more important texts clarifying Rav Kook's theoretical ideologies are in *'Orot Hakodesh*, *'Arpalei Tohar* and writings of a similar nature (some still in manuscript form) rather than letters and articles written for publication in newspapers and journals. This contention is strengthened by the fact that all of the sources on which Goldman bases himself in his article are of a purely publicist nature. In his own publicist articles Rav Kook indeed refrained, for understandable reasons, from using kabbalistic style and terminology, yet as stated, this does not prove he only later adopted kabbalistic phrases or did so for purely tactical reasons. On this point see Goldman's "Hitgabshut Hashkefotav ha-Mercaziyot shel ha-Rav Kook—ha-Ketavim me-ha-Shanim 1906–1909" ("The Structuring of Rabbi Kook's Thought: 1906–1909"), *Bar-Ilan Sefer ha-Shana* 22–23 (1988): 870–120. See also Y. L. Ashkenazi, "Shimush be-Musagim Kabbaliyim be-Mishnato Shel ha-Rav Kook" ("The Cabbalistic Sources of Rabbi Kook"), *Yovel 'Orot*, ed. B. Ish-Shalom and S. Rosenberg (Jerusalem, 1985), p. 123.

18. This is also true of Rav Kook's understanding of *will*, despite the external resemblance to R. Moshe Cordovero and Ibn Gabirol's apprehension

of this concept, a likeness that has blinded certain researchers to the uniqueness of Rav Kook's conception. See Z. Yaron, *Mishnato shel ha-Rav Kook* (Jerusalem, 1974), pp. 62–63 and note 14.

19. Consider H. Clark, *The Philosophy of Albert Schweitzer* (London, 1962).

20. See Schatz-Uffenheimer, "Utopiya," p. 24.

21. S. H. Bergman, "'Al Torah ha-Hitpatchut be-Mishnato Shel ha-Rav Kook," *Anashim ve-Derachim* (Jerusalem, 1967). IN the same book a chapter is devoted to Teilhard de Chardin and the concept of evolution. Also consider Marcel Dubois, "Dat u-Mada'-Torato Shel Teilhard de Chardin ve-Ha'arakhata," *Petahim* (Spring 1969). Teilhard de Chardin himself treats these subjects in his book, *Le phenomene humain* (Paris, 1955).

22. S. H. Bergman, "Ha-Lohem be-Malkhut Shaday," *Hogim U-Ma'aminim* (Jerusalem, 1959), pp. 171–195. And M. Mattmueller, *Leonhard Ragaz und der reliogiose Sozialismus*, 1–2 (1957). Ragaz had great affection for the Jewish people; he and Martin buber were friends. See M. Buber, "Le-'Ish Britainu (le-Yom Huladeto Ha-75 Shel Leonhard Ragaz)," *Ha-Po'el ha-Za'ir*, 14, no. 46 (August 5, 1943), M. Buber, "Ragaz ve-Yisrael," *Ba'ayot*, 7, no. 6 (1946), pp. 241–245. Consider also the collection, Y. Levi, ed. *Leonhard Ragaz—Yisrael, Yahadut, Nazrut* (Petah Tikvah, 1968). (In the collection, Ragaz's essay appears with articles by S. H. Bergmann, M. Buber, and D. Flusser.)

23. *Igrot Rayah* vol. 1, p. 45.

24. Characteristics of the crisis of this period were expressed in various fields including philosophy, art, and literature, especially in the "Decadence" genre of French literature of the late nineteenth century, which coined the period as *Fin de siecle*. See K. W. Swart, *The Sense of Decadence in Nineteenth Century France*, (The Hague, 1964). Also see A Shapiro, "Dual Structures in the Thought of Martin Buber," diss., Tel Aviv, 1984, pp. 23 ff. and note 1, p. 207. On the intellectual, societal, and political repercussions in Europe 1890–1914, see H. S. Hughes, *Consciousness and Society* (New York, 1958), pp. 33–66; R. Link-Salinger (Hyman), *Gustav Landauer: Philosopher of Utopia* (Indianapolis, 1977), pp. 7–8; and in other sources cited in "Mivnim Du'aliyim" notes 9–19. See also L. S. Feuer, *Einstein and the Generations of Science*, trans. G. Levi (Tel Aviv, 1979).

25. Y. Kaufman *Bekhevle ha-Zeman* (Tel Aviv, 1936), p. 41.

26. B. Croce, *Toldot Europa be-Me'a ha-Tesh' Esre* (Jerusalem, 1962), p. 47.

27. I. Berlin, *'Arba' Massot 'Al Herut* (Tel Aviv, 1971), p. 193.

28. These thoughts are documented in the memoirs of Rav David Cohen: "*Nezir 'Ehav*, Divrey Torah, Hagot, Mehkar ve-ha'arakhah." *Zikaron le-Nezir ha-Elohim Maran ha-Rav David Cohen (Ha-Rav ha-Nazir) z"l*, vol. 1 (Jerusalem, 1922), pp. 287–288.

29. See Chapter 2, note 56.

30. An example is the question of Rav Kook's attachment to European philosophy. Rav David Cohen, Rav Kook's student and close friend, editor of *'Orot Hakodesh,* speaks explicitly of such an attachment (*Nezir 'Ehav,* pp. 362–363). However, Rav Kook himself was apparently unaware of the influence European philosophy had on him and claimed that the sources of his philosophy "flow . . . solely from the tents of Shem, from the wellspring of Torah—its public and hidden revelations" (from a letter to Dr. Kaminka, *IG"R,* vol. 2, p. 132).

31. For a description of the historical background, see E. Luz, *Makbilim Nifgashim* (Tel Aviv, 1985); I. Etkas, *Rav Yisrael Salanter ve-Reyshitah Shel Tenu'at ha-Mussar* (*Rabbi Israel Salanter and the Beginning of the "Mussar" Movement*) (Jerusalem: 1982); Y. Solomon, "Ha-'Imut Beyn ha-Haredim la-Maskilim be-Tenu'at Hibat-Ziyon be-Shenot ha-Shemonim," *Ha-Ziyyonut,* 5 (1979): 43–77; S. Eisenstadt, *Toldot Tenu'at ha-Po'alim ha-Yehudit,* vols. 1–2 (Tel Aviv, 1970).

32. On this concept and the first use of the term consider M. Friedman, *Hevra ve-Dat* (Jerusalem: 1978), p. 1, note 1; See also I. Bartal, "'Yishuv Yashan' ve-'Yishuv Hadash'—Ha-Dimu'i ve-ha-Mezi'ut" ("The 'Old' and 'New' Yishuv—Image and Reality"), *Cathedra* 2 (Heshvan 1976): 3–19; J. Katz "'Od 'Al Yahasey ha-Yishuv ha-Yashan ve-ha-Yishuv he-Hadash" ("More on the Relations Between the 'Old Yishuv and the 'New Yishuv'"), *Cathedra* 12 (*Tamuz 1979*): 31–33; E. R. Malakhi, *Perakim be-Toldot ha-Yishuv ha-Yashan* (Tel Aviv, 1971); Y. Kaniel, *Hemshekh ve-Temura, ha-Yishuv ha-Yashan ve-ha-Yishuv he-Hadash be-Tekufat ha-'Aliya ha-Rishona ve-ha-Sheniyah* (*Continuity and Change: Old Yishuv and New Yishuv During the First and the Second Aliyah*) (Jerusalem, 1982); Y. Kaniel, "Ha-Munahim Yishuv Yashan ve-Yishuv Hadash be-'Eyney Beney ha-Dor (1882–1914) u-ve-'Eyney ha-Historiyographi'a" ("The Terms 'Old Yishuv' and 'New Yishuv' in Contemporaneous Usage [1882–1914] and in Historiographical Usage), *Cathedra* 6 (1978): 3–19.

33. Friedman, *Hevra ve-Dat,* p. 2.

34. Responsa of Hatam Sofer, Jerusalem, 1970. OH no. 203, p. 251.

35. M. Eliav, *Ahavat Tzion ve-Germania* (Jerusalem, 1966), p. 326.

36. Rav Zvi Hirsch Lehren in *Emet me-Ere'z,* vol. 3. Amsterdam, 1843.

37. Consider Y. Peres, "Le-Toldot ha-isur 'Al Batey ha-Sefer be-Yerushalayim," in the collection *Minha ie-David* (Jerusalem, 1935); likewise L. A. Fraenkel, *Yerushalayma* (Vienna, 1860), p. 202.

38. Fraenkel, ibid., pp. 249–250.

39. See *Igrot Rabbi 'Azriel Hildesheimer,* comp. and ed. M. Eliav (Jerusalem, 1966), p. 51. Rav Akiba Lehren (1795–1876) was one of the main supporters of the yishuv in Eretz Israel. The friendship between him and Rav

Hildesheimer grew colder in the wake of Hildesheimer's plans to build an orphanage in Eretz Israel where secular studies would also be taught. See ibid., p. 98, no. 153.

40. See M. Friedman, *Hevra ve-Dat*, p. 18, and no. 43.

41. Ibid., p. 22.

42. Ibid., p. 27.

43. Consider D. Cana'ani, *Ha-'Aliya ha-Sheniya ha-'Ovedet ve-Yahasah la-Dat ve-la-Masoret* (Tel Aviv, 1977); *Tenu'at ha-'Avoda ve-Yahasah la-Dat*. Protocol from a seminar (in light of D. Cana'ani's book), Institute for Studies On Labor and Society, founded by the Histadrut and Tel Aviv University, 1976; S. Zemah, "Sifrut ve-Nekhar," *Shedmot* 30 (Summer 1968), especially pp. 18–25.

44. Cana'ani, *Ha-Aliya ha-Sheniya*, pp. 28, 48–55.

45. Ibid., pp. 31–32.

46. Ibid., pp. 100–101.

47. Consider E. Don-Yahya, "Hilun, Shelila ve-Shiluv Tfisot shel ha-Yahadut ha-Mesoratit u-Musageyha be-Zionut ha-Sozialistit," *Kivunim* 8 (Summer 1980): 35.

48. The Eyn Gev Haggada, 1940. A selection of texts from Kibbutz Passover Haggadot that exemplify the secularization of the language is found in the addendum to Avshalom Reich, "Changes and Developments in the Passover Haggadot of the Kibbutz Movement 1935–1971," dissertation, University of Texas at Austin, 1972, Haggadat Eyn Gev, p. 395.

49. Ibid., p. 199.

50. This definition is Bialik's. B. Ben-Yehuda, "Le-Toldot ha-Hinukh be-Erez Yisrael" ("On the History of Education in Israel"), *Ha-Hinukh be-Yisrael* (Jerusalem: Ministry of Education, 1973), p. 22. These facts are recorded by E. Don-Yahya ("Hilun, Shalila ve-Shiluv Tfisot"), and see his other comments on this subject ibid., pp. 42–44.

51. "Be-Hayim u-va-Sifrut," *Kol Kitvey J. H. Brenner*, vol. 2, p. 61.

52. *Reshafim* (February 1910).

53. D. Ben-Gurion, "Le-She'aylat ha-Yishuv ha-Yashan" ("The Question Regarding *Yishuv ha-Yashan*"), *Ha-Ahdut* 2 (1910).

54. D. Cana'ani, *Ha-'Aliyah ha-Sheniya*, pp. 106–111.

55. 12 Sivan 1933. Agudat Yisrael Archives, no. 140.

56. 4 Av 1933. Agudat Yisrael Archives, no. 140.

57. M. Friedman, *Hevra ve-Dat*, p. 359.

58. Ibid., p. 362.

59. Manuscript, Collection D, p. 18b. This paragraph has recently been published in *'Orot ha-Emunah*, pp. 67–68.

60. *IG"R*, vol. 1, p. 139.

61. *IG"R*, vol. 2, p. 12.

62. *IG"R*, vol. 1, p. 148.

63. Ibid., p. 139.

64. *IG"R*, vol. 2, p. 265.

65. Ibid., p. 268.

66. *IG"R*, vol. 1, p. 197.

67. See J. Avneri, "Ha-Rav Kook u-fe'iluto ha-Hinukhit be-Tekufat Yaffo" ("Rabbi Kook and His Educational Activities During His Jaffa Tenure"), *Niv ha-Midrashia* (1984): 181–182.

68. *IG"R*, vol. 2, pp. 27, 340.

69. Y. Avneri, "Ha-Rav Kook u-Fe'iluto," p. 183 and no. 15.

70. *IG"R*, vol. 2, p. 340.

71. Ibid., p. 97.

72. Ibid., p. 269.

73. Y. Avneri, "Ha-Rav Kook u-Fe'iluto," p. 191. See also D. Tidhar, *Encyclopediya le-Haluzey ha-Yishuv u-Vonav* (Tel Aviv, 1947), vol. 7, p. 766, and see Rav Y. L. Maimon, *Azkarah*, loc. cit., p. 111.

74. See Avneri, "Ha-Rav Kook u-Fe'iluto," p. 191; in more detail, see *IG"R* vol. 1, pp. 52, 66, 122, 131, 140, 185, 189, 195.

75. Y. Avneri, ibid., p. 192. The curriculum in the upper division would include philosophy, Kabbalah, Aggadah, Midrash, Mussar (ethics), and "all aspects of historical investigation."

76. Ibid., p. 193.

77. Ibid. In fact, the yeshiva did not create a great stir, probably due to its sparce achievements. At the outset there were four to five students in the yeshiva. Later the number reached approximately ten. Rav Kook saw the lack of success as a result of financial difficulties; he was satisfied with the quality of students and the level of studies. The yeshiva operated for only a short time, 1909–1914, and closed when Rav Kook went abroad during World War I.

78. *IG"R*, vol. 1, p. 185. One must not forget that Rav Kook himself, although a member of the Second Aliyah, dressed like a man of the old Yishuv. On Rav Kook as a man of the Second Aliyah, see E. Shapira, "Ha-Rayah Kook ke-'Ish ha-Aliya ha-Sheniya" ("Avraham Y. Kook as a Member of the Second Aliya"), *Ha-Do ar* 10 (Adar I 1978): 230–231.

79. M. Madan, "Igeret be-'Inyaney Lashon" ("Letters on Linguistic Subjects"), *Zikhron Rayah*, ed. Y. Raphael (Jerusalem, 1986), p. 15.

80. See Y. Fried, "Igrot ve-Te'udot" ("Letters and Documents"), *Zikhron Rayah*, p. 243.

81. In Rav Zvi Yehuda's letter to Brenner he asks the latter to study Rav Kook's book closely and review it in *Ha-me'orer*. On this journal, see H. Matras. "Ha-Me'orer" *Ketav Et ve-Arikhato* (Jerusalem, 1984): see also A. Beilen *J. H. brenner be-Tekufat ha-Me'orer*, (Meraveya, 1943).

82. S. Kushnir, *HaRoeh le-Merachok* (Tel Aviv, 1972), p. 68.

83. D. Cana'ani, *Ha-Aliya ha-Sheniga*, p. 199. *Ha-Po'el ha-Za'ir* 27a (1920) and 14 (1919); *Ha-Aretz ve-ha-'Avoda* 5 (1919).

84. Cana'ani, ibid.

85. *Ha-Po'el ha-Za'ir* 40 (1909). Similar criticism is levelled in the same magazine, vol. 4 (1911).

86. *Ha-'Ahdut* 9 (1914). See also P. Peli, "Ha-Rav Kook u-Brenner: Or ve Hoshekh," *Davar* (August 31, 1984); N. Tutmann and A. Ben-Ezer, *Beyn Holot ve-Kehol Shamayim* (Yavnen, 1980), p. 88; See also Rav Zvi Yehuda Kook's letter to Brenner, Matras, "Ha Me'orer," Chapter 1.

87. G. Hafner, "Darki le-Merhaveya," *Sefer Merhaveya ha-Ko'operaziya* (Tel Aviv, 1961), pp. 95–96.

88. "Mikhtav me-ha-Galil ha-takhton," *Ha-Po'el ha-Za'ir* 11 (1914). It seems that the rabbis were moderately successful in some of the settlements: in Poriya *mikva'ot* were fixed and the kitchen was made kosher; in Zikhron Ya'akov, Kefar Tabor, Yavni'el and Rosh Pina, "talmud torahs" (religious primary schools), were established. The "talmud torah" in Yavniel was especially successful, and it attracted most of the local student body. For more on the results of the mission in the areas of education and *halacha*, see Kaniel, *Hemshekh ve-Temura*, pp. 236–237. See also *Hoveret 'Eleh Mas'ey*, a journal of the mission of the rabbis from the Ve'idah le-Haramat Keren ha-Dat ve-ha-Yahadut (Council for Raising the Prestige of Religion and Judaism), Frankfurt, 1916.

89. Y. Fried, "Igrot ve-Te'udot," published a letter in which he invited Rav Kook "and other national giants" to his house "to consult on matters effecting the spiritual state of the *yishuv.*" The list of those invited included Rabbis Berlin, Uzziel and Fishman as well as Menahem, Ussishkin, Itzhak

Ben-Zvi, David Ben-Gurion, Joseph Sprinzak, Moshe Glickson, Asher Beilin and Berel Katznelson.

90. Among the members of the Zionist organization some viewed it as a movement for cultural revival as well, which would engage in education and ideological propaganda. However, the polar opposites in the movement allowed no consensus and the question of "culture" was tabled as a compromise measure. See Luz, *Makbilim Nifgashim*, pp. 187–196. On the position of "Mizrahi" on this issue see ibid., pp. 299–324.

91. *IG"R*, vol. 4 (Jerusalem, 1984), pp. 24–25. Rav Kook also wrote about this matter to the rabbi of Gur in a letter dated 11 Nissan 1921 (ibid., pp. 102–103).

92. *IG"R*, vol. 1, p. 169. He came to this realization near the time of his aliya to Israel.

93. *IG"R*, vol. 3, p. 200.

94. From the call to found Ha-Yeshiva ha-Mercazit ha-'Olamit (the Central Universal Yeshiva), Elul 1922, *IG"R*, vol. 4, p. 138.

95. Ibid., p. 231.

96. From "Ha-Yeshiva ha-Mercazit ha-'Olamit be-Yerushalayim, me-'et Rabenu ha-Gadol Maran Avraham Yizhak Ha-Cohen Kook, ha-Rav ha-Rashi le-Erez Yisrael." This booklet was printed in Jerusalem but is undated.

97. On education and enlightenment in general in Rav Kook's conception, see Yaron, *Mishnato shel ha-Rav Kook*, pp. 189–230.

98. *IG"R*, vol. 1, p. 86.

99. Ibid., p. 132.

100. Actually, already in the 1930s, despite the ban imposed on secular studies, the rabbi of Gur permitted the study of English as a foreign language in the "talmud torah" of the Gur Hassidim in Tel Aviv, on condition that the studies would be held in a room separate from the school. See Friedman, *Hevra ve-Dat*, pp. 267–268.

101. On the ideology of the Hesder yeshivot, see Rav A. Lichtenstein, "Zot Torat ha-Hesder," *'Alon Shevut* 100 (1982): 9 ff.

2. *Reality and Truth—Epistemology and Ontology*

1. *Orot ha-Kodesh* (*OH"K*), vol. 1, pp. 218–219. It is interesting to compare Rav Kook's views on the theory of knowledge to the outlook of Rabbi Nahman of Bratslav, especially on the question of doubt ("the question") and its place. See J. Weiss, *Mehkarim be-Hassidut Bratslav* (*Studies of the Hassidut of*

Breslov) (Jerusalem, 1975), pp. 109–149; A. R. Green, *Tormented Master* (New York: Schocken Books, 1981), pp. 285–330.

2. See *IG"R*, vol. 1, pp. 47–48: "We have always known, and did not need Kant to reveal this secret, for *all* human *knowledge* is subjective and relative." Also *Eder Hayakar*, p. 42: "Concepts are attainable only in a relative way."

3. See note 33.

4. *OH"K*, vol. 1, pp. 218–219.

5. Compare Spinoza's various kinds of knowledge: *Ma'amar Katzar al Elokhim ha-'Adam ve-'Oshro*, ed. Ben Shelomo, pp. 268–272.

6. *OH"K*, vol. 1, p. 219; see also pp. 6–7. Compare Weiss *Mehkarim*, pp. 116–119. Of interest in this context are Irving M. Kopi's remarks in his book *Mevo le-Logika* (Tel Aviv, 1977), p. 423: "Scientific explanation is always presented in a tentative and temporary fashion. Any explanation is considered as no more than a hypothesis, verified by ready facts or relevant testimony. The scientist's vocabulary is misleading on this point. When what was originally proposed as an 'hypothesis' is well fortified, it is frequently elevated to the status of 'theory.' And when, based upon a large quantity of evidence it receives a good deal of general recognition, it is advanced to the lofty position of a 'law.' This terminology is not always carefully followed: Newton's discovery is still called 'the law of gravity' whereas Einstein's contribution, which essentially replaced Newton's or at the least improved upon it, is called the 'theory of relativity.' The lexicon 'hypothesis,' 'theory' and 'law' is an unfortunate one for it obscures the important fact that all of science's general claims are regarded as conjecture, certainly never as dogma."

7. *OH"K*, vol. 2, p. 363.

8. *OH"K*, vol. 1, p. 217.

9. Ibid., p. 219. Rav Kook's opinion, based on his kabbalistic worldview, is that human perceptive faculties draw their power from the highest spiritual modes of being, in the "*sefirot*" in the kabbalistic terms; those faculties are actually directed to these supreme entities on their various levels. This world-view offers another dimension helpful in explaining the truth and value attributed to conjecture and imagination in Rav Kook's thought; the matter will be discussed further later.

10. *Arpalei Tohar* (hereafter, *A"T*), (all citations are from the 1914 edition, printed by Rav Kook himself; in 1983 a second edition of the book was published in Jerusalem, with some changes inserted), p. 32. Elsewhere Rav Kook ascribes the virtue of certainty to tradition, see ibid., p. 56. (Also *OH"K*, vol. 1, p. 102.) More on the relationship between doubt (or, "the question") and certainty is found in *OH"K*, vol. 1, pp. 203–204, 205–206, 207, 210, 211. Compare Rav Nahman of Bratslav, (see 323, note 1).

11. See Chapter 3, p. 323.

12. *OH"K*, vol. 2, p. 367. See Chapter 9, note 43.

13. *OH"K*, vol. 1, p. 259.

14. *IG"R*, vol. 2, p. 41. It is interesting to note the similarity between Rav Kook's understanding of "will" and A. D. Gordon's remarks on that subject. See A. D. Gordon, *Mikhtavim u-Reshimot* (Jerusalem, 1954), p. 203; E. Schweid, *Ha-Yachid: 'Olamo shel A. D. Gordon* (Tel Aviv, 1970), pp. 116–119. Also see note 87.

15. *A"T*, p. 22.

16. Ibid.: "The act of being is necessarily engendered by God." In other words the premise that all of existence originates in God, is evident; even more evident is the necessity of existence of an absolute entity. Rav Kook expressed the same in his essay "Kirvat Elohim," *Tahkemoni*, p. 4: "We find knowledge of absolute wholeness deep within ourselves, and do not need to ask: Whence does it come?—'the necessity of existence' of ancient philosophy is well explained by the concept that the entire question of our cause was only born within us because we are forever dealing with an incomplete reality, which by nature must have a cause. Were we ever to perceive absolute reality we would at once recognize that the question of its cause is irrelevant. It is worthy of being, is the cause of all causes and itself needs no cause. Were it not for our habit of always seeing things which need a cause in order to exist, we would never have conceived the idea that something needs a reason for existence. And this absolute godly wholeness is not only sufficient in and of itself, but also always awakens a desire to strive to become close to it."

17. *A"T*, ibid. This basic understanding cannot be inferred from Kabbalah, and it shows the degree of Rav Kook's connection to kabbalistic metaphysics.

18. *OH"K*, vol. 1, p. 243. The idea of "equivalence" is ancient; one version of it is found as early as Rav Azriel. See G. Scholem, *Reyshit ha-Kabbalah* (Jerusalem and Tel Aviv, 1948), p. 139. On the principle of structural parallelism between the upper and lower worlds according to Rav Moshe Cordevero, see I. Ben-Shelomo, *Torat ha-Elokhut shel R. Moshe Kordevero*, p. 28. And yet, the actual background to Rav Kook's theory of "equivalence of values" is apparently similar to ideas found among scientists and philosophers of his time. For example, see S. H. Bergmann, "Höffding," *Encyclopediya ha-'Ivrit*, vol. 15, column 73: Hoffding explained the relationship between body and soul as two parallel expressions of the same entity; just as one thought can be conveyed in two different expressions ("the parallelist theory"). The theory Hoffding presents ("the assumption of similarity"), according to which the material and the spiritual are identical, differing only according to the vantage point, whether internal or the external, was first expressed by Spinoza. Spinoza, in his theory of attributes taught that all material phenomena are also spiritual and all spiritual phenomena are also material. Sim-

ilarly, Hoffding also assumed an encompassing and universal parallelism, according to which all bodies have a spiritual existence as well. But Hoffding was not always consistent and was sometimes content to demonstrate experiential parallelism, which assumes the parity between body and soul only where it is possible to prove this likeness through experience. Compare Feuer, *Einstein and the Generations of Science* p. 105. The stir generated by the theories of psychophysical parallelism is also found in Rav David Cohen's letter to Rav Kook's son, see *Nezir 'Ehav* XI, p. 352. Also compare R. Schatz-Uffenheimer, "Peyrush ha-Ḥassidut ke-Bitui la-Hashkafa ha-'Idi'alistit shel Gershom Scholem," *Gershom Scholem: al-ha-'Ish u-fo'alo* (Jerusalem: 1983).

19. *OH"K*, vol. 2, p. 519; see also p. 416. There Rav Kook deduced the movement of being from the living organism. See also *OH"K*, vol. 3, p. 150: Everything that happens to the individual happens on a macrocosmic level in all the worlds. This is also the source of the demand that one synchronize one's own human life with eternity. See ibid., p. 152, and Chapter 6 of this book, p. 236 and p. 239.

20. *OH"K*, vol. 2, p. 519.

21. That is to say, the equalized values are "internal and essential," that is, express the essence; as for *En-sof*, or absolute unity, all is essence. Here already we find a hint of the acosmic tone of his writings.

22. *A"T*, pp. 44–45; parallel source, *OH"K*, vol. 2, p. 391. See *OH"K*, vol. 1, p. 103 (Chapter 87). There speculation is understood as revelation, which bolsters its measure of truth. This aspect will be dealt with in Chapter 3. Another point is worthy of attention: There is a discrepancy between Rav Kook's concept of emanation and the parallelism he maintained (on the problematic logic involved in this issue, see J. Schlanger, *Ha-Philosophiya shel Shlomo ibn-Gevirol* [Jerusalem, 1980], p. 251). In the course of our study it will become clear that this discrepancy is an illusion as Rav Kook's "parallelism" itself is, in fact, illusory. In Rav Kook's view of reality, there really is no parallelism but rather an infinite continuum. Parallelism, therefore, is only methodological, a means to discuss the nature of realms unattainable through knowledge using tools from other realms available to knowledge; the basic assumption is of monism and a continuum, which is another aspect of that assumption. The question of the continuity of existence in relation to the unique and individual forms of existence is, in Hoffding's opinion, the fundamental question of philosophy. See L. Feuer, *Einstein and the Generations of Science*, p. 109. See also A. O. Lovejoy, *The Great Chain of Being* (1936; reprinted New York: Harper, 1960).

23. *OH"K*, vol. 1, p. 91.

24. Ibid., p. 135. See Chapter 9, pp. 315–316.

25. Private records of discussions held by Rav Kook's circle ("Hug ha-Rayah") of 1937 were given to me to examine, I quote from Rav David Cohen ("ha-Nazir"), the editor of *Orot Hakodesh*, in reference to the last words of this

passage: At the end of the chapter, the text spoke for itself, but persuaded by the comments of friends, Rav Kook agreed to make his language more veiled. For further clarification of this idea see Chapter 3.

26. See Scholem, *Reyshit ha-Kabbalah ve-Sefer ha-Bahir* (Synopses of lectures given at Hebrew University), ed. R. Schatz-Uffenheimer (Jerusalem, 1979), pp. 5–6.

27. On Rav Kook's awareness of the innovativeness of his thought and his legitimization of this, see Chapters 9 and 4, also notes 105 and 113. On the tension between innovation and preserving continuity, also see *Orot ha-Emunah* (Jerusalem, 1985), pp. 64–65. See also G. Scholem, "Revelation and Tradition as Religious Categories in Judaism," *The Messianic Idea in Judaism* (New York: 1971), pp. 282–303 (This article appeard in German in *Uber einige Grundbegriffe des Judentums* (Frankfurt am Main, 1970), pp. 90–120. G. Scholem, "Masoret ve-Hidush be-Ritu'al shel ha-Mekubalim," *Pirkey Yesod be-Havanat ha-Kabbalah u-Semaleha*, pp. 113–152. S. Rosenberg, " 'Ha-Hitgalut ha-Matmedet'—Shelosha Kivunim" ("'Permanent Revelation'—Three Variants"), *Hitgalut, Emuna, Tevuna* (*Revelation, Faith, Reason*), ed. M. Halamish and M. Schwarcz (Ramat Gan, 1976), pp. 131–143 and n. 27; S. Rosenberg, "Beyn Peshat le-Derash: Perakim al Parshanut ve-Idiologia," *De'ot* 37 (1969): 91–99; see essays by E. E. Urbach, U. Simon, M. Cohen, and S. Rosenberg in the collection *Ha-Mikra ve-'Anahnu*, ed. U. Simon (Tel Aviv, 1979); Z Levi, *Hermenutica* (Tel Aviv, 1987); N. Rotenstreich, *Tradition and Reality* (New York, 1972); J. Barr, *Fundamentalism* (London, 1977); E. Rackman, "A Challenge to Orthodoxy," *Judaism* 18, no. 2 (Spring 1969): 143–158; D. Weiss Halivni, "Revelation and Zimzum," *Judaism* 21 (1972): 205–210. See also articles by M. Greenberg, M. Fishbane, and N. Rotenstreich in the collection *Contemporary Jewish Religious Thought*, ed. A. A. Cohen and P. Mendes-Flohr (New York, 1987). Also see a discussion of this question in connection with the theory of education, M. Rosenak, *Commandments and Concerns—Jewish Religious Education in Secular Society* (Philadelphia, New York, and Jerusalem, 1987); A. Holtz, *Be-Olam ha-Mahshava shel HaZ"aL* (Tel Aviv, 1978), pp. 45–67 and no. 4. One example of the treatment of the relationship between tradition and rational understanding is found in Rambam, "Hakdama le-Perek Helek," *Hakdama la-Mishna*, M. D. Rabinowitz edition (Jerusalem, 1961), p. 122; also B. Ish-Shalom, "Tanin, Livyatan ve-Nahash—le-Fesharo shel Motiv Aggadi" ("Tanin, Leviathan, and Nahash—On the Meaning of a Legendary Motif"), *Da'at* 19 (Summer 1978): 79–101.

28. *OH"K*, vol. 3, p. 127.

29. *Eder ha-Yakar* (hereinafter *Eder*) (Jerusalem, 1967), p. 38. Rav Kook's statements give rise to a position at odds with the anthropological-sociological approach to religion; that is, an approach that rejects any connection to metaphysical questions, interested solely in humankind. Humankind interests Rav Kook as well, but, as we shall see later, in his opinion the only meaning existence has is in relation to what is beyond it. Rav Kook wrote

more on the moral purpose of metaphysical ideas in "Ma'amar Meyuhad" on Maimonides (see Chapter 8, note 7).

"And as a rule, this sort of general abstract question [the question of the purpose of creation], which has become a system of Jewish faith, should not be decided one-sidedly. Even mystical kabbalah, based upon the Zohar and the teachings of R. Isaac Luria also maintained (in Etz ha-Hayim, heikhal Adam Kadmon, 1:2 discourse entitled "Igulim ve-Yosher'), that there are two opinions on the question of whether the spheres are of a higher metaphysical order than the earth, or vice versa, that the earth is loftier and more important. And they certainly cannot be accused of being drawn away from the wisdom of Israel by Greek influences, rather in truth all of these thoughts on the general purpose of existence can only be said to whet the appetite, in order to *clarify* through them man's *lofty moral connections* and his adherence to his Creator, may He be blessed, for at times the theological idea connected to man's creation and the meaning of his life causes him to be uplifted, while at other times the recognition of man's nullity and insignificance before all of creation, God's awesome handiwork, causes him to be clothed in greatness and well-founded modesty—both positions are the words of the living God, and it would be a travesty to say either of these thoughts were external and foreign to the wisdom of Israel."

30. *A"T*, p. 23.

31. Ibid.

32. See later below note 213 and also Chapter 6, p. 429 n. 213 and p. 239.

33. *OH"K*, vol. 2, pp. 395–396. Note his understanding of spiritual pleasure as proof of the truth-value of an idea. Compare the concept of spiritual pleasure in Habad Hassidism: I. Tishby and J. Dan, "Hassidut," *Encyclopediya ha-'Ivrit*, p. 96; also M. Halamish, "Mishnato ha-Iyunit shel Rav Shneur Zalman me-Liadi" (dissertation, Jerusalem, 1976), pp. 189, 190, 192 and no. 54, also p. 327; R. Schatz-Uffenheimer, *Ha-Hassidut ke-Mistika (Quietistic Elements in Eighteenth Century Hassidic Thought)* (Jerusalem, 1980), p. 127, no. 22. See also *OH"K*, vol. 2, p. 399: "Less tiresome for man than this (monotheistic) outlook is the monotheistic outlook that leans to pantheism, especially noticeable in the rational side of the new Hassidism, wherein there is nothing but God." He no doubt refers to Habad Hassidism.

34. *A"T*, p. 46.

35. *OH"K*, vol. 2, p. 401.

36. Compare *IG"R*, vol. 1, p. 319 (letter to Moshe Zeidel): "In just-law we always link 'rights' to choice. When man chooses good and his endeavors succeed in comparable proportion to the measure of his goodness, this vision pleases our sense of justice." Also *A"T*, p. 63: "Will tells more about he who wills." See also *Orot*, pp. 19–20.

37. Compare Plotinus, *Enneades* 307, 8 VI. In his opinion, good is the purpose of freedom and that which makes one free.

38. Compare R. Schatz-Uffenheimer, *Ha-Hassidut ke-Mistika*, Chapters 1 and 2. For further discussion see Chapter 4, pp. 172–178.

39. See later, p. 120.

40. *OH"K*, vol. 1, p. 103.

41. On Rav Kook's understanding of revelation, see Chapter 3.

42. On the ontological aspects of his thought see pp. 105 ff.

43. See note 10.

44. *OH"K*, vol. 1, p. 91, also p. 252: "There is room even for the contention that emotion is rational." See further Chapter 8, p. 296 and note 55.

45. See p. 66 and note 29. Rav Kook did not seem to think he was transforming religious consciousness into a means or that he had marred its religious worth. In his opinion it is pontless not to admit that religious consciousness has two components—the purely religious element and the practical one: "There are two elements necessary to know God in this world. The first is that necessary for the benefit of society and individual peace of mind . . . the second is yet higher, the supreme, noble elevation itself."

46. *OH"K*, vol. 1, p. 212 (parallel source: *A"T*, p. 4; there the sentence ends "to criticize themselves").

47. See S. Carmi, "Rav Kook's Theory of Knowledge", *Tradition*, no. 1–2 (1975): 195.

48. See J. Guttmann, "Ba'ayat Mikriyut ha-Mezi'ut be-Philsophiyat ha-Rambam," *Dat u-Mada'* (*Religion and Knowledge*) (Jerusalem, 1979), p. 121.

49. Ibid., p. 119.

50. Ibid., p. 122.

51. *OH"K*, vol. 1, p. 213.

52. Compare I. Ben-Shelomo's introduction to the Hebrew translation of Spinoza's book, *A Short Treatise on God, Man and His Happiness*, ed., with introduction and commentary, I. Ben-Shelomo (Jerusalem, 1978), p. 41. There Ben-Shlomo discusses the positions of Spinoza and Giordanno Bruno, similar on this topic to those of Rav Kook.

53. *OH"K*, vol. 1, p. 114. See also *Olat Re'ayah*, vol. 1, p. 36 (on the words "Sanctify unto Me all the first-born" [Exodus 13:2]): "What is potential rather than actual truly is incomplete and profane, for the supreme holy. . . . He is always actuality, and regarding the Most-High, nothing at all exists potentially, all is complete actuality." Compare Maimonides, *Guide for the*

Perplexed, trans. S. Pines, (Chicago: University of Chicago Press, 1963), Part I, Chapter 68.

54. See note 16.

55. Compare A. Bergson, *Ha-Hitpatchut ha-Yotzeret* (Jerusalem, 1978), pp. 193–207, on reality and nothingness.

56. Elsewhere Rav Kook explicitly maintained that opposites make knowledge possible. See *Ikve Hatzon*, p. 43: "Not only can the world not exist without the great expanse of all branches of knowledge and feeling, but, moreover, no one part can be fully understood without including all of the different aspects seemingly distant from that part. Only thus will the throne of the Kingdom of ideas be established 'Great is knowledge since it was placed between two names [literally, letters], as it says, 'for a God of knowledge is the Lord' [I Samuel 2:3] (BT Berakhot 33a)."

57. *OH"K*, vol. 1, i.

58. *A"T*, p. 27.

59. See *OH"K*, vol. 3, p. 27: "And since there truly is nothing but Him, therefore all is necessary, for all that is possible does not come into existence." The acosmic tone expressed in this excerpt does not contradict the contention that all that is possible exists, for the passages refer to different aspects of reality; the divine aspect and the cosmic aspect.

60. On ibn Tabul's attempt to define deficiency as an immanent part of the concept of completeness, see R. Schatz-Uffenheimer, "Ramak ve-ha-'ari: Beyn Nominalizm le-Re'alizm" ("R. Moses Cordevero and and the Ari: Between Nominalism and Realism"), *Mehkarey Yerushalayim be-Maheshevet Yisrael (Jerusalem Studies)* 3 (1982); hereinafter, "Ramak ve-ha-Ari."

61. *OH"K*, vol. 1, p. 212.

62. Ibid., p. 17. On the consequences of this understanding, see Chapter 3, pp. 152 ff.

63. The "law of contradiction" maintains that no argument can be simultaneously true and false; the law of the "impossible third" maintains that all arguments are either true or false.

64. There is no unequivocal proof of his sources, but the influence of Maimonides, Kant, and Hegel is clearly recognizable. Without discounting kabbalistic motifs, echoes of modern developments in the field of formal logic at the beginning of this century are audible in one of his arguments. See note 73.

65. *IG"R*, vol. 1, p. 133.

66. *A"T*, pp. 56–57 (and in *OH"K*, vol. 1, p. 16). Also see pp. 39, 66 in *A"T* Compare Rav Nachman Krochmal, *Moreh Nevukhey ha-Zeman*, ed.

Rawidowicz, pp. 16–17, on the "deep introspection" through which opposites become nullified.

67. *OH"K*, vol. 1, pp. 103–104. Nonetheless, this division into domains is not absolute, for later in the same section Rav Kook spoke of a dialectical relation between the two levels. See also *OH"K*, vol. 3, pp. 30, 31. Rav Kook established that the distinction between will and necessity belongs to a realm where there is some sort of restriction. In this section Rav Kook went so far as to identify the concepts of freedom and necessity with good and evil. Compare this with Kant's approach on p. 133.

68. *A"T*, p. 22.

69. Ibid., p. 31 (also *OH"K*, vol. 3, p. 26).

70. *OH"K*, vol. 2, p. 548.

71. Ibid., pp. 532–533, also pp. 464–465 and 530. On this topic, see J. Ben-Shelomo, "Shelemuth ve-Hishtalmut be-Torath ha-Elokhim shel ha-Rav Kook" *Iyyun* 33 (1984): 289–309.

72. Ibid., p. 353. On the definition of the complete in incompleteness see Schatz-Uffenheimer, "Ramak ve-he-Ari."

73. *OH"K*, vol. 2, p. 527; also see p. 377 on temporal existence as a spark of eternity. It is interesting to compare these ideas to the approach of the Polish logistician Jan Lokshevitz, who wished to overturn logical certainty and philosophical determinism. He constructed a three-dimensional logical system that annulled the law of "the impossible third," maintained until then by philosophers. According to that law, a sentence is either true or false and there exists no third alternative. In the logical system developed by Lokshevitz a statement may be true, false, or uncertain. This new logic had consistent rules and procedures of its own. See Feuer, *Einstein and the Generations of Science*, pp. 175–176. Rav Kook himself pointed out the similarity between his understanding of the concept of the "complete" and that of Rav ʿAzriel of Gerona. See page 19.

74. See note 71.

75. *A"T*, p. 45; *OH"K*, vol. 1, p. 38.

76. *A"T*, p. 10; *OH"K*, vol. 1, p. 29.

77. *A"T*, p. 45.

78. Ibid., p. 10; *OH"K*, vol. 1, p. 29, also p. 177. The comparison between Rav Kook and Spinoza on the subject of evident knowledge is of great interest. See Spinoza's *Ethics*, Part II, Proposition 43, schol.: "Just as light reveals both itself and the darkness, so truth reveals the standard of itself and of the false." Similarly in Spinoza's *Igrot*, No. 76, p. 272:) "Truth is a touchstone both for itself and for falsehood." This idea appears as well in *A Short*

Treatise, Part II, Chapter 15, section 3: "Anyone who grasps truth cannot doubt whether o not it is actually in his domain."

79. *OH"K*, vol. 1, p. 277, also p. 281.

80. Ibid., p. 115.

81. Ibid., p. 280.

82. Ibid., p. 248.

83. Ibid., p. 249.

84. Ibid., p. 281.

85. I cannot ascertain the chronology of his writings, but what draws our attention is the fact that Spinoza, too, in his earlier discussion of the levels of knowledge in *A Short Treatise*, variously lists both three and four levels of knowledge, and in his later work, *Ethics* lists only three. See *A Short Treatise*, Part II, Chapter 1, and Chapter 4, section 9; also see J. Ben-Shelomo's notes in these areas and on pp. 268–272. See also *ethics* II, proposition 40, schol. 2 and propositions 41 and 42. See further *On the Improvement of the Understanding*.

86. *OH"K*, vol. 1, p. 251.

87. *A"T*, p. 14. See also *OH"K*, vol. 1, p. 213 (paragraph 44). The concept of "instinct" is also prevalent in the writings of A. D. Gordon, usually in the sense of "vital force." Nonetheless in Gordon's writings as well, instinct sometimes appears as synonymous, or at least similar, to feeling. For example, "We worked with no clear consciousness, without clear and sharp, deep and encompassing understanding; we were led to our goals by virtue of unmediated feeling, by instinct" (*Ha-'Uma ve-ha-'Avoda* [Jerusalem, 1952], p. 396). And, "When [people] touch each other in a positive way, they awaken or recreate positive feelings and instincts in one another, just as, conversely, confrontations between them intensify or instill within them negative instincts and feelings" (ibid., p. 457). Gordon's relationship with Rav Kook was already suggested by E. Schweid (note 14). On this topic, see also A. Shapiro "Beyn Shlomo Zemah ve-Aharon David Gordon le-ha-Rayah Kook," *Ha-Doar* 34 (Tamuz 1978).

88. We find parallels of this understanding of "instinct" in Spinoza's conception of the third type of knowledge, intuition; similarly, there are likenesses to Bergson's understanding of the relationship between mind and instinct, see H. Bergson *Ha-Hitpatchut ha-Yozeret*, pp. 106–137. Also see later, pp. 147 and note 35.

89. *IG"R*, vol. 1, p. 135.

90. See *OH"K*, vol. 1, p. 232: "God created everything with its corresponding element."

91. Ibid., p. 223.

92. Ibid., p. 239, see also p. 229.

93. Ibid., p. 234.

94. Ibid., p. 237.

95. Ibid., p. 234.

96. Ibid., p. 227.

97. Ibid., p. 237.

98. Ibid., p. 91.

99. Ibid., p. 232.

100. Ibid., p. 235.

101. Ibid., p. 252.

102. Ibid. Compare Joseph Gikitila, *Sha'arei 'Orah,* ed. Joseph Ben Shelomo (Jerusalem, 1971), pp. 53 ff.

103. *OH"K,* vol. 1, p. 237, see also p. 231. Rav Kook's discussion is reminiscent of Maimonides's doctrine of prophecy and the relationship between mind and "the imaginative faculty" in his thought. Yet it is important to highlight the essential difference between the models each of them outlined. Maimonides viewed imagination as essentially inferior to intellect, and at the supreme level of prophecy, that of Moses, it is absent altogether. In contrast, Rav Kook viewed intellect and imagination as diverse aspects, united in their sublime source; the distinctions in this relationship and status depend on the perspective of the evaluator: for some, imagination is superior to intellect; whereas for others, it is a subordinate aspect of intellect.

104. Ibid., p. 233.

105. Ibid., p. 225. An inverse usage of this saying is found in Chapter 7, pp. 280–281.

106. Ibid., p. 247.

107. Ibid., p. 277; *OH"K,* vol. 2, p. 334; *OH"K,* vol. 1, p. 100; ibid., p. 44; *A"T,* p. 64.

108. *OH"K,* vol. 1, p. 186, see also pp. 185 and 275. *A"T,* p. 62. Compare Maimonides, *Guide for the Perplexed,* trans. S. Pines, Foreword, p. 5.

109. *OH"K,* vol. 1, p. 275.

110. Ibid.

111. This variation is according to Rav David Cohen, editor of *OH"K.* From the context and the content of the entire chapter, this is indeed the

original version, for Rav Kook compares *aggadah* to prophecy, stating that *aggadah*, like prophecy, stems from human "soulfulness"; i.e., from the inner self. Also see Chapter Three, p. 167 and note 99.

112. *OH"K*, vol. 1, p. 23. Also see *Orot*, p. 121 (*"Hakkham 'adif me-navi"*).

113. *OH"K*, vol. 1, p. 275.

114. Ibid., p. 277.

115. Ibid., p. 275.

116. See *Zohar*, Part I, p. 36: "Because they knew and became aware of the knowledge of evil, they knew they were naked, that they had lost the divine brightness which had covered them and now eluded them, and they were left stripped of it." See *A"T*, p. 12 and *OH"K*, vol. 2, p. 298 (note the variations to the text printed in *OH"K*). Also see G. Scholem, *Shabetai Zvi ve-Hatenu'a ha-Shabeta'it biyemey Hayav* (Tel Aviv, 1970), p. 180.

117. *OH"K*, vol. 2, p. 493.

118. Ibid. vol. 3, p. 143; also see: A. D. Gordon, *Ha-Ummah ve-ha-Avodah* (Jerusalem, 1952), pp. 373–374; and see E. Schweid *HaYahid: Olamo shel A. D. Gordon* (Tel Aviv, 1970), p. 180.

119. *OH"K*, vol. 1, p. 279.

120. See p. 96.

121. On the role of vision in divine inspiration see *OH"K*, vol. 2, pp. 446, 520.

122. Rav David Cohen developed an entire thesis on the accoustical nature of Jewish thought in general. See his work, *Kol ha-Nevu'a—ha-Higayon ha-'Ivri ha-Shim'i* (Jerusalem, 1970). Compare M. Idel, "Ha-perush ha-Magi ve-ha-Te'urgi Shel ha-Musica be-Tekasim Yehudiyim me-Tekufat ha-Renaissance 'Ad ha-Hassidut" ("The Magical and Theurgic Interpretation of Music in Jewish Sources from the Renaissance to Hassidism"), *Yuval* 4 (1982): 33; also see "Music and Prophetical Kabbalah," ibid., p. 150. On the role of music in Habad Hassidism, see Halamish, "Mishnato ha-Iyunit shel Rav Shneur Zalman me-Liadi," p. 194. Rav Kook did not refer to actual music, rather mystical perception is described in terms borrowed from the realm of music. Compare W. James, *The Varieties of Religious Experience*, pp. 420–421: "They prove that not conceptual speech, but music rather, is the element through which we are best spoken to by mystical truth." Further readings on music in Rav Kook's thought are found in J. Gellman, "Ha-'Estetica be-Mishnato Shel ha-Rav Kook," in *Yovel 'Orot, Haguto shel ha-Rav A. I. ha-Cohen Kook*, ed. B. Ish-Shalom and S. Rosenberg (Jerusalem, 1988), p. 162.

123. *A"T*, p. 27. Also see *OH"K*, vol. 3, p. 213: "Complete harmony of divine song comes about through them (through the thirstings of the heart)." Also ibid., p. 229: "[The *zaddik*'s] desires, passions, inclinations, thoughts,

actions, conversations, customs, movements, sorrows, joys, anguishes, pleasures—all of them are *chords of the holy music,* for God's life force by virtue of imbuing within all the worlds, emanates its voice, a strong voice, through them."

124. Manuscripts, Collection E, p. 110a. The image of striking the rock to draw forth water refers to the scene described in Exodus (17:6). On the principles of parallelism expressed here, see note 18.

125. *OH"K,* vol. 2, p. 334; also see *A"T,* p. 20.

126. Ibid.

127. *OH"K,* vol. 2, p. 428.

128. Ibid., pp. 515–516.

129. Compare *A"T,* p. 44: "The essence of listening to God's voice is in hearing the entire procession along the paths of life. . ."

130. *OH"K,* vol. 1, p. 268.

131. Ibid., p. 248. Compare *Zohar,* Part I, p. 246b and p. 74a. See I. Tishby, *Mishnat ha-Zohar,* vol. 1, pp. 177–178.

132. *OH"K,* vol. 2, p. 515.

133. *OH"K,* vol. 1, p. 116.

134. *OH"K,* vol. 3, p. 273, also see pp. 274, 275, 276 and 179. Compare *OH"K,* vol. 1, p. 79, and vol. 2, p. 297. See M. Halamish, "'Al ha-Shetika ba-Kabbalah u-va-Hassidut" ("On Quiet in Kabbalah and Hassidut"), *Dat U-Sap-ha,* ed. M. Halamish and A. Kasher (TelAviv, 1982), pp. 79–89.

135. *OH"K,* vol. 3, p. 139.

136. Ibid., p. 273. Compare R. Schatz-Uffenheimer, *Ha-Hassidut ke-Mistika,* p. 107; and Chapter 9.

137. *OH"K,* vol. 1, p. 116.

138. Ibid., p. 248.

139. Hegel's name is not mentioned anywhere in Rav Kook's writings; however, this concept was prevalent in his day and Rav Kook may have encountered it in R. Nachman Krochmal's *Moreh Nevukhe Hazman.* A Hegelian influence on Rav Kook's view of the development of thought in the course of history is clear in his article, "Le-Mahalakh ha-'Idey'ot be-Yisrael," *Orot* (Jerusalem, 1973), pp. 102 ff.

140. *Genesis Rabbah,* Ed. Theodore Albeck, Chapter 9, p. 68.

141. Rav Zvi Yehudah, Rav Kook's son, testified to his students that the changes were made only after consultation with Rav Harlap and with Rav

Kook's own assent. It seems that the passage was reformulated to mitigate the radical implications of the original version.

142. *OH"K,* vol. 1, p. 152. Manuscripts, Small Collection, Chapter 24, p. 59. Compare *OH"K,* vol. 2, p. 214: "Holiness may be destructive . . . , destroying in order to build something more lofty than what has already been built." Also see, *Orot ha-Tehiah,* Chapter 66: "We are called to the wellsprings of prophecy. . ." Also compare *A"T,* p. 29: "Without the *chutzpa* of the pre-Messianic age it would not be possible to explain the secrets of Torah with utter clarity. Only by the condensation of feelings, brought on by this *chutzpa,* will it be possible to receive sublime intellectual enlightenment, and will everything finally return to complete perfection." Also, on page 12: "The impudent sons, path breakers and breechers of fences will become prophets of the highest order, on the level of Moses and the supreme luminousness of Adam ha-Rishon, the First Man. The Tree of Life, in its profound goodness will be revealed by them and through them." See note 116 and Chapter 9, note 21. Also see Schatz-Uffenheimer, "'Utopiya," pp. 24–25. On the concept of the decaying seed and the dialectic of the growth, see R. Schatz-Uffenheimer, ed., *Maggid Devarav le-Ya'acov,* Sect. 78, p. 134; Sect. 173, pp. 208–209. Yet for Rav Kook there was also a level wherein there is no need whatsoever for destruction; See *OH"K,* vol. 1, p. 59.

143. See H. A. Wolfson, "Torat ha-Emuna ha-Kefula Lefi Rav Sa'adia, ibn Roshad ve-Thomas Aquinas" ("The Concept of Double Belief According to Saadya Gaon, Ibn Rushid and Thomas Aquinas"), in *Ha-maheshava ha-Yehudit Biymey ha-Beynayim (The Jewish Philosophy of the Middle Ages)* (Jerusalem, 1978), pp. 196–216.

144. See Maimonides, *Guide for the Perplexed,* vol. 2, 25. Maimonides steadfastly maintained that the concept of creation encompasses the idea of will or freedom and forms the conditional basis for the possibility and very existence of the Torah.

145. See J. Schlanger, *Ha-Philosophia shel Shlomo ibn Gevirol* (Jerusalem, 1980), especially pp. 200–228; J. Guttmann, *Ha-Philosophiya shel ha-Yahadut (The Philosophy of Judaism)* (Jerusalem, 1941), pp. 97–100; S. Pines under "Gabirol" in *Encyclopediya ha-'Ivrit,* vol. 10, column 227; J. Guttmann, *Die Philosophie des Salomon Ibn Gabirol* (Gottingen, 1889), pp. 200–269.

146. Ibid.

147. Schlanger, *Ha-Philosophiya,* p. 93.

148. Ibid., pp. 223–228. On the attempt to preserve the principle of God's immutability, which caused Lurianic Kabbalah to split from Cordovero's doctrine, see Schatz-Uffenheimer, "Ramak ve-ha-'Ari," pp. 122–136.

149. J. Guttman, "Torat ha-Elohim shel ha-Rambam," *Dat u-Mada' (Religion and Knowledge)* (Jerusalem, 1979), p. 104.

150. Maimonides, *Guide for the Perplexed*, vol. 1, 55. Interestingly, in Rav Sa'adia Gaon's writings the adjective *alive* is substituted for the word *desiring*. See *Emunot ve-De'ot*, Article II, Chapter 4.

151. Maimonides, ibid., pp. 2 and 18 ("the second meaning").

152. Ibid., pp. 3, 13.

153. This understanding also influenced Maimonides's position on a tangential subject: the necessity or possibility of existence. See Guttmann, *Dat u-Mada'*, p. 119.

154. See Scholem, *Reshit ha-Kabbalah*, p. 140.

155. I extend my gratitude to Professor J. Dan, who guided me in this matter in *Sefer ha-Bahir*.

156. Azriel of Gerona, *Peyrush ha-'Aggadot le-Rabbi 'Azriel* (*Commentary on Talmudic Aggadot*), ed. I. Tishby (Jerusalem, 1945), Chapter "Eyn Dorshim" from Tractate Hagigah, esp. p. 81 line 15; p. 107, lines 3 and 12; and p. 110, line 13. Due to the difficulty entailed in uncovering Rav Azriel's position, it seems fitting to justify my conclusions here. Rav Azriel maintained that in the case of will "there is nothing other than it." I. Tishby pointed out (ibid., p. 81, no. 14) that this language is unique to Rav Azriel and appears often in his writings, usually in connection with the first *sefira* and occasionally with reference to *En sof*. It appears that the expression *there is nothing other than it* represents will as the all-encompassing foundation, and this phrase seems more appropriate than any other to describe *En-sof*; when it is used regarding the first *sefira*, it designates the aspect of *En-sof* to that *sefira*. Therefore, to the best of my knowledge, there is truth to the contention that "will," according to Rav Azriel, is identical with *En-sof*; the accepted configuration: *En-sof, keter, hokhma* parallels, in his writings, the hierarchy of will, intellect, and wisdom. In his words, "Will emanates intellect and intellect emanates wisdom" (ibid., p. 107, line 12). This contention is reinforced by his description of will as, "Air that is inconceivable and cannot be divided; it is a single entity without differentiation, and all desires were united in that primary unity of will." This implies that will is an essential characteristic of *En-sof* itself. Therefore, intellect does not seem to be an intermediary level between *keter* and *hokhma*, as I. Tishby interpreted in n. 9, ibid., and G. Scholem's assertion that intellect is "a sublime aspect of wisdom" is thus difficult for me to accept (see "Kabbalah," *Encyclopediya ha-'Ivrit*, vol. 29, column 101).

Indeed, in Rav Yehuda Ben Yakar's commentary on prayer (Schechter, *Jewish Quarterly Review* 4: p. 248) one may understand intellect to be an intermediary level between *keter* and *hokhma*, and Rav Azriel's definition of intellect implies that it is essentially identical to *hokhma* in its connection to things dependent on it. Yet it seems to me that Rav Azriel's thoughts do not correspond with these. Rav Azriel made a clear distinction between intellect and *hokhma*, and it is unlikely that he would give symbolic expression to an entity that is not an independent *sefira* without explicitly stating that its status is different from that of the *sefirot*. In some instances, qualities of a *sefira* may be mentioned that are actually the extension of some aspect of a superior *sefira*, and in this sense one can view them as a connection between the two *sefirot*. However, to my knowledge, no independent intermediary levels assigned symbolic language are mentioned. What we find is a clear hierarchy of will, intellect, and *hokhma* with no mention that these elements are ontologically different. Explicitly stated: "Will emanates intellect and intellect emanates wisdom". Furthermore, the entire sefirotic system is a system of emanations. If there is doubt whether *keter* is an emanation, this hinges on the question whether *keter* is identical to *En-sof*. (See: Joseph Gikatilla, *Sha'are Orah* ed. Joseph Ben Shlomo [Jerusalem, 1971], p. 30.) Here Rav Azriel explicitly stated that will is *not an emanation;* rather it is boundless and indifferentiated, and all the *sefirot* emanate from it: "the order of being is controlled by will, yet this was not revealed until the right time came for their visible manifestation. So too the *sefirot*" [the author agrees the footnote should be deleted], (*Perush ha-'Aggadot*, p. 110, line 13). On Rav Kook's connection to Rav Azriel see p. 21, compare their thoughts on the subject of will and its status.

157. Asher Ben David, *Sefer ha-Yichud* (Jerusalem, 1934), "Perush shem ha-Meforash," p. 56.

158. Ibid., p. 6, line 15.

159. Ibid., p. 5, line 40; p. 6, line 1.

160. Ibid., p. 5, line 6.

161. See Ben Shelomo, *Sha'are 'Orah.*

162. Y. Gikitilia, *Sha'are 'Orah*, Sha'ar Five, pp. 187–188; also see Sha'ar Nine, vol. 2, pp. 87–88, 89.

163. Ibid., p. 91.

164. Ibid., p. 92.

165. R. Schatz-Uffenheimer, *Ramak ve-he-Ari*, p. 123.

166. Ibid., 124.

167. The same is true of Rav Kook's understanding of "will," despite the outward similarity to the approaches of R. Cordevero and R. Shlomo Ibn Gabirol, a similarity that has blinded certain scholars to the uniqueness of Rav Kook's approach. See Z. Yaron, *Mishnato shel ha-Rav Kook* (Jerusalem, 1974), pp. 62–63 and no. 14.

168. The reference is apparently to R. Mordechai Rosenblatt of Ushmina, with whom Rav Kook discussed kabbalistic matters. See Y. L. Fishman, *Ha-Rayah* (Jerusalem, 1965), p. 62.

169. On the intellectual aspects of the revelation of the prophet Eliyahu, see *OH"K*, vol. 3, p. 362; also Cohen, *Kol ha-Nevu'a*, p. 312.

170. *Orot ha-Teshuva* (hereinafter, *OH"T*), (Jerusalem, 1970), p. 99.

171. Ibid., p. 57. Also see *OH"K*, vol. 3, pp. 88–90, 91, 95–98; and *A"T*, p. 76.

172. See *OH"K*, vol. 1, p. 259: "When inner will is tainted, this cannot help but manifest itself in the intellect and attributes . . . therefore, the light of *hokhma*, and the light of Torah cannot shine in man with brilliant clarity until he has fully repented, correcting his spiritual self; repentence causes the revelation of will to be clear and brilliant and then illumine the branches of the intellect and attributes as well, and the light of Torah grows brighter and brighter, like the perennial spring and unending river." Here Rav Kook seems to express "actuality" of the theory of will.

173. See p. 115.

174. *OH"K*, vol. 1, p. 260.

175. See Chapter 8, pp. 297–298, notes 24, 25.

176. *OH"K*, vol. 1, p. 258.

177. Ibid., pp. 56 and 260.

178. Also see *OH"K*, vol. 2, p. 430.

179. *OH"K*, vol. 1, p. 260.

180. Compare Maimonides, *Guide for the Perplexed*, vol. 1, Chapters 2, 5, 32, 34. Also see Maimonides, *Introduction to Tractate Avot*, Chapter 7.

181. See p. 76.

182. *OH"K* I, p. 258.

183. In form, this point too merits comparison to Maimonides's approach, although it is impossible to ignore the essential differences between the two authors. See J. Guttmann, *Ha-Philosophiya shel ha-Yahadut* (Jerusalem, 1963), pp. 163–164: "Morality, which was previously subservient to knowledge, here becomes the ultimate content and purpose of knowledge of God." An alternate interpretation of Maimonides's view: Z. Harvey, "Political Philosophy and Halachah in Maimonides," *Iyyun* 29 (1980): 211–212.

184. *OH"K*, vol. 2, p. 430.

185. *OH"K*, vol. 3, p. 92.

186. *OH"K*, vol. 2, pp. 283–284.

187. Compare Y. Gikitilia, *Sha'arei Ora*, p. 83: "Know that in the Torah this *sefira* is called 'Yesh' [literally, 'being'], and you must understand the reason, for the first *sefira*, which is *keter*, hidden from all living beings and beyond human gaze, is called 'Ayin' [En] [literally, 'nothingness'] . . . but the

beginning of the expansion of thought and revelation of order is the second *sefira* called 'hokhma,' and there it is possible to question; although on the surface unrevealed, it is not absolutely hidden like the first."

188. Compare ibid., p. 102: "Eden" [pleasure] is the *sefira* of "*hokhma*".

189. *OH"K*, vol. 3, p. 27.

190. *OH"K*, vol. 2, p. 365. Also compare *IG"R*, vol. 2, pp. 41–42, where Rav Kook rebutted the Plotinian concept that "cause is linked to effect as light originates from the sun."

191. *OH"K*, vol. 2, p. 367.

192. *OH"K*, vol. 3, pp. 108–110.

193. *A"T*, p. 11. Also see *Orot*, p. 132: "There must be some interruption between the content of the abstract ideal of ultimate purpose and that which is revealed [of the ideal] in actuality. If not for this separation between levels, the form of all creation would be blurred, the nature of being would become unstable, rules and boundaries would not last, constant qualities and limiting values that form the foundation of the entire world would not endure."

194. *OH"K*, vol. 3, p. 92. Like the distinction between will and *hokhma*, associated with "truth" and "good," Rav Kook differentiated between free will and necessity, associated with "good" and "evil." See ibid., p. 31.

195. Schopenhauer's view appears in his *The World as Will and Idea*, trans. R. B. Haldone and John Kemp (London: 1906), vol. 2, especially pp. 399 ff. (on the possibility of knowing the thing-in-itself), pp. 411 ff. (on self-awareness of will), and p. 468 (actualization of will in the body). Also see S. H. Bergmann, *Todot ha-Philosophia ha-Hadasha—Shitot ba-Philosophia she-le-ahar Kant* (Jerusalem, 1979), pp. 64 ff.

196. *OH"K*, vol. 2, p. 484. See Chapter 9, p. 328 and note 58.

197. *OH"K*, vol. 2, p. 482.

198. Nietzsche regarded himself as Schopenhauer's successor and even expressedly noted this in *The Will to Power*, trans. W. Kaufman and R. S. Hollingdale (New York: Vintage, 1967), p. 255.

199. *OH"K*, vol. 2, p. 367.

200. *OH"K*, vol. 3, p. 110.

201. *IG"R*, vol. 2, p. 41. Compare this to Plotinus' conception of freedom, *Enneades*, 9–10, III (translated into Hebrew by N. Speigel [Jerusalem: Bialik Foundation, 1978–1981]); Also see B. Spinoza, *Ethics* Part I, Definition 7.

202. *OH"K*, vol. 2, p. 544.

203. On the identification of freedom with good, compare Plotinus, *Enneades* 3–7, I VI. Also see *A"T*, p. 2 and *OH"K*, vol. 2, p. 289: "The laws of life, of heaven and earth shine with a supernal light, the light of greatness, the light of life's made manifest in all being in its highest form, broader and full, the light of eternal life and the source of life itself, all theories, laws, ideas, morals, natures, orders, customs, wisdom, songs, desires, life tremors, movements of being, its existence ["*hitkaymut*" according to the version in *OH"K* and manuscripts, however in *A"T* the word appears as "*hitkadmuta*" — its progress], its grasp of the essence of being are but treasures filled with happiness, in which *will*, supreme in the strength of its splendor (*gevurat 'uzo*) and the majesty of its eternity (*u-ve-hod nizho*), in the foundation of its glory (*be-yesod tif'arto*) and the exalted desire of its glorious kingdom (*malhuto*), will be revealed and made visible in them in full brightness, from the most humble movement, all progress step by step without pause to the highest heights."

204. This view lead Maimonides to establish that the concept of creation is imperative for the existence of a normative Torah. See *Guide for the Perplexed*, vol. 2, 25.

205. See *OH"K*, vol. 2, p. 559: "The aspect of will relates to the desire to fulfill a certain aim." Also see *OH"K*, vol. 3, p. 85: "The aspiration in its aspect of *azilut* is the composition of intellect and will." We saw the diametric opposite of this view in the Geronese Kabbalah and in Maimonides's system, in which will is identified with *hokhma* (see Chapter 2, p. 107. There it was will that introduced the element of freedom into a system of imperative order, and the identification of will with *hokhma* was meant to mitigate and limit this freedom, making it "rational" or "intellectual."

206. *OH"K*, vol. 2, pp. 366–367, 370; *OH"K*, vol. 3, p. 41–44.

207. *OH"K*, vol. 3, p. 26; *A"T*, p. 31.

208. *OH"K*, vol. 2, p. 484.

209. Ibid.

210. *OH"K*, vol. 3, pp. 33–34: "When the holy light is diminished, unrefined nature rules, its hidden rules enwrap being, and man is drawn after his bestial side; and the world, likewise, follows its course, for its systems are also ordered like the stars in their orbit, the energies and forces exerted in their orderly constellation according to their regimen. But when the inner intellect overcomes, when good will, in imitation of divine will, gains power, everything is raised, and when this occurs in man, the world as well is no longer ruled by hidden laws but by the exacting reign of the intellect."

211. *OH"K*, vol. 3, p. 30. Compare Kant's idea of the realms of freedom and necessity. Rav Kook's formulation ("truth in and of itself") is no doubt influenced by Kantian concepts.

212. *OH"K*, vol. 2, p. 362. The consequences of this view are discussed in Chapter 3.

213. *OH"K*, vol. 3, p. 30. The source of the phrase *to be drawn into the body of the King* is found in the Zohar I, p. 217b, where the soul is described as clinging to God after death. Here the expression means the return of all existence to a state of adherence to God; that is, to absolute unity. More on the phrase is found in Y. Liebes, "Perakhim be-Milon Sefer ha-Zohar" (later, Chapter 9, note 43), pp. 226–227. See pp. 67–68 and note 31.

214. *OH"K*, vol. 2, p. 365.

215. *A"T*, p. 11.

216. Ibid., p. 2; *OH"K*, vol. 2, p. 288.

217. *A"T*, p. 11; *OH"K*, vol. 2, p. 289.

218. The symbols of "line" and "circumscribing" correlate to "linearity" and "circles" later. Compare "Etz Hayim," 1:1:3, exposition on "Igulim ve-Yosher"; Rave Moses Hayyim Luzzatto, *Kelah Pithei Hokhma*, Petah 27, 28; *Sefer ha-Kelalim*, in *Da'at Tevunot*, ed. H. Friedlander (Benei Barak, 1973), p. 249. On the significance of this symbol in Habad Hassidism, see R. Elior, *Torat ha-Elohut be-Dor ha-Sheni shel Hassidut Habad* (Jerusalem, 1982), pp. 69–70.

219. "Kirvat Elohim" *Tahkemoni* II, 1911, p. 6.

220. *OH"K*, vol. 3, p. 24.

221. Ibid., p. 25. We must remark that here is yet another example of symbols of mythological significance utilized for abstract concepts.

222. See p. 70 and Chapter 10, p. 338. Compare Luzzatto, *Kelah Pithey Hokhma*, Petah 1. It seems that in this instance Luzzatto's influence is decisive. See Rav David Cohen, *Kol ha-Nevuah*, pp. 283–284.

223. *OH"K*, vol. 3, p. 59. Also see *OH"K*, vol. 2, p. 369: "[Will] is revealed as the animate spirit of existence, active and striving, whose extensions are revealed in all forms of life [inanimate, vegetative, animal, and human], in most minute detail, and in the greatest generality."

224. *OH"K*, vol. 2, p. 416 and 347.

225. Ibid., p. 518, also see p. 515.

226. Ibid., p. 416.

227. See J. Schlanger, *Ha-Philosophia shel Shlomo ibn Gevirol*, p. 136.

228. *OH"K*, vol. 2, p. 416.

229. Earlier, p. 78.

230. See *OH"K*, vol. 3, p. 34: "Overt choice as embodied in people . . . is but a drop in the sea compared to the hidden choice that guides the
entire system ordering all existence."

Also ibid., p. 39: "The marvel of man's will in all its glorious freedom
can only be understood as but one spark from the great flame of the larger
will of all existence."

Further ibid., p. 40: "Good will, free of all oppression, the spirit of God
that hovers in all existence, is revealed in the hearts of the righteous and
upright in all its majesty."

And in *OH"K*, vol. 2, p. 559: "Our intellect and will, like everything in
existence, is a spark of the All and from the source of All does it flow. And
that draws us to think analagously about the supernal light."

231. Spinoza, *A Short Treatise*, first argument, Section 90.

232. Ibid., Sections 11, 12. To clarify this view Spinoza posited the
metaphor of the relationship between the sea and its waves, the relationship
between free space and the various subdivisions it contains, or the relationship between a line and the dots that compose it. That is to say, the many
details of reality are substantial, yet their substance and presence is not to be
understood as separate from their connection to the whole of which they are
part.

233. Spinoza, *Ethics*, Part I, Definition VI, Proposition 16, and Proposition 29, schol. The distinction Spinoza drew between *natura naturans* and
natura naturata in his note to Proposition 29, does not mean they are two
different essences, but two avenues through which the one all-encompassing
substance is grasped. See ibid., Part V, Proposition 29, schol.

234. To mention only the static element of Spinoza's onthology is an
incomplete representation of his conception; however, this is not the place to
delve further into the matter. In any event, the element in Spinoza's thought
that makes it deterministic is the static nature of reality; the dynamic principle
expressed in the theory of movement and rest was adapted after the fact to
the deterministic-logical view derived from the concept of a static "substance." See also *Ethics*, Part I, Proposition 33, schol. 6: "There is no when,
nor before nor after in eternity."

235. Of interest in this context is E. Lewin's comment that, along with
ability, Spinoza created the absolute obligation to obey . . . as opposed to
Spinoza's true objective as defined in the introduction to his theorlogical-
political essay," see E. Lewin, "A Note on Obediance to Law in Spinoza's
Tractus Thelogico-Politicus" Iyyun (Tishrey 1979): 296.

A. Shmueli already pointed out this paradox in Spinoza, *Letters*, ed. A.
Shmueli (Jerusalem, 1964), p. 313: Spinoza's necessity-determinism theory
attempted to grant man freedom from awareness of his dependency on his
material environment. It sought to fight the religious fatalism of the Reforma-
tion churches and its philosophical expression in "occasionalism" nurtured
by some of Descartes's students. This theory also disputed Descartes's own

"volunteerism," which taught that will deviates from the bounds of intellect, it stemmed from the desire to free man from the terror of dependence on God and the world, especially from supernatural decree. It defended the necessity of rules in the world, guarding them from that miracle-working transcendental force. See Spinoza, *Letters*, p. 21, and many other references in his writings. It is interesting to compare Spinoza's aim with the attitude of Maimonides, who viewed the Torah as a rational alternative to free man from the superstitions and arbitrariness of idolatrous belief. See *Guide for the Perplexed*, vol. 3, Chapters 26, 29, 30, 37, 46, and 47.

236. M. Schwarcz, *Safah Mitos 'Emunot* (Jerusalem and Tel Aviv, 1967), p. 90. Schwarcz attributed this turn about to Leibniz, but it seems to me that Spinoza's contribution to this revolution should not be dismissed. It is noteworthy that Rav Kook attributed the upset of the idea of freedom both to the Catholic Church and rationalistic philosophy, although in his opinion the Church's role was decisive: "Only the stupification of the heart and deadening of the person by the gloom of life of the Middle Ages, whose imprint is recognizable even in modern times . . . that alone caused the feeling of freedom to be silenced so utterly, especially by Papal influence, until philosophy—ironically rationalistic philosophy, which should flow from life itself—lost its life force and thunderous courage and could not raise a hand to resist, to demand what the healthy spirit requires, what the whole stream of human life pronounces unanimously, saying: 'How on earth can man deny the reality of divine, universal freedom when, at the same time, internal and external freedom are his most treasured ideals and his heart's desire.'— 'Engraved (*harut*) on the tablets' (Exodus 32:10) do not read 'engraved' (*harut*) but rather 'freedom' (*herut*) (*Mishna* Avot, 6:2)." (*Ikve Hatzon* [Jerusalem, 1967], p. 153).

237. Schwarcz, *Safah Mitos 'Emunot*, pp. 91–92.

238. Compare B. Spinoza, *Ethics*, Part I, Definition VII: "That thing is called free which exists from the necessity of its own nature alone and is determined to action by itself alone." In other words, substance alone, that is, God, is free, for He alone is His own cause (ibid., Definition I).

239. See Schwarcz, *Me-Mitos le-Hitgalut* pp. 89 ff. (Tel Aviv, 1978), Chapter 3. N. Rotenstreich, "Ha-'Ikaron ha-Dinami shel Schelling," *Mehkarim be-Kabbalah u-ve-Toldot ha-Datot Mugashim le-Gershom Scholem be-Melo'ot Lo Shiv'im Shana* (Jerusalem: 1968), p. 197.

240. See M. Schwarcz's introduction to L. P. V. Schelling's *Shitat ha-Idialism ha-Transendentali*, trans. M. Schwarcz (Ramat Gan, 1980), p. 165.

241. The following is based on A. Schopenhauer, *The world as Will and Idea* (London, 1906), vol. 2, especially pp. 399 ff. (on the possibility of knowing the thing-in-itself); pp. 411 ff. (on self-awareness of will); and p. 468 (on the will in the body). Also see Bergmann, *Toldot ha-Philosophiya ha-Hadasha*, pp. 64 ff.

242. Compare Spinoza, *Ethics* Part I, Definition VI: "By God I understand Being absolute infinite, that is to say, substance consisting of infinite attributes, each one of which expresses eternal and infinite essence." And, in Definition IV: "By attributes I understand that which the intellect perceives of substance as constituting its essence." Spinoza thereby established the possibility of knowing the essence. He argued that of God's infinite attributes we can know but two, yet that does not mean our knowledge is only partial; we know God fully in respect of thought and expansion for these attributes convey his essence.

243. Schopenhauer, *The World as Will and Idea*, Vol. 2, Sect. 28.

244. Ibid.

245. F. Nietzsche, *The Will to Power*, vol. 1, p. 255.

246. Ibid., p. 14.

247. Ibid., p. 16. Compare Rav Kook, *A"T*, p. 34; *OH"K*, vol. 2, p. 15: "Morality will not withstand without its source."

248. F. Nietzsche, *The Will to Power*, p. 11.

249. Ibid., p. 11.

250. Ibid., vol. 2, p. 513.

251. Ibid., vol. 1, p. 196.

252. K. Jaspers, *Der Philosophische Glaube* (Zurich, 1948), s. 7.

253. L. S. Feuer, *Einstein and the Generations of Science*, p. 12.

254. Ibid., pp. 101–224.

255. Based on the testimony of the editor of *Orot ha-Kodesh* in his introduction to the third volume.

3. *Revelation as a Principle*

1. Y. M. Grintz, "Hitgalut" ("Revelation"), *Encyclopedia ha-'Ivrit*, vol. 15, column 613.

2. S. Rosenberg, "'Ha-Hitgalut ha-Matmedet'—Shelosha Kivunim" ("'Permanent Revelation'—Three Variants"), *Hitgalut, 'Emuna, Tevuna* (*Revelation, Faith, Reason*), ed. M. Halamish and M. Schwarcz (Ramat Gan, 1976), p. 131.

3. Ibid., p. 136.

4. Ibid., p. 138. Also see BT Berakhot 19b. Here the authority of the rabbis to determine *halacha* is based on the verse: "According to the law which

they shall teach thee, and according to the judgment which they shall tell thee, thou shalt do; thou shalt not turn aside from the sentence which they shall declare unto thee, to the right hand, nor to the left (Deuteronomy 17:1).

5. Ibid., p. 143, no. 30.

6. See Chapter 7, p. 280. See G. Scholem, *Pirkey Yesod be-Havanat ha-Kabbalah u-Semaleha*, p. 11: "Every mysticism has two opposing complimentary sides: one conservative and the other revolutionary".

7. *A"T*, p. 11. See Chapter 7, p. 251 ff.

8. Compare Chapter 2, pp. 87 ff.

9. Similar tension was not unknown to Hassidism but there is a fundamental difference in how the bounds of the problem are drawn. See R. Schatz-Uffenheimer, *Ha-Hassidut ke-Mistika*, Chapters 5, 15.

10. *OH"K*, vol. 2, p. 369.

11. Ibid., p. 367.

12. *IG"R*, vol. 2, p. 41. This view is expressed in numerous passages; I believe those quoted express it adequately. For additional reinforcement, see also *OH"K*, vol. 2, pp. 366–367, 370, and 412; *OH"K*, vol. 3, pp. 26, 27, 109, and 110; *IG"R*, vol. 3, p. 4; "Kirvat Elohim," pp. 3–5.

13. *A"T*, p. 2.

14. See *A"T*, p. 10: "And the hour is important, for it is one of the revelations of eternity; the world is important because it is one of the infinite forms, through which the light of divine being is revealed." Also ibid., p. 36: "Our temporal existence is but a spark of the eternal existence of the majesty of the Everlasting [*hod nezah ha-nezahim*]."

15. "Its progress" = *hitkadmuta;* the manuscript reads: *hitkaymuta* = "its being." Also printed thus in *OH"K*, vol. 2, p. 289.

16. *A"T*, p. 2; *OH"K*, vol. 2, p. 289.

17. *A"T*, p. 5.

18. *Orot*, p. 119.

19. See *A"T*, p. 4, on the ontological status of the "possible"; compare *OH"K*, vol. 3, p. 27. Also see Chapter 2, pp. 55 ff., and compare Spinoza, *A Short Treatise*, p. 41.

20. See *OH"K*, vol. 3, pp. 109–110. Both will and *hokhma* are understood as revelations.

21. *Kirvat Elohim*, p. 5. *Small [ze'ir]* and *long [arich]* allude to the kabbalistic symbols *Ze'ir 'Anpin* and *Arich Anpin;* here, though Rav Kook altered their original meaning and attributed them to the material world.

22. Ibid., pp. 3–4.

23. *OH"K*, vol. 3, p. 39.

24. *OH"K*, vol. 2, p. 559.

25. *A"T*, p. 7. Rav Kook took the same stance on the question of the relationship between the holy and the profane in general. See ibid. pp. 6–7; also see *OH"K*, vol. 1, p. 145.

26. *OH"K*, vol. 3, p. 59.

27. *A"T*, p. 7.

28. Ibid.

29. Ibid., p. 24.

30. See note 8. See especially *OH"K*, vol. 2, p. 362.

31. *A"T*, p. 24.

32. Ibid.

33. *OH"K*, vol. 2, pp. 364–365. Compare Claude Levi-Strauss's view on the value of primitive cultures: Claude Levi-Strauss, *The Savage Mind* (London: Weidenfeld and Nicolson, 1962), especially Chapter 9; Z. Levi, *Structuralism* (Tel Aviv, 1976), p. 119.

34. *OH"K*, vol. 1, p. 251.

35. *A"T*, pp. 7, 14. See Chapter 2, p. 87.

36. *OH"K*, vol. 1, p. 231.

37. *A"T*, pp. 9–10.

38. Ibid., p. 3; and *OH"K*, vol. 2, p. 291. In *OH"K* the words "magic, strange and impure beliefs" were omitted. This passage no doubt echoes the Hassidic idea of "elevating the sparks."

39. *OH"K*, vol. 2, p. 358.

40. See Chapter 2, p. 78.

41. *OH"K*, vol. 1, p. 17.

42. *OH"K*, vol. 2, p. 312.

43. *IG"R*, vol. 2, p. 39. See chapter 9, p. 327.

44. *OH"K*, vol. 2, p. 393; *A"T*, p. 33. Compare the two versions. In *A"T* the statement appears in singular form whereas in *OH"K* it appears in plural form: "I can make no division"; "We can make no division". The original version is that found in *A"T*; compare the words of Goethe, Chapter 1, note 4.

45. *A"T*, pp. 2, 3; *OH"K*, vol. 2, p. 289.

46. *A"T*, p. 1.

47. Despite numerous reservations and criticism. See *IG"R*, vol. 1, p. 146 (on the desecration of the Sabbath in Eretz Israel: "Our heart's wound is deep and very serious." "Ignorance and vulgar, contemptible apostacy"); "Te'udat Yisrael u-Le'umiyuto," p. 62; *OH"T*, p. 40 (apostacy devoid of moral validity); *IG"R*, vol. 1, pp. 21, 369; *IG"R*, vol. 2, pp. 90, 67; *Orot*, pp. 91–101 (apostacy distorts humankind's natural aspiration); *OH"K*, vol. 3, Heading, p. 24.

48. *Orot*, pp. 84–85; "Te'udat Yisrael u-Le'umiyuto," p. 62.

49. *Eder*, p. 32; *IG"R* I, p. 50; *Orot*, pp. 87, 79, 124–127; *OH"K*, vol. 1, p. 14.

50. *A"T*, p. 32, also p. 19: "All moral ideals must be revealed in God's management of the world, and one of these revelations is the element of *hesed* [loving kindness], simple and ideal, which contains no room for gratitude, unbelief is thus one basic revelation of the ideal in the divine, and the blasphemy and scorn it yields are the higherest level of that revelation." Also see *Orot*, p. 127: "Whoever knows unbelief from within, sucks its honey and returns it to the source of its holiness". See note 38. Also see Rav Kook's words in *Orot ha-Emunah*, p. 21: "Occasionally an unbeliever is found who has strong, inner and luminous faith, stemming from the source of supreme holiness, more intense than a thousand believers of little faith . . . and of them all it is said 'but the righteous shall live by his faith' [Habakkuk 2:4]."

51. *OH"K*, vol. 2, p. 544.

52. *A"T*, p. 47. Also see *Ne'edar ba-Kodesh*, p. 14: "The culture superior to all language and tongue in our times, is an important revelation of vital secular value. One must probe it, know its branches, its aspirations and its roots, and this knowledge will guide us in building the edifice where the holy in culture can be revealed, holiness that surpasses the value of secular culture like the supremacy of the sky over the earth." Also in *Orot ha-Emunah*, p. 21: "Books written by those of little faith may ruin a man . . . whereas books written by complete unbelievers, permeated with the spirit of the impure power of unbelief, will mend him."

53. "Ma'amar Meyuchad" (photocopy edition, together with "Me'orot ha-Emunah"), p. 10. See Chapter 8, note 7.

54. See *A"T*, pp. 73, 23 ("The source of the inclination to idol worship is in holiness"); *IG"R*, vol. 1, p. 142; "Tallelei Orot," *Tahkemoni* 2 (1910): 17. Also see the discussion in Chapter 5.

55. Rav Kook recognized that "there are very lovely things that can be revealed only as disadvantages," and therefore, "We respect those disadvan-

tages for they point to the good cause which engenders them." See: *A"T*, pp. 13 and 48.

56. *OH"K*, vol. 3, Heading, p. 34.

57. See: R. Shatz-Uffenheimer, Utopia and Messianism p. 24.

58. Based on Mishna *Sota* 9:15.

59. *A"T*, p. 1. compare p. 20. Rav Kook saw additional reasons for this insolence (*chutzpa*), but they are less essential; see *OH"K*, vol. 2, p. 298; *A"T*, p. 60; *Orot*, p. 83.

60. For example, in Kant's conception of morality, an act is considered moral and concurrently also rational only if it fits both versions of the categorical imperative; that is, the rational imperative. See Immanuel Kant, *Fundamental Principles of the Metaphysics of Ethics*, trans. Thomas Kingsmill Abbot (London: Longman's Green and Co., 1946), pp. 46, 47, 56. See S. H. Bergmann, *Ha-Philosophia shel Emmanuel Kant* (Jerusalem, 1980), pp. 89–100. Alfred North Whitehead claimed the underlying force motivating speculative reason is the assumption that any individual phenomenon can be understood as exemplifying a general principle of its nature; A. Whitehead, *The Function of Reason* (Princeton, N.J., 1929), p. 29.

61. *A"T*, p. 1, also see p. 74; and R. Schatz-Uffenheimer, p. 25, n. 9. See also *Orot ha-Emunah*, p. 29: "The insolence preceding the coming of the Messiah is expressed through unbelief. And the source of this unbelief is in the lack of inclination toward belief. This lack has arisen because the world awaits a great illumination, in which all most hidden secrets will become clear. . . . The aptitude of belief thus makes way for a higher and loftier aptitude which is that of knowledge . . . and if the aptitude of belief is thereby impoverished . . . belief is raised to yet a loftier place . . . and in this way they go from strength to strength. . ."

62. See S. Rosenberg, "Ha-Hitgalut ha-Matmedet," pp. 133–137, amd "Cheker ha-Mikra ba-Machshava ha-Yehudit ha-Datit ha-Chadasha," p. 102, in the anthology *Ha-Mikra ve-ʿAnahnu*, ed. U. Simon ed. (Tel Aviv: 1979).

63. *A"T*, p. 45.

64. Ibid., pp. 2–3.

65. Ibid., p. 8.

66. Ibid., pp. 39–40.

67. Ibid., p. 10.

68. See, for example, J. Gikitilia, *Shaʾarei Ora*, vol. 1, p. 89. More on *Knesset Israel* as the *sefira* of *malkhut*can be found in G. Scholem, *Pirkey Yesod be-Havanat ha-Kabbalah u-Semaleha*, pp. 259 ff.

69. In rabbinic literature, sleep is so described; it is considered a tinge [literally, "one-sixtieth"] of death.

70. The *sefira* of *malkhut* is also called *Eretz Israel*. See J. Gikitilia, *Sha'arei Ora*, p. 90.

71. *OH"K*, vol. 3, p. 117.

72. Ibid., p. 30.

73. *OH"K*, vol. 2, p. 300.

74. Ibid., 103.

75. See R. Schatz-Uffenheimer, "Utopiya," p. 23.

76. *A"T*, p. 1.

77. *OH"K*, vol. 2, p. 103. More on Rav Kook's nationalistic view can be found in Y. Ben-Nun, "Le'umiyut ve-'Enoshut ve-Knesset Yisrael" ("Israel and the Nations—Rabbi Kook's Idea of Nationalism"), in *Yovel 'Orot*, pp. 169–208.

78. R. Schatz-Uffenheimer contended that, in the word *deliberately*, he referred to willful assimilation in the nineteenth century.

79. *A"T*, pp. 5–6.

80. *OH"K*, vol. 3, p. 67. The similarity between this view and the Aristotalian concepts of "active intellect" and "passive intellect" should be noted.

81. Ibid., p. 69.

82. *OH"K*, vol. 1, pp. 135. Also see Chapter 9, p. 323–324 and Chapter 2, pp. 152–155.

83. On the parallel between the Torah and *Knesset Israel* as mystical organisms, see G. Scholem, *Pirkey Yesod*, p. 49. Regarding both *Knesset Israel* and the Oral law as denoting the *sefira* of *malkhut*, see J. Gikitilia, *Sha'arei Ora*, p. 86.

84. *Eder*, pp. 38–39.

85. On the kabbalistic roots of the outlook maintaining the dependency of the written Torah on the Oral Torah and, ultimately on the nation's interpretation see, G. Scholem, *Pirkey Yesod*, p. 52.

86. *A"T*, p. 37.

87. *OH"K*, vol. 3, p. 69.

88. *OH"K*, vol. 1, p. 179.

89. Chapter Two, note 94.

90. *Orot ha-Torah,* Chapter 2, Section 2, p. 11. Also see *A"T,* p. 1, beginning with the words, "Ikar limud torah li-shema'" and following.

91. *Ikve Hatzon,* p. 25.

92. *IG"R,* vol. 2, p. 39.

93. *Olat Re'ayah,* vol. 2, p. 57.

94. See R. Schatz-Uffenheimer, *Utopiya,* p. 19.

95. *A"T,* p. 37.

96. See G. Scholem, "Mashma'uta Shel ha-Torah ba-Mistika ha-Yehudit," *Pirkey Yesod,* pp. 36 ff.; G. Scholem, "Hagigim 'Al Te'ologiya Yehudit," *Devarim be-Go* (Tel Aviv, 1976); "Offenbarung und Tradition als religioese Kategorien in Judentum", *Uber einige Grundbegriffe des Judentums,* (Frankfurt am Main: Suhrkamp Verlag, 1970), pp. 90 ff.

97. Manuscripts, Collection D p. 32a.

98. *OH"K,* III, p. 3; Compare (ibid.) pp. 6–7.

99. Orot Haemunah, p. 25. See chapter 2, p. 96, n. 111.

4. The Concept of "Freedom" and the Category of "Self"

1. Space does not allow us to survey the abundance of philosophical inquiries and studies dedicated to this subject, but noteworthy is S. Pines's recently published article, "'Al Gilgulim shel ha-Munah Herut," *Iyyun* 23, nos. A–B (Studies in honor of Natan Rotenstreich's seventieth birthday) (Tevet–Nisan 1984): 247–265. On various aspects of the concept of "freedom," see I. Berlin, *Arba' Massot 'al Herut,* trans. Y. Sharett (Tel-Aviv, 1971); B. P. Weltsch, *Gnade Unde Freiheit* Munich, 1920; N. Rotenstreich, "Hekhre'ah ve-'Ahrayut," *Behinot* 9 (1956): 62–71; N. Rotenstreich, "'Al Hekre'ah ve-Hofesh," *Iyyun* 13, nos. C–D (1962): 139–146; N. Rotenstreich, "Freedom as a Cause and as a Situation," *Revue Internationale de Philosophie* 24 (1970): 53–71; H. Bergson, *Zeit und Freiheit* (Jena: 1912); K. Joel, *Der Freie Wille* (Munich, 1908); E. Nagel, "Determinism in History," *Philosophy and Phenomenological Research* 20, no. 3 (1960): 311–317; W. Kersting, *Wohlgeordnete Freiheit* (Berlin, 1984); A. N. Whitehead, *An Adventure of Ideas* (Cambridge, 1935), pp. 54–86.

2. See Berlin, *'Arba Massot,* p. 137.

3. Spinoza, *Ethics,* Part I, Definition 7.

4. I. Kant, *Hanahat Yesod le-Metaphizika shel ha-Middot,* trans. M. Shafi (Jerusalem 1933), p. 100. And see A. Messer, *Kants Ethik: Eine Einfuehrung in ihre Haputprobleme und Beitrage zu ihrer Loesung* (Leipzig, 1904), pp. 354 ff.

5. Spinoza, *Ethics* Part IV, Proposition 68; *Tractatus Theologico-Politicus* (London, 1862), pp. 111–112.

6. Maimonides, *Guide for the Perplexed*, vol. 3, 17. This rule, however, has an exception, see J. Guttman, "Hasdai Crescas," in *Ha-Philosophiya Shel ha-Yahadut* (*The Philosophy of Judaism*) (Jerusalem, 1951), pp. 217–218.

7. This matter is discussed further in Chapters 7 and 10.

8. *Ikve Hatzon*, p. 153.

9. *IG"R*, vol. 2, pp. 41–42.

10. J.-P. Sartre, *Mivhar Ketavim*, ed. M. Brinker (Tel-Aviv, 1977), vol. 1, p. 6.

11. See Chapter 2, pp. 118ff.

12. See Maimonides, *Sefer Ha-Madda*, Hilkhot Teshuva, Chapter 5.

13. Mishna *Avot*, Chapter 3, Mishna 15. Also see *Eruvin* 54a [regarding the scriptural text, "Engraven upon the tablets" (Exodus 32:16), "read not 'engraven' (*harut*) but 'freedom' (*herut*)].

14. See Plotinus, *Enneades* VI, 7, 9; VI, 7, 34–35; V, 5, 6. See Chapter 8, note 38.

15. See R. Schatz-Uffenheimer, *Ha-Hassidut ke-Mistika*, especially Chapters 1, 2, and 7.

16. *Ha-Yesod* (13 Nissan 1935), folio 126–127.

17. *A"T*, p. 41.

18. *OH"K*, vol. 1, p. 175.

19. *OH"K*, vol. 2, p. 314.

20. *A"T*, p. 63. See *OH"K*, vol. 1, p. 259. There will is understood as the first revelation of spiritual essence, and the intellect and attributes are second and third revelations. But no conclusion can be drawn from this, for in *OH"K*, vol. 1, p. 270, a distinction is made between "secular intellect" and "holy intellect"; and "holy intellect" is understood as the source of will. This problem is linked to the relationship between will and *hokhma* as metaphysical principles, and this is explored in Chapter 2.

21. *A"T*, p. 46.

22. See note 7.

23. Rav Kook refers here to Plotinus' concept of emanation.

24. His reference seems to be to Spinoza's view of reality as logically derived from the concept of "essence."

25. On the lack of decisiveness regarding metaphysical questions and the reason for it, see Chapter 2, pp. 60–61.

26. *IG"R*, vol. 2, pp. 41–42.

27. An analysis of the concept of the "absolute" or "complete" is found in Chapter 2, pp. 81–83.

28. See later, p. 182.

29. *OH"K*, vol. 3, p. 34.

30. *A"T*, p. 2.

31. From a letter to M. Zeidel, *IG"R*, vol. 2, p. 41.

32. *OH"K*, vol. 2, p. 368.

33. *IG"R*, p. 319 (letter to M. Zeidel).

34. I reached this understanding of Rav Kook's words with the aid of Prof. Adi Zemah, who spoke of the relationship between art and morality and of moral judgment as esthetic judgment.

35. *Orot ha-Teshuvah*, p. 114.

36. *OH"K*, vol. 3, p. 297.

37. The only exception to this rule, in Rav Kook's opinion, is the Jewish people, endowed with complete freedom as a collective and not just as individuals. This freedom was granted them at the momonet of exodus from Egypt and expressed in the "divine servitude of the Lord, God of Israel." See *OH"K*, vol. 3, p. 35.

38. *OH"K*, vol. 1, p. 177. The yearning for wide open spaces finds poetic expression in Rav Kook's poem, "Merhavim"

Merhavim

Expanses, Expanses
for God's expanses my soul longs,
close me in no cage,
Material or spiritual.
My spirit soars in the wide heavens,
the walls of the heart cannot contain it,
Nor can stony walls of action,
Morals, reason or law
Above all these she soars in flight
Higher than all that has a name,
All delight,
All lovliness and beauty,
Beyond the most sublime and emanated.

(quoted in Z. Yaron, *Mishnato shel ha-Rav Kook*, p. 24.)

39. See p. 173.

40. See Chapter 3.

41. See chapter 2, p. 66.

42. Ibid.

43. *OH"K*, vol. 1, p. 99.

44. See chapter 9.

45. *OH"K*, vol. 1, p. 84.

46. Ibid., p. 191.

47. Ibid., pp. 168, 173. Autobiographical expressions of this appear in *IG"R*, vol. 1, p. 154: "I am not a learned man . . . rather gifted by God with original talent, but that talent must expand from within with total confidence, unfettered, to the outside." Z. Yaron cited a similar comment in *Mishnato shel ha-Rav Kook*, p. 23: "I must be a poet, but a free poet; I cannot be found in the fetters of meter and rhyme."

48. *OH"K*, vol. 1, p. 176.

49. *A"T*, p. 43; parallel source, *OH"K*, vol. 1, pp. 95–96. In *OH"K* the formulation is slightly different: "for each and every *zaddik* has a separate Eden." At the same time it is improtant to note that Rav Kook negated no outside influences absolutely, and he recognized some positive aspects of such an influence may have. See *OH"K*, vol. 1, p. 67.

50. Based on the *midrash* in *Genesis Rabbah*, 9: "As the fruit was edible so the tree as well, until the sin and the damage it caused." Compare *OH"K*, vol. 3, p. 294.

51. *OH"K*, vol. 3, pp. 140–141.

52. See *Bereyshit Rabbah*, "Theodore—Albeck" edition (Jerusalem, 1965), pp. 74, 78, 218, 452. Also M. Jastrow, *A Dictionary of the Targumim, the Talmud Babli and Yerushalmi, and the Midrashic Literature*, p. 305.

53. "Kirvat Elokhim," in *Tahkemoni* 1, Berlin 1910. p. 2.

54. Ibid., p. 3.

55. See p. 158; Compare A. Altman, *Panim shel Yahadut* (Tel Aviv, 1983), pp. 11–30.

56. Leviticus 22:33. Compare *Olat Harayah*, II, p. 286 (on the Passover Haggadah). We may assume this verse also suited Rav Kook's idea because the words *I am the Lord* appear at the beginning and end of the verse. Rav Kook may have viewed this as support for his association of the "self" with God.

57. *OH"K*, vol. 3, p. 119.

58. Also see p. 174.

59. *OH"K*, vol. 3, p. 115.

60. Ibid., p. 117. More on the identification of *Knesset Israel* with the *sefira* of *malkhut* is found in Chapter 9, p. 326 and note 51.

61. See *OH"K*, vol. 2, pp. 414–415.

62. *OH"K*, vol. 3, pp. 46, 53, 39, 43, 41, and 40; *OH"K*, vol. 2, p. 302; *A"T*, pp. 2, 51–52, and 65; *Ikve Hatzon*, p. 146.

63. See *OH"K*, vol. 2, pp. 395–396, 399–401; also see R. Schatz-Uffenheimer, *Ha-Hassidut ke-Mistika*, Chapters 1 and 2.

64. *OH"K*, vol. 3, p. 39.

65. *OH"K*, vol. 2, p. 297.

66. *OH"K*, vol. 3, p. 77.

67. See Chapter 7.

68. *OH"K*, vol. 2, p. 297.

69. Ibid., p. 292.

70. See *A"T*, pp. 13, 60, and 61.

71. *OH"K*, vol. 3, p. 75.

72. It is interesting to compare his approach with that of Maimonides, who saw the Torah as freeing humankind from the superstitions and arbitrariness of pagan belief. See *Guide for the Perplexed*, vol. 3, pp. 26, 29, 30, and 37.

73. *A"T*, p. 40.

74. Ibid.

75. *OH"K*, vol. 3, Heading, p. 26.

76. Ibid., pp. 28 and 30.

77. *A"T*, p. 32. These words are not merely theoretical, they reflect the reality he knew intimately.

78. *OH"K*, vol. 3, Heading, p. 28.

79. Ibid. Compare ibid., p. 27: "Fear of heaven must not repress man's natural morality, for then it is no longer pure fear of heaven."

80. *Olat Harayah*, vol. 2, p. 261 (on the Passover Haggadah).

81. Ibid., p. 289.

82. *Zohar*, vol. 2, pp. 22, 109.

83. "Kirvat Elohim," p. 2; compare E. Cassirer: "The entirety of human culture may be described as a process of gradually freeing man. Language, art, religion and science are stages in this process" (*Masah 'al ha-'Adam [Essay on Man]* [Tel Aviv, 1972], p. 230). Rav Kook's understanding of the religious phenomenon will be discussed further in Chapter 5.

84. "Kirvat Elohim," p. 2.

85. Compare this with Plato's theory of recollection. See *Meno*, pp. 81a–86a. Also see R. Schatz-Uffenheimer, *Ha-Hassidut ke-Mistika*, p. 171. Rav Kook was no doubt influenced in this matter by the romantic-idealistic trend in pedagogical theory. A detailed description of the emphasis on the individual and individualism as a basic tendency in the romantic revolt, accompanied by caustic criticism, is found in I. babbit, *Rousseau and Romanticism* (1928). Also see: Y. Talmon, *Romantika u-Meri* (Tel Aviv, 1973); also Y. Talmon, "Herder ve-ha-Ruach ha-Germanit," in *Achdut ve-Yichud* (Tel-Aviv, 1965).

86. *OH"K*, vol. 3, p. 137.

87. Ibid.

88. See *OH"K*, vol. 2, pp. 381–384.

89. Ibid. Also see *Orot ha-teshuva*, p. 10. On Rav Kook's understanding of death, see S. H. Bergmann, "Mavet ve-al-Mavet be-Machshavto shel ha-Rav Kook," in *Hogim u-Ma'aminim* (Tel Aviv, 1959), pp. 101–111.

90. *OH"K*, vol. 2.

91. *OH"K*, vol. 1, p. 197.

92. Ibid., pp. 83–84.

93. Job 2:4.

94. *IG"R*, vol. 1, p. 174.

95. See R. Schatz-Uffenheimer, *Ha-Hassidut ke-Mistika*, Chapter 2.

96. See G. Scholem, "Ra'ayon ha-Ge'ula ke-Kabbalah," *Devarim be-Go*, pp. 195, 199.

97. Schatz-Uffenheimer, *Ha-Hassidut ke-Mistika*, p. 171.

98. *OH"K*, vol. 3, p. 120; *Eder*, p. 39.

99. Chapter 7.

100. "Tallelei Orot," *Tahkemoni* (1910): 14–15.

101. *Oh"K*, vol. 3, Heading, p. 31.

102. *OH"K*, vol. 3, p. 66.

103. See N. Rotenstriech, *Iyyunim be-Machshava ha-Yehudit ba-Zeman ha-Zeh* (Tel-Aviv, 1978), p. 42; Rotenstreich, *Ha-Machshava ha-Yehudit ba-'Et ha-Hadasha* (Tel-Aviv, 1966), pp. 254, 261.

104. F. Neitzsche, *The Will to Power*, volume 1, p. 11.

105. *OH"K*, vol. 3, pp. 13 and 12.

106. *OH"K*, vol. 2, p. 568.

107. *OH"K*, vol. 3, p. 140.

108. Ibid., p. 221.

109. Ibid., p. 139, also see p. 137. Compare "Masekhet Hibut ha-Kever," *Bet ha-Midrash A. Jellinek* ed. (Jerusalem, 1967), vol. 1, p. 150. Here *punishment after death* refers to the suffering involved in an individual's struggle to build his or her spiritual world; that is, affirmation of selfhood. Compare p. 196; alienation is described there as "like the slain who lies in the grave" (Psalms 88:6).

110. *OH"K*, vol. 3, p. 120.

111. *OH"K*, vol. 1, pp. 91–92.

112. *A"T*, p. 22.

113. *OH"K*, vol. 3, p. 122. A discussion of the halakhic aspects of Rav Kook's view is found in Z. Kaplan, "Le-Darko ba-Halakha" ("His Approach to Halacha"), *Kovez ha-Rayah* (Jerusalem, 1966), p. 71.

114. The kabbalistic basis for this idea is the identification of *Knesset Israel* and the Oral Torah with the *sefira* of *malkhut*. See Chapter 9, p. 326 and Chapter 3, p. 157.

115. *OH"K*, vol. 3, p. 122.

116. *A"T*, p. 35.

117. *OH"K*, vol. 2, p. 447.

118. *A"T*, p. 36.

119. See *Orot*, p. 144; *A"T*, p. 59; *OH"K*, vol. 3, p. 147.

120. *OH"K*, vol. 1, pp. 165–166. See G. Scholem, *Devarim be-Go*, p. 565.

121. *Orot ha-Teshuvah* (*OH"T*), pp. 75 and 134 (from "Ha-Tor," Rosh Hashana folio, 1927).

122. Ibid., p. 111.

123. *OH"K*, vol. 1, p. 173.

124. *OH"T*, pp. 72–73.

125. Ibid., p. 26.

126. Ibid., p. 36.

127. *A"T*, p. 73.

128. *OH"K*, vol. 2, p. 492.

129. *OH"T*, p. 66.

130. Ibid., p. 54.

131. Ibid., p. 44.

132. *OH"T*, p. 37; also see *OH"K*, vol. 3, p. 11.

133. *OH"T*, p. 70.

134. Ibid., p. 41. Compare Rav Kook's thoughts to those of the Polish logistician Jan Lokshevitz, in Chapter 2, note 73. More on Rav Kook's view on repentance is found in S. Sterlitz, "Ha-Teshuva le-'Or Histakluto shel Rabbenu" ("Repentance as Perceived by Rav Kook"), *OH"T* p. 139; N. Arieli, "Ha-Teshuva be-Mishnato shel ha-Rav Kook" ("Repentance in the Philosophy of Rav Kook"), *Teshuva ve-Shavim* (Jerusalem, 1980), pp. 81–98. Repentance as distinctive of twentieth century thought is discussed in E. Schweid, "Ha-Teshuva ba-Mahshava ha-Yehudit shel Me'a ha-Esrim" ("The Concept of Teshuva in Modern Jewish Thought"), *Yovel 'Orot*, ed. B. Ish Shalom and S. Rosenberg (Jerusalem, 1988), pp. 277–294; E. Goldman, "Darkei Teshuva be-Yameinu," *Teshuva ve-Shavim*, pp. 117–122; S. B. Auerbach and Hillel Zeitlin, "Hayyim shel Mevakshe Hashem," *Teshuva ve-Shavim*, pp. 123–130; A. Neher, "Demuto shel Franz Rosenzweig ke-Ba'al teshuva" (A Profile of Franz Rosenzweig as a 'Ba'al Teshuva' "), *Teshuva ve-Shavim*, pp. 131–138.

5. *Man and the Origin of the Religious Phenomenon*

1. E. Cassirer, *An Essay on Man*, in Hebrew. (Tel-Aviv: 1972), pp. 227–228.

2. See Chapter 2, pp. 56–73.

3. In this vein it is interesting to note Albert Einstein's thoughts (p. 455; Ch. 5, n. 3). He contends that a yearning exists for understanding, just as there is a yearning for music. This sort of desire is very common among children, though later most people lose it. Without that yearning, there would be no mathematics and no natural sciences. See: A. Einstein, "On the Generalized Theory of Gravitation," *Scientific American* 182 (1950).

A similar argument is made by Rav Kook with regard to the desire for closeness to God found in most children, which usually disappears with maturity. See "Kirvat Elokhim," p. 1. Clifford Geertz also regards the human need to understand, to find meaning as a biological need. Meaning, for him, does not bear the existential sense it has for Victor Frankl, yet little separates his understanding from the existential sense. See C. Geertz, *The Interpretation of Cultures* (New York, 1973), especially pp. 140–141. Also see V. Frankl, *Man's Search for Meaning* (Tel-Aviv, 1970).

More on Rav Kook's position on this subject is found in *Ne'edar ba-Kodesh*, pp. 7–8; "Orot Hatehiyah," *Orot*, pp. 72–73.

4. *A"T*, p. 36; parallel source: *OH"K*, p. 377, also see *OH"K*, p. 222. Compare F. Rosenzweig, *The Star of Redemption* (Jerusalem, 1970), p. 3: "All cognition of the All originates in death, in the fear of death." See that paragraph in its entirety. Also see S. H. Bergmann, "Mavet ve-'al Mavet be-Mishnato Shel ha-Rav Kook," *Hogim u-Ma'aminim* (Tel-Aviv, 1959), p. 101.

5. BT *Berakhot* 17a. This is another term for the evil impulse (*yezer ha-ra*).

6. "Kirvat Elokhim", pp. 1–2. Also see *Orot*, p. 119: "The only secure place for the spirit is in the air of God."

7. "Kirvat Elokhim," pp. 6–7.

8. The term was coined by S. H. Bergmann in reference to A. D. Gordon's idea. Further discussion on this subject is in Chapter 9 and note 61.

9. "Kirvat Elokhim," p. 3.

10. *OH"K*, vol. 2, p. 375. Compare *Orot*, p. 119: "Our resting place is in God alone."

11. *A"T*, p. 45.

12. *OH"K*, vol. 2, p. 561.

13. However, in Rav Kook's monistic view, the absolute dimension of reality is immanent in concrete existence. Nevertheless, the distinction among the various dimensions is important. See *OH"K*, vol. 3, p. 141.

14. *A"T*, p. 9.

15. "Kirvat Elokhim," p. 3.

16. *Meorot ha-Emunah*, p. 11.

17. *Manuscripts*, Collection E, p. 57a.

18. *Manuscripts*, Collection B, p. 55a. More on the status of practical *mizvot* is discussed in Chapter 7. Also see R. Schatz-Uffenheimer, "Ha-Tefisa ha-Mishpatit shel ha-Maharal: Antithesis to Natural Law," *Da'at* 2–3 (1978–1979).

19. *Manuscripts*, Collection D, p. 31b.

20. *OH"K*, p. 129. Compare Maimonides, *Guide for the Perplexed*, vol. 1, p. 1. A radically different approach to the *mizvot* is found in my article, "Ha-

Mizvot u-Ma'amadan ba-Philosophia ha-Datit shel Rav Nahman Krochmal" ("The Significance of the Commandments in the Philosophy of Rabbi Naehman of Krochmal"), *Tarbiz*, (Nissan–Sivan 1987): 373–383.

21. *A"T*, p. 1. See Chapter 3, p. 186.

22. Ibid., p. 17.

23. Ibid., p. 1.

24. *Ne'edar ba-Kodesh*, p. 19.

25. See W. James, *The Varieties of Religious Experience* (Jerusalem, 1969), pp. 479–480.

26. *Ne'edar ba-Kodesh*, p. 19.

27. See A. Even-Shoshan, *Ha-Milon he-Hadash*, under the listing "n.b.k."

28. *Manuscripts*, Early Collection, p. 57.

29. *A"T*, p. 60.

30. *Ne'edar ba-Kodesh*, p. 4.

31. See Chapter 3.

32. See Chapter 3, p. 184 and note 50.

33. *Manuscripts*, Collection C, p. 21. Still, Rav Kook did not refrain from serious criticism of unbelief and apostates. See Chapter 3, note 47. In the *Manuscripts*, Collection B, p. 34b Rav Kook's language is biting; he called the unbeliever a "lost man," whose "life is not a life". Also see *A"T*, pp. 20 and 75; *OH"K*, vol. 3, Introduction, p. 34.

34. *OH"K*, vol. 3, p. 15.

35. "Tallelei Orot," p. 17.

36. On tolerance and Jewish tradition, see A. Altmann, *Panim shel Yahadut* (Tel Aviv, 1983), p. 217. I also address this subject in my article, "Ha-Sovlanut be-Mishnat ha-Rav Kook ve-Shorasheha ha-'Iyuniyim" ("Tolerance and Its Roots in the Thought of Rav Kook"), *Da'at* 20 (Winter 1987–1988): 151–168.

37. "Tallelei Orot," p. 17.

38. See R. Otto, The Idea of the Holy, London, 1959, p. 15. Rav Kook also saw the rationalistic principle as one of the elements of the religious phenomenon, but his analysis of the components of the phenomenon differs from that of Otto. See also note 51.

39. *Manuscripts*, Collection E, p. 76b. Also see Chapter Three, note 54. More in the distinction Rav Kook drew between the emotional and rational principles is found in note 51.

40. *A"T*, pp. 32–33.

41. *Manuscripts*, Early Collection, p. 128.

42. "Tallelei Orot," p. 17.

43. *Manuscripts*, Small Collection, p. 97.

44. See Chapter 3, pp. 187–189 and Chapter 9, p. 326 and note 51.

45. See note 43; also "Tallelei Orot," p. 17. Compare R. Yehuda ha-Levi's view of the organic connection between Israel and the nations in *Kuzari* 2, p. 36. More on Rav Kook's nationalistic views: Y. Ben-Nun, "Le'umiyut ve-'Enoshut ve-Knesset Yisra'el" ("Israel and the Nations—Rabbi Kook's Idea of Nationalism"), in *Yovel 'Orot*, pp. 169–208.

46. *Ikve Hatzon*, p. 148. Despite serious differences on other matters, on this point Rav Kook's view was very close to that of Hermann Cohen. Rav Zvi Yehuda Kook made that observation in his letter to Brenner (see Chapter 1, p. 12).

47. *OH"K*, vol. 2, p. 488, 486 (also *A"T*, p. 68), and 491.

48. *Manuscripts*, Collection B, p. 15b.

49. Ibid., Collection E, p. 103b.

50. *Ikve Hatzon*, pp. 147–148.

51. Ibid. It is interesting to compare Rav Kook's analysis of this issue to Otto. In the article, "Le-Demut Diyokno shel ha-Rambam," published in *Ha-Aretz* newspaper on April 16, 1935, Rav Kook, like Otto, maintained that the religious phenomenon encompasses two elements, the emotional and the rational. In his opinion, the emotional element is expressed in the natural desire to come close to God, a desire that also has deleterious side effects. The rational element serves to restrain the emotional and purify religious thought. The difference between Rav Kook and Otto lies in their understanding of these two elements. For Otto the emotional element, or in his words "das 'Numinose'," is expressed in terror of the divine and mysterious (*mysterium tremendum*), whereas the rational element finds ways to describe and conceptualize, allowing a rational understanding of God. For Rav Kook, in contrast, the emotional element expresses desire and striving rather than terror, whereas the rational element actually negates all description or conceptual formulation in the attempt to purify religious thought. An excellent treatment of Otto's philosophy of religion is found in I. Ben-Shelomo's articles: "Ha-Raziyonali ve-ha-'Iraziyonali be-Philosophiat ha-Dat shel Rudolph Otto" ("The Rational and Irrational in the Philosophy of Rudolph Otto"), *Ha-*

Raziyonali ve-ha-'Iraziyonali, ed. M. Daskel and E. Porush (1975), and "Le-Ba'ayat Yihudah shel ha-Dat ba-Philosophiya Shel Rudolph Otto", *Sefer ha-Zikaron le-Ya'akov Friedman*, a collection of studies edited by S. Pines (Jerusalem, Beer-Sheva, 1974); also see Y. Shechter, "Iyunim be-Tefilot Rosh ha-Shana ve-Yom ha-Kippurim," *Shedemot*—56 (Winter, 1974–1975): 61–72 and *'Al ha-Kedusha, Iyunim be-Maheshevet Zemanenu* (Yahdav, 1977); B. Leiser, "The Sanctity of the Profane: A Pharisaic Critique of Rudolph Otto," *Judaism* 20, no. 1 (Winter 1971): 87–93; Z. Yaron saw Rav Kook's thought as "normal mysticism" and opposed to Otto's view of the sacred as mysterious and nonrational. See Yaron's, *Mishnato shel ha-Rav Kook* (Jerusalem, 1974), pp. 108–109, n. 4. The term *normal mysticism* was coined by M. Kadushin in his book, *The Rabbinic Mind* (New York, 1965). On Kadushin's thought, see A. Holtz, *Be-'Olam ha-Maheshava shel ha-ZaL* (Tel Aviv, 1979), in this context especially chapter 8, "Avoda she-ba-Lev" and "Mistika Normalit."

52. *Ikve Hatzon*. Further discourse on the subject of godly ideals can be found in J. Ben-Shelomo, "Ha-'Idiyalim ha-'Elohiyim be-Torat ha-Rav Kook" ("The Divine Ideals in Rav Kook's Teaching"), *Bar Ilan sefer ha-Shana* (Sefer Schwarcz), ed. M. Halamish (Ramat Gan, 1988), pp. 73–86.

53. It should be noted that Shleirmacher also stressed the feeling of dependence as a central and characteristic element of the religious phenomenon. See Rav Kook's discussion of the subject in *Ikve Hatzon*, p. 145.

54. Ibid.

55. See *OH"K*, vol. 3, p. 75: "One of the goals of the divine Torah is to lessen burdens."

56. *Manuscripts*, Collection C, p. 9.

6. The Purpose of Man and Existence

1. *Meorot ha-Emunah*, p. 11; see also *OH"K*, vol. 3, p. 24: Fear of God is the deeper wisdom, based on a more internal world-view, and that which, whether holy or secular, invests every science and teaching with a foundation of profound thought."

2. These questions have been addressed in Chapters 2 and 4 and will be considered from a different angle in the last chapter. In his seminal letter of 1793 Kant defined the scope of philosophy as that which provided answers to humankind's four questions: "What can I know? What can I do? What may I hope for? What is man?" Yet Kant did not posit the question of purpose, which lies beyond the realm of philosophy.

3. See I. Tishby, *Mishnat ha-Zohar* (Jerusalem: 1970), Part 2, pp. 280–306; G. Scholem, "Devekut u-Hitkashrut 'Intimit 'im 'Elochim be-Reyshit ha-Hassidut (Halakha u-Ma'ase)," in *Devarim be-Go* (Tel Aviv, 1976), pp. 325–350; M. Pachter, "Tefisat ha-Deveykut ve-Te'ura be-Sifrut ha-Derush ve-ha-Mussar

shel Hakhmey Zefat ba-Me'a ha-Shesh-'Esrey" ("The Theory of *Devekut* in the Writings of the Sages of Safed in the Sixteenth Century"), *Mehkarei Yerushalayim be-Maheshevet Yisra'el* 4 (1982): 51–121.

4. See G. Scholem, *Devarim be-Go*, pp. 326–327.

5. See M. Pachter, p. 121.

6. G. Scholem, *Devakim be-Go*, p. 236.

7. Ibid., p. 340.

8. In *Ne'edar ba-Kodesh*, p. 7, the word is printed as *me-ha-tokhen* (literally, *"from* the content").

9. *Manuscripts*, Small Collection, Section 196.

10. *Manuscripts*, Collection C, p. 12.

11. See Chapter Four, p. 173 and Chapter Five, pp. 220–221.

12. *Manuscripts*, Early Collection, p. 173.

13. *Manuscripts*, Collection D, p. 65.

14. *Manuscripts*, Collection B, p. 56.

15. *Manuscripts*, Collection B, p. 7.

16. In *Manuscripts*, Collection E, p. 46 Rav Kook spoke of love founded on knowledge and understanding: "all the happiness of souls, all the luster of life and all virtues are branches growing from the divine love embedded deep in every living soul. And this love develops more and more, branching out, rising and glowing through the labours of the spirit in reason and in deed.

"The masses are nourished by the hidden core, drawn from this divine, natural love to goodness and uprightness and their soul is gradually prepared until it is ready to base this delicate principle of unending love *on the foundations of knowledge and rational thought."*

In the same collection, on page 86, Rav Kook spoke of the need to purify the concept of divine love, by applying the theory of negative attributes: "After the process of refinement by which pure science must cleanse the attribute of intellect, we come to speak of godliness; and because such profound differences separate our intellect from the sublime, divine intellect, we need negative description, for it offers us a basis for all positive descriptions in their purity.

"And our hearts are glad, for we know we dwell in the shadow of the Almighty, delighted by one highest truth, the source of all blessings and the spring of all happiness, for which all souls yearn evermore.

"And again, unimpeded, we turn to the tradition of divine knowledge, knowing that everything handed down in faith, whether esoteric or manifest, is sincere, and the pure heart aims and strives toward greatness and the lofty light of absolute truth, which is its inheritance forever.

"In the same way, yet more intensely, we must discern the concept of divine love, that it may serve as a guiding light, delighting, warming, its tens of thousands of tributary flames arousing, after we have purged our form; we must make those intellectual distinctions that should be made between wordly kinds of love. They are nebulous and restricted, crushed and obscrue compared to boundless divine love, filled only with great and lofty light, drenched in supernal delights; even the shadows of shadows in God's love are enough to illumine great and everlasting lights.

"Then, at last, after the purging, and after negative shielding [see Hebrew, "*tahara*, A. Even-Shoshan, *Hamillon he-Hadash* Jerusalem, 1966], we reach the depths of this love in its glorious splendor: 'and let those who love Your name be joyful in You. For You, Lord, do bless the righteous; you encircle him with favor as with a shield' (Psalms 5, 12)."

17. *A"T*, p. 22. In an unmarked manuscript this idea appears explicity: "The spiritual revelation of love and fear, in their divergent forms, is but one general revelation. In its appearance in the upper worlds, it sparkles with greatness [. . .] and the most sublime pleasure; as it weakens and descends it is manifest as love, and as it drops yet lower it appears as awe and then as fear, until it takes the form of external fear. Spiritual ascent raises the thought of it, drawing it from the abject depths of external fear up to the pinnacle of glory."

18. *OH"K*, vol. 2, p. 442.

19. *Manuscripts*, Collection E, p. 86. Also see *Manuscripts*, Early Collection, p. 149: "This sweet and necessary force of love must inevitably bear actual fruit, to love actively and overtly all that relates to the good, to attaining God's light, love the Torah, the *mitzvot* . . . love uprightness and justice . . . we cannot help being filled with love for all creatures."

20. *Manuscripts*, Collection E, p. 86.

21. *Manuscripts*, Early Collection, p. 128. In the same paragraph, based on this idea, Rav Kook explained why King Solomon had numerous wives and the Torah generally condoned of polygamy: "And this is the secret of the king's eighteen wives and of Solomon's thousand, and the overall nonlimitation of wives by the Torah. The male soul is more encompassing, longer, expansive and deeper than the female soul. And the fullness of love becomes more complete when all the disparate parts are drawn together by that masculine force."

22. Ibid., 149.

23. See note 20.

24. *OH"K*, vol. 2, pp. 522, 524.

25. *A"T*, p. 13.

26. *Manuscripts*, Half Collection, p. 12.

27. See Chapter 4, pp. 197 ff.

28. A"T, pp. 51–52. The idea of humankind as the fountainhead of holiness is linked to a broader view of the expansion of revelation of holiness in the world in three dimensions: human, place, and time. See OH"K, vol. 2, pp. 303–304: "We must always remember the importance of the lights of holiness, sparkling somewhere, secretly expanding in every direction, spreading on hidden paths and concealed streams, until they come to be revealed at that very luminary place.

"*The Holiness of a man of Israel* is latent in every man, in all of humanity, in the most secret depths, and it flows . . . until illumination is revealed in the soul of Israel.

"*Holiness of place* fills the world, yet it is hidden and unknown; the secret streams of holiness strive toward the place of their revelation and are finally revealed in Eretz Israel, the zenith of the world, and from there to the locus of holiness, the Temple—and the foundation stone [*even hashetiya*].

"*Holiness of time* spreads over all of time, may God be blessed daily, and the threads of the light of holiness mysteriously drawn forward, to be expressed and revealed at holy points in time, on the Sabbath. . . An example of this is the senses' illumination of the soul—the eye that sees and the ear that hears their light does not come from within them but from that same illumination of life that flows from the light of the soul, animating the entire body, granting the vital gifts of sight and hearing. For when this power bursts forth, when it reaches the choicest point to reveal itself, it is transformed from potential to actual, in the form of sight through the eyes and hearing through the ears. . . Whatever happens at any particular time is but the concentrated revelation of the multitudinous forces secretly stored all along."

29. A"T, p. 19. Also see Chapter 10, on man's metaphysical ability.

30. Ibid., p. 22: "The idea that everything connected with man, be it his food, drink, tools, movements or any of his property, is all essentially related to his true being—this idea is reasonable; here, future, present and past are no different, everything contains a revelation of being, and every manner of being lives in some way and has some form of cognition. Life surrounds us on all sides: when we are uplifted, so is everything, and when we are degraded, all is brought low."

31. OH"K, vol. 3, p. 339 and 332; OH"K, vol. 3, p. 42; A"T, pp. 53, 61.

32. OH"K, vol. 2, p. 434. Also see Chapter 10, pp. 159–160.

33. OH"K, vol. 3, p. 61.

34. Ibid., p. 64. Also OH"K, vol. 1, pp. 217, 249.

35. On the role of the "microcosm–macrocosm" analogy in Greek philosophy see: J. Moreau, *L'ame du Monde de Platon aux Stoiciens* (Paris: 1939). See index under the heading "microcosm."

36. *OH"K*, vol. 2, p. 560. On the kabbalistic understanding of man's status see: A. Gottlieb, "Ha-Yesod ha-Te'ologi ve-ha-Misti shael Tefisat Ye'ud ha'Adam ba-Kabbalah", *Mehkarim be-Sifrut ha-Kabbalah* (Tel Aviv: 1976), pp. 29–37. See also Chapter 10, note 31. Note the relationship of Nietzsche's *uebermensch* to Rav Kook's conception, and the difference between the two.

37. See J. Schlanger, *Ha-Philosophiya shel Shlomo ibn Gevirol* (Jerusalem: 1980), pp. 251–254.

38–39. *OH"K*, vol. 3, p. 156. *OH"K*, vol. 2, pp. 522–524. In certain places this idea is formulated in terms borrowed from Lurianic kabbalah, see *OH"K*, vol. 3, p. 81; *OH"K*, vol. 2, p. 527.

40. Chapter 4, p. 99.

41. See *OH"K*, vol. 2, p. 517: "The appearance through which man experiences creation, not as something finished and complete, but as something which is continuously becoming, rising, developing and elevating, that appearance is what raises him from a position of 'beneath the sun' [Ecclesiastes] to 'above the sun', from a place where nothing is new to a place where nothing is old, where all is renewing, where joy of heaven and earth is as the day they were created."

42. Ibid., p. 557: "We thirst only for the ideal of knowledge, whose very greatness is beyond contemplation—that ideal itself is the quality of knowledge of Gods and worship of God, qualities which, for us, are of supreme importance. The secret of Israel is simply a dark process that gradually purifies itself, patiently and over time, quietly, persistently and ceaselessly."

43. Ibid., p. 565.

44. See Chapter 4, pp. 169 ff.

45. Compare p. 234.

46. *Manuscripts*, Half Collection, p. 11.

47. *Manuscripts*, Collection B, p. 31.

48. *OH"K*, vol. 2, p. 525.

49. Ibid., p. 69; parallel source, *A"T*, p. 35.

50. *OH"K*, vol. 3, p. 32. Also see *OH"K*, vol. 2, pp. 375, 377; *A"T*, pp. 44, 61, 25–26, etc. . . . See N. Rotenstreich on the idea of "correspondence" in Rav Kook's thought, *Iyunim ba-Machshava ha-Yehudit be-Zeman ha-Zeh* (Tel Aviv, 1978), p. 50. See chapter 2, note 18.

51. *OH"K*, vol. 3.

52. See *Manuscripts*, Collection E, p. 54: "And we go from strength to strength adapting ourselves to infinite light (*En-sof*); we grow accustomed to

the glow of majesty [*hod*], and greatness and exultation fill our souls, and our whole being is broken by the mighty beating within us, and we delight in the pleasantness of love, the sweet friendship that penetrates us, and in fear we yearn for joy, our souls filled with unbounded happiness.

"We sense a fountain of life welling up from the force of our being, showering us with an abundance of eternity. 'For you are the source of life and in your light shall we see light' [Psalms 36:10]."

Also see *Manuscripts,* Collection B, p. 38: "As man overcomes and rises in holiness and repentence *all his disparities are united,* and he begins to feel how *all things are connected to one another, and all is rooted in the supreme spiritual source.* The great *demand* that his higher soul demands of him, *that he live in a world of unity, harmony, and correspondence,* begins to be fulfilled.

"And the desire to dwell always in the tent of Torah, recalling laws and exacting in commandments, awakens in all its loveliness, with grace and good sense in the spirit of loving kindness filled with generosity and honesty, from the source of supreme love, full of knowledge and fear of God."

Likewise, in unmarked *Manuscripts:* "Just as man must accustom himself to physical nature and its powers, learn its ways and actions in accordance with the general laws that govern the world, and realize that those laws rule within him just as they rule outside of him, so, too, he must "adjust" to the spiritual laws of nature, which rule, to an even grater extent, over all of existence, of which he is part.

"And the beginning and end of this adaptation is that supreme point of cleaving [*devekut*] to God in all his paths and actions, all his feelings and thoughts, *for the adaptation to spiritual existence, which encompasses all*—all originates in that point, and all returns there. . ."

Also see *OH"K,* vol. 2, pp. 333, 377; *OH"K,* vol. 3, p. 152, etc.

53. *OH"K,* vol. 2, p. 397. It is difficult to ignore the resemblance to Kant's two "critiques": Critiques of Pure Reason and Critique of Practical Reason.

54. *A"T,* p. 49. Also see Chapter 2, p. 126 and note 207.

55. *OH"K,* vol. 2, pp. 376 and 537.

56. Ibid., p. 397.

57. See R. Schatz-Uffenheimer, "'Utopiya," p. 22.

58. *A"T,* p. 34; *OH"K,* vol. 1, p. 94.

59. *A"T,* p. 37.

60. *Ne'edar ba-Kodesh,* pp. 5–6.

61. *A"T,* p. 37.

62. Ibid., p. 59.

63. Ibid., p. 47. Also see *OH"K,* vol. 3, p. 58.

64. *OH"K,* vol. 3, p. 85.

65. *OH"K,* vol. 2, p. 427; *A"T,* p. 10.

66. *Manuscripts,* Collection C, p. 8.

67. See *OH"K,* vol. 2, pp. 397–398, 395–396; *OH"K,* vol. 3, pp. 19–20.

68. *A"T,* p. 34.

69. *OH"K,* vol. 3, p. 86.

70. See note 57.

71. *OH"K,* vol. 1, p. 128. On the mutual dependence between will and intellect and their unity at the source, see also *OH"K,* vol. 1, pp. 44, 56, 259, 258, 260; *OH"K,* vol. 2, pp. 430, 327; *OH"K,* vol. 3, pp. 58, 85, 86, 87, 88, 89, 90, 98, 91, 95; *A"T,* pp. 11, 43, 76; *Orot ha-Teshuvah,* pp. 57, 99.

72. *A"T,* p. 7.

73. Ibid., p. 53; parallel source, *OH"K,* vol. 3, p. 58.

74. *OH"K,* vol. 3, pp. 50, 52, 47, 49; *A"T,* p. 50.

75. "Ha-Tefila ha-Matmedet shel ha-Neshama," *Olat Re'ayah* (Jerusalem, 1963), vol. 1, p. 11. For an anthology on prayer from Rav Kook's writings, see M. Z. Neriah, *Orot ha-Tefila,* by Mara"N ha-Rav Abraham Isaac ha-Cohen Kook z"l (Jerusalem, 1979).

76. *Olat Re'ayah,* vol. 1, pp. 11, 13.

77. Ibid., p. 13. It is remarkable that this aspect of Rav Kook's understanding of prayer has not yet been a subject of research. See Y. Morial, "Prayer in the Philosophy of ha-Rav Kook," *Be-'Oro* (Jerusalem: 1986), p. 49. Rav Kook, in his vision of prayer as a cosmic aspiration, went far beyond other mystical and kabbalistic thinkers, who view prayer as a means to mystical unification with God; prayer, for them, remained in the realm of human activity and was not described as a cosmic force. See, for example, R. Yehuda ha-Levi, *Kuzari,* vol. 3, p. 5; R. Yosef Albo, *Ikkarim,* Fourth Discourse, Chapter 19; *Perakim be-Hazlaha* (attributed to Maimonides) Jerusalem 1939, pp. 6–8; Meir ibn Gabbai, *Tola'at Ya'akov* (Warsaw, 1877), p. 4a; *24 Sodot* (in Oxford Ms. 1610, 3), Sod 15; J. Ben-Shelomo, *Torat ha-Elokhut,* pp. 38, 41, 43 (and note 17), 44, 231–232.

A summary of prayer in Kabbalah is found in I. Tishby, *Mishnat ha-Zohar,* vol. 2, pp. 247–280. This subject deserves more attention, and I hope to address it elsewhere.

78. See Chapter 2, p. 111.

79. *Olat Harayah,* p. 14.

80. *Ikve Hatzon,* p. 145.

81. Ibid.

82. *OH"K*, vol. 3, p. 8. see also *A"T*, p. 25.

7. *The Way of the Holy*

1. See Chapter 8, note 1. Also see N. Rotenstreich, "Cosmos u-Ma'asim"; Y. Amital, "Mashma'uta shel Mishnat ha-Rav Kook le-Dorenu" ("The Meaning of Rav Kook's Thought to Our Generation"), *Yovel 'Orot*, pp. 333–342.

2. *OH'K*, vol. 3, p. 221. See Chapter 4, pp. 203–204.

3. *OH"K*, vol. 3, p. 86.

4. *OH"K*, vol. 1, p. 249.

5. Ibid., p. 247.

6. *OH"K*, vol. 3, p. 203.

7. Ibid., p. 69.

8. *A"T*, p. 49.

9. Chapter 2, p. 84.

10. *OH"K*, vol. 1, pp. 66–67.

11. See *A"T*, p. 60, 68–69. Also Chapter 8, pp. 31–32.

12. *A"T*, p. 39.

13. *OH"K*, vol. 3, p. 205; Also p. 206.

14. Ibid., p. 204.

15. Ibid., p. 203.

16. *Manuscripts*, Small Collection, p. 170. The Maharal maintains a similar position. See R. Schatz-Uffenheimer, "Ha-Tefisa ha-Mishpatit shel ha-Maharal: Antithesis to Natural Law," p. 154. On the source of this view in Kabbalah, see A. Gottlieb, *Studies in the Literature of the Kabbalah*.

17. *Manuscripts*, Small Collection, p. 21.

18. *OH"K*, vol. 3, p. 180.

19. See Rav Harlap's testimony to this in Chapter 10, pp. 358–359.

20. *OH"K*, vol. 3, pp. 103–104.

21. *OH"K*, vol. 1, p. 106.

22. *Manuscripts,* Small Collection, p. 160.

23. *OH"K,* vol. 1, p. 106.

24. *A"T,* p. 52.

25. *OH"K,* vol. 3, p. 360.

26. *A"T,* p. 54.

27. *Manuscripts,* Collection B, p. 55a.

28. *OH"K,* vol. 3, p. 70. Compare R. Moshe Haim Luzzato, *Da'at Tev-onot,* ed. H. Friedlander (Benei Barak, 1973), pp. 3–4.

29. *Manuscripts,* Collection D, p. 27a.

30. *OH"K,* vol. 3, p. 125. The relationship between study and action and the necessity of action to balance excessive spirituality are discussed in *Arpalei Tohar,* p. 9. Also see Manuscripts, Early Collection, p. 73: "The righteous are ever bound up with adhesion to God (May his name be blessed), they cannot imagine life devoid of the sweetness of cleaving to God. However, since deceptive imagination intrudes in all human ideas, and with it many negative qualities, which spread as branches stemming from one small root, and as many sprouts of one seed, they must therefore *clarify* their adhesion to God *by way of Torah and mitzvot,* that it be entirely pure and holy."

31. I. Tishby discusses the Lurianic concept of "raising the sparks" in *Torat ha-Rav ve-ha-Kelipa be-Kabbalat ha-AR"I* (Jerusalem, 1960), pp. 82–84, 124–125.

32. *A"T,* pp. 63, 66; *OH"K,* vol. 3, p. 184.

33. *A"T,* pp. 3–4 (parallel source, *OH"K,* vol. 2, pp. 290 ff.), 14–15. Compare R. Elior on the concept of "distinctions", *Torah ha Elokhut be-Dor ha-Sheni shel Hassidut Habad* (Jerusalem, 1982), p. 56.

34. See R. Schatz-Uffenheimer, "'Anti-Spiritualism in Hassidut: Studies in the Thought of Rabbi Schnuer Zalman of Liadi," *Molad* 171 (1962): 513–528.

35. *A"T,* p. 34.

36. *OH"K,* vol. 3, p. 203.

37. *Manuscripts,* Small Collection, p. 245. One important element in the context of this effort is the sacrificial service in the Temple. Thus Rav Kook in the *Manuscripts,* Collection D, p. 19b said: "Godly thought in living and actual form is linked to the Temple service, for only through actual sacrificial worship can it become complete."

38. *Manuscripts,* Collection B, p. 22.

39. *OH"K*, vol. 3, p. 58.

40. See A. Even -Shoshan, *Ha-Millon he-Hadash* under *lakot* and *lakota* ["flaws"]. Compare *Orot*, p. 82; BT *Zevahim* 18b; BT *Sota* 12b, Rashi, ad loc.

41. *Manuscripts*, Collection B, p. 46, also see p. 35: "There are two types of *devekut* [adhesion] in man: one comes from the *Torah*, and although he may only feel some inward spiritual light with no trace of halacha [law] or *mitzva* [commandment], this comes from the force of *practical Torah*. The second type stems from the soul's illumination itself, relative to divine light in the world. The minute aspects of these two types of adhesion to God sparkling in man's soul are used in various ways. And at times one must be *combined* with the other."

Also see *Manuscripts*, Collection D, p. 40: "When one cleaves to Torah, one cleaves to the tree of life itself. As man becomes more rooted and his soul absorbs the light of Torah in its innermost depths, the significance of his cleaving to the tree of life through the Torah will become clear, until [the soul] will feel the Torah's expansiveness with the same naturalness as it senses the expansiveness of life.

"And then the soul will need no intermediary to awaken within it the sense of its divine vitality. For it will draw from the stream of delights, flowing with life, true life, eternal life, containing all aspects of temporal life in sublime and eternal form."

We must stress here that, for Rav Kook, cleaving to Torah does not imply learning Torah in the usual sense. See *Manuscripts*, Early Collection, p. 94: "It is false to demand of the soul *true adhesion to God*, without the exultation plumbing the depths of the esoteric Torah.

"And, when one has already approached the antechamber, if he distances himself, even for a short while, he becomes ensnared in the net of abandoned study, though he might engage in the other branches of Torah; the same is true, all the more, were he to stop learning Torah completely for any reason."

42. Chapter 3, pp. 157–158.

43. *A"T*, p. 60; parallel source, *OH"K*, vol. 1, pp. 123–124. Compare this view to Franz Rosenzweig's understanding of the *mitzvot* as expressed in his letter of 1923 to M. Buber: "Ha-Bonim", *Neharayim* (Jerusalem, 1977), pp. 80–93, especially pp. 86–87. Rosenzweig expanded the domain of the *mitzvot* and denies the existence of a neutral category known as *heter* ("permitted"). In his view, a Jew must always be conscious of his or her status as one "commanded," thus transforming all actions into *mitzvot* (good deeds).

See also S. H. Bergman, *"Ha-Bonim* le-Franz Rosenzweig", *Ma'aznaim*, (Sivan, 1961): 5–9; Z. Levy, *Mevaser Existensializm Yehudi—Franz Rosenzweig* (Tel-Aviv, 1970), pp. 138–143; *On Jewish Learning*, ed. N. N. Glatzer New York, (1955).

44. See R. Schatz-Uffenheimer, *Ha-Hassidut ke-Mistika*, Chapter 5.

45. *OH"K*, vol. 3, p. 129. Autonomy replaces the normative element. This idea resembles Schelling's claim that the ultimate goal of the "self" is to transform laws of freedom to laws of nature and laws of nature to laws of freedom, to instill nature into the "I" and instill the "I" in nature. See F. W. J. Schelling, "Vom Ich als Prinzip der Philosophie" [1795], *Werke*, ed. Otto Weiss (Leipzig, 1907), vol. 1, p. 50 (14).

Also compare Kant's understanding of morals in his book, *The Fundamental Principles of the Metaphysics of Ethics* (London, 1946) and *Critique of Practical Reason*, p. 8, note, Hebrew trans. and annotation S. H. Bergman and N. Rotenstreich (Jerusalem, 1973). Also see S. H. Bergman, *Ha-Philosophia shel Immanuel Kant*, p. 94.

Maimonides's influence on Rav Kook's understanding of the "primal sin" in the garden of Eden is clear. See *Guide for the Perplexed*, vol. 1, p. 2.

46. See Chapter 9, p. 318 and note 21.

47. According to Rav Kook, there is no opposition between freedom and necessity of natural tendencies or natural causality. Spinoza also saw freedom as "internal" necessity as opposed to some external compulsion. See B. Spinoza, *Ethics*, Part I, Definitions, Definition 7. Kant, too, saw no contradiction between the concepts of freedom and necessity born of natural causality; see *Critique of Practical Reason*. Also see A. Messer, *Kants Ethik* (Leipzig, 1904), pp. 354 ff.

48. *OH"K*, vol. 3, p. 125.

49. Ibid., p. 128.

50. *OH"K*, vol. 1, p. 23.

51. *A"T*, p. 12.

52. *Manuscripts*, Small Collection, p. 74.

53. Ibid. Rav Kook expressed the same idea less radically in *Manuscripts*, Small Collection, Chapter 222, p. 64; "Such *zaddikim*, are driven by an inward demand that every word of Torah, all knowledge and learning be absorbed in the profound desire of their innermost love and supernal awe, in their adhesion to God. They cannot be held from this holy delight, even though it may diminish their formal study. As it is said, 'it is the same whether a man offers much or little [as a sacrifice], so long as he directs his heart toward heaven' (TB Ber. 5b).

"But every person, even if he feels his desire to cleave to God is pure, must *accustom himself to intellectual pursuits*, to love for the Torah, drawing the light of his own faith to the desire for Torah, until the influence of love, awe and true adhesion to God flows over, permeating *every aspect of the Torah* itself."

Compare *A"T*, pp. 24, 25, 46: *OH"K*, vol. 3, p. 259.

54. *A"T*, p. 1. See R. Schatz-Uffenheimer, "'Utopiya," p. 16: "This was a crisis of the unknown, rather than the 'superfluous': Not 'excess' in the normative system of *mitzvot*, but the limit of transparency of the entire system on the metaphysical plane."

55. Ibid.

56. Ibid.

57. Ibid., p. 54. Compare Chapter 8, pp. 325–327 and p. 278 and p. 161.

58. *OH"K*, vol. 1, p. 178.

59. *A"T*, p. 44. Also see *OH"K*, vol. 2, p. 334.

60. Chapter 2, pp. 84–86.

61. Compare F. Rosenzweig, *The Star of Redemption*, pp. 176–178; M. Buber, *Be-Sod Siah*, (Jerusalem, 1959), pp. 85–86. Also see G. Scholem, "Hagigim 'Al Te'ologiya Yehidit," *Devarim be-Go* (Tel Aviv, 1976), pp. 568–569.

62. Compare G. Scholem, *Pirkey Yesod*, pp. 213 ff., and I. Tishby, *Mishnat ha-Zohar*, vol. 2, pp. 655 ff.

63. *A"T*, p. 12; parallel sources, *OH"K*, vol. 2, p. 298.

64. *OH"K*, vol. 4, p. 305.

65. *A"T*, p. 12.

66. *OH"K*, vol. 3, p. 123. The idea is qualified later in the same passage: "Of course they are exacting in their actions," and reiterated on pp. 124 and 259. These remarks might be part of a polemic. On the criticism against him, see R. Schatz-Uffenheimer, "Reysit ha-Masa' Neged ha-Rav Kook" ("The First Campaign against Rav Kook").

67. See pp. 262–263.

68. *AT*, p. 12.

69. *OH"K*, vol. 3, p. 330.

70. Ibid., p. 42.

71. *A"T*, p. 11.

72. On affirmation of the world in Rav Kook's thought, see *Arpalei Tohar*, new edition (Jerusalem, 1983), pp. 114–117. Also see *OH"K*, vol. 4, p. 136; *A"T*, pp. 24–46.

73. *OH"K*, vol. 2, pp. 292–293, also p. 297: "He [the holy man of silence] does not become holy in seclusion; he lives [in the world]." For Rav Kook, social involvement is essential; although he did not reject solitude out of

hand, it is a path suited only for "the man of character" (in *OH"K*, vol. 2, p. 439). The distinction is made between this term and two other descriptions he often invokes, the *zaddik* and the *holy man of silence*, for whom solitude is not recommended. See *OH"K*, vol. 3, pp. 268, 267, 270, 271, 272.

74. *OH"K*, vol. 3, p. 78; also *A"T*, p. 24. Compare *OH"K*, vol. 3, p. 289. Fasts and mortification are justified here only as a temporary measure.

75. *A"T*, pp. 9, 13, and elsewhere.

76. Ibid., p. 71. See also *Manuscripts*, Collection B, p. 47: "Every member of the people of Israel is righteous and holy in his connection to the nation as a whole; everything Jewish is a dwelling place of holiness and divine emanation."

77. *OH"K*, vol. 2, p. 298.

78. Ibid., p. 297.

79. *A"T*, p. 20, also see pp. 8–9.

80. See R. Schatz-Uffenheimer, "'Utopiya.'" The author shows the centrality of the utopian and messianic dimension in Rav Kook's thought. See note 124.

81. *A"T*, p. 55; parallel source, *OH"K*, vol. 1, p. 147.

82. *A"T*, pp. 3–4; parallel source, *OH"K*, vol. 2, pp. 290 ff.

83. *A"T*, p. 12; parallel source, *OH"K*, vol. 2, p. 298. Note the variations between texts: In *Arpalei Tohar:* "The impudent sons, path breakers and breachers of fences, will become prophets"; whereas in *OH"K*, "their children will become prophets. . ."

84. See Chapter 9, p. 318 and notes.

85. *A"T*, p. 9, also see p. 5.

86. Ibid., pp. 8–9; *Orot*, p. 84.

87. See I. Tishby, *Mishnat ha-Zohar*, vol. 2, Introduction, p. 11.

88. Also see *A"T*, p. 48: "Certain rectifications the world must undergo cannot be engendered by the righteous, but only by the wicked and those whose views and actions are imperfect. . . . Some of these rectifications are in the social realm; developing agricultural implements, waging wars that the world sometimes sorely needs; in the world and practical inventions. Other rectifications are in the spiritual, concerning practical and intellectual knowledge; a soul encompassed in piety and lofty holiness of the spirit cannot penetrate the details of such sciences."

89. See Tishby, *Mishnat ha-Zohar*, pp. 12–13.

90. *IG"R*, vol. 2, p. 19: "The disparity between thought and deed cannot be completely eliminated, because actions are drawn, even involuntarily and to a greater or lesser extent, after thought."

91. *A"T,* p. 19, compare p. 17 (on the eternal nature of the Torah according to Maimonides); also see p. 11. In *Manuscripts*, Small Collection, p. 270, Rav Kook wrote: "The degree of awe corresponds with physical force. [But] the mind must sparkle in bright splendor, in the might of its pure freedom."

92. According to Deuteronomy 28:10.

93. *Eder*, p. 52.

94. *OH"K*, vol. 1, p. 177.

95. *OH"K*, vol. 3, Heading, p. 26. See Chapter 4, pp. 191–194, and Chapter 5, p. 221.

96. *A"T*, pp. 32–33. See *OH"K*, vol. 1, p. 217; *Ikve Hatzon*, p. 129.

97. In a letter to Rav Meir Berlin dated 1911, Rav Kook deprecated apologetics and plemical criticism and maintained that "Truth is more precious that anything else; it is through truth alone that God may be praised, and the faith uplifted." See *IG"R*, vol. 2, p. 20.

98. See *OH"K*, vol. 1, pp. 120–121; *Olat Re-ayah*, pp. 330–331; *OH"K*, vol. 2, pp. 544, 545. Also see Chapter 5, pp. 222–223.

99. *OH"K*, vol. 3, pp. 327 and 100.

100. *A"T*, p. 13.

101. *IG"R*, vol. 1, pp. 19–20.

102. Compare J. Stuart Mill, *On Freedom* (Jerusalem, 1966), pp. 14–15. In Rav Kook's opinion, freedom of expression should be limited not by fanatical insistence on any one view but by a sense of responsibility that perceives many aspects and considers a number of implications. See *OH"K*, vol. 3, p. 282: "One should refrain from expressing anything that could weaken another's moral code. Even if the idea itself seems right, it harms the listener if his moral framework is at odds with what he hears."

103. See note 101.

104. *OH"K*, vol. 3, p. 130.

105. See p. 260.

106. *IG"R*, vol. 2, pp. 250–251.

107. *IG"R*, vol. 1, p. 51.

108. *OH"K*, vol. 3, pp. 106–107.

109. The symbol of the "tree of life" is further explored in Chapter 9, pp. 317–318 and note 21.

110. See note 108.

111. On the utopian aspect of the Torah as a function of freedom, symbolized by the "tree of life," see note 109. The identification of freedom with life is discussed in Chapter 4. The verse at the close of the chapter "Your testimony is for me a conversation" (Psalms 1198:99) hints that the testimony (i.e., the Torah) will become "speech" (i.e., freedom). Compare *OH"K*, vol. 3, p. 129.

112. See note 108.

113. *A"T*, p. 96.

114. Unless we greatly expand the connotations of a "halakhic reason." Rav Kook wrote a halakhic analysis of the question of *shmita* in his book *Shabbat ha-'Arez*.

115. See *IG"R*, vol. 1, pp. 289, 311; M. Friedman, "Le-Mashma'uto shel Pulmus ha-Shmitah (1888–1989)" ("On the Social Significance of the Polemic on Shmitah 1888–89"), *Shalem* 1 (1974): esp. pp. 470 ff.

116. See Chapter 3, pp. 151–155 ff.

117. *A"T*, p. 11. In the newer edition of *Arpalei Tohar*, the editors "corrected" the original, more radical text by deleting four words and changing two, making it read: "But when the light of prophecy has been obstructed, this *repair* is effected through *revolt*, which grieves the heart itself, and gladdens it *in its ultimate goal*. (New edition, p. 15).

This change completely reverses the meaning; the word *itself* (its essence, its inwardness), replaces *externally*, and *inwardly* is replaced by *its ultimate goal*; that is, its purpose or function, something external and certainly not "its essence."

118. See *IG"R*, vol. 1, pp. 102–103; also pp. 175–176. M. Klein wrote about Rav Kook's basic approach to halacha in "'Ekronot Tefisato ha-Ra'ayonit shel ha-Rayah et ha-Halakha" ("Rabbi Kook's Philosophical Grasp of Halacha"), *Be-'Oro*, pp. 153–166.

119. See *IG"R* I, p. 139. In a letter to Rav Yitzhak Isaac ha-Levi, Rav Kook admits that, counter to common practice, he overlooks certain Jews' rejection of halakhic decisions made by the Rishonim [rabbinic authorities who lived before the Shulhan Arukh]. His "overlooking" is not to be considered an *a priori* halakhic decision but rather acceptance of a second best after the fact. Compare Chapter Nine, pp. 152–153 and note 45.

120. BT *Shabbat* 112b.

121. JT *Shevi'it*, 6:1, Venice edition, p. 36b; JT *Kiddushin* 1:9, p. 81c.

122. *OH"K*, vol. 3, pp. 218–219.

123. *OH"K*, vol. 2, pp. 381–384.

124. Ibid., p. 384.

8. *The Dynamic of Rationalism and Mysticism in Rav Kook's Thought*

1. M. Schwarcz, "Polmus ha-Pantheism ve-ha-Theologiya shel Shlomo Ludwig Steinheim" ("The Pantheism Controversy and the Theology of Solomon Ludwig Steinheim"), in *Hitgalut, Emunah, Tevunah* (*Revelation, Faith, Reason*), p. 119.

2. On some aspects of the problematic nature of the concept of "reason," see the collection of essays *Ha-Ratzionali ve-ha-Iratzionali* (*The Rational and the Irrational*), ed. M. Daskal and A. Porush (Beer-Sheva, 1975).

3. See *Encyclopaedia Britannica: Macropaedia.* "Philosophical Schools and Doctrines—"Rationalism."

4. These two possibilities are not mutually exclusive, and Spinoza indeed makes a heroic attempt to unite them. See A. Shmueli, "Ha-Methoda ha-Geometrit, Ideal ha-Hinuch ve-Torat ha-Zehirut," in *Baruch Spinoza*, ed. M. Brinker, M. Dascal, and D. Nesher (Tel-Aviv, 1979).

One might say that rationality is intrinsic to a rationalistic outlook, due to its assumption that the intellect is the exclusive source and measure of all perception. A viewpoint that can responsibly be accused of irrationality cannot be considered rationalistic. Of course, not every rational system holds the intellect as the unique source and measure of perception. The extensive influence of Kant's "Copernian revolution," on the one hand, and the logical-analytical philosophy of positivism, on the other, engendered a new sort of rationalism, methodological rationalism, which takes experience into account and rejects the very possibility of a priori ontological contentions. Influenced by Wittgenstein, logical positivists shared a similar view, with the following principles: comprehensive empiricism, sustained by modern logical theory, admiration of the achievements of modern science, absolute rejection of metaphysics based on logical and linguistic considerations, which they saw as meaningless, and limitation of philosophy to the task of solving its own problems through a logical analysis of language. A good example of such a thinker is Rudolph Carnap. See his *Logical Syntax of Language*, trans. A. Smeaton and K. Paul (London, 1937). See also K. R. Popper's definition of *rationality* as openness to criticism in *The Logic of Scientific Discovery* (New York, Harper 1957), preface to Chapter 1. Popper also claimed that rationalism itself, in its dependence on irrational choice and obligation, is as irrational as any other form of obligation. See J. Agassi, "Ratzionaliut ve-Ta'anat ha-Gam Ata" ("Rationality and the Tu Quoque Argument"), in *Ha-Ratzionali ve-ha-Iratzionali* (*The Rational and the Irrational*), p. 17. Strident criticism of analytic philosophy for having artifically constricted the concept of rationality to the point of driving important philosophical questions out of its domain entirely and dealing only with trivial problems is found in Y. Yoval, *Kant ve-Hidush ha-Metaphysica* (Jerusalem, 1973), introduction, Section 2. In any case, a narrow definition that identifies rationality with logic, that is, with acceptance of valid arguments and acts according to them, cannot explain the concept of "rationality" in all its historical metamorphoses. See also M. Kroi, "Razionalit Kolelet ve-Ratzionalit Helkit," in *Ha-Ratzionali ve-ha-Iratzionali*, pp. 43, 45.

5. A. N. Whitehead, *The Function of Reason* (Princeton, N.J., 1929), p. 51.

6. See Yoval, *Kant ve-Hidush*, Section 4.

7. Ibid., pp. 42–43.

8. There are a number of similarities between Whitehead's concept of reason and that of Kant: for both reason is dynamic and attributed the ability or tendency to generalize. See A. N. Whitehead, *Process and Reality* (New York, 1941), pp. 22–23.

9. See N. Rotenstreich, *Al Techuma shel ha-Philosophia* (Jerusalem, 1969), pp. 80–81.

10. Ibid., Chapter 1.

11. See the classic works of Rudolph Otto, *Das Heilige*, and Max Weber, *Das Antike Judentum;* the former seeks to uncover the connection between rational and irrational elements of religion, and the latter, the rationalistic processes of the world's major religions. See also J. Ben Shelomo, "Ha-Ratzionali ve-ha-Iratzionali be-Philosophiyat ha-Dat shel Rudolph Otto" ("The Rational and the Irrational in the Philosophy of Rudolph Otto"), in *Ha-Ratzionali ve-ha-Iratzionali*, n. 2, p. 78. Also S. N. Eisenstadt, "Ha-Yahadut ha-Kedumah shel Weber ve-Defus ha-Historiya ha-Yehudit" (*"Weber's Ancient Judaism* and the Format of Jewish Civilization"), *Tarbiz* 49, nos. 3–4 (Sivan–Elul 1980): 386, 396.

12. R. Otto, *The Idea of the Holy*, trans. John W. Harvey (London, 1959), p. 15.

13. Ibid., p. 20.

14. Ibid., p. 15. See Ben Sehlomo, "Ha-Ratzionali," p. 79.

15. Ibid., pp. 80–81.

16. D. Luce and H. Raiffa, *Games and Decisions* (New York, 1957), Chapter 2.

17. S. I. Benn and G. W. Mortimore, eds., *Rationality and the Social Sciences* (London 1976).

18. W. R. Inge, *Mysticism in Religion* (London, 1969), p. 32.

19. See R. Otto, *Mysticism East and West (London 1932); W. T. Stace, Mysticism and Philosophy* (London, 1960); S. T. Katz, ed., *Mysticism and Philosophical Analysis* (London, 1978); B. A. Sharfstein, *Ha-Havayah ha-Mystit* (Tel-Aviv, 1972); J. Sermoneta, "Yehuda ve-Emanuel ha-Romi—Ratzionalizm she-Sofo Emunah Mysitit" ("Yehuda and Immanuel Haromi—Rationalism Culminating in Mystic Faith"), *Hitgalut, Emunah, Tevunah.*

20. For an example of an extreme mystical approach, see Z. Werblowski, "'Al he-Dehiya ha-Mystit shel Hearot ve-Giluyei-Razim, le-Birur Torato shel Yokhanan min ha-Tzlav" ("On the Mystical Rejection of Mystical Illuminations"), *Iyyun* 14, nos. 2–4 (1964). W. Stace, in his opposition of mysticism and reason, considered reason to be the three famous rules of logic (*Mysticism and Philosophy*, p. 252).

21. Compare J. Ben Shelomo, *Torat ha-Elokhut shel Rav Moshe Cordovero,* p. 32.

22. Gershom Scholem described mystical experience thus in the name of a great poet of his youth. See his book, *Ha-Kabbalah be-Gerona* (Jerusalem, 1978), p. 1. Consider Al Gazali's contention that "He who has not tasted this through inner experience cannot attain true prophecy; he knows it by name only," in *Ha-Podeh min ha-T'iyah ve-ha-Ta'ut ve-ha-Movil el Ba'al ha-'Oz ve-ha-Malkhut* (Tel-Aviv, 1965), p. 59, see also p. 64. The English scholar of religion W. R. Inge claimed that in German the distinction can be made between mysticism and what he considers unauthentic mysticism, which we term *mystical philosophy;* the terms are *Mystik* versus *Mysticismus* (*Mysticism in Religion*), p. 31.

23. See W. R. Inge, *Christian Mysticism,* first published in 1899, and his proposal of twenty-six definitions of mysticism, thus demonstrating the difficulty in describing the subject.

24. See G. Scholem, *Pirkey Yesod,* p. 9. Mysticism is usually perceived as a discipline of intent, that is, a conscious appeal to the absolute, the objective of which is complete merging with that higher power. See E. Underhill, *Mysticism* (New York, 1957), pp. 81, 170.

25. Otto, *The Idea of the Holy,* chapters 4, 5. A brief analysis of the differences between the religious experience of "the sensation [or terror] in the presence of the holy" and mystical illumination by means of spiritual disciples can be found in F. J. Streng, *Understanding Religious Life* (Encino, Calif., 1976), Chapters 5, 8.

26. *The Varieties of the Religious Experience,* p. 379.

27. Ibid., p. 513.

28. E. Neumann, "Der mystische Mensch," *Kulturentwicklung und Religion* (Zurich, 1953).

29. G. Scholem, *Ha-Kabbalah be-Gerona; Reshitha-Kabbalah,* p. 115. Scholem claimed that all of Jewish thought, both philosophical and kabbalistic,

avoids neo-Platonic formulations of the absolute union of the soul with the One. In his view, even in the most intimate cojoining of the soul and the divine essence, something remains of the mutual relationship between two separate agents. Scholem saw this as a typically Jewish tendency to avoid breaching boundaries even at that supreme level, in contrast to mystics of other religions. The same approach is also expressed in "Mistika ve-Chevra," published in a new collection of his essays, *Od Davar*, ed. A. Shapira. Yet there are exceptions to this rule as well; Y. Tishby has challenged this un-equivocal characterization in *Mishnat ha-Zohar*, vol. 2, pp. 252 ff., 292–293. A. Gottlieb also indicated a text unavailable to Scholem and Tishby, which shows us there were individuals who penetrated beyond the boundaries most kabbalists drew for themselves. The source is by R. Itzhak of Acre, presented by Gottlieb in *Mehkarim be-Sifrut ha-Kabbalah* (*Studies in the Literature of the Kabbalah*), p. 41. On this issue in Hassidism, see R. Schatz-Uffenheimer, *He-Hassidut ke-Mystika*, Chapter 9. A. Altmann supports Scholem's opinion on the subject; see his *Panim shel Yahadut* (Tel-Aviv, 1983), pp. 87, 89. In contrast, M. Pachter introduces another example demonstrating the phenomenon evaluated by Tishby and Gottlieb. See "Tefisat ha-Devekut ve-Tiura be-Sifrut ha-Drush ve-ha-Musar shel Hakhmei Zefat be-Mea ha-17" ("The Theory of *Devekut* in the Writings of the Sages of Safed in the Sixteenth Century"), *Mehkarei Yerushalayim be-Mahshevet Yisrael* (*Jerusalem Studies in Jewish Thought*) 3 (1982): 114–115.

30. R. C. Zaehner, *Concordant Discord* (London, 1970), p. 194.

31. See S. T. Katz, *Mysticism and Philosophical Analysis*, p. 36. For more on *devekut* in Kabbalah, see G. Scholem's essay, "Devekut o Hitkashrut Intimit 'im Elokhim be-Reshit ha-Hassidut," *Devarim be-Go*, p. 325.

32. Schwarcz, "Polmus ha-Pantheism."

33. G. Scholem, *Pirkey Yesod*, p. 86.

34. Ibid., p. 87.

35. Ibid., p. 88.

36. Ibid., p. 94. Also I. Tishby, "Le-Birur Netivei ha-Hagshamah ve-ha-Hafshata be-Kabbalah," *Netivei Emunah ve-Minut* (*Paths of Faith and Heresy*) (Tel-Aviv, 1964).

37. My thanks to Prof. R. Schatz-Uffenheimer for bringing this general characterization to my attention. See for example I. Ben Shelomo, *Torat ha-Elokhut*, pp. 32–34. Also Maharal, *Tiferet Israel* (Jerusalem, 1970), Chapter 10.

38. *Ne'edar ba-Kodesh*, p. 5, see also p. 25.

39. *OH"K*, vol. 1, p. 102.

40. *A"T*, pp. 6–7; *OH"K*, vol. 1, p. 64. Compare Maimonides, *Guide for the Perplexed*, vol. 1, Chapters 2, 5, 32–34, and the introduction to his commentary on tractate Avot, Chapter 7.

41. *OH"K*, p. 33. Rav Kook claimed that sometimes even overtly intellectual thought may be mystical; though it seems to originate in the human, its source is divine.

42. *OH"K*, vol. 1, p. 128, see also p. 219.

43. Although Rav Kook did not hesitate to criticize philosophy on many issues, his criticism is not a rejection of philosophy per se. See, for example, his comments on the concept of divine providence in philosophical terms, *OH"K*, vol. 2, p. 549, and his condemnation of German philosophy as "anarchic and worthless ideas" (perhaps in reference to Nietzsche and Schopenhauer) in *Eder*, p. 58. In a few instances, Rav Kook contends with Maimonides or Spinoza, Nietzsche, Schopenhauer, and Bergson; and in every case his criticism is specific. See *'Ikve ha-Zon*, in *Eder*, p. 135, and p. 42; also *OH"K*, vol. 2, pp. 532–533, and pp. 330, 464–465, 472, 474. See also his defense of Maimonides in "Ma'amar Miyuhad" in Z. Yavetz, *Toldot Israel* (Tel Aviv, 1935), vol. 2, pp. 211–219; reprinted in *Ma'amarei ha-Rayah* (Jerusalem, 1980), p. 105. Compare also "Le-Demut Diyukono shel ha-Rambam," *Ha'aretz* (1935) (reprinted in *Ma'amerei ha-Rayah*, p. 113).

44. *Ne'edar ba-Kodesh*, p. 5; and in *OH"K*, vol. 1, p. 9: "Philosophy extends only to a certain part of the spiritual world." Also in *A"T*, p. 45: "It is impossible to live without the influence of faith in holiness. Human thought is too narrow to plumb the depths of being on its own . . . it needs assistance from higher powers."

45. *Ne'edar ba-Kodesh*, ibid. See also *OH"K*, vol. 1, p. 11, and compare the use of the term *shadows* for the object of perception in Plato's cave parable, *The Republic*, Book 7, pp. 514a–518b.

46. *Ne'edar ba-Kodesh*, p. 12.

47. Ibid. pp. 16–17. His view of equalization and the disappearance of value differences will be discussed further in Chapter 10.

48. *OH"K*, vol. 1, p. 25.

49. Ibid., p. 9.

50. Ibid., also p. 41. See *Ne'edar ba-Kodesh*, pp. 2–3.

51. We have no explicit record of the books Rav Kook read. In certain places in his writings, he did mention the names of philosophers to whom he referred, such as Spinoza, Kant, Schopenhauer, and Bergson. Hegel's hermeneutical thought exerted a clear influence on his conception of history (see p. 418 note 137), and the influence of Moshe Hess is recognizable as well (as R. Schatz-Uffenheimer has pointed out in "Utopya") although neither name appears in his writings. Rav Kook may have read their works himself, but his knowledge may also be second- or thirdhand; in any case, philosophical motifs popular in his day are found throughout his writings, as we have

pointed out in a number of contexts. On Rav Kook's public image as an alert individual interested in general culture, see R. Neriah's description in his biography, *Harav* (Jerusalem, 1938), p. 23. See also Chapter 1, notes 4 and 17.

52. *OH"K*, vol. 1, p. 105.

53. *Ne'edar ba-Kodesh*, p. 2: "In the normal world of thought, principles must contradict each other."

54. *OH"K*, vol. 1, p. 105.

55. Ibid., pp. 105–106.

56. Ibid., p. 16. I am doubtful whether this distinction and claim of the clear superiority of mysticism is immune to criticism. I am unable to understand the difference between mysticism and any monistic, pantheistic, or panatheistic philosophy on this subject.

57. Ibid., p. 105; compare pp. 44, 126.

58. Ibid., p. 25.

59. *Ne'edar ba-Kodesh*, p. 25.

60. Ibid., p. 4. Also *OH"K*, vol. 1, p. 263.

61. *OH"K*, vol. 1, pp. 9–10.

62. Ibid., pp. 1 and 260. Also *Ne'edar ba-Kodesh*, p. 6. Compare Loewe, *Tiferet Israel*, Introduction, p. 4: "Through the Torah man can cleave to God . . . and that *devekut* is total rather than partial; . . . through the Torah one can cleave to Him completely, in all aspects." And in Loewe, Judah (Maharal), *Netivot 'Olam*, "Netiv ha-Torah," Chapter 9, p. 40: "The Torah is intellectual; through it, one can free oneself of corporeality and cleave to God, blessed be He." See also Chapter 4, p. 17.

63. *OH"K*, vol. 1, p. 1. See also p. 272 on the difference between knowledge and prophecy.

64. Ibid.

65. See Luzzato, Moses Ḥayyim *Kelah Pithei Ḥokhma* (Jerusalem, 1961), Introduction p. 2: "Thus we know that the Torah is truly one single light, given to Israel for their enlightenment, unlike alien wisdom and secular knowledge, which is no more than what the intellect can grasp. The Torah, though, is holy, for it partakes of the highest reality; when a person occupies himself with Torah in the lower worlds, its light shines in his soul, leading him to the hidden and sublime secrets of the Creator, may His Name be blessed; the Torah is a powerful force upon him. The wise man said, 'For the commandment is a lamp, and the Torah light' (Proverbs 6:23)—light itself, not knowledge alone; rather than the appearance or image of light, he perceives light itself in its higher state, and it enters his soul as a flash of sunlight

comes into a house. This has been compared, with great precision, to fire: you see an ember, and although it does not blaze, the flame is hidden within it; when it is fanned, it expands and bursts into flame, growing and spreading, and within the flame many colors can be seen—although they were invisible in the ember, all of them emerge from it. The same is true of the Torah . . . this is no analogy, but must be understood literally, for all the letters of the Torah that we see, all of them teach us of the twenty-four sublime lights."

66. See *OH"K*, vol. 3, pp. 108–110: "The source of rationality is in the revelation of the creature as divine wisdom, and the source of mystery is in its revelation as His will."

67. Compare R. Moshe Cordovero's view of the relationship between philosophy and mysticism: J. Ben Shelomo, *Torat ha-Elohut*, pp. 31–36.

68. Italics mine (author).

69. Double in the manuscript.

70. *Manuscripts*, column 4, p. 12.

71. *OH"K*, vol. 1, p. 10.

72. Compare ibid., p. 135. We will return to this question later.

73. *Meorot ha-Emunah*, p. 10, see Chapter 5 as well.

74. Ibid., p. 11. See also *OH"K*, vol. 3, pp. 108–110.

75. The matter has been discussed in detail in many chapters of this book.

76. Rav Kook clearly invested the term *faith* with kabbalistic connotations, yet he did not identify it with a particular *sefira*; this, as we shall see later, is characteristic of his thought. Compare R. Moshe Cordovero's view of faith on the esoteric level as the attribute of *Malkhut* "the Divine Presence [*Shekhina*] in the lower worlds, and from the *Schekhina* man believes in *malkhut* [divinity]." Faith is *malkhut* in its unity with *En-sof*, and "all faith is in this secret." See J. Ben Shelomo, *Torat ha-Elohut*, p. 25. Compare R. Elior, *Torat ha-Elokhut be-Dor ha-Sheni shel Hassidut Habad*, pp. 225–243.

77. *OH"K*, vol. 1, pp. 66–67.

78. Ibid., p. 260.

79. Ibid., pp. 66–67.

80. See note 46.

81. Compare the view of R. Naḥman of Breslav: A. Green, *Tormented Master*, pp. 285–336.

82. See our discussion in Chapter 2, p. 116 and p. 120.

83. See note 70. See *OH"K*, vol. 2, pp. 283–284; *OH"K*, vol. 1, pp. 178, 17, 144, 179.

84. An extensive examination of the relation between will and *hokhma* is found in Chapters 2 and 3.

85. *Arpalei Tohar*, p. 49. See *OH"K*, vol. 1, p. 268.

86. *OH"K*, p. 247.

87. Ibid., p. 249. For more details see Chapter 7.

88. Ibid., pp. 68–69.

89. *Manuscripts*, Collection B, p. 53.

90. *A"T*, p. 60.

91. Ibid., p. 74. In the text found in *Manuscripts*, Collection D, p. 18b, Rav Kook expressed vehement criticism of the ultraorthodox tendency to repress the intellect on religious grounds. See Chapter 1, p. 21.

92. *Manuscripts*, Collection B, p. 23.

93. *IG"R*, vol. 1, p. 48. Compare Spinoza, *Ethics* I, Prop. XI, Another Proof, trans. A. Boyle (London, 1910, and New York, 1967): "From which it follows that that must of necessity exist concerning which no reason or cause is granted which could prevent its existence. If thus no reason or cause can be granted which could prevent the existence of God or take his existence from him, it must certainly be concluded that he does exist of necessity."

94. See "Kirvat Elokhim," *Taḵemoni* 2 (1911): 4: "Absolute reality . . . should exist, for it is the supreme cause and needs no other cause for its existence. If it were not for our habit to see things that cannot exist without a cause, the idea would never occur to us that things need a cause in order to exist."

95. *Critique of Pure Reason*, Chapter 3, "The Ideal of Pure Reason," Section 4, "The Impossibility of an Ontological Proof of the Existence of God."

96. See Z. A. Bar-On, "Ha-Reiya ha-Ontologit: Girsato shel Spinoza be-Hashva'a le-Girsotehem shel Anselm ve-Descartes" ("The Ontological Proof: Spinoza's Version Compared with Anselm's and Descartes's Versions"), in *Baruch Spinoza*.

97. *'Eder*, p. 134. The influence of Kantian philosophy is clear and conscious; reference is neither to Maimonides's theory of negative attributes nor to kabbalistic teachings. In another context, Rav Kook mentioned Kant by name, but there his claim was that nothing is new about Kant's innovation;

see Chapter 2, note 2. In any case, the very statement shows Rav Kook himself was aware of the Kantian influence in his thought.

98. *Orot*, p. 154, also p. 119: "Is God not beyond all reality; how could any sense or idea of Him enter us?"

99. There are three aspects of Rav Kook's criticism of Spinoza on this issue: theoretical, moral, and metaphysical. From a theological point of view, Rav Kook saw philosophy that deals with "essence" as "pagan confusion" (*Ikve ha-Zon*, in *Eder*, p. 133), because the very claim that the human mind can grasp the essence of God is idolatrous. (Z. Yaron, in *Mishnato shel ha-Rav Kook*, p. 59, referred in a footnote to Y. Kaufman: "In Spinoza's system, an outstanding crystallization of pagan thought, the Godhead is bound with the iron chains of geometric criteria and its eternal reign".) In moral terms, Rav Kook saw the Spinozian rejection of the principle of freedom as a destruction of the values on which religious and moral behavior are founded and as the forebearer of materialism (*Ikve ha-Zon*, in *Eder*, p. 135). As for epistemology and metaphysical contemplation, Rav Kook discounted the possibility of perception of the thing-in-itself (ibid., pp. 42, 134).

100. *OH"K*, vol. 2, p. 283.

101. Ibid., p. 391. Compare J. Gikitilia, *Sha'arei Ora*, vol. 2, pp. 92–93 and no. 53.

102. See N. Rotenstreich, *Iyunim be-Machshava ha-Yehudit be-Zeman ha-Zeh*, pp. 41–42.

103. *OH"K*, vol. 2, pp. 537–538. See also *A"T*, p. 45: "Common sense [*ha-sekhel ha-yashar*] is the basis of everything. The impression of good and of truth in inward understanding, which no force in the world leads astray, is the *path* of light which leads the collective and the individual to everlasting happiness, and to temporal happiness corresponding to that eternal state." Compare Maimonides, *Guide for the Perplexed*, vol. 1, Chapter 54. There Maimonides spoke of מקום עיון from which Moses attained "the aim which man can attain." In his Hebrew translation, R. Kapah renders the Arabic term "נט'ר" as מבט; that is, that a "subject of speculation" was revealed to Moses, rather than the "מקום עיון" as ibn Tibon translated. According to this translation, and on the basis of Maimonides's interpretation of the verb "הביט" in Chapter 4 of the *Guide*, we may understand that the only goal one may hope to attain is the very process of perception and thought itself, rather than any particular static level of perception. See E. Schweid, *Ta'am ve-Hakasha* (Ramat Gan, 1970), p. 119. According to Schweid, Maimonides "considers the aspiration to perceive God as man's supreme aim, and as a religious obligation of the first degree."

104. See A. Altmann, *Panim shel Yahadut*, p. 87: "Divine unity is not conjecture but rather something to be realized." And "unification is forever but a *task* and never actual merging" (ibid., p. 89).

105. Compare Maimonides's view in note 103.

106. The state in which this aspiration is most fully expressed, when all oppositions, contradictions, and shadows fade away, is the state of adhesion with the source of wisdom, with what cannot be grasped: "The only complete correspondence of all perception is in the source of wisdom, He alone 'who is perfect in knowledge' (Job 37:16). The source of wisdom, also termed in this passage as 'the treasure of the supreme intellect' or 'the soul's brillance,' is the site of 'inward divine *devekut*, the foundation of all knowledge; this cleaving heals all wounds and blows . . . and there, it is called peace." See *OH"K*, vol. 1, pp. 11–12. A discussion of *devekut* in Rav Kook's system is found in Chapter 5. Another aspect of his definition of Jewish mysticism is discussed in Chapter 2.

107. See Stace, *Mysticism and Philosophy,* pp. 37–39. Compare W. James, *The Varieties of Religious Experience,* p. 389 and n. 1. I prefer the term *philosophical mysticism* to *mystical interpretation* for two main reasons. First is to distinguish clearly between mythical or symbolic interpretation and mystical interpretation, which develops explicit and comprehensive theories formulated in conceptual terms and which, in contrast to the two former types is, in my opinion, the only type of interpretation that can be considered "philosophy." This distinction is mandatory, for as we have seen, the history of Kabbalah contains two parallel trends, mythic and abstract; we associate Rav Kook's thought with the speculative trend of Jewish mysticism. (For discussion of the various trends in the Kabbalah, see Y. tishby, "Le-birur Netivei." in *Nitivei Emunot u-Minut,* p. 23 ff. See also R. Schatz-Uffenheimer ("Ramak ve ha-Ari," pp. 122–136), who claimed that the Lurianic Kabbalah as well, commonly considered "mythic," has a philosophical thesis expressed in the system of rationalization and abstration.

The second reason for our preference of the term *philosophical mysticism* is our assumption, contrary to Stace's view, that philosophical mysticism is much more than mere interpretation of mystical experience. Rather, it is the product of the mutual relationship between the entire content of Jewish cultural-religious tradition, including the general cultural and intellectual climate in which the mystic lives and works, and his own emotional and intellectual reaction to what his culture holds as the object of perception and of religious experience. The term *mystical interpretation* implies a one-way connection between experience and interpretation, ignoring the dialectical relationship just described. The majority of G. Scholem's writings demonstrate the marked influence of Jewish tradition on kabbalistic thought, which explains, as well, the fundamental differences between the Kabbalah and other mystical traditions. See Scholem, *Major Trends in Jewish Mysticism* (New York, 1954); *the Messianic Idea in Judaism; Kabbalah* (New York, 1974); and, in Hebrew, *Pirkey Yesod,* p. 86; *Devarim be-Go,* vol. 1, "Morasha ve-Tehiya" (Tel-Aviv, 1977); *Reshit ha-Kabbalah* (Jerusalem and Tel-Aviv, 1948). See also S. T. Katz, "Language, Epistemology and Mysticism," in *Mysticism and Philosophical Analysis.*

108. For examples of the first trend, see Stace, *Mysticism and Philosophy*, pp. 37–39; and B. Sharfstein, *He-Havayah ha-Mystit*, pp. 53–73. For an example of the second trend, see J. Sermoneta, "Yehuda ve-Emanuel ha-Romi."

109. *OH"K*, vol. 1, p. 71. As R. Schatz-Uffenheimer pointed out to me, these two concepts are fundamental in Lurianic dialectics.

110. Compare J. Ben Shelomo, *Torat ha-Elokhut shel Ramak*, pp. 268–274. For R. Moshe Cordovero, the "*or hozer*" is related to divine knowledge of the created world, which for R. Shelomo Alkabez, "*or hozer*" represents the attribute of judgement (*din*) in the world of *atzilut*. For R. Moshe Hayyim Luzzatto, these symbols designate the emanation of the sefirot. See *Kelah Pithei Hokhma*, p. 14: "The *sefirot* have two kinds of light: *or yashar* and *or hozer*; in the first, [*or yashar*], after the descent through all the stages from *keter* to *malkhut*, *malkhut* returns and becomes *keter*, and then once again *keter* becomes *malkhut*—this evinces the perfection of *En-sof*, blessed be He, from whom all emanates and to whom all returns. Thus 'I am the first and the last'; He is revealed at the beginning as at the end, and the closer each stage comes to him, the greater it grows; what was *malkhut* becomes *keter*." The second kind of light (*or hozer*) does not raise all the *sefirot* to the level of *keter*; rather, it rises alone, leaving the *sefirot* behind at their various levels. Compare the conception in Hassidism: R. Schatz-Uffenheimer, *Ha-Hassidut ke-Mistika*, p. 25; R. Elior, *Torat ha-Elokhut*, p. 340.

111. *OH"K*, vol. 1, pp. 68–69: "Intellectual activity can be divided into two basic approaches. The first wishes to clothe the effulgence of divine inspiration in the garb of human logic and reason . . . and the second wishes to bring the rational strivings of the heart, loyal to their own nature and order, to the supreme *atzilut* of divine inspiration."

112. *A"T*, p. 34.

113. *OH"K*, vol. 1, pp. 68–69. In contrast to this view, Rav Kook said elsewhere that the crude intellect impedes "the emanated constructs that appear from the higher source of holiness." See *OH"K*, vol. 3, p. 133.

114. *A"T*, p. 34.

115. *OH"K*, vol. 1, p. 75.

116. Compare Maimonides, *Guide for the Perplexed*, vol. 2, Chapter 33. He wrote that when the Torah was given at Sinai, the Israelites heard only a voice without articulated words, and Moses explained the contents of the voice to them.

117. *OH"K*, vol. 2, p. 334.

118. *OH"K*, vol. 1, p. 177.

119. Ibid., p. 137. All these expressions allude to the metaphysical dimension according to kabbalistic symbolism.

120. In *OH"K*, vol. 1, p. 101, Rav Kook mentioned another path to reach truth: "Reception from superior individuals, whose souls are penetrated by divine light," followed by "internal conjecture" that "arranges the matters upon the heart, until they become as concepts in the simple and natural intellect."

121. Ibid., p. 177. See *Meorot ha-Emunah*, p. 11: "Faith grants the final stage of being, and science the means by which it can be perceived."

122. *OH"K*, vol. 1, pp. 6–7; see also p. 219.

123. Messianism may be generated by longing for an ideal past and desire for its renewal within a concrete period, whereas utopia is founded on a vision of the future. For more on the distinction between the two concepts, see G. Scholem, "Le-Havanat ha-Ra'ayon ha-Meshihi be-Israel," *Devarim be-Go*, pp. 115–190; "Ra'ayon ha-Geulah be-Kabbalah," in ibid., pp. 191–216. See also E. Bloch, *Geist der Utopie* (Munich, 1918); Bloch, *Das Prinzip Offnung* (Berlin, 1954–1959); H. Cohen, *Religion of Reason out of the Sources of Judaism*, trans. S. Kaplan and F. Ungar (New York, 1972), p. 311. The similarity between Rav Kook's view and that of Hermann Cohen on matters of utopia, morality, and epistemology is striking, despite the disparity between their basic metaphysical assumptions. On the question of the Messiah and messianism, see also *Ha-ra'ayon ha-Meshihi be-Israel* (Jerusalem, 1982); A. Ravitzki, "Ha-tzapui ve-ha-Reshut Netuna," *Israel Likrat ha-Mea ha-21*, ed. A. Hareven (Jerusalem, 1984), p. 135.

124. *OH"K*, vol. 1, p. 368.

125. *OH"K*, vol. 2, p. 348. See *OH"K*, vol. 1, p. 7.

126. Compare Plato's cave parable in *The Republic*.

127. *A"T*, p. 45.

128. *OH"K*, vol. 1, p. 75.

129. *O"T*, p. 10. *OH"K*, vol. 1, p. 209. See also *Meorot ha-Emunah*.

130. *A"T*, p. 35.

131. *OH"K*, p. 75.

132. In an essay about Maimonides published in the newspaper *Ha'aretz* ("Le-Demut Diyokono shel ha-Rambam") Rav Kook contended that the mystical element of religion, in and of itself, leads to deterioration, whereas the rational element leads to doubt and uneasiness; a balance must be struck between the two. It is interesting to compare Rav Kook's view of the relationship between mysticism and reason, and Rav Nahman of Breslav's adamant opposition to philosophy and to any form of rational thought (in A. Green, *Tormented Master*).

9. *Mystical Language, Myth, and Symbol*

1. G. Scholem, "Kabbalah," *Ha-Encyclopedia ha-'Ivrit*, p. 72.

2. See W. R. Inge, *Mysticism East and West*, p. 32 and his extensive discussion "Symbolism and Myth," on pp. 73 ff. On the distinction between symbol and sign, see p. 96.

3. Chapter 1, p. 4 and note 3.

4. A. Steinsaltz, "Ha-Ba'ayatiut be-Orot ha-Kodesh" ("Problematics of Orot ha-Kodesh"), *ha-Re'ayah*, ed. I. Raphael (Jerusalem, 1966), p. 103. E. Schweid's position is similar to Steinsaltz's on this question. See his *Ha-Yehudi ha-Boded ve-ha-Yahadut (The Lonely Jew and Judaism)* (Tel-Aviv, 1974), p. 179.

5. *OH"K*, vol. 1, p. 86. Although Rav Kook wrote in *Ikve ha-Zon*, in *Eder*, p. 54, of the need "to express more profound matters in simple, popular style in order to quench thirsting souls," that statement cannot be applied to all his writings. Rav Kook did indeed write a great many essays in popular, publicist style, which were published in newspapers, and even the style of his letters is clear and simple. Yet *Orot ha-Teshuvah*, oriented to a general audience, does not reflect his desire to present esoteric matters in popular language. There, he in fact deliberated "just how much to explain cosmic secrets and where the boundary should be drawn before esoteric matters" (*IG"R*, vol. 2, pp. 36 and 11). We must remember, though, that only the first three chapters of the book were published in the order they were written. The vast majority of Rav Kook's writings, published for the most part in the three volumes of *Orot ha-Kodesh*, in *Arpalei Tohar*, and in many as yet unpublished manuscripts make no claim to "simple, popular style." We can thus conclude that in them Rav Kook did not deliberate the question of how overtly he should treat profound and esoteric matters. Most of his writings are not in modern style, which in his opinion contradicts the depth of his ideas. See *IG"R*, vol. 2, p. 7, and vol. 1, p. 151. Yet nonetheless, he did not use classical kabbalistic formulations.

6. *OH"K*, vol. 1, p. 108. See *Rosh Milin*, p. 140; there Rav Kook stated that the *gematria* [numerical value] of "translation" [תרגום] is "slumber" [תרדמה]; that is, the original idea is not revealed in translation.

7. *OH"K*, vol. 1, p. 111. On the interesting question of the ontology of language, see P. Ricoeur, *Hermeneutics and the Human Sciences* (Cambridge, 1983). My gratitude to Schatz-Uffenheimer for calling my attention to that book. See also Z. Levi, *Hermeneutica*, pp. 155–173, 106–134; Z. Levi, "Al ha-Hermeneutica shel Paul Ricoeur," *Iyyun* 33, nos. a–b (1984): 156–171; J. Golomb, "Me-Phenomenologiya le-Hermeneutica 'al Shitato ha-Parshani shel P. Ricoeur" ("From Phenomonology to Hermeneutics—On the Parshanut of Paul Ricoeur"), *Iyyun* 29 (1980): 22–36.

8. *OH"K*, pp. 6–7, and see p. 219.

9. "Utopiya," p. 19.

10. See Chapter 2, p. 66 and Chapter 3, p. 140 ff.

11. *IG"R*, vol. 1, p. 154.

12. *OH"K*, vol. 1, p. 84: "Gaze upon the lights in their inwardness. The names, phrases and letters will not swallow up your soul. They are delivered into your hand, and not you into theirs." See also ibid., pp. 168, 173, 191.

13. See *Perakim be-Mishnato ha-Iyunit shel ha-Rav Kook*, ed. I. Hadari and Z. Singer (Jerusalem, 1961), vol. 2, pp. 55–56.

14. *A"T*, p. 59, and *OH"K*, vol. 1, p. 99. In this context it is interesting to compare Rav Kook's comments in manuscripts not yet published: Manuscripts, Collection B, p. 55): "A person can know nothing at all about the life of another superior to him, because the only way he can imagine the essential and delicate nobility of the latter's spiritual world-view is by using the tools he himself has acquired; what is beyond him, even by a hairsbreadth, he cannot conceive."

15. *A"T*, p. 40. See also *OH"K*, vol. 1, p. 6, 192. *Ne'edar be-Kodesh*, p. 2.

16. *IG"R*, vol. 1, p. 131, see also p. 127. In a letter to Dr. Benjamin Menashe Levin, 1919, Rav Kook attributed his difficulties in expressing himself to the subjects he treats and said he does not envy those who speak eloquently and overtly, for "if someone is willing to reveal everything, it is a sure sign of the poverty of his innermost spirit."

17. On his need to express himself Rav Kook wrote: "I am impelled to speak of everything, of sublime things high above my own senses and apprehension, for I am called to that inward spiritual level, 'I will create a new expression of the lips: Peace, peace, both for far and near, says the Lord. And I will heal him' (Isaiah 57:19). Manuscripts, Collection B, p. 22.

18. *Ne'edar ba-Kodesh*, p. 2. For a detailed discussion of Rav Kook's conception of revelation, see Chapter 3, and on his view of the prophetic nature of his thought, see Chapter 10.

19. Ibid., p. 9. See also Ibid., pp. 1, 2, 14, 16, 17–18.

20. *A"T*, p. 29.

21. Ibid., p. 12. Printed, with changes in *OH"K*, vol. 2, p. 298. In the kabbalistic works *Ra'aya Mhemana* and *Tikkunei Zohar*, the Tree of Knowledge and the Tree of Life symbolize constriction or *tsimtsum*, prohibitions and restrictions, on the one hand, and freedom and lack of distinction between good and evil, on the other. The Tree of Life is the Tree of freedom, and symbolizes the utopian aspect of the Torah. See G. Scholem, *Pirkey Yesod*, p. 69.

22. *Ne'edar ba-Kodesh*, p. 2. Also *OH"K*, vol. 1, p. 143. See Chapter 2, notes 112 and 113.

23. Ibid.

24. See *Zohar*, vol. 3, 239a–b, and vol. 1, 35a. See also Y. Tishby, *Mishnat ha-Zohar* vol. 1, pp. 204–205.

25. See G. Scholem, *Pirkey Yesod*, p. 69.

26. Ibid., p. 77.

27. On the distinction between esoterics and mysticism, see G. Scholem, *Reshit ha-Kabbalah ve-Sefer ha-Bahir*, ed. R. Schatz-Uffenheimer (Jerusalem, 1979), p. 1. In *OH"K*, vol. 1, p. 127, Rav Kook spoke of two sorts of mystical perceptions: "essential secrets and accidental secrets." "Essential" concealed things cannot be revealed in common language, because they are not part of discursive thought. "Accidental" hidden matters, although perceivable, cannot be revealed either, due to the "spiritual atrophy of language, which cannot muster the strength to pronounce thoughts with expressive content." In any case, Rav Kook's writings are clearly not *intentionally* esoteric. See also *IG"R*, vol. 1, p. 267. Compare J. Weiss, *Mehkarim be-Hasidut breslav* (*Studies in the Hassidut of Breslov*) (Jerusalem, 1975), in the chapter on "Gilui ve-Kisui be-Torat Breslav uv-Sifruta."

28. See S. H. Bergmann, "Torah ha-Hitpatchut be-Mishnato shel ha-Rav Kook," in *Shitato shel ha-Rav Kook* (Jerusalem 1963), p. 69.

29. See T. Ross, "Musag ha-Elohut shel ha-Rav Kook" ("Rav Kook's Concept of God") Parts 1–2, *Da'at* (Winter 1982; Summer 1982).

30. *OH"K*, vol. 2, p. 348.

31. *OH"K*, vol. 1, pp. 83–84.

32. *OH"K*, vol. 2, p. 402, and *OH"K*, vol. 1, pp. 110–111; *A"T*, p. 50.

33. *OH"K*, vol. 2, pp. 403–404. On Gikitilia's and Cordovero's attempts to divorce their thought from all mythical understanding of sefirotic symbolism, see Y. Tishby, *Mishnat ha-Zohar*, vol. 1, p. 147. See also G. Scholem, *Pirkey Yesod*, pp. 86–112.

34. *OH"K*, vol. 2, pp. 403–404.

35. Rav Kook took the same stance on other questions as well; see, for example, *A"T*, p. 32: "Compared to supreme, divine truth, there is no difference between mythical faith and atheism, for neither offers the truth. . . . Relative to the light of *En-sof*, everything is equal." And in *OH"K*, vol. 3, p. 26: "And necessity is not necessity but rather something completely beyond will" (parallel source, *A"T*, p. 31). See p. 327 and note 54. The question is discussed further in Chapters 2 and 3.

36. Compare J. Ben Shelomo, *Torat ha-Elokhut*, pp. 174–178.

37. See *A"T*, p. 2 (parallel, *OH"K*, vol. 2, p. 289), p. 33 (parallel, *OH"K*, vol. 2, p. 393), and p. 61; "Kirvat Elokhim," p. 7; *OH"K*, vol. 1, p. 274; *OH"K*, vol. 2, p. 571, *A"T*, p. 336.

38. See Scholem, *Pirkey Yesod*, pp. 153 ff.

39. *OH"K*, vol. 2, p. 368.

40. On the role of the symbol in mysticism in general see Inge, *Mysticism in Religion*, pp. 93 ff.

41. *OH"K*, vol. 3, p. 10.

42. For more on his concept of the *mitzvot*, see *OH"K*, vol. 3, pp. 69, 96; *Ikvei ha-Zon, Eder*, p. 25; *IG"R*, vol. 2, p. 39; *Olat ha-Re'ayah*, vol. 2, p. 57; *Arpalei Tohar*, p. 60 (parallel, *OH"K*, vol. 1, pp. 133–134).

43. *OH"K*, vol. 2, p. 367. The term *Adam Kadmon* is prevalent in Lurianic teaching, in which it designates the path of light in its descent from *En-sof* after the *tsimtsum*, and takes the form of the human figure. See Y. Tishby, *Torat ha-Rah ve-Ha-Kelipa be-Kabbalat ha-Ari*, p. 145. Compare Y. Liebes, "Perakim be-Milon Sefer ha-Zohar," pp. 37–43. The expression "the soul of Adam ha-Rishon usually represents the *sefira* of *hokhma* (Liebes pp. 39–40) and thus Rav Kook's identification of it with will is puzzling. For further discussion of these symbols, see Chapter 2.

44. Examples may be found in *A"T*, p. 11; *OH"K*, vol. 2, pp. 283–286, 407 (parallel, *A"T*, p. 61); *OH"K*, vol. 3, p. 258; *OH"K*, vol. 1, p. 57.

45. *A"T*, p. 16.

46. See G. Scholem, *Pirkey Yesod*, p. 50.

47. *A"T*, p. 54.

48. G. Scholem, *Pirkey Yesod*, p. 52.

49. Midrash *Canticles Rabbah* (Warsaw, 1867), Chapter 1, p. 5b (trans. M. Simon [Soncino, N.Y., 1983], I.2, 2, p. 32): "The scholars said in the name of R. Johanan: The injunctions of the Scribes are more beloved than those of the [written] Torah, as it says, 'For thy love (*dodeka*) is better than wine' (Song of Songs 1:2). If a man says: 'There is no command to put on phylacteries,' thus transgressing a precept of the Torah, he is subject to no penalty. But if he says 'there are five compartments [in the phylacteries],]' thus transgressing the injunction of the Scribes, he is subject to a penalty." See also BT Eruvin, 21b; JT Berachot, 1:4.

50. *Eder*, pp. 38–39. Further discussion in Chapter 6.

51. *OH"K*, vol. 3, p. 117. *A"T*, pp. 2–3, 8, 10, 39, 40. Compare *OH"K*, vol. 3, p. 23: Rosh Davar, re God-fearingness, which is also related to *malkhut*.

Malkhut is perceived not only as a metaphysical entity but as a certain trait or characteristic. See Chapter 3, pp. 156–157.

52. See note 50.

53. *OH"K*, vol. 1, p. 135. See also Chapter 2, pp. 34–35

54. See, for example, *A"T*, pp. 5–6, 15.

55. *IG"R*, vol. 2, p. 39.

56. *Genesis Rabbah*, 8, p. 60 in Theodor-Albeck ed.

57. Another example of the abstraction of a mythic midrash is found in Chapter 4, note 102. On the abstraction of the messianic idea, see p. 184; on abstraction of the midrash recounting the sin of the moon, see *OH"K*, vol. 1, p. 253.

58. *OH"K*, vol. 2, p. 484. Chapter 2.

59. This symbol appears frequently in *Sefer ha-Kanah, Sefer ha-Peliya*, and the Zohar. The source is apparently in the work of R. Itzhak ben Ya'akov ha-Cohen, "Ma'amar 'al ha-Atzilut ha-Smalit" (Cambridge Ms. 505, Add., fol. 16b–23a. An Ashkenazic manuscript, dated 5289 [1529]. In the Jewish National- al and University Library of Jerusalem, Microfilmed Manuscript Collection, no. 16798. Published by G. Scholem in *Mad'ai ha-Yahadut II* [1937], pp. 244– 264). On the *tannin* in the Zohar, see Y. Tishby, *Mishnat ha-Zohar*, vol. 1, pp. 302–303. We must point out, though, that in the writings of the kabbalists, especially R. Itzhak ha-Cohen, the *tannin* does not represent will. On the contrary, in the future, the *tannin* will be nullified by will. Only one thinker, the Maharal of Prague, transformed the figure of the *tannin* into the *leviathan*, a symbol of divine will. See Ish Shalom, "Tannin, Leviathan, ve-Nahash—le-Perusho shel Motiv Aggadi" ("Tanin, Leviathan, and Nahash—On the Mean-ing of a Legendary Motif"), *Da'at* (Summer, 1987). On the *tannin* in Rav Kook's conception, see S. Rosenberg, "Ha-Rayah ve-ha-Tannin ha-Iver," in *Be-Oro*, ed. H. Hamiel (Jerusalem, 1976), pp. 317–352.

60. On "מיתת המלכים", the death of the Kings, see *Zohar* III, 135a–b, "Idra Rabba." Y. Tishby, *Mishnat ha-Zohar*, vol. 1, p. 183; *Torat ha-Rah*, pp. 21– 34; G. Scholem, *Devarim be-Go*, p. 215.

61. Manuscripts, Collection E, p. 54.

62. S. H. Bergman characterized A. D. Gordon's thought as "an ethic of self-realization" in an introductory essay to Gordon's *Ha-Adam ve-ha-Teva* (Tel-Aviv, 1951). In the wake of A. D. Gordon, N. Rotenstreich (*Iyyunim be-Machsheva ha-Yehudit be-Zeman ha-Zeh* [Tel-Aviv, 1978], pp. 190, 200) and E. Schweid ("Ahriut le-Klal Yisrael, Hagshama 'Atzmit ve-Mimush 'Atzmi," *Iyyun* 33, nos. a–b (Tevet–Nisan 1984), pp. 327 ff.) distinguished between *self-realization* (מימוש עצמי) and *self-actualization* (הגשמה עצמית). According to Ro-tenstreich, *self-realization* means the individual's definitive preference of one-

self, demanding that society recognize one's authority to express oneself as one wishes; *self-actualization* means that "if you act for the good of the collective, you actualize yourself." Clearly, in the context of Rav Kook's thought, the expression *self-actualization* is the more appropriate of the two. Yet I prefer to use the term *self-realization*, in the sense of realization of personal potential, and consciously ignore the preceding distinction; my objective is to preserve the dialectical tension, pervasive in Rav Kook's writings, between the two poles of individuum and collective, with no absolute preference of one over the other. As we have seen (Chapter 7), various formulations throughout emphasize either the demands of the individual or the value of the collection. Of course, in Rav Kook's view, the term *self-realization* is not to be understood as "satisfaction of needs" and "giving vent to one's drives and desires") (see Schweid, "Ahriut le-Klal Yisrael," p. 332), but rather as use of one's talents, freedom of thought, personal path in serving God, and so on.

63. See Chapter 1, note 19.

10. *Before the Secret of Existence*

1. L. S. Feuer, *Einstein and the Generations of Science,* p. 115.

2. B. A. Sharfstein, *He-Havaya ha-Mystit,* p. 155.

3. G. Scholem, *Pirkey Yesod,* p. 86.

4. See, for example, J. Ben-Shelomo, *Torat ha-Elokhut shel Rav Moshe Cordovero;* G. Scholem, *Avraham Cohen Herera Ba'al "Sha'ar ha-Shamayim"* (Jerusalem, 1978); M. Halamish, "Mishnato ha-Iyunit shel Rav Shneur Zalman me-Liadi"; R. Elior, *Torat ha-Elokhut be-Dor ha-Sheni shel Hassidut Habad.*

5. *OH"K,* vol. 2, p. 391.

6. *OH"K,* vol. 3, p. 3. See later, p. 429 and note 70. There Rav Kook identified the *zaddik*'s pain at his lack of *devekut* with the anguish of the *Shekhinah,* a cosmic sorrow or yearning for completeness. The *zaddik*'s suffering is perceived as a manifestation of the anguish of the *Shekhinah.*

7. As Schatz-Uffenheimer pointed out, in kabbalistic thought the word *differentiated* (מופרד) is a technical term signifying the world differentiated from the divine; in antique philosophy, on the other hand, it implies what is differentiated from materiality.

8. *A"T,* p. 37. See Chapter 2, pp. 80 ff.

9. *A"T,* p. 39. See also pp. 56–57 (and parallel, *OH"K,* vol. 1, p. 16), 66, 69; *OH"K,* vol. 1, pp. 11–16; *OH"K,* vol. 2, p. 527; *Ne'edar ba-Kodesh,* par. 3, etc.

10. *OH"K,* vol. 3, p. 103. See Chapter 2, p. 61.

11. See Chapter 3.

12. See Chapter 2, pp. 66 ff., note 27.

13. Se Chapter 2, note 58, and Chapter 3.

14. See Chapter 4.

15. *OH"K*, vol. 2, p. 517, also pp. 484, 487, 537, 542–543, etc.

16. Ibid., p. 374.

17. Ibid., p. 416.

18. Compare Chapter 9, p. 150.

19. On silence and attentiveness, see Chapter 2, pp. 99–101. Compare W. James, *Varieties of the Religious Experience*, p. 250.

20. *OH"K*, vol. 1, pp. 60–79. In passages in which Rav Kook described the internal battles and contradictions of his world, the dynamism of his inner world also comes to the fore. See Preface, p. viii.

21. See Chapter 2, note 33.

22. See Chapter 2, note 35. See the discussion there pp. 69–70 and note 38. See also Chapter 6.

23. *OH"K*, vol. 3, p. 214.

24. Ibid., p. 122.

25. *OH"K*, vol. 1, p. 173.

26. *OH"K*, vol. 3, p. 214.

27. See note 24.

28. Compare Green, *Tormented Master*, p. 278.

29. *OH"K*, vol. 3, p. 172.

30. Perhaps the text should read תבש׳, "despair," rather than תבכי, "weep".

31. Unnumbered manuscript. This statement may echo Rav Kook's distress over the reactions of many of his contemporaries, from both the ultra-orthodox and secular communities: their lack of understanding, mocking, and attacks. See Preface, note 5.

32. Rav Kook said as much explicitly in *OH"K*, vol. 2, p. 339. On the perception of humankind and the *zaddik* in Hassidism, see G. Scholem, "Kabbalah," *Ha-Encyclopedia ha-'Ivrit*, vol. 29, pp. 119–122; *Pirkey Yesod*, Chapter 7; Y. Tishby and J. Dan, "Hassidut," *Ha-Encyclopedia ha-'Ivrit*, vol. 17, p. 774; Y. Tishby, *Mishnat ha-Zohar*, vol. 1, pp. 3 ff; A. Gottlieb, "Ha-Yeshod ha-Teologi ve-ha-Mysti shel Tefisat Ye'ud ha-Adam be-Kabbalah," *Mehkarim be-Sifrut ha-*

Kabbalah (*Studies in the Literature of the Kabbalah*), pp. 29 ff.; N. Leam, *Torah le-Shma* (Jerusalem, 1972), pp. 64–65; A. Altmann, "Tzelem Elokhim be-Theleologia ha-Yehudit ve-ha-Notzrit," *Panim shel Yahadut* (Tel-Aviv, 1983), pp. 11–30 and in the same collection "Elokhim ve-'Atzmuto shel Adam be-Mystica ha-Yehudit," pp. 76–81; R. Schatz-Uffenheimer, "Torat ha-Zaddik etzel Elimelech me-Lijansk," *Molad* (1960): 144–145, 379–390. A. Ravitsky demonstrated the development of the idea of humankind's wondrous abilities in medieval Jewish philosophy. See "Ha-Adam ha-Shalem ke-Po'el Nif-la'ot: Gilgula shel Theoria be-Philosophia ha-Yehudit be-Yemai ha-Benayim," (Jerusalem, 1982). Y. Liebes pointed out, following the previously mentioned lecture by Ravitsky, that such a theory is already found in some rabbinic statements as well as *Sefer ha-Yetzira* and presented some examples. See BT Sanhedrin 65b ("אי בעו צדיקיא ברו עלמא"). Consider the rabbinic remarks drawing an analogy between divine decisions and decisions pronounced by the *zaddik:* BT Ta'anit 23a; TY Ta'anit 3.12, 67a; BT Shabbat 63a; Shabbat 59a; BT Mo'ed Katan 17b; BT Baba Metziya 85a.

33. *OH"K*, vol. 2, p. 339. See *A"T*, p. 22: "The idea is not far-fetched that everything related to man in any way at all . . . everything is related to his very essence."

34. *OH"K*, vol. 2, p. 299.

35. Ibid., p. 434. See also pp. 560, 332; *OH"K*, vol. 1, p. 216; *OH"K*, vol. 3, pp. 31, 66, 153; *A"T*, pp. 19, 29, 65, and so on. A detailed discussion of the subject is found in Chapter 6.

36. *A"T*, p. 12.

37. On Rav Kook's view of his own prophetic abilities, see p. 347.

38. *OH"K*, vol. 3, p. 357.

39. See *OH"K*, vol. 2, pp. 434, 560.

40. Compare A. Ravitsky, "Ha-Adam ha-Shalem."

41. Manuscript D, p. 11b. On the connection between human meta-physical ability and degree of *devekut*, see Rav Kook's essay, "Kirvat Elokhim," pp. 3–4.

42. *OH"K*, vol. 3, p. 42.

43. See Chapter 2, p. 116 ff.

44. *A"T*, p. 43 (and *OH"K*, vol. 1, p. 95).

45. See chapter 2, p. 116.

46. Manuscripts, Small Collection, p. 60.

47. Manuscripts, Collection B, p. 35.

48. Manuscripts, Collection D, p. 11.

49. *A"T*, p. 50.

50. *OH"K*, vol. 3, p. 156.

51. See note 44.

52. See note 37.

53. Ibid.

54. Chapter 9, note 18.

55. *OH"K*, vol. 3, p. 355.

56. *Orot*, p. 95.

57. *OH"K*, vol. 1, p. 157.

58. See Katz, *Mysticism and Philosophical Analysis*.

59. Ibid., p. 26.

60. See Chapter 8, p. 309, where we remarked that Rav Kook considered the mystical phenomenon itself as *aspiration*.

61. Moshe Tzvi Neriya, ed., *Sichot ha-Re'ayah* (Tel-Aviv, 1979), p. 352.

62. *OH"K*, vol. 1, pp. 47, 36–37.

63. *A"T*, pp. 20–21; *Oh"K*, vol. 1, pp. 36–37.

64. *OH"K*, vol. 1, p. 47.

65. Ibid.

66. *A"T*, pp. 20–21 (and *OH"K*, vol. 1, pp. 36, 37).

67. *A"T*, p. 21 (and *OH"K*, p. 37).

68. *OH"K*, vol. 3, p. 211.

69. Ibid.

70. Manuscripts, Half Collection, p. 11. See note 6.

71. Manuscripts, Collection D, p. 41.

72. *OH"K*, vol. 1, p. 45. On the suffering created by confinement of thought, see also *A"T*, p. 61; *OH"K*, vol. 3, p. 186.

73. Manuscripts, Small Collection, p. 224.

74. Ibid., pp. 205, 60.

75. *OH"K*, vol. 1, pp. 31–32. These terms are borrowed from the Kabbalah.

76. *OH"K*, vol. 3, p. 259. On the relationship to details in actual practice, see Chapter 7.

77. Manuscript, Collection B, p. 49. The passages is inspired by biblical language; among the allusions are (Psalms 27:4): "One thing have I desired of the Lord, that will I seek after; that I may dwell in the house of the Lord all the days of my life, to behold the beauty of the Lord, and to inquire in his temple." The phrase *the God of my father* echoes many similar expressions in Genesis 31:5, 32:9; Exodus 15:2, 18:4, and so on. The desire "to contemplate the Temple of the eternal King" recalls the search of the shepherd, and that of God himself described in Ezekiel 34:12.

78. *OH"K*, vol. 3, p. 210. It is important to remember that Rav Kook recognized a characteristically Jewish ability or quality inherent in mysticism and the aspiration toward unity. See also *OH"K*, vol. 1, p. 21 and *A"T*, p. 4.

79. *A"T*, p. 49.

80. Unnumbered Manuscripts.

81. Compare G. Scholem, *Pirkey Yesod*, pp. 9 ff. ("Mystika ve-Samkhut Datit").

82. *OH"K*, vol. 3, p. 130. Rav Kook addressed the question of the relationship between mysticism, practical life and the natural world in a passage in the manuscript of *Arpalei Tohar* not published in the first edition; it appears in the new edition of the book, Jerusalem 1983: "At first sight, it may seem that esoteric thought, so deep within the concealed reaches of being, so able to raise man's worth to the highest heavens, actually weighs him down with a moral burden, denies him his natural freedom, annuls his desires by its very greatness, robs the earth from him, and in its stead offers him heavens so infinitely supreme that no human being could ever hope to reach them in union. But such an impression is superficial. . . . The initial vision is almost overwhelming, in a storm wind, great cloud and blazing fire, but as מתחוללת הדיעה, as reason gets used to these tremendous things . . . morality finds a place in the human spirit, and the world becomes precious and beloved ten times over what it was in his former, unenlightened estimation of material and spiritual being, in his view of himself and his essence based on mere overt theories."

83. *A"T*, p. 11.

84. Manuscripts, Small Collection, p. 224.

85. Unnumbered Manuscripts.

86. Both the Ba'al Shem Tov and Rav Nahman of Breslav spoke of the possibility of bringing oneself to the point of death in ecstatic prayer. See A. Green, *Tormented Master*, p. 33 and notes 34, 35. The concept of "כלות הנפש", the soul's consumation in spiritual ecstacy, does not refer to prayer alone. It is seen as the highest achievement of mystical experience or perception, and its

nature is thus ambivalent. Compare R. Schneur Zalman of Lyady, *Likkutei Amarim, Tanya,* chapter 3.

87. On the relationship between moral wholeness and mystical perception, see Chapter 8, pp. 295, and note 44.

88. *A"T,* p. 11.

89. *OH"K,* vol. 3, p. 239, see also p. 240.

90. See note 78.

91. *A"T,* p. 50.

92. Manuscripts, Collection D, p. 20.

93. The word is unclear in the manuscript.

94. Manuscripts, Collection D, p. 41. Compare note 75.

95. Manuscripts, Small Collection, p. 224.

96. Ibid.

97. Ibid.

98. *A"T,* p. 42. See also p. 13: "The [soul's] action must not be impeded by excessive effort, neither physical nor spiritual; grace beyond measure must not be wearied by backbreaking labor. She is accustomed to expanding and rejoicing in the volatility of her inner life, and that is the path she must find and shall find; with a mighty hand, she will break all the iron walls that stand in her way."

99. See chapter 2, p. 91 and note 235. Like many who fought for the ideal of freedom in the modern age, Rav Kook saw both eccesiastical tyranny and philosophical determinism as factors to be combatted. See *Ikvei ha-Zon,* pp. 153–154: Like many advocates of the idea of freedom in the modern age, Rav Kook perceived both the despotism of the Church and philosophical determinism as elements to combatted. See Ikvei haTson pp. 163–154: "The heart's stupor and self denial alone, engendered by the life forces of the Middle Ages, whose traces remain visible even in modern times to the individual who prepares himself to touch that dark malaise—those alone caused the feeling of freedom to be so silenced, particularly through the Papal influence. Until philosophy—rational philosophy, in fact, which must emerge from life itself—lost its life force and sublime strength, and could no longer courageously raise its arms and demand the breath of health, when all the streams of human life would join in saying: How could such a man deny the reality of complete, divine freedom when internal and external freedom is *his highest ideal and his heart's desire*—'"Engraved on the tablets"—do not read "engraved" [*harut*] but "freedom" [*herut*]' (Avot 6:2)?

"... When we envision the abundance and the might, the glory and the splendour in every side and corner of reality, indeed, then man's great spirit will be returned to him, filled with brave freedom. We shall not destroy our own image, and we will not offer our understanding to the diviners."

100. *OH"K*, vol. 1, p. 97.

101. Ibid.

102. Ibid., p. 135.

103. Ibid., p. 99, and *A"T*, p. 59.

104. Manuscripts, Collection B, p. 35.

105. Ibid. See also Manuscripts, Half Collection, p. 11: "The extent and the pleasures of this revelation [of sublime divine completeness] is *conditional*, for it requires the perfection of man's free will."

106. *A"T*, p. 40.

107. *OH"K*, vol. 3, p. 186. See also *OH"K*, vol. 1, p. 107: "When the soul is wearied of all the constraints imposed by מדעי הגבול, of all the strivings shut up in narrow places, it comes to hide itself from the stream in the cool shadow of contemplation, thinking on the world's secrets and the holy wonders latent in the secrets of Torah."

108. *OH"K*, vol. 3, p. 97.

109. *OH"K*, vol. 1, p. 111.

Afterword

1. The works of R. Nahman Krochmal and Hermann Cohen reflect this view.

2. R. Sigad, *Existentialism*, p. 7.

3. On the development of spiritualism in Europe as a reaction to materialism, see G. W. Butterworth, *Spiritualism and Religion* (London, 1944). Materialism is in fact not unique to the nineteenth century, and even then many other views were polarly opposed to it. Still, materialism flourished at that time, and along with existential philosophy, it posed a formidable theological challenge to Rav Kook. See, for example, *Eder ha-Yakar*, p. 135: "Human understanding has been systematically swept away from knowing God's ways, because the light of freedom, the source of ideals, has been blocked out. Human idealism sunk little by little until it was forced to turn to materialism, which robbed it of its vital luster. . . . Now the time has come for Israel to recognize its own might and glory, whether aggressively, by utterly eradicating the goddess who negated idealism and divine freedom, or constructively, by elevating idealism, the love of God's ways that is implanted deep within the soul of the nation." It is interesting to remark that Rav Kook saw materialism as a result of Spinozist determinism. He mentions Spinoza by name at the

beginning of the previous paragraph in the same section, p. 133. Compare Chapter 8, p. 305 and note 99.

4. See the extensive bibliography in note 2.

5. See D. Canaani, *Ha-Aliyah ha-Shenia*, pp. 36, 55. Compare also Chapter 1, the last two sections.

6. On an approach that broadens the bounds of hermeneutics in a similar way, see P. Ricoeur, *Freud and Philosophy, An Essay on Interpretation* (New Haven, Conn., 1970), p. 25. For criticism of this approach, see I. Golomb, "Me-Phenomenologiya le-Hermeneutika—al Shitato ha-Parshanit shel Paul Ricoeur," ("From Phenomenology to Hermeneutics—On the Parshanut of Paul Ricoeur"), pp. 32–33. See also Chapter 9, note 7.

7. See Chapter 8, p. 310 and note 123.

8. In this connection, it is interesting to compare a statement in his conversation "Ahdut ve-Shniut" recorded by "a listener" and published in *Ha-Nir* (1929): 45–47: "When spirituality dominates, people find meaning in life . . . because for great and exalted spirituality . . . the material world is not separate from the spiritual. . . . Yet shortsighted people, when they detect a tendency toward material life, fall upon that view, and in their obsession with materialism seek to wipe out spirituality completely, fearing it opposes the materialism so dear to them. . . . And the People of Israel . . . the unique nation . . . senses that the separation between the material and spiritual causes it profound sorrow, and searches for a way to return to unity [i.e., to a balance between the two]. . . . And the sinners of Israel . . . they too cannot bear this dualism and are thus the first to destroy. . . . They begin by demolishing the divided spirituality above materialism . . . showing all its falsehood and הפסדה. . . . Their lack of trenchant distinctions even makes them suppose they have already eradicated all spirituality . . . although they have really only managed to destroy the idol of spirituality, illusory spirituality . . . and not true spirituality. . . . And after they have finished demolishing the idol of spirituality they are brought, against their will, to destroy the idol of materialism as well, for after materialism is separated from spirituality, the former is also no more than a idol, with no justification for its existence [as the concept is one of wholess, a balance between the two—recorder]. Then the wars between parties and candidates begin . . . materialism in and of itself is cheapened. . . . Those consumed by doubt and stricken with boredom find no other way out than suicide. . . . People search for some purpose in life and find none. . . . Thus sinners of Israel smash the idols of the times by themselves, smash and shatter and clear away all fake spirituality and all empty and degraded materialism, and make way for the highest holiness. . . . Truly, in the sphere of great, wide faith, spirituality does not contradict materiality, nor the opposite, but rather both combine to aggrandize and multiply the faith of our soul, which so yearns for unity. . . . Even materialism, when it cleaves to spirituality, is purified of its primitive and beastial courseness and takes the graceful form of supreme majesty."

9. Rav Kook's position often fascillated between an idealistic view of reality and existentialist views and expressions; this is a clear example. On the question of the relationship between the two perspectives, see J. Guttman, "Existentzia ve-Idiliya," *Da'at u-Mada* (*Religion and Knowledge*), pp. 281–304.

10. R. Sigad, *Existentialism,* pp. 263–264.

11. Compare Jasper's view, H. Tanan, *Tefisat ha-Ethika ha-Existentialit be-Mishnat Karl Jaspers* (Ramat Gan, 1977), p. 287.

12. See *IG"R*, vol. 1, pp. 19–20.

13. For an important approach to this subject, see Y. Amital, Mashma'uta shel Mishnat ha-Rav Kook le-Dorenu" ("The Meaning of Rabbi Kook's thought to Our Generation"), *Yovel Orot*, ed. B. Ish Shalom and S. Rosenberg, pp. 333–342.

14. For an interesting treatment of this issue, see "Symposium: Terumata shel Mishnat ha-Rav Kook le-Hagut Yehudit Mithadeshet," with the participation of R. Schatz-Uffenheimer, M. Pruman, A. Ravitzki, S. Rosenberg, and N. Rotenstreich, in *Yovel Orot*, p. 349.

GLOSSARY OF SELECTED NAMES AND TERMS

Explanations of other kabbalistic and philosophical terms may be found in the text itself and in the notes.

Adam ha-Rishon. Literally "primordial man," a symbol in kabbalistic literature, representing all of existence, being the embodiment of the system of the sefirot.

Aggadah. Most commonly designates the legends of the sages, but in Rav Kook's teaching it refers to the entire domain of non-philosophical rabbinic thought.

Azriel of Gerona. One of the earliest Spanish kabbalists of the thirteenth century and one of the most profound speculative thinkers in kabbalistic mysticism. His works reflect the process whereby platonic thought penetrated into the original kabbalistic tradition as it reached Provence in the *Sefer ha-Bahir.*

Berlin, Naphtali Zvi Yehuda ("Netziv"; 1816–1893). Rabbi, halachic authority, and biblical commentator. Head of the Volozhin yeshiva for thirty years until it was closed by the government. One of the first activists of the movement "Hovevei Zion."

Binah. "Understanding," third of the ten *sefirot.* The second stage of intellectual process; symbolically corresponds to the heart.

Devekuth. "Adhesion" or "being joined" to God. Regarded as the ultimate goal of religious perfection.

Distinctions (ברורים). Has many connotations in kabbalistic and Hasidic literature, most commonly the distinction between good and evil in the world. Through this distinction the ideal of effecting the worlds *tikkun* is fulfilled in God's name.

En-Sof. "The Endless" or "Infinite." Frequently used in the Zohar and later kabbalistic works to indicate the Unknowable God.

331

Forehead and eyes. Kabbalistic symbols adopted from the description in the *Idrot* of the Zohar of the personified Divine Mercy (*Arikh Anpin*).

Gikatilla, Joseph. Born in Castille in 1248, died in the first third of the 14th century. Author of the seminal kabbalistic work *Sha'are Orah*.

Halukkah. Charity distribution. Halukkah, after the end of the 18th century, was the financial allowance for the support of the inhabitants of Eretz Israel from the contributions of their coreligionists in the Diaspora.

Hildesheimer, Azriel (1820–1899). German rabbi and leader of Orthodox Jewry. Advocated a synthesis between religious and secular studies and established a Rabbinic seminary along these lines. An opponent of the Reform movement, he was an enthusiastic supporter of Palestine Jewry and the building of the *yishuv*.

Hirsch, Samson Raphael (1808–1888). Rabbi, founder and leader of the New German Orthodoxy. Stood for the combination of Torah and secular knowledge, and for observing the mitzvot with integration in secular society and culture, a view called "*Torah im derkh-eretz.*"

Hirschenson, Hayyim (1855–1935). Rabbi, writer, and Zionist activist. Born in France, he emigrated to the United States in 1904 and served there as a Rabbi.

Hokhma. "Wisdom," the first of the ten Sefirot. First of the intellectual powers of the soul.

Kalam. A philosophical movement concerned with interpretation of the Koran and defense of Islam by philosophical-rational means.

Kelipah. Literally "Shell." Frequently used in Kabbalah to denote evil and the source of sensual desires in human nature.

Keter. "Crown," intermediate category between the essence of, or En-Sof (the Emenator), and the emanations. Also identified with "Supernal Will." The first of the ten *sefirot.*

Knesset Israel. Literally "The Assembly of Israel." Denotes the heavenly image and the Divine Spirit of the entirety of the People of Israel. Represents the *sefira* of *malkhut.*

Lurianic Mysticism. Named after R. Itzhak ben Shlomo Luria ("Ha-Ari" יצחק האלוהי רבי), 1534–1572. A great kabbalist and founder of the Lurianic school of kabbalistic thought, Ha-Ari's influence on Jewish intellectual history was tremendous.

Malkhut. "Royalty," the tenth and lowest of the sefirot. Identified with Shekhinah, the immanent category of Divine Presence.

Maskil. "Intellectual," an adherent of the Haskallah—the enlightenment movement and ideology which began within Jewish society in the 1770s.

Haskallah in particular maintained that secular studies should be recognized as a legitimate part of the curriculum in the education of a Jew.

Menachem Mendel ben Shalom Shachnah ("Zemah Zedeq"; 1789–1866). The third rabbi of the Habad dynasty, grandson of R. Schneur Zalman of Lyady. He wrote essays on Hasidic thought, halachic interpretations and rulings, and was recognized as a Torah sage even by Mitnagdim.

Mitnagged. Opponent of Hasidism.

Pilpul. Sharp, academic arguments; Talmudic casuistry.

Schneur Zalman of Lyady (1745–1813). Founder of Habad Hasidism.

Sefer ha-Bahir. A collection of kabbalistic midrashim on various subjects, presented in the name of Tannaim and Amoraim. First appeared in southern France in approximately 1200. Also known as "Midrash R. Nehuniah ben Hakaneh."

Sefira, Sefirot. Potencies or agencies by means of which, according to the Kabbalah, God manifested His existence in the creation of the universe.

Shekhinah. "The dwelling" or "resting." Refers to the majestic immanence of God in the world.

Sofer, Moshe ("Hatam Sofer"; 1762–1803). Rabbi and great halachist of the nineteenth century. Leader of Hungarian Orthodox Jewry.

Torah she-be'al-peh. Usually designates the Oral Torah, but in the kabbalah it is a mystical symbol representing the *sefira* of *malkhut*.

Tsimtsum. Denotes the act that enabled emanation, suggesting that God, the en-sof, infinity, contracted, as it were, and withdrew into Himself, or limited Himself, to make room for the creation of the world.

The thing-itself. A technical term used by Kant. It means the real object which is in fact the ideal and is not seen or discerned. Its opposite is "the phenomenon," that is, that which is discernible; the object as it is seen.

Tykocinski, Jehiel (1872–1955). Rabbi and head of the Etz Hayyim Yeshiva in Jerusalem. He specialized in the halachic laws of Eretz Israel and published an annual calender of laws and customs.

BIBLIOGRAPHY

Primary Works of Rabbi Kook Cited in this Volume

Arpalei Tohar. Jaffa, 1914, incomplete printing; cited as *A"T.* All citations are from this edition unless otherwise indicated.

Arpalei Tohar, ed. Issac Shilat. Jerusalem: Hamchon al shem Harav Zvi Yehuda Kook Zal, 1983.

Eder ha-Yakar ve-Ikvei ha-Zon. Jerusalem, 1967; cited as *Eder.*

Hazon ha-Geulah. Jerusalem: Association for Publishing the Works of the Chief Rabbi A. I. Kook, 1941.

Iggerot ha-Re'ayah, 4 vols. Jerusalem: Association for Publishing the Works of the Chief Rabbi A. I. Kook with the aid of Mossad Harav Kook, 1962–65; cited as *IG"R.*

Ma'amarei ha-Re"ayah, ed. Elisha Aviner. Jerusalem, 1980.

Ne'edar ba-Kodesh. Jerusalem, 1933.

Orot. Jerusalem: Mossad Harav Kook, 1973.

Orot ha-Emunah. Jerusalem, 1985.

Orot ha-Kodesh. Jerusalem: Mossad Harav Kook, 1963–64; cited as *OH"K.*

Olat Re'ayah, 2 vols. Jerusalem: Mossad Harav Kook, 1963.

Orot ha-Teshuva. Or Etzion: Merkaz Shapira, Jerusalem, 1970; cited as *OH"T.*

Orot ha-Torah. Jerusalem: Hayeshiva Hamercazit Ha'olamit, 1940.

335

Articles and Essays by Rabbi Kook

Ha-Mahshavah ha-Yisraelit ed. Elhanan Kalmanson Jerusalem, 1920.

Ha-Mispeid be'Yerushalayim. (eulogy delivered for Dr. Theodore Herzl, 20 Tammuz 5564 [1904]), *Sinai* 47 (1960). Idem. B'Oro, ed. H. Hamiel.

"Kirvat Elokhim." *Tahkemoni* 2 (Berlin, 1911).

"Le-Demut Diyukono shel ha-Rambam." *Ha'Aretz,* Passover edition, 1935.

"Ma'amar Meyuchad [al ha-Ramabam]." In Ze'ev Ya'avetz, *Toldot Yisrael.* Tel Aviv, 1935.

Meorot ha-Emunah, offset edition, with *Ma'amar Meyuchad,* no bibliographic data.

"Perurim mi-Shulchan Gavoah." In *Yizre'el,* a Literary Collection edited by Alexander Ziskind Rabinovitz. Jaffa, 1913.

"Tallelei Orot." *Tahkemoni* (Berlin, 1910).

"Te'udat Yisrael u'Le'umyuto." *Ha-Peless* (Bern, 1901).

Manuscript Code

A considerable number of Rabbi Kook's writings remain in unpublished manuscript form. The author wishes to thank all those responsible for allowing access to these manuscript collections. They are referred to under the following names.

Early Collection (*Kovetz Kadum*).

Collection B (*Kovetz Bet*).

Collection C (*Kovetz Gimmel*).

Collection D (*Kovetz Daled*).

Collection E (*Kovetz Heh*).

Small Collection (Kovetz "katan").

Half Collection (Kovetz ½).

Unnumbered Manuscripts.

Articles on the Philosophy of Rav Kook

Amital, Yehuda. "The Meaning of Rabbi Kook's Thought to our Generation." In *Yovel 'Orot,* ed. B. Ish Shalom and S. Rosenberg. Jerusalem, 1985.

Avneri, Joseph. "Rabbi Kook and His Educational Activities During His Jaffa Tenure." *Niv ha-Midrashia* (1984).

Arieli, Nahum. "Repentance in the Philosophy of Rav Kook." *Teshuvah ve-Shavim*. Jerusalem, 1980.

Ashkenazi, Yehuda. "The Kabbalistic Sources of Rabbi Kook." In *Yovel 'Orot*, ed. B. Ish Shalom and S. Rosenberg. Jerusalem, 1985.

Ben-Nun, Yoel. "Israel and the Nations—Rabbi Kook's Idea of Nationalism." In *Yovel 'Orot*, ed. B. Ish Shalom and S. Rosenberg. Jerusalem, 1985.

Ben-Shelomo, Joseph. "Shelemuth ve-Hishtalmut be-Torath ha-Elokhim shel ha-Rav Kook." *Iyyun* (Studies in Honor of N. Rotenstreich) 33 (1984).

_____. "The Divine Ideals in Rav Kook's Teaching." In *Bar Ilan Sefer ha-Shana* (Moshe Schwarcz Anniversary Volume). ed. M. Halamish. Ramat Gan, 1988.

Bergman, Samuel H. "Torat ha-Hitpatchut be-Mishnato shel ha-Rav Kook." In *Anashsim u-Derakhim*. Jerusalem, 1967; *Shitato shel ha-Rav Kook* (Jerusalem, 1963).

_____. "Mavet ve-al-mavet bemachshavto shel ha-Rav Kook." In *Hogim u'm-a'aminim*. Tel-Aviv, 1959.

E'leh Masei: Reshimat Masa Harabanim. (Frankfurt-am-Main: Have'ida Leharamat Keren Hadat Be'eretz Hakodseh, 1914.

Fishman, Yehuda Leib. *Ha-Reayah*. Jerusalem, 1965.

_____. "Toldot ha-Rav." In *Azkarah*, ed. Y. L. Fishman. Jerusalem, 1936–38.

Fried, Yohanan. "Letters and Documents." In *Zikhron Re'ayah*. Jerusalem, 1986.

Friedman, Menahem. "On the Social Significance of the Polemic on Shmitah 1888–89." *Shalem* 1 (1974).

Goldman, Eliezer. "Secular Zionism, the Vocation of Israel and the Telos of the Torah: Rabbi Kook's Articles Published in Ha'Peless Between 1901–1904." *Da'at* (1983).

_____. "Rabbi Kook's Involvement with European Philosophy." *Yovel 'Orot*, ed. B. Ish-Shalom and S. Rosenberg. Jerusalem, 1988.

_____. "The Structuring of Rabbi Kook's Thought: 1906–1909." *Bar-Ilan* 22–23. ed. M. Halamish. Ramat Gan, 1988.

_____. "'Aesthetics' in Rav Kook's Writings." In *Yovel 'Orot*, ed. B. Ish Shalom and S. Rosenberg. Jerusalem, 1985.

Hamiel, Haim, ed. *Be-Oro: Iyunim be-Mishnato shel ha-Rav Kook*. Jerusalem, 1986.

Ish-Shalom, Benjamin. "Religion, Repentance and the Freedom of Man in the Philosophy of Rabbi Kook." In *Yovel 'Orot*, ed. B. Ish Shalom and S. Rosenberg. Jerusalem, 1985.

————. "Tolerance and Its Roots in the Thought of Rav Kook." *Da'at* 20 (1988).

Kaplan, Zvi. "His Approach to the Halacha." In *Kovez ha-Rayah*, ed. Yitzchak Rapahel. Jerusalem, 1966.

Klein, M. "Rabbi Kook's Philosophical Grasp of Halcha." In *Be-'Oro*, ed. H. Hamiel. Jerusalem, 1986.

Kook, Zvi Yehuda, ed. *Li-Shlosha be'Elul*. Hapoael ha-Mizrahi City Press, 1947.

Madan, Meir. "Letters on LInguistic Subjects." In *Zikhron Re'ayah*, ed. Yitzchak Raphael. Jerusalem, 1986.

Morial, Yehuda. "Prayer in the Philosophy of Rav Kook." In *Be'Oro*, ed. H. Hamiel. Jerusalem, 1986.

Nezir Echav: Essays and Articles in Memory of Rabbi David Ha-Cohen. Jerusalem, 1977.

Neriah, Moshe Zvi. *Harav*. Jerusalem, 1938.

————, ed. *Sichot ha-Re'ayah*. Tel-Aviv, 1979.

Peli, Pinhas. "Ha-Rav Kook u-Brenner: Or ve-Hoshekh." *Davar* (August 31, 1984).

Raphael, Issac, ed. *Zikhron ha-Re'ayah*. Jerusalem, 1966.
Rosenberg, Schalom. "Ha-Rayah ve-ha-Tannin ha-Iver." In *Be-Oro*, ed. H. Hamiel. Jerusalem, 1986.

Ross, Tamar. "Rav Kook's Concept of God." *Da'at* (Winter 1982; Summer 1982).

Rotenstreich, Nathan. "Ha-hashva'a ve-ha-Shiva." *Hamakhshavah ha-Yehudit Be'ait ha-Chadasha*. Tel-Aviv, 1966.

————. "Kosmos u-ma'asim." *Iyunim be'Machshava ha-Yehudit be-Zeman ha-zeh*. Tel-Aviv, 1978.

Schatz-Uffenheimer, Rivka. "Utopia and Messianism in the Teachings of Rav Kook." *Kivunim* 1 (November 1978); cited as "'Utopiya."

————. "The First Campaign against Rav Kook." *Molad* (n.s.) (Tevet 1974).

Schweid, Eliezer. "Secularism from a Religious Perspective." In *The Lonely Jew and Judaism*. Tel-Aviv, 1974.

Shapiro, Abraham. "Avraham Y. Kook as a Member of the Second Aliya." *Ha-Doar* 10 (Adar I 5738 [1978]).

Shapiro, Abraham. "Beyn Shlomo Zemah ve-Aharon David Gordon le-ha-Rayah Kook." Ha-Doar 34 (Tamuz 1978).

Steinsaltz, Adin. "Problematics of Orot ha-Kodesh." In *Ha'reayah*, ed. Issac Raphael. Jerusalem, 1966.

Sterlitz, Shim'on. "Repentance as Perceived by Rav Kook." In *Orot ha-Teshuva*. Jerusalem, 1970.

Yaron, Zvi. *Mishnato shel ha-Rav Kook*. Jerusalem, 1974.

Yovel 'Orot: Haguto shel Harav Avraham Yitzchak Hacohen Kook Z'tzal, ed. Benjamin Ish-Shalom and Shalom Rosenberg. Jerusalem: Ha'histadrut Hazionit, 1985; referred to as *Yovel 'Orot*.

Zikhron Re'ayah, ed. Issac Raphael. Jerusalem, 1986.

Zeitlen, Hillel. "Hakav Hayesodi Bakabalah shel Harav Kook Zal." In *Safran shel Yehidim*. Jerusalem, 1979.

Sources—Philosophic, Kabbalistic and General

Asher ben David. *Sefer ha-Yichud*. Jerusalem, 1934.

Azriel of Gerona. *Commentary on Talmudic Aggadot*, ed. Y. Tishby. Jerusalem, 1945.

Ben-Gurion, David. "The Question Regarding the *Yishuv ha-Yashan*," *Ha-Achdut* 2 (1910).

Bergson, Henri. *Ha-Hitpatchut ha-Yotzeret*, trans. into Hebrew Y. Or. Jerusalem, 1978.

_____. "Philosophical Intuition." In *Mevo Le-Metifisika*, trans. J. Levy. Tel-Aviv, 1947.

Brenner, Y. H. "Be-hayim u-vasifrut." In *Kol Kitvei J. H. Brenner*, vol. 2, Tel-Aviv 1924–1930.

Buber, Martin. *Be-Sod Siah*. Jerusalem, 1959.

Cassirer, Ernst. *Essay on Man* [in Hebrew]. Tel Aviv, 1972.

Cohen, Hermann. *Dat Hatevunah mi-Mekorot Hayahadut*, trans. Zvi Wislowsky. Jerusalem, 1972.

_____. *Iyyunim Beyhadut Uveba'ayat Hador*, trans. Zvi Wislowsky. Jerusalem, 1978.

_____. *"Yisud Katedraot le-Etika u-Philosophia Datit Bevatei Hamidrash Harabanim,"* ed. Joseph Kalusner and Hayyim N. Bialik. Hashiloah 13 Cracow, 1904.

Fraenkel, Ludwig August. *Yerushalayma* Vienna, 1860.

Ghazali, Abu Hamid [El-Gazali], *The Deliverer from Error,* trans, H. Yaffe-Lazarus. Tel-Aviv, 1965.

Gikitila, Joseph. *Sha'arei Ora,* ed. Joseph Ben Shelomo, Jerusalem, 1971.

Gordon, A. D. *Ha-'Uma ve-ha-'Avoda.* Jerusalem, 1952.

_____. *Ha-Adam ve-ha-Teva.* Tel-Aviv, 1951.

_____. *Michtavim u-Reshimot.* Jerusalem, 1954.

Ha'achdut, no. 9 (1914).

Hildesheimer, Azriel. *Letters,* ed. M. Eliav. Jerusalem, 1966.

Hapoel Ha'zair 27a (1920); 40 (1909); 11 (1914).

Hayyim of Vholozin. *Nefesh Hahayyim.* Jerusalem, 1973.

Krochmal, Naḥman. *Moreh Nevukhe Hazman,* ed. S. Rawidowicz. Waltham, MA: 1961.

Lichtenstein, Aaron. "Zot Torat ha-Hesder" *Alon Shevut* 100 (1982).

Loewe, Judah *(Maharal). Tifferet Yisrael.* Jerusalem, 1970.

_____. *Netivot Olam.* Jerusalem, 1970.

Luzzatto, Moses Hayyim. *Kelah Pithei Hokhmah.* Jerusalem, 1961.

_____. *Da'at Tevunot,* ed. H. Friedlander. Benei Barak, 1973.

Maimonides, Moses. *Moreh Nevukhim* [The Guide for the Perplexed]. trans. S. Pines Chicago, 1963.

Maimonides, Moses. *Moreh Nevukhim,* trans. Joseph Kepakh. Jerusalem, 1972.

Mill, John Stuart. *On Freedom.* Jerusalem, 1966.

Nietzche, Fredrich. *The Will to Power,* trans. W. Kaufman and R. S. Hollingdale. New York: Vintage, 1967.

Pekidim and Amarcalim. *Emet me-Eretz,* Amsterdam, 1843.

Plato. *Meno* [Hebrew]. Tel-Aviv, 1975.

_____. *The Republic* [Hebrew]. Tel-Aviv, 1975.

Plotinus. *Enneads,* trans. N. Spiegel. Jerusalem, 1978.

Rosenzweig, Franz. *The Star of Redemption*. Jerusalem, 1970.

———. *Naharayim*. Jerusalem, 1977.

Sa'adia b. Joseph Gaon. *Hanivkhar Be'Emunot ve-Daot*, ed. J. Kepakh. Jerusalem, 1970.

Sartre, J.-P. *Herut Nusach Descartes*, Writings. Tel-Aviv, 1977.

Schelling, L. P. V. *Shitat ha-Idialism ha-transcendentali*, trans. M. Schwartz. Ramat Gan, 1980.

Schneur Zalman of Lyady. *Likkutei Amarim, Tanya*. Kfar Habad, 1966.

Spinoza, Benedict. *Ma'amar Katzar al Elokhim Ha'Adam ve-Orsho (A Short Treatise on God, Man and Happiness)* [Hebrew], ed. Joseph Ben-Shelomo. Jerusalem, 1978; cited as *A Short Treatise*.

———. *Torat Hamidot*. Ramat Gan, 1967.

———. *Igrot* [Hebrew], ed. A. Shmueli. Jerusalem, 1964.

———. *Ma'amar al Tikkun ha-Sehel* (On the Improvement of Understanding), ed. Joseph Ben-Shelomo. Jerusalem, 1977.

General Works

Agassi, Joseph. "Rationality and the Tu Quoque Argument." In *The Rational and the Irrational*, ed. M. Daskal and E. Porush. Beer-Sheva, 1975.

Altmann, Alexander. *Panim shel Yahadut*. Tel-Aviv, 1983.

Auerbach, S. B., and Zeitlin, H. "Hayyim shel Mevakshe Hashem." In *Teshuva Veshavim*. Jerusalem, 1980.

———. *Toldot Tenuat Hapoalim Hayehudim*, 2 vols. Tel-Aviv, 1970.

Bar-On, Arieh Z. "The Ontological Proof: Spinoza's Version Compared with Anselm's and Descartes's Versions." In *Barukh Spinoza*, ed. M. Brinkner, M. Dascal, and D. Nesher. Tel-Aviv, 1979.

Bartal, Israel. "The 'Old' and the 'New' Yishuv—Image and Reality." *Cathedra* 2 (1976).

Ben Shelomo, Joseph. "The Rational and the Irrational in the Philosophy of Rudolph Otto." *Ha-Ratzionali ve-ha-Iratzionali*, ed. M. Daskal and E. Porush. Beer-Sheva, 1975.

———. *Torat Ha-Elokhut shel R. Moshe Cordevero*. Jerusalem, 1965.

Ben-Yehuda, B. "On the History of Education in Israel" *Hakhinukh Be-Yisrael*. Jerusalem, 1973.

Bergman, Samuel Hugo. *Hogim U-Ma'aminim.* Jerusalem, 1959.

_____. *"Ha-Bonim le-F. Rosenzweig."* *Ma'aznaim* (Sivan 1961).

_____. *Ha-Philosophia shel Immanuel Kant.* Jerusalem, 1980.

_____. "Hoffding." *Encyclopaedia Haivrit* [Hebraica], vol. 15 (1962 ed.)

_____. *Toldot ha-Philosophia ha-hadasha—Shitot ba-Philosophia she-le-ahar Kant.* Jerusalem, 1979.

Berlin, Isaiah. *Arba' Massot al Herut,* trans. Y. Sharrett. Tel-Aviv: Reshafim, 1971.

Buber, M. "Leish Be'ritainu" ("birthday Anniversary Issue to Leonard Ragatz") *Hapoel Hatzair* 14, no. 64 (August 5, 1943).

_____. "Ragatz Veyisrael." *Ba'ayot* 3, no. 6 (1946).

Cana'ani, David. *Ha-Aliya ha-Sheniya ha-Ovedet ve-Yahasah la-Dat ve-la-Masoret,* Tel-Aviv, 1977.

Croce, Benedetto. *Toldot Europa be-Me'a ha-tesha-Esre,* trans. E. Shmueli, Jerusalem, 1962.

Don Yahya, E. "Hilon Shelili ve-Shiluv Tfisot shel ha-Yahadut ha-Mesoratit u-Musageyha be-Zionit ha-Sozialistit." *Kivunim* 8 (1980).

Eisenstadt, S. N. "Weber's *Ancient Judaism* and the Format of Jewish Civilization." *Tarbiz* 49 (1980).

Elior, R. *Torat ha-Elokhut be-Dor ha-Sheni shel Hassidut Habad.* Jerusalem, 1982.

Etkes, Immanual. *Rabbi Israel Salanter and the Beginning of the "Mussar" Movement.* Jersalem, 1982.

Even-Shoshan, Avraham. *Hamillon he-Hadash,* Jerusalem, 1966.

Feuer, Lewis. *Einstein and the Generations of Science,* trans. G. Levi. Tel-Aviv, 1979.

Frankl, Victor. *Man's Search for Meaning,* trans. H. Issac. Tel-Aviv, 1970.

Friedman, Menahem. *Society and Religion: The Non-Zionist Orthodox in Eretz-Israel 1918–1936.* Jerusalem, 1977; cited as *Hevra ve-Dat.*

Golomb, Jacob. "From Phenomenology to Hermeneutics—On the Parshanut of Paul Ricoeur." *Iyyun* 29 (1980).

Gottlieb, A. *Studies in the Literature of the Kabbalah.* Tel-Aviv, 1976.

Green, Abraham. *Ba'al Hayisurim* (*tormented Master*). Tel-Aviv, 1981; New York: Schocken Books, 1981.

Grintz, Y. M. "Revelation." *Encyclopedia Hebraica* [*ha-Ivrit*], 1962 ed.

Gutmann, N., and Ben-Ezer, A. *Beyn Holut ve-Kahol Shamayim.* Yavneh, 1980.

Guttmann, Julius. *Ha-Philosophiya Shel ha-Yahadut.* Jerusalem, 1951.

_____. *Religion and Knowledge.* Jerusalem, 1951.

Hafner G. "Darki le-Merchaveya," *Sefer Merhaveya ha-co'operaziya.* Tel-Aviv, 1961.

Halamish, Moshe. "Mishnato ha-Iyunit shel Rav Schneur Zalman me-Liadi." Dissertation, Jerusalem, 1976.

_____. "On Quiet in Kabbalah and Hasidut." *Dat u-Sapha* ed. M. Halmish and A. Kasher. Tel-Aviv, 1982.

Histadrut Ha'Ovdim, Tel-Aviv University. Hamachon Lekhikrei Avoda: *Tenuat Havoda Veyachasa Ladat* (a conference). Tel-Aviv, 1976.

Holtz, Abraham. *Rabbinic Thought.* [Hebrew]. Tel-Aviv, 1978.

Idel, Moshe. "The Magical and Theurgic Interpretation of Music in Jewish Sources from the Renaissance to Hassidism." *Yuval* 4 (1982).

_____. "Music and Prophetic Kabbalah." *Yuval* 4 (1982).

Ish-Shalom, Benjamin. "Tanin, Leviathan, and Nahash—On the Meaning of a Legendary Motif." *Da'at* 19 (1987).

_____. "The Significance of the Commandments in the Philosophy of Rabbi Nachman of Krochmal." *Tarbiz* 56 (1987).

James, William. *The Varieties of Religious Experience,* trans. J. Koflivetz Jerusalem, 1969.

Kaniel, Yehoshua. *Continuity and Change: Old Yishuv and New Yishuv During the First and the Second Aliyah.* Jerusalem, 1981.

_____. "The Terms 'Old Yishuv' and 'New Yishuv' in Contemporaneous Usage (1882–1914) and in Historiographical Usage." *Cathedra* 6 (1978).

Katz, Jacob. "More on the Relaitons Between the 'Old Yishuv' and the 'New Yishuv.'" *Cathedra* 6 (1978).

Kaufman, Yekhezkel. *Bekhevle ha-Zeman.* Tel-Aviv, 1936.

Kopi, A. M. *Mevo le-Logika.* Tel-Aviv, 1972.

Kroi, M. "Ratzionalit Kolelet ve-Ratzionalit Helkit." In *Ha-Ratzionali ve-ha-Iratzionali,* ed. M. Daskal and A. Porush. Beer-Sheva, 1975.

Levi, Y., Ed. *Leonard Ragatz—Yisrael, Yahadut, Natzrut.* Petah Tikvah, 1968.

Levi, Ze'ev. *Structuralism.* Tel-Aviv, 1976.

_____. *Hermeneutica*. Tel-Aviv, 1987.

_____. *Mevaser Existentialism Yehudi: Franz Rosenzweig*. Tel-Aviv, 1970.

Liebes, Y. "Perakhim be-Milon Sefer ha-Zohar." Dissertation, Jerusalem, 1977.

Lovejoy, Arthur. *Sharsheret ha-Havaya ha-Gedolah*, trans. E. Emir. Tel-Aviv, 1969.

Luz, Ehud. *Makbilim Nifgashim*. Tel-Aviv, 1985.

Malachi, Eliezer. *Perakhim be-Toldot ha-Yishuv ha-Yashan*. Tel-Aviv, 1971.

Mieses, Fabius. *Korot ha-Philosofia ha-Hadasha*. Leipzig, 1847.

Neher, Andre. "*A Profile of Franz Rosenzweig as a 'Ba'al Teshuva.'*" In *Teshuva Veshavim*. Jerusalem, 1980.

Pachter, Mordekhai. "The Theory of *Devekut* in the Writings of the Sages of Safed in the Sixteenth Century." *Jerusalem Studies in Jewish Thought* 3 (1982).

Pines, Shlomo. "Gabirol." *Encyclopaedia Hebraica* [ha-Ivrit]. Tel-Aviv, 1955.

Press, Isaiah "On the History of the Ban on Secular Schools in Jerusalem." *Minchah le-David*. Jerusalem, 1935.

Ravitzky, Aviezer "Ha-Adam ha-shalem ke-Po'el Nifla'ot: Gilgula shel Teoria be-Philosofia ha-Yehudit be-yemai ha-Benayim." Jerusalem: Hebrew University, 1982.

_____. "Ha-Tzapui ve-ha-Reshut Netuna." In *Yisrael Likrat ha-Mea ha-21*, ed. A. Hareven. Jerusalem, 1984.

Rosenberg, Shalom. "'Permenant Revelation'—Three Variants." In *Revelation, Faith, Reason*, ed. M. Halamish and M. Schwarcz. Ramat Gan, 1976.

_____. "Beyn Peshat le-Darash: Perakim al Parshanut ve-Idiologia." *De'ot* 37 (1969).

_____. "Cheker ha-Mikra be-Machshava ha-Yehudit ha-Datit ha-chadasha." In *Ha-mikra ve-Anachnu*, ed. U. Simon. Tel-Aviv, 1979.

Rotenstreich, N. *Ha-Machshava ha-Yehudit be'Et ha-hadasha*. Tel-Aviv, 1966.

_____. *Al Techuma shel Ha-Philosophia*. Jerusalem, 1969.

_____. *Iyyunim be-Machshava ha-Yehudit ba-Zeman ha-Zeh*. Tel-Aviv, 1978.

Segal, C. "Orot Be'ofel." *Nekudah*, (September 1987).

Schatz-Uffenheimer, Rivka. *Quietistic Elements in Eighteenth Century Hassidic Thought (Ha-Hassidut ke-Mistika)*. Jerusalem, 1980.

———. "Torat Hazadik etzel Elimelech me-Lyzansk." *Molad* (1960).

———. "R. Moses Cordevero and the Ari: Between Nominalism and Realism." *Jerusalem Studies* 3 (1982); cited as "Remak ve-ha-Ari."

———. "Peyrush ha-hassidut ke-Bitui le-hashkafa ha-Idialistit shel Gershom Scholem." In *Gershom Scholem: al ha-Ish u'fo'alo.* Jerusalem, 1983.

———. "Anti-Spiritualism in Hassidut: Studies in the Thought of Rabbi Schneur Zalman of Liadi." *Molad* (1962).

———. "Ha-Tefisa ha-Mishpatit shel ha-Maharal: Antithesis to Natural Law." *Da'at* (1979).

———, ed. *Maggid Devarav le-Ya'acov.* Jerusalem and Tel-Aviv, 1972.

Schlanger, J. *Ha-Philosophia shel Shlomo ibn Gevirol.* Jerusalem, 1980.

Scholem, Gershom. *Devarim be-Go.* Tel Aviv, 1976.

———. "Mistika ve-Chevra." In *Od Davar,* ed. A. Shapira. Tel-Aviv, 1989.

———. *Pirkey Yesod be-Havanat ha-Kabbalah u-Semaleha.* Jerusalem, 1977.

———. *Reshit ha-kabbalah.* Jerusalem and Tel-Aviv, 1948.

———. *Reshit Hakkabalah ve-Sefer ha-Bahir,* ed. Rivka Schatz-Uffenheimer. Jerusalem: Akadamon 1979.

———. *Avraham Cohen Herera Ba'al "Sha'ar ha-Shamaim."* Jerusalem, 1978.

Scholem, Gershom. *Shabbetai Zevi ve-ha-Tenu'ah ha-Shabbeta-it biyimei Hayyav,* Tel-Aviv, 1970.

Scholem, Gershom. *The Messianic Idea in Israel* (Conference). New York, 1971; Jerusalem, 1982.

Schwarcz, Moshe. *Me-Mitos le-Hitgalut.* Tel-Aviv, 1978.

———. *Safah Mitos Emunot.* Jerusalem and Tel-Aviv, 1967.

———. "The Pantheism Controversy and the Theology of Solomon Ludwig Steinheim." In *Revelation, Faith, Reason,* ed. M. Halamish and M. Schwarcz. Ramat Gan, 1976.

Sermoneta, Joseph. "Yehuda and Immanuel Haromi—Rationalism Culminating in Mystic Faith." In *Revelation, Faith, Reason.* Ramat Gan, 1976.

Sigad, Ron. *Existentialism.* Jerusalem, 1982.

Schweid, Eliezer. *Ta'am ve-Hakasha.* Ramat Gan, 1970.

———. *Ha-Yachid: Olamo shel A. D. Gordon.* Tel-Aviv, 1970.

———. "The Concept of Teshuva in Modern Jewish Thought." In *Yovel 'Orot,* ed. B. Ish Shalom and S. Rosenberg. Jerusalem, 1988.

Shmueli, A. "Ha-Metoda ha-Geometrit, Ide'al Hachinukh ve-Torat ha-Zehirut." In *Barukh Spinoza*.

Shapiro, A. "Dual Structures in the Thought of Martin Buber." Disseration, Tel-Aviv, 1984.

Sharfstein, Ben Ami. *He-Havaya ha-Mistit*. Tel-Aviv, 1972.

Shulman, Y. "Ha-Imut bein ha-Haredim le-Maskilim be-Tnuat Hibat Zion be-Shnot ha-Shmonim." *Hazionut* 5 (1979).

Straus, Claude Levi. *Hachashiva ha-pera'it*. Merhavia, Tel-Aviv: n.d.

Talmon, Jacob. *Romantica u-Meri*, trans. Y. S. Levi, Tel-Aviv, 1973.

———. "Herder ve-ha-Ruach ha-Germanit." In *Achdut ve-Yichud*. Tel-Aviv, 1965.

Tanan, Hanokh. *Tefisat ha-Ethika ha-Existentialit Be-Mishnat Karl Jaspers*. Ramat Gan, 1977.

Tidhar, David. Encyclopedia Lehaluzei Hayishuv, vol. 17, 1963.

Tishby, Isaiah. *Nitivei Emunah u-Minut*, Tel-Aviv, 1964.

———. *Torat ha-rah ve-ha-kelipa be-Kabbalat ha-AR"I*. Jerusalem, 1960.

———. *Mishnat ha-Zohar*. 2 vols. Jerusalem, 1970.

Weiss, Joseph. *Studies in the Hassidut of Breslov*. Jerusalem, 1975.

Werblowski, Zvi. "On the Mystical Rejection of Mystical Illuminations." *Iyyun* 14–15 (1964).

Wolfson, Harry A. "The Concept of Double Belief According to the Philosophy of Saadya Gaon, Ibn Rushid and Thomas Aquinas." In *The Jewish Philosophy of the Middle Ages*. Jerusalem, 1978.

Yoval, Yirmiahu. *Kant ve-Hidush ha-Metiphysica*. Jerusalem, 1973.

———. *Kant ve-Hachidush shel ha-Historia*. Jerusalem, 1988.

Zemah, Shlomo. "Sifrut ve-Nelchar." *Shedmot* 30 (Summer 1968).

Non-Hebrew Works Cited

Works originally written in other languages of which Hebrew translations were utilized, have been included in the Hebrew works section.

Agus, Jacob. *Banner of Jerusalem*. New York, 1964.

Baar, J. *Fundamentalism*. London, 1977.

Babbitt, Irving. *Rousseau and Romanticism*. 1928.

Benn, S. I., and Mortimore, G. W., eds. *Rationality and the Social Sciences*, 1976.

Bloch, Ernst. *Geist der Utopie*. Munich, 1918.

Butterworth, George. *Spiritualism and Religion*. London, 1944.

Carmy, Shalom. "Rav Kook's Theory of Knowledge." *Tradition* 15 (1975).

Carnap, Rudolph. *Logical Syntax of Language*. London, 1937.

Clark, Harry. *The Philosophy of Albert Schweizer*. London, 1962.

Cohen, Arthur A., and Mendes-Flohr, Paul, eds. *Contemporary Jewish Religious Thought*. New York, 1987.

Einstein, Albert. "On the Generalized Theory of Gravitation." *Scientific American* 182 (1950).

Encyclopaedia Judaica. Jerusalem, 1972.

Geertz, Clifford. *The Interpretation of Cultures*, (Selected Essays). New York, 1973.

Glazer, Nahum N., ed. *On Jewish Learning*. New York, 1955.

Guttmann, Julius. *Die Philosophie des Salomon Ibn Gabirol*. Gottingen, 1889.

Halivni, David. "Revelation and Zimzum." *Judaism* 21 (1972).

Hoffding, Harold. "Philosophy and Life." *International Journal of Ethics* 12 (1902).

Hughes, H. S. *Consciousness and Society*. New York, 1958.

Inge, William R. *Christian Mysticism*. London, 1899.

Inge, William R. *Mysticism in Religion*. London, 1969.

Jaspers, Karl. *Der Philosophische Glaube*. Zurich, 1948.

Kadushin, Max. *The Rabbinic Mind*. New York, 1965.

Katz, S. T., ed. *Mysticism and Philosophical Analysis*. London, 1978.

Likutei Amarim Bi-Lingual Edition. Glossary. London, 1981.

Link-Salinger, Hyman. *Gustav Landauer: Philosopher of Utopia*. Indianapolis, 1977.

Luce, D., and Raiffa, H. *Games and Decisions*. New York, 1957.

Mannheim, Karl. *Ideology and Utopia*. New York, 1936.

Mattmuller, M. *Leonhard Ragaz and der Religiose Sozialismus*. volx. 1–11, 1957.

Messer, August. *Kants Ethik*. Leipzig, 1904.

Neumann, E. *Kulturentwicklung und Religion*. Zurich, 1953.

Otto, Rudolph. *Mysticism East and West*. London, 1932.

———. *The Idea of the Holy*. London, 1959.

"Philosophical Schools and Doctrines—Rationalism." *Encyclopaedia Britannica: Macropaedia*. 1985 ed.

Popper, Karl R. *The Logic of Scientific Discovery*. New York, 1957.

Rackman, Emmanuel. "A Challenge to Orthodoxy." *Judaism* 18 (1969).

Reich, Avshalom. "Changes and Developments in the Passover Haggadot of the Kibbutz Movement 1935–1972." Ph.D. Diss., The University of Texas at Austin, 1972.

Ricoeur, Paul. *Freud and Philosophy, An Essay on Interpretation*. New Haven, 1970.

Ricoeur, Paul. *Hermeneutics and the Human Sciences*. Cambridge, 1983.

Rosenak, Michael. *Commandments and Concerns, Jewish Religious Education in Secular Society*. Philadelphia–New York–Jerusalem, 1987.

Rotenstreich, Nathan. *Tradition and Reality*. New York, 1972.

Schelling, Friedrich. *Von Ich als Prinzip der Philosophie, Werke*. Edited by Otto Weis. Leipzig, 1907.

Scholem, Gershom. *Kabbalah*. Jerusalem, 1974.

———. *Major Trends in Jewish Mysticism*. New York, 1954.

———. *Offenbarung and Tradition als Religiose Kategorien im Judentum, Ueber einige Grundbegriffe des Judentums*. Frankfurt, 1970.

———. *The Messianic Idea In Judaism*. New York, 1972.

Schopenhauer, Arthur. *The World as Will and Idea*. Vol. 2. London, 1906.

Stace, K. W. *Mysticism and Philosophy*. London, 1960.

Strengt, F. J. *Understanding Religious Life*. Encino CA, 1976.

Swart, K. W. *The Sense of Decadence in Nineteenth Century France*. The Hague, 1964.

Underhill, Evelyn. *Mysticism*. New York, 1957.

Whitehead, Alfred N. *The Function of Reason*. Princeton, 1929.

———. *Process of Reality*. New York, 1941.

Zaehner, Robert C. *Concordant Discord*. London, 1970.

Note: Works by contemporary scholars mentioned in the endnotes are not listed in this index. However, references to scholars in the body of the text as well as all references to classical works apart from bibliographical references in the notes, are listed here.